The Urban Predicament

Edited by
WILLIAM GORHAM
NATHAN GLAZER

The Urban Institute
Washington, D.C.

THE URBAN INSTITUTE is a nonprofit research organization established in 1968 to study problems of the nation's urban communities. Independent and nonpartisan, the Institute responds to current needs for disinterested analyses and basic information and attempts to facilitate the application of this knowledge. As a part of this effort, it cooperates with federal agencies, states, cities, associations of public officials, and other organizations committed to the public interest.

The Institute's research findings and a broad range of interpretive viewpoints are published as an educational service. The interpretations or conclusions are those of the authors and should not be attributed to The Urban Institute, its trustees, or to other organizations that support its research.

CONTENTS

TABLES

Chapter 4. CRIME

Chapter 5. EDUCATION

FIGURES

xiii

Preface

In the fall of 1974, a large foundation asked The Urban Institute whether it would be interested in preparing a comprehensive social report on the present quality of life in America, for completion during the bicentennial year. It was an alluring proposal, but—as with many alluring proposals—when the full costs were estimated it was abandoned. Left in its place was the seed of this venture, whose theme is also the "quality of life in America" but whose focus has been narrowed into the range of feasibility.

The Urban Predicament is thus a volume in which a stable of expert contributors bring together much of what is known about some of the city's major problems. Two of the authors and one of the co-editors are from the university community—Nathan Glazer and James Q. Wilson of Harvard University and James Coleman of the University of Chicago. The rest are members of The Urban Institute staff.

This book does not present a complete picture of the situation in cities. Rather, it throws a number of shafts of light into "areas of major concern." More cannot be claimed, for this effort, like every other, is bounded by time, by the knowledge of the authors and the editors, and by the more generally limited ability of scholars and analysts to understand more than a part of complex human problems.

Within each chapter, the topics included are those which, in the opinion of the authors and the editors, are justified on the basis of the following criteria: (1) the topic is important in that it affects many people or is on many people's minds; (2) it is *not* transient; and (3) the authors bring to it new insight about the nature of the problems, about their malleability, or about the effects which different courses of action have had or might have on them.

The finance chapter presents a comprehensive analysis of the circumstances through which most of the largest cities got into their fiscal bind and suggests what each level of government can do, whether in the short run or the long run, to ease the bind.

The housing chapter surveys a number of past and current aspects of housing: what has happened to the quality of housing in this country over the past several decades; why the average cost of housing has risen since 1969; the changing patterns of residential segregation and why more racial integration has not occurred; and, finally, the reasons for slum formations and the prospect of its continuing. The chapter suggests how all these aspects of housing relate to each other in the operation of the housing market. In recognizing this gestalt, it also indicates how changes that occur in one sector of the housing market inevitably produce changes in other sectors of the housing market.

While the thesis that improving the general conditions of society will reduce crime is only scantily documented, many people believe it is true. That, however, is a long-term solution. The crime chapter focuses on the nearer-term methods of reducing street crime, particularly robbery. The authors approach this question from two sides: what can the individual do to avoid being victimized, and what can local government do (through building codes, the police force, the court system) to increase the risks for the criminal, to divert the might-be criminal to other pursuits, and to confine those who do commit crimes. The chapter also presents an analysis of the effect that a higher arrest rate and incapacitation might have on the crime rate.

The bulk of the education chapter is devoted to an analysis of desegregation in the public schools since 1968. The chapter shows that while marked desegregation has occurred in the South, segregation has increased in most of the largest metropolitan areas throughout the nation. The chapter also discusses, but less extensively, the problems of finance, violence in the school, student achievement, and the changes that are occurring in the governance of schools.

The transportation chapter covers most of the problems on the passenger transportation scene. The central foci are the issues surrounding public investment in urban passenger transportation and schemes for reducing congestion in downtown areas.

In the Introduction and Overview, Nathan Glazer and I try to place the other chapters in the context of recent attempts by the federal government to influence conditions in the cities. We trace some important demographic trends, and offer our view of an appropriate government stance with regard to these trends. The trends we deal with are: (1) the shift in regional economic vitality toward the West and South; (2) the declining population and fortunes of major central cities; and (3) the persistence of large, low-income minority ghettos with low opportunity levels in and around most of the large central cities.

This book will kindle varying degrees of controversy, as would any serious book about our cities and their problems. While I judge that all of the authors are sound scholars, their values inevitably color their choice of issues, the way they "see" those issues, and the conclusions they draw from their analyses. Both their objective analyses and their views support the purpose of this volume, which is to contribute to an understanding of the problems and to the dialog concerning their importance and ways of affecting them.

William Gorham
President
The Urban Institute

Acknowledgment

The intellectual forebears of this book are legion. Those specifically relied upon are acknowledged either in the footnotes to the individual chapters or in a chapter bibliography. Beyond our large collective debt to these colleagues, past and present, we benefited from the reading of the manuscript by a number of individuals, particularly many researchers of The Urban Institute. Of these we are particularly indebted to Robert Harris and Timmy Napolitano, who read several successive drafts and provided helpful suggestions and critiques of each. In addition we were extremely fortunate in having a formal expert review panel composed of William Alonso, Ellen Bozman, Herrington Bryce, and Francine Rabinovitz, who read drafts of all chapters, save the introduction, and suggested extensions which improved the coverage and quality of this final product. Ernest Strauss provided an invaluable service with a close edit of the entire manuscript. Finally, we are grateful to Cecelia Fong for the superb administrative support she provided throughout the period this book was underway.

The research behind three of the chapters was supported by two federal agencies: the housing and finance chapters by the Office of the Assistant Secretary for Policy Development and Research, Department of Housing and Urban Development; the crime chapter by the National Institute of Law Enforcement and Criminal Justice, Law Enforcement Assistance Administration, Department of Justice. That support is most gratefully acknowledged and appreciated. The research on which the other chapters are based was supported with institutional funds provided by the Ford Foundation. Without that support this effort would simply not have been possible. Needless to say, responsibility for any errors in this volume rests solely on the chapter authors and the co-editors.

W. G.
N. G.

Chapter 1

Introduction and Overview

William Gorham
Nathan Glazer

In 1975 the financial crisis in New York City brought the city back into public view. It was a loud new note—amid diminished old ones—reminding us that urgent problems are still to be found in American cities. Some obvious questions were raised around the country: Which cities would be next? What really lay behind New York's fiscal collapse? Was it the recession, the less benign attitude of the Republican administration, or was it mostly bad management and profligate habits? With the door opened by fiscal problems, wider questioning followed: Are central cities alive and well *generally*—and even if so, is the clock ticking toward a rude awakening? And what ever became of the urban problems of the 1960s and the profusion of remedial programs they spawned?

The Urban Predicament is about these and related questions. It is about conditions in the cities—finance, housing, crime, passenger transportation, and schooling—and about some of the underlying forces which are responsible for those conditions. It is also about the role of government— what government has done and what it can do in affecting the forces which shape cities and the conditions in them. In roughly equal measure the book aims to further the search for more effective government policies and to temper public expectations as to what government can accomplish.

We should say at the outset that in 1976 there is less consensus on the ultimate causes of many serious urban problems, and even less consensus on the measures that would ameliorate them, than there was in 1966, or

1

in 1956. Confidence in our ability to frame solutions has declined as understanding of problems has grown. As explanations have become more tentative, so the proposals put forth these days are more modest than the programs launched with such high expectations in the 1960s. One can say at least about the domestic sphere of government action—that we now know more than we did but, deprived of our hubris, are less confident in our ability to shape a future as we will. Our national mood is different in 1976.

But, despite the wariness about government intervention that has emerged, it is clear that something beyond the complex structure of federal aid that has been built and rebuilt since the early 1960s is going to be necessary. Government interventions will continue to be called for in response to current and future problems. In defining and applying those interventions, moreover, the various fates of previous attempts are still to be heeded since they not only reveal the pitfalls but also serve the more positive function of suggesting the way to firmer ground.

I. WHAT WE HAVE TRIED—A BRIEF HISTORY OF FEDERAL INTERVENTION

Twenty years ago, individual cities for the most part were left to cope with their own problems. Apart from mortgage insurance and implicit subsidies written into federal tax laws, federal involvement in urban development was modest. There was a federally subsidized public housing program dating from the 1930s, but it was small, and there was a more substantial federally subsidized program for urban renewal. The problems of the urban poor were addressed by what were then modest programs of federally assisted welfare and local public assistance. Since then we have lived through an explosion of federal programs, followed by an effort to retrench, reorganize, and consolidate. The cry of the mayors now concentrates, not on a demand for programs in this or that functional area—planning, housing, poverty, environment, crime, or what you will—but rather on a demand for unconstrained cash to spend on traditional city services and basic capital programs. While the mayors clamor, urban experts are, on the whole, silent—or when their voices are raised, it is without accord.

It was not always so. Urban policies over the past 20 years grew out of a shifting consensus among urban experts on what was needed to make a substantial contribution to easing the problems of cities. Almost every idea that has had some modest level of sponsorship has been tried.

Admittedly, not everything has been tried in the specific form and volume that experts or interest groups believed sufficient. But undoubtedly one of the barriers to doing more for cities today is that the ground is already occupied by scores of programs, each having its own interest group, employees, and rationale. Anything new will have to be accommodated to much that is old.

It is impossible in brief compass to give a complete picture of the evolution of urban policies, but for this historical prologue a sketch of broad directions will suffice. Since about 1950, insofar as we have had an urban policy it has been generated and fueled by the federal government. States, it is true, have sometimes shown the way—in housing, finance, or in welfare policies—but the chief thrusts of urban policy have come at federal initiative. It has been assumed that the states and cities are too poor, too poorly administered, or too poorly organized, to manage more than the traditional city services. Promoting positive change has been seen as requiring guidance and an infusion of funds from the federal center. For the most part, guidance has not been prescriptive but it has been forcefully suggested to states and localities through the financial incentives built into specific federal programs.

Cities in the American political system are still the creatures of states. The federal government did not, and indeed could not, take direct responsibility for the cities, as national governments do in other countries, intervening directly to correct actions, to set city borders, or to determine urban plans and projects. Nor do states commonly take such responsibility —except in a negative way by limiting cities' taxing or borrowing power, or by setting the ground rules for their political expansion through annexation. Keeping in mind the limits to federal intervention, we can glean a historical perspective on these gropings toward an urban policy by looking briefly at the *federal* government's attempts to deal with housing, planning, metropolitan governance, poverty, income maintenance, and revenue sharing.

Housing

In the 1930s, slums were seen as *the* problem of cities. The public housing program, designed to replace those slums, began in the late 1930s and was resumed in the postwar period. With broad public acceptance, it provided modestly subsidized housing for the working poor. By providing new housing, it would clear slum areas and provide better neighborhoods.

In 1949, urban renewal was added to the housing programs, supported by grants from the federal government. Urban renewal was not a housing-for-the-poor program, though many saw it as such and were outraged when it turned out that many of the poor were being evicted so their houses could be torn down to make way for new developments designed for higher-income groups. The objective of urban renewal was to eliminate substandard and inadequate housing through clearance of slums and blight and to provide a stronger tax base for cities by attracting private investment to the cities' older parts.[1]

In many cities urban renewal had an unfortunate impact on public housing, because those who lost their homes, usually from the worst slums in the city, had first claim on public housing. These new tenants, it is generally believed, contributed to a decline in the environments public housing provided. By the mid-1950s, public housing, which never housed more than a few percent of the nation's low-income households, had lost its glow: it was said the projects were too big and too uniform, that they concentrated the problem population, that they did not provide good living environments. All through the 1960s we tinkered with public housing, which nonetheless had become so unpopular that in many communities no further construction of public housing was undertaken—except for special groups, such as the aged.

As early as 1961 new subsidy programs were enacted which called for the building and management of housing for low-income groups by private nonprofit and limited-profit corporations, and for subsidized homeownership for the poor. These programs, greatly expanded in 1968,[2] were remarkably successful in producing a great quantity of housing—far greater than had been built or made available under traditional public housing. But part of their success apparently was also owing to the ease with which money could be made from these programs, legally and illegally. Scandals multiplied so rapidly that the programs were suspended in 1973. In 1974, Congress emerged with a new housing program[3] which provides rental assistance to low-income families. It also gives local communities a great deal of flexibility to adapt their programs to local housing market condi-

---

[1] The Housing Act of 1949 (P.L. 81-171), Title I: "Slum Clearance and Community Development and Redevelopment." Revised and renamed "urban renewal" in the Omnibus Housing Act of 1954 (P.L. 83-560).

[2] Section 235 of the National Housing Act of 1934 as amended by section 101 of the Housing and Urban Development Act of 1968, P.L. 90-448; Section 236 of the National Housing Act of 1934 as amended by section 201 of the Housing and Urban Development Act of 1968, P.L. 90-448.

[3] Housing and Community Development Act, 1974, P.L. 93-383.

tions. The new program maintains the movement away from large public housing projects, the once-great reform of the 1930s and 1940s.

Today, the limited problem of housing, conceived as adequate shelter, is almost solved in this country. But the direct contribution of federal housing programs to that solution has been modest. Housing has dramatically improved since the 30s, primarily because income has dramatically increased and because a large share of that higher income has gone into better housing. For those who are either retired or dependent and do not rely on earnings, the even greater improvement in transfer payments has allowed them to share in the general upgrading of physical housing conditions.

While the housing–shelter problem was being solved, a less widespread but much more complex housing-related problem was emerging—the problem of neighborhood. Housing is more than shelter. It is fixed in a place in a neighborhood. The place and the neighborhood supplement the shelter of the house by meeting other needs and desires: personal security, information, access to jobs, credit, friends, as well as standard public services. It is infinitely more difficult to improve neighborhoods than it is to improve shelter. Few people in 1976 see further housing improvement as making more than a modest contribution to improving neighborhoods.

Planning

If poor housing was the most visible malady of our cities, it was admittedly just one aspect of an intricate pattern of decline taking place in some of our major cities. By the 1950s, many analysts of urban problems saw the answer to urban deterioration in expanded agencies and instruments of planning. Cities, as they existed, were a hodge-podge. They lacked order in their development. Residential areas were to be found where developers could make a profit. Occupational opportunities of various kinds in various places grew out of the decisions of individual entrepreneurs to locate in those places they judged most advantageous to their enterprises. Transportation between residence and work in most places had become dominated by private automobiles because public fixed-rail transportation facilities were expensive and could not easily be expanded, or were poorly placed to serve the new residential areas. Schools in the old parts of cities suddenly were half-empty, while in new residential areas they were few and overcrowded. It seemed clear that a more coherent urban development was possible, which would improve upon the wholly independent development of housing, job-creating facilities, urban services, and transportation.

"Planning" can mean many things. At the one pole, there is strong government direction and control, which has never been popular in this country. At the other, there are "wish lists" having little to do with reality. Planning in the United States has been nearer the latter pole. In 1949, the federal government began to provide money for the development of overall plans for communities. To obtain urban renewal and other funds, cities were obliged to prepare master plans—for which federal assistance was available. Planning departments grew apace, and many development master plans were created.

This was only the beginning of a veritable explosion in planning aid. "Categorical aids for open space (1961), mass transportation (1964), sewer and water grants (1965) and advanced land acquisition (1965) were all conditioned on consistency with comprehensively planned development of the area. . . . Legislation passed in 1966 and 1968 requires review-and-comment by a regional planning agency of federal aid projects with regional impact. . . . In 1966 . . . Congress provided additional support for planning through Title II of the Demonstration Cities and Metropolitan Planning Act . . ."[4] More recently, air and water quality legislation and housing and community development laws call for extensive planning elements. Each burst of federal grants to cities—for housing, manpower development, transportation, open space, poverty, health facilities—now required its own planning agencies, at city, regional, and/or state levels. All this planning, in turn, now required still more planning to coordinate between the functional areas that were being planned for as well as between different regions covered by planning authorities. By 1974, the White House could report, "There are 37 major planning assistance authorities [programs] funded in the aggregate at an annual level of $450 million."[5]

By this time the earlier enthusiasm about what planning could accomplish for city development was gone. Each plan, and each part of a plan, inevitably created conflicts between different interests: homeowners, developers of housing, developers of industry, lovers of nature, the poor, the well-to-do, and so on. The plan that might evoke harmonious agreement

---

[4] Morton Schussheim, *The Modest Commitment to Cities* (Lexington, Mass.: Lexington Books, 1974), pp. 172, 174.

[5] *Report on National Growth and Development, 1974,* Committee on Community Development, The Domestic Council (U.S. Government Printing Office), p. 89.

did not exist, it appeared—or existed only while its details were unclear and each interest could still read into the outline the specifics that were most satisfactory to that interest. But perhaps most damaging to the success of planning is the limited power of government over the processes which shape our cities. Those who had high hopes for planning did not appreciate that fact. Whatever the achievements of planning in other political systems, it appeared that planning in the United States, whether for master plans or for urban renewal, achieved only marginal improvements over what had gone before. While planning is now fixed as part of the urban government process, it would be the rare urban specialist who would place much weight on it.

Metropolitan Government

The late 1950s and early 1960s saw an emphasis on urban political development. Many urban specialists then viewed the problems of the city as rooted in a growing imbalance between the central cities (hemmed in by fixed boundaries, at least in the Northeast and Midwest) and the surrounding politically independent suburban areas. The boundary problem was created when the states began to protect communities contiguous to cities from annexation. The initial position of the experts was that there were substantial economies of scale in the provision of services to be reaped by joining several local jurisdictions into a single governmental unit. Over time, this emphasis has been superseded by a concern for equalizing resources between city and suburb. The suburban communities are newer, with a higher-income population, and with fewer of the social problems stemming from a low-income population. Thus, they can tax themselves relatively lightly for essential services, compared to the central city. It is argued that the central city provides unreimbursed services (roads, police protection, cultural facilities, etc.) to the suburbs and suburbanites.[6] Cooperation and coordination between a city and its suburbs in the delivery of many urban services seemed sensible. Thus both equity and efficiency call for suburb and central city to attack together the com-

---

[6] It has been difficult to demonstrate the actual "balance of trade" between central cities and suburbs. For a recent review of the literature, and an effort to plunge deeper into the issue of whether suburbs and suburbanites "exploit" central cities and central city dwellers, see Kenneth V. Greene, William B. Neenan, and Claudia D. Scott, *Fiscal Interaction in a Metropolitan Area* (Lexington, Mass.: Lexington Books, 1974). The matter is complicated, but from the evidence of this book one can say of this thesis, "not proven."

mon problems of a metropolitan area. Here is a means whereby the resources of the relatively prosperous suburbs can be recaptured for the benefit of the pinched central cities.

There are other advantages to bringing central city and suburbs together in a common political framework: If planning has values for an urban area, then clearly it must be metropolitan planning, because the entire metropolis forms a single market at least for jobs, for transportation, for recreation and culture, and usually a single environment for air, water, and waste. Such planning would best be done within common political institutions.

Many approaches to bringing together the central city and its suburbs have been proposed: amalgamation, strengthened countywide government, special-function authorities to cover the areas where cooperation was most insistently required (transportation, recreation, sewer and water, health facilities). Considerable professional enthusiasm has existed for creating such metropolitan-wide governments, and some were indeed created. One cannot say this approach is a failure or a success, since it has been so little tried. There are some examples of new kinds of metropolitan political organization in which several city and suburban political functions were consolidated. This was done in Dade County (Miami) (1957), Nashville (1962), Indianapolis (1969), and the Minneapolis-St. Paul region (1967). But even quite limited metropolitanization of governmental functions has been widely opposed by suburbs eager to retain their fiscal and other advantages. In some cases, black political interests have opposed amalgamation because it meant losing the reality or opportunity for black political control of the central city.

One modest form of metropolitan coordination has had much wider application. Under federal prodding and pressure, "councils of governments" (COGs) have been created in every major metropolitan area. The council is made up of the elected heads of each government in the metropolitan area. The local COG comments on how newly applied-for federally funded projects would fit into (or conflict with) existing metropolitan plans. It can recommend against approval. But this is practically never done. Both because of its political structure and because of absence of strong federal backing, the power of the COGs to bring order and rationality to decisions and projects in metropolitan areas is very limited.

Short of a compelling state interest to change the governance of metropolitan areas—and it is hard to imagine how that would arise—widespread movement toward metropolitan-wide government is unlikely.

Poverty

By the 1960s, the suburbanization of middle-income whites and the northward migration of low-income southern blacks were changing the racial composition of cities in the Northeast and North Central States. It became clear to many that the most serious present and future urban problems would have to do with race and low income. The violent riots that began in 1964 universalized that belief, but in that same year the widest efforts to improve conditions for the urban poor were launched under the Economic Opportunity Act of 1964, better known as the "poverty program." Clearly poverty was more than an urban problem: indeed, in the mid-60s there was proportionally more poverty in nonurban areas than in the cities. But the worst problems of the cities were associated with poverty. "If some real disaster impends in the city, it is not because parking spaces are hard to find, because architecture is bad, because department store sales are declining or even because taxes are rising. If there is a general crisis, it has to do with the essential welfare of individuals. . . . It is clear . . . that poverty, ignorance, and racial (and other) injustices are among the most important of the general conditions affecting the welfare of individuals." [7]

This was the view of a political scientist in 1968. An urban economist in 1974 saw the problem more starkly: "Simply stated, our fundamental urban problem is the low income, or poverty, of many of the residents of our cities. In the 1930s President Franklin Roosevelt asserted that the South was the nation's number one economic problem. Today many would argue that our cities are. . . . The problem has moved from the rural South to the urban North." [8]

When the war on poverty was declared in 1964, of the 34 million people counted as poor, 16 million lived within SMSAs and of those 10 million lived in central cities.[9] Despite the fact that only about 30 percent of the poor lived in central cities when the poverty program was started, it is fair to say that the Economic Opportunity Act constituted a major federal "urban" policy.

The poverty program and the subsequent "model cities" program

---

[7] Edward C. Banfield, *The Unheavenly City* (Boston, Mass.: Little, Brown, 1968) pp. 10-11.

[8] Richard F. Muth, *Urban Economic Problems* (New York, N.Y.: Harper and Row, 1974) p. 2.

[9] Robert A. Levine, *The Poor Ye Need Not Have With You* (Cambridge, Mass.: Massachusetts Institute of Technology Press, 1970) table 2, p. 22.

(1966) focused funds, activities, and ingenuity on particular areas of cities—those characterized by relatively high concentrations of the poor. A variety of things would be done in these areas: local community organizations would be formed, work training programs would be launched, children would be enrolled in special educational programs, comprehensive health programs and centers would be created, housing would be improved; and many other programs would also be launched—some that experts thought necessary, some that local inhabitants of poverty and model cities areas themselves developed.[10]

The ferment created by these programs was tremendous. The poverty program established, through Community Action Agencies and the legal services programs, the wherewithal for the evolution of new centers of power. The old centers, the regularly elected political authorities and the civil servants responsible for the traditional services, were threatened. This conflict emerged immediately with the launching of the poverty program and raged through the late 1960s. It has since moderated, first because the old and the new political forces have learned to live with each other, and second because federal support for the new neighborhood political forces has been gradually withdrawn, especially after Richard Nixon became President.

The overall evaluation of poverty programs and model cities will probably always be in dispute. Reliable evaluation is hindered by the fact that the poverty programs were only a few of a large number of factors affecting income and "opportunity." Of the other forces that were increasing income, perhaps the most important was the very high

---

[10] The books on the poverty program are too numerous to list, but for recent evaluations, see "The Great Society: Lessons for the Future," a special issue of *The Public Interest* edited by Eli Ginzburg and Robert Solow, Winter, 1974; Robert D. Plotnick and Felicity Skidmore, *Progress Against Poverty: A Review of the 1964-1974 Decade* (New York, N.Y.: Academic Press, 1975). For studies of the poverty program, see Sar D. Levitan, *The Great Society's Poor Law* (Baltimore, Md.: Johns Hopkins Press, 1969); James C. Donovan, *The Politics of Poverty* (Indianapolis, Ind.: Bobbs-Merrill [Pegasus], 1976); James Sundquist, ed., *On Fighting Poverty* (New York, N.Y.: Basic Books, 1969); Robert A. Levine, *The Poor Ye Need Not Have With You* (Cambridge, Mass.: MIT Press, 1970); Daniel P. Moynihan, *Maximum Feasible Misunderstanding* (New York, N.Y.: Macmillan, [Free Press], 1969); and this is the merest sampling. Two on the model cities program: Bernard J. Frieden and Marshall Kaplan, *The Politics of Neglect: Urban Aid from Model Cities to Revenue Sharing* (Cambridge, Mass.: MIT Press, 1975); and Charles M. Haar, *Between the Idea and the Reality: A Study in the Origin, Fate, and Legacy of the Model Cities Program* (Boston, Mass.: Little, Brown, 1975).

economic growth the United States was experiencing during the late 1960s. Equal opportunity was given a great boost by the passage of new civil rights legislation in 1964 which banned discrimination in employment. Sorting out the contribution of each of these factors is, at least for the present, beyond our most perceptive evaluators. However, few doubt that some of the changes that reduced poverty from 19.3 percent in 1964 to 12.8 percent in 1968 could be traced in part to the poverty program. It hired tens of thousands of people to inform the poor of their rights and opportunities. This recruiting, plus the success of the legal services program in easing eligibility rules, contributed substantially to the increase in welfare recipients in the late 1960s and early 1970s. Further, the simple creation of so many agencies which were required to make a special effort to employ people from poverty areas and poverty backgrounds created many new jobs and many new careers.

Even though much of the poverty program was dismantled in the early 1970s, much survived. Many erstwhile poverty workers found themselves in new occupations—government service (appointive and elective), private employment, consultantship—that they would never have entered had it not been for the poverty program.

Income Maintenance

One achievement of the poverty program—signing up eligible welfare recipients for payments—became an incentive for the reform of welfare in the early Nixon years. The chosen instrument, the Family Assistance Plan (FAP), involved a federal takeover of welfare cash payments up to a national minimum, and the extension of cash support to the working poor, to reduce the gap between their circumstances and the circumstances of families supported by welfare. It was also expected to discourage welfare-induced family splitting and to encourage work.

The idea was spawned in the academic community and the Johnson administration. Some of its protagonists expected it to make an indirect contribution to easing the problems of cities: If city problems were caused by poverty, and if some cities provided more assistance to the poor than others, by that token alone these generous cities would have more poor, and more problems. One hope for a national FAP was that it would reduce the flow of the poor—black and white—from states with low welfare payments to cities in the North, Midwest, and far West, with high welfare payments. There was yet another possible, though hypothetical, contribution FAP might make—one might expect it to help equalize employment opportunity by reducing the risk which job-seeking welfare recipients incur when they leave places with poor job prospects to go where the jobs are. While the contribution of different welfare payments to the mobility or immobility of the urban poor was not known, the logic of the prospective benefit of more uniform welfare payments had much to recommend it.

The reform was never passed by Congress. Once close examination of FAP began, it was realized that, since it was to be an add-on to the existing income-conditioned federal benefits (for medical care, housing, and the like), it would not greatly increase work incentives (or decrease work disincentives). Additional income from work would still reduce income-conditioned benefits by almost as much as (and sometimes more than) the income earned. While FAP did not reduce work incentives as much as the programs it was designed to replace, it paradoxically focused attention on this problem and on the interaction of all the income-related programs to benefit the poor.[11]

The urgency of welfare reform has abated in the middle 1970s. On the one hand, the rapid increase of the welfare population in the more generous states (New York, California, Massachusetts, and others) led them finally to institute more restrictive administrative practices to reduce the numbers on welfare and the benefits they received. On the other hand, a national food stamp program, whose benefits came completely from the federal government, grew from a modest $36 million in 1965 to $3.6 billion in 1975. To a large extent this program did what FAP proposed—it extended to all families of given size below a certain income a substantial income supplement, irrespective of place of residence, family make-up, and relationship to the labor force. A partial reform which established national minimum support for the aged, blind, and disabled and placed them under the Social Security System, was passed in 1972.[12]

Income maintenance programs—even perfectly designed—are unlikely to rescue the country from serious urban problems of the kinds analyzed in this book. No level of income support consistent with maintaining a

---

[11] For analyses of these and other issues surrounding FAP, see Vincent and Vee Burke, *Nixon's Good Deed* (New York, N.Y.: Columbia University Press, 1974); Daniel P. Moynihan, *The Politics of a Guaranteed Income* (New York, N.Y.: Random House, 1973).

[12] Social Security Amendment of 1972 (P.L. 92-603), Supplemental Security Income.

reasonable incentive to work would be high enough to make much of a dent in those problems.

Revenue Sharing

FAP was never tried; but the general philosophy that called for the federal government to back away from specific interventions in specific cities to deal with specific problems did prevail. Thus, housing subsidies, as we have pointed out, shifted from projects constructed and administered by local agencies to supporting homeownership and rental programs of existing housing or encouraging new construction by private and non-profit builders.

The new federalism of the Nixon administration called for further substantive withdrawal. The administration proposed and Congress passed general revenue sharing in 1972. Revenue sharing was an old idea—states had been doing it for decades. Federal revenue sharing was accorded intense public debate in the 1960s, in the heady days when the difficult problem foreseen by many economists was "fiscal drag"—a tendency for federal revenues to build up faster than expenditures, depressing economic demand and ultimately GNP. The excess income could be used to reduce federal taxes or the surplus could be passed on to lower levels of government. Passing the surplus to state and local governments would relieve the pressure on them to meet their expenditure demands by raising local taxes, which are more regressive than federal revenue sources. Thus, from the point of view of its early protagonists, the merit of federal revenue sharing lay in its "progressive" tax consequences, and its guarantees of steadily growing state and local revenues.

Revenue sharing was philosophically appealing to others, including the Republican administration, because it moved public decision-making responsibility away from Washington and seemed to be a way to ease out the narrowly targeted "categorical" programs of the 1960s, many of which were regarded as alien, ineffective, or mischievous.

General revenue sharing (passed into law in 1972) was to be paired with a group of special revenue-sharing packages which were to combine individual grant programs in each functional area and award on a formula basis a single grant to state and local governments. Several of these were enacted into law: The Comprehensive Employment and Training Act (CETA) in 1973; the Housing and Community Development Act in 1974; and Title XX of the Social Security Act in 1974 (P.L. 93-647), which provides a block grant for social services. By 1976 about

25 percent of the federal support to states, counties, and cities was in the form of revenue sharing or block grants.[13]

But general revenue sharing started and has remained a relatively small program. And the special revenue sharing programs have remained at about the same funding levels as the categorical grants they replaced. In 1976 general revenue sharing will amount to $6.3 billion, less than a single year's annual growth in the budgets of the local governments receiving it. Once general revenue sharing was in place, the growth of federal government support to state and local governments slowed sharply and the federal "presence" in local urban problems was reduced. The coincidence of this slowdown and the economic recession and inflation of 1974-75 has added to the variety of traditional city woes one with overriding urgency: meeting the budget.

* * *

In summary, 20 years ago federal direct intervention in cities was minimal; it reached its height in the late 1960s and has been on the decline since then. Although there are mixed views about the justification and merit of spending more money, practically no voices at the moment are arguing for more substantive federal intervention in city problems. The arguments over block grants are about providing assurances that a fair share will go to this or that group, to this or that purpose, or to this or that city—they deal with target groups and formulas, not with program philosophy. This is not to say that there is widespread satisfaction with the state of our cities, only that a smaller percent of the population care about the cities, while even fewer have confidence that the federal government (or any other level of government for that matter) knows how to make things better.

Such is the national mood today.

And a good time, we think, to sharpen the discussion not only about urban conditions themselves but also about what should be expected of government to improve those conditions. To provide a backdrop for that discussion, we turn, now to some of the major trends shaping our urban society.

---

[13] For a fundamental analysis of revenue sharing see also Charles Goetz, *What Is Revenue Sharing?* (Washington, D.C.; The Urban Institute, 1972); Richard P. Nathan, Allen D. Manvel, Susannah E. Calkins, and associates, *Monitoring Revenue Sharing* (Washington, D.C.: The Brookings Institution, 1975); and "The Future of General Revenue Sharing," *Nation's Cities,* vol. 13, no. 2 (Feb. 1975), pp. 14-24.

II. DEMOGRAPHIC AND INCOME TRENDS AFFECTING THE CITIES

Over the past 25 years the total U.S. population has increased by 40 percent, from 152 million in 1950 to 213 million in 1975. The rate of increase per year has dropped sharply, however, from almost 2 percent in the fifties to less than 1 percent in the seventies. During the same period, there has also been a shift toward the West and most recently toward the South, away from the Northeast and North Central regions.

Figure 1
Percent Change in Population Growth
by Region, 1950-1975

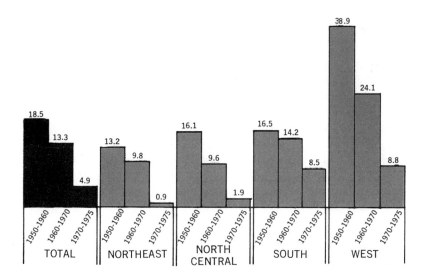

Source: Based on *U.S. Census of Population, 1970,* Characteristics of the Population, Part 1, United States Summary, section 1, table 8, and *Current Population Reports,* Population Estimates and Projections, Series P-25, no. 615.

The distribution of nonagricultural jobs among regions has also been changing: the older Northeast and North Central regions have steadily lost ground to the West and the South.

Figure 2
Percent Distribution of Nonagricultural Employment
by Region, 1949-1974

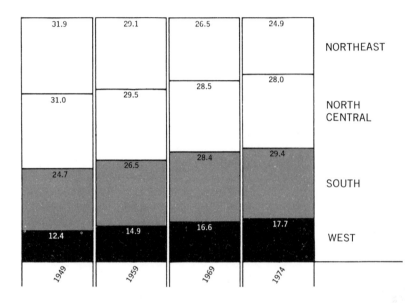

Source: Based on *1976 Report on National Growth and Development: The Changing Issues for National Growth,* The Committee on Community Development, The Domestic Council, February 1976, table II-5.

Figure 3
Net Black Migration from South
to Northeast and North Central Regions (in thousands)
1955-1975

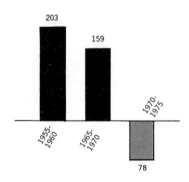

Source: Based on *Current Population Reports,* Population Characteristics, Series
P-20, no. 285, table 28; *U.S. Census of Population, 1970,* Mobility for
States and the Nation, PC (2)-2B, table 42; and *U.S. Census of Population, 1960,* Mobility for States and Economic Areas, Final Report PC
(2)-2B, table 14.

Metropolitanization, which increased from 63 percent in 1950 to 68 percent by 1974, has begun to taper off, and in some of the largest SMSAs, population is declining. Between 1970 and 1974 the population of *all* SMSAs increased by about 5 million or 3.6 percent. However, in the Northeast and North Central regions, the population of SMSAs remained unchanged. Five SMSAs—Pittsburgh, Cincinnati, Cleveland, New York, and Detroit—declined in population.

One reason for the recent decline in the SMSAs of the Northeast and North Central regions is the reversal of the net migration of blacks from the South.

Within metropolitan areas, suburbanization has continued apace. By 1960 the suburban population had grown to equal that of the central city, and by 1970 (and through 1974) 7 percent more of the U.S. population lived in the suburbs than in the central cities.

Figure 4
Percent Distribution of Population
by Metropolitan and Nonmetropolitan Residence
1950-1974

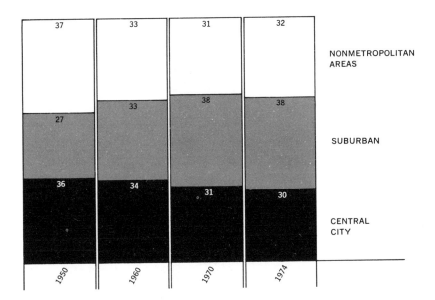

Source: Based on *Current Population Reports*, Special Studies, Series P-23, no. 55, table E; *General Demographic Trends for Metropolitan Areas, 1960 to 1970*, Bureau of the Census, report PHC (2)-1, pp. 1-23; and *State of the Cities: 1974*, National League of Cities, Washington, D.C., 1974, p. 12.

The growth of the suburbs relative to the central city has been more pronounced in the West, North Central, and Northeast regions than it has in the South, where, unlike the other regions, the central cities have been able to adjust their boundaries to encompass contiguous population growth.

The suburbanization has historically been largely of white, middle-income persons. That, plus the post World War II migration of southern blacks and the higher fertility rate of blacks, has changed the racial make-up of central cities, most sharply in the Northeast and North Central regions.

Figure 5
Percent of Blacks in Central Cities
by Region, 1940-1970

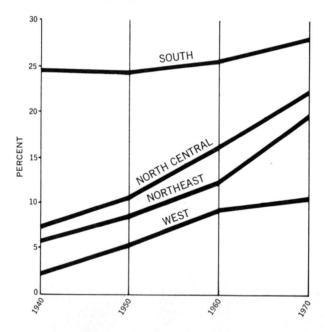

Source: Based on "The Changing Distribution of the Population of the United States in the Twentieth Century," Irene B. Taeuber, in *Population Distribution and Policy,* Sara Mills Mazie, ed., vol. 5 of reports of Commission on Population Growth and the American Future, Washington, D.C., U.S. Government Printing Office, 1972, table 19.

Real income per capita has increased nationally by two-thirds since 1950. It still differs substantially among regions, but these differences are diminishing.

Figure 6
Regional Personal Income Per Capita as a Percentage of U.S.,
1950-1974

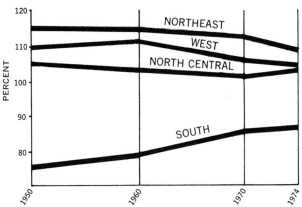

Source: Based on data in *The Statistical Abstract of the United States*, Washington, D.C., U.S. Government Printing Office, 1961, 1974, and 1975 editions.

The median income of families nationally differs substantially by race
and by place of residence. Black families earn less than white families.
(Black family income as a percentage of white family income increased
from 55 percent in 1960 to 64 percent in 1970. Since then it has dropped
slightly.) Earnings of suburban families outstrip the earnings of central
city and nonmetropolitan families.

Figure 7
Median Income of Families in 1973
by Race and Residence

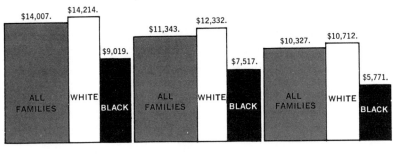

Source: Based on "The National Setting: Regional Shifts, Metropolitan Decline,
and Urban Decay," Vincent P. Barabba, in *Post-Industrial America:
Metropolitan Decline and Inter-Regional Job Shifts*, George Sternlieb and
James W. Hughes, eds., The Center for Urban Policy Research, Rutgers-
The State University of New Jersey, New Brunswick, New Jersey, 1975,
p. 60.

Income differences between central city and suburban families are increasing. In 1970 the average income of all families living in central cities was $13,349. Between 1970 and 1974 the average income of families moving out of central cities was $14,169, while the average income of families moving into central cities was only $12,864. The effect has been to reduce the average income of central city residents relative to that of

Figure 8
Impact of Migration on
Average Family Income in Central Cities
1970-1974

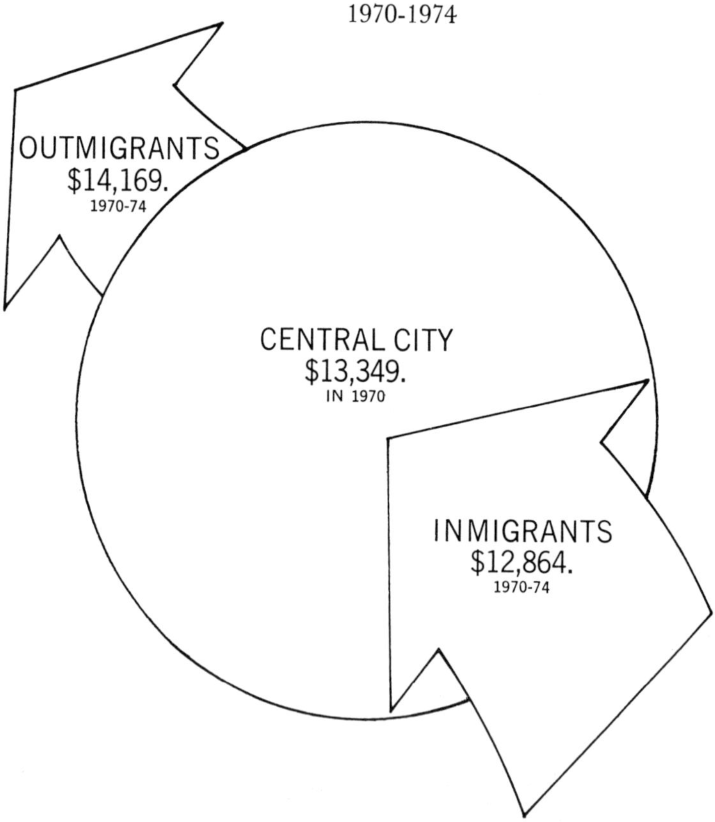

OUTMIGRANTS
$14,169.
1970-74

CENTRAL CITY
$13,349.
IN 1970

INMIGRANTS
$12,864.
1970-74

Source: Based on Barabba, op. cit., p. 55.

the suburbs (see figure 8). For example, between 1960 and 1970 the median income of central city residents as a percent of the median income of the entire metropolitan area declined from 94 to 91 percent in Pittsburgh, from 90 to 87 percent in Cincinnati, from 85 to 80 percent in Cleveland, from 93 to 89 percent in New York, and from 89 to 83 percent in Detroit.

Poverty has moved to the city. Although the proportion of central city residents in poverty has declined, a higher percentage of the poor now reside in the central city.

Figure 9
Percent Distribution of Population below Poverty Line
by Residence, 1959-1974

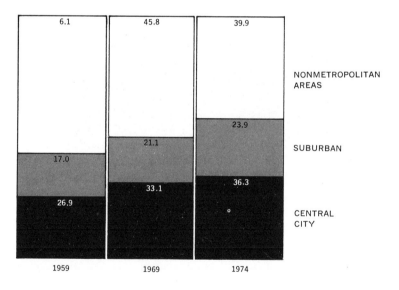

Source: Based on *Current Population Reports,* Consumer Income, Series P-60, no. 102, table 3.

Of the poor in the central city, the percentage who are black has increased dramatically, from 37 percent in 1959 to 47 percent in 1974.

(An overwhelming number of the poor blacks living in central cities—
4.1 million in 1974—live in black ghettos.)

Figure 10
Percent of Central City Poor
Who Are Black, 1959-1974

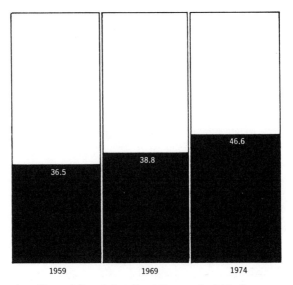

Source: Based on *Current Population Reports,* op. cit., table 3.

III. TOWARD DEFINING THE GOVERNMENT ROLE

Here we will examine three of the several trends we illustrated in the
previous section: the regional shift in population and economic activity
from the Northeast and North Central regions into the West and most
recently into the South; the relative economic decline and the loss of
middle-income population from the major central cities in the Northeast
and North Central regions; and the increasing concentration in these
cities of blacks, a large percentage of whom are of low income.

The forces behind these trends are not the only ones that contribute
to the urban predicament, but in the 1970s their close interrelationship
and pervasive impact seem to give them special significance. Hardly a
single major urban problem can be understood without acknowledging
their role, and thus they invite the careful attention of government.

The Economy

Before turning to these trends, we must first emphasize the paramount importance of the overall economy to the well-being of cities. More than anything else the state of the economy has determined, and will continue to determine, the rate at which urban conditions improve or deteriorate. A strong economy will not, in and of itself, alleviate many urban problems—crime has continued its upward path for several decades in good times and bad—but it is a necessary condition for progress against most of them. National economic prosperity probably is the most important contribution that the federal government can make in behalf of the cities.

The intricate relationship between national prosperity and the condition of the cities has been aptly illustrated in the past few years. The economic *recession* of 1974-75 squeezed municipal revenues as receipts from municipal tax sources reflected the reduction of business activity and consumer spending, and forced an increase in expenditures for social programs. The accompanying *inflation* increased the pressure from municipal workers for wage increases and raised other costs of government, particularly energy costs. These twin pressures have affected virtually all local governments. But stagflation has thrown those cities facing long-term declines in population and jobs, the most notable of which is New York City, into profound discomfort. In the absence of greatly increased state or federal help, most of these cities have been forced to respond with such measures as raising taxes and reducing services—which will exacerbate the underlying trends that account for the cities' *long-term* fiscal problems. These measures tend to encourage further loss of higher income residents and job-creating enterprises.

What of the effects of stagflation on the poor of the cities? While it is true that in the past ten years federal income transfer programs have become much better equipped to hold things together for households that suffer economic hardship, the poor and near-poor continue to bear the brunt of a weak economy because they have the least slack for absorbing price increases and reductions in earned income.

We would have liked to present a full report on the effects that recession and inflation have had on specific urban ills. But the research findings for such a discussion are spotty and inconclusive. It must suffice to note that what findings do exist support the intuitive view that a weak economy contributes to street crime (probably white collar crime as well), to a disproportionate increase in unemployment among those who live in urban poverty areas, to the deterioration of low-income housing, and to a decline in the quality and quantity of social services for individual recipients.

Beyond the benefits of a stable and strong economy what can be said about the impact on the cities of the methods used in trying to achieve those conditions? Which of the macro-economic measures used to control inflation or reduce unemployment have secondary effects that help or hinder peculiarly urban interests? The question is important and should receive attention in shaping the nation's economic policies. Some examples of such policies and their possible outcome for cities are:

- In fattening the federal budget to promote aggregate demand, such measures as revenue sharing, community development block grants, and Comprehensive Employment and Training Act programs obviously serve urban interests better than they are served by expanding public works programs generally, or augmenting expenditures on federal highway construction, or defense and space spending.
- In paring down federal budgets to reduce inflationary pressures, preserving the revenue-sharing and block grant programs would be most beneficial to the cities in trouble.
- Monetary policies affect the cost of municipal borrowing and the cost of local government, and can be more harmful or less harmful depending on the degree to which that impact is considered. Whether those policies are intended to promote the expansion or contraction of the money supply or to increase the supply of government or government-insured debt, they should take into account the repercussions on the tax-exempt credit markets which are so important to municipal governments.

Although we state these illustrations simply, to determine what policies actually benefit or hurt which sorts of cities is very complex. Our most talented and experienced economists still do not have a firm grasp on how many of these measures work their way through the economy and produce effects over time. (If they understood such things well, our ability to achieve much closer realization of overall economic goals would be closer at hand.) Nonetheless, however incomplete are the estimates of how different macroeconomic policies affect the city, they should be made and be taken into account in choosing among those policies.

The Declining Northeast and North Central Regions

As we have seen, the Northeast and North Central regions are losing population. They are faring less well in terms of new economic activity than either the West or the South. This condition, on top of a recent sharp reduction in overall U.S. population growth, has led to the first absolute population declines in a number of older metropolitan areas and their central cities.

Shifts in the location of jobs reflect the choices which employers make in trying to improve their profits. Correspondingly, most individuals who migrate do so to improve their economic circumstances. Such mobility is one important way in which productivity and average economic well-being are improved in our economy. But not only private entrepreneurs and individuals make locational decisions: government also locates enterprises and contracts that generate economic activity. As a side effect of achieving their public purpose, government activities and spending generate jobs, income, and wealth. Thus, government influences regional employment patterns and migration and, ultimately, the relative vitality of the different regions. For example, in preparation for World War II and in the course of the two successive wars that were fought in the Far East, enterprises of enormous economic significance to the overall development of the West Coast were generated by government decision. Also, starting in the 1930s and continuing to the present time, the South has been a favored area for the flow of federal funds. In the latter case, the regional pattern of economic well-being was a definite consideration in the locational decisions: the South was poor and federal money, flowing there for military and other purposes, would help it catch up. Beyond equity, indeed usually before equity, such decisions flow from the same considerations that drive private locational choices—efficiency and political power. The full impact of federal government investment on regional economic development and well-being has never been determined. However, few doubt that the effects have been, and are, highly significant.

So long as the less prosperous regions of the country are on the receiving end of the advantages of federal investment—as has been true of the South during the past several decades—public equity seems to have been served. However, when government-induced economic stimulation bolsters better off regions at the expense of others in inferior circumstances, there is at least an argument for reducing the negative effects in the latter regions or for distributing the stimuli more even-handedly. Developing even-handed regional policies is not easy. And regional equity is only one consideration in determining the geographical location of government investments or purchases. How much efficiency should be traded for increased equity is no mean question. Moreover, why should the consideration of regional equity begin and end with government procurement and the location of government facilities? All government regulatory action and spending have regional economic implications. And what about equity between different-sized places irrespective of region? None of these questions is simple. In spite of the difficulty in answering such questions about the net advantages that the federal government bestows on differents places, the effort should be undertaken to legitimate current practices or to modify them.

Of course—even apart from the actions of government—in a system of national markets every regional economic trend carries within it the seeds for its reversal. Thus, if the major reason for the relatively larger employment and income gains of the South is the difference in costs of production (and living) between it and the losing region, then, as the job and population flows continue, these differences will tend to shrink. Signs of this adjustment are already appearing. For example, property values and other costs in the declining cities of the Northeast and North Central regions have generally been increasing much less rapidly than those in the South and West—in some cases they have declined absolutely. Also the cost of labor, which has been lower in the less unionized South, has been climbing relative to the Northeast and North Central regions. As these cost adjustments continue, they will tend to lessen the relative economic gains of the South and West.

Declining Central Cities

As is pointed out in chapter 2, the decline in the central cities of the Northeast and North Central regions stems from a long-term trend toward decreasing density in all of the old cities. What responsibility has the larger society toward this development?

Many feel that the decline taking place not only reduces the quality of life for the remaining population but also leads to the inevitable running down of the capital plant of the city, depriving present and future residents and nonresidents of the esthetic, cultural, and even social pleasures of a healthy city. They argue that preserving an option for the dense city is of great importance and that "saving" such places from extreme decline therefore deserves high national priority. They also instance the earlier interventions of both the federal and the state governments which accelerated the trend toward suburbanization. The tax benefits of homeownership, the facilitation of financing home mortgages through the Federal Housing Administration, and the federal highway program are usually cited as the major interventions of the federal government; the restriction of annexation, as the major state intervention.

In response to these and other arguments in recent years federal (and some state) programs have been developed which direct (disproportionate) financial aid to the cities. These programs were briefly described earlier. Whether, in some way, they match the merit of the case probably cannot be determined. It is by no means clear how much government interventions actually accelerated the movement out of cities. Even if that were estimated, to determine just compensation for government-induced losses would be very difficult, if not ultimately arbitrary.

A number of actions which seem worthwhile have been under consideration or have recently been suggested to ameliorate the short-term financial problems. These include the revision of revenue-sharing formulas, introducing counter-cyclical aid, increasing federal financial responsibility for welfare cash payments and the state financial responsibility for elementary and secondary education. These and other measures are detailed in the next chapter.

None of these measures would allow declining cities to live much beyond their own means. Most of them would therefore have to accept much more stringent municipal budgets, holding the line on wage and benefit increases for municipal employees, extracting increased productivity, and—if this does not align spending with receipts—making the hard choices of which services to reduce or eliminate. Mayor Kenneth Gibson of Newark put the case sharply:

> Before dealing with this fiscal crisis—when you talk about that now, you talk about New York City—it would be good to talk about, first, what city government is or what it should be, or the purpose of the city government, because therein lies the possibility of a solution. I firmly believe that the purpose of city government is to provide basic services to people. That has to start with those services that are absolutely necessary in the city and progress to another order of priority, and once you define what those basic, absolutely needed services are in the city and you go to some point where you're to going to say, "At this point we stop," then you have to decide where you get that money to provide those basic services. There's not much beyond that. We're not now rebuilding any city, unless you find someplace out in the far West where the city planners are taking a nice oasis and making a city —we're not at that stage. The older cities in this country have to take another look at redefining what the purpose of the city government is, what services are absolutely necessary, which ones are maybe not necessary [but] should be provided, and get to some level and say, "That's it, at least for the time being." [14]

---

[14] In Special *New York Affairs* Conference, "The New Politics of Less," *New York Affairs*, vol. 3, no. 1 (Fall 1975).

What can city government do to improve its *long run* prospects?

In general, declining cities will find it in their interest to work against the conditions which deter enterprises and middle-income people from moving in or supply an impetus for them to move out. These include crime, poor public education, declining service, relatively high taxes, ugliness, congestion, and the like—all formidable problems. It is by no means clear that central city government can work effectively against these forces. Some city governments will have allies—the increased relative cost of suburban living, a trend toward smaller households, and some renewed interest in the architecture of the cities and the mode of life they offer—and will be aided substantially by these factors, others will not.

The most intractable problem is the net loss of jobs occurring in many of the central cities. Public employment provides at best a temporary expedient which cannot substitute for the benefits of a vibrant local economy. Special programs which provide tax and other incentives to business also may help in some places. And, of course, the general conditions which encourage households to locate or stay in the city will also tend to maintain the employment base.

The declining cities are going through a period of urban natural selection. The most likely outcome: some will pull out, stabilize, and even revitalize; others will continue to weaken and will eventually stabilize at a much lower level of activity. Many of the federal and state programs will facilitate the positive process of stabilization and even revitalization where the other forces conducive to it are present; where they are not, aid from above will not halt or reverse the decline.

Ghettos

The third trend is the continuing departure of middle-income white population from the central cities and the inner suburbs and the increasing population of blacks in old central cities. Residential segregation in large metropolitan areas is probably increasing. While the legislation of 1964 and 1968 provides a firm legal bar against racial discrimination in the rental and sale of housing, the commitment to integrated housing is not widespread. In the absence of such a commitment, the persistence of racial segregation is likely to continue in the foreseeable future.

The total costs of racial segregation to our society are, by the calculation of most students of the subject, very high—much higher than most people realize. This, however, is not the place to detail them. In any case, widespread appreciation of the costs would probably do little to offset the individual and institutional actions which lead to segregation. We should expect, although we do not always get, aggressive enforcement of antidiscrimination laws. But even with rigorous enforcement, racial segregation would persist (and grow in some places). There are two major reasons for this: (1) even very mild but widespread preference for neighbors of the same race leads to rental, buying, and selling behavior which tends strongly toward racial segregation,[15] and (2) there is a strong aversion among both black and white middle-income families to neighbors of lower socioeconomic status. Since blacks are greatly over-represented among the poor, the income preferences reinforce the racial preferences. Therefore, a necessary, though by no means sufficient condition for substantial residential integration would seem to be full equality of income among the races. Unfortunately, one of the greatest obstacles to realization of more equality is the condition of segregation itself. And this is the Catch 22 of American interracial life.

The upshot is that we have, and will continue to have, large urban ghettos, substantial sections of which are in sharp decline. By most standards of urban well-being, these declining areas offer unsatisfactory living environments and distinctly inferior opportunities for improved income and greater social mobility. It is clear that progress toward equal opportunity and adequate living standards will have to take place in the ghettos themselves. We have little new to add on how this is to be done, but before even addressing that question we should offer a firmer footing on who should share that responsibility, and why.

What are the arguments for spending public funds to improve low-income ghetto areas? There have been several. For one, it has been argued that the negative attributes of particular areas "spill over"—that is, the negative attributes are not confined to those areas but have effects elsewhere. Thus, the edges of a bad neighborhood inevitably tend to expand into the adjoining neighborhoods; crime engendered within the neighborhood bounds does not stay there but invades fringe areas and spreads far into other sections of a metropolitan area. Therefore, it is argued, improvement in the low-income ghettos provides a positive benefit to the residents in the surrounding area. That is a respectable argument for the participation of surrounding communities but not for the participation of distant ones. Why should the residents of Gallup, New Mexico, be taxed to aid the south Bronx? We think the best answer is that, although the

---

[15] Thomas C. Schelling, "On the Ecology of Micromotives," *The Public Interest* (Fall 1971), p. 82 ff.

concept is vague, our society is committed to equal opportunity, and that even very limited definitions of that concept would indicate that in such places as the south Bronx or the Woodlawn section of Chicago opportunity is well below an acceptable minimum. Few would doubt that it is very hard for an "average" child to get an "average" education in core city ghettos. The youngsters who do are truly exceptional. Personal and property insecurity is also vastly higher—a ghetto dweller is about 4 times more likely to be robbed, 1.3 times more likely to be burglarized, and about 7 times more likely to be murdered than an average American.

Beyond education and security, the opportunity in ghettos to earn a living and to accumulate personal wealth is substantially less than the average opportunity elsewhere. First, most ghettos are increasingly poorly located with respect to new job opportunities. The large black ghettos of Chicago, Philadelphia, and Cleveland are not where the incremental jobs are being created. The locational handicap is exacerbated by the weakness of the information resources of ghetto communities. Informal informational channels have always played a large role in finding jobs, but these channels are not as well developed in the modern black and chicano urban ghetto as they were in ghettos of old or are in the remainder of the urban community. This limits opportunity for ghetto job seekers. On the other hand, good information for illicit activities is on the average probably better, which is also a handicap for ghetto dwellers.

When the national economy was doing very well in 1969, the overall black unemployment rate in urban areas was 7.2 percent, twice the national average; the rate for black teen-age youth was 27.9 percent, 8 times the national average. In the third quarter of 1975, with overall average unemployment at 8.3 percent, black unemployment in urban poverty areas was 17.7 percent and black teen-age unemployment was 41.4 percent. While many different reasons can be offered to explain these extraordinarily high unemployment rates, almost all of them stem from the dual handicaps of race and place.

Employment provides income, but it is usually not the road to a financial cushion. Most Americans (and perhaps other peoples as well) who have managed to develop net worth in the past 30 years have done so through homeownership. The owned home has been the means by which persons of low income, through "sweat" equity (i.e., enhancing the value of the property by working on its maintenance and improvement) and market appreciation, put something aside for a rainy day. The opportunity to do that in most parts of our urban ghettos is extremely limited.

For one thing, the housing market in most central city ghettos has a relatively high proportion of rental units, and the tax and savings advantages of home owning are not available to the renter. Moreover, since ghetto property values are not increasing as much as they are in other neighborhoods, the incentive for individual homeowners to make improvements is relatively low. High crime, poor schools, poorer than average amenities, all undermine the promise of property appreciation in exchange for the struggle of investing in homes and maintaining them.

Personal security and educational and economic opportunity are decidedly inferior in low-income ghettos. A society committed to equal opportunity must back its commitment with tangible efforts. Once the legal bars to equality of opportunity are overcome, those efforts take the form of programs aimed at intervening positively in the process or conditions which constitute the barriers to equal opportunity. But effective strategies or programs are elusive.

We know that many things will not work: a simple expansion of expenditure, under which the greater share must inevitably go to the professionals in the fields of employment, crime, education, and housing, may offer little improvement in the quality of life or opportunity in declining neighborhoods; the creation of new community organizations through the infusion of outside funds seems to hold little promise at this point in history; the imposition of a *great plan* from the outside cannot, it seems, be responsive to the complex, interlinked problems that are dragging these neighborhoods down.

It has been argued that a major barrier to doing better against ghetto problems has been the social, ethnic, and geographic distance between those making the decisions and those affected. It is very hard in our multi-ethnic society for one group to acquire the necessary insight, good will, legitimacy, and authority to carry out programs that will effectively solve the problems of another. Much of the leadership in the 1960s consisted of an elite body of planners and experts in Washington, combined with an inexperienced, partially fabricated, and semi-manipulated group of neighborhood organizations. It did not appear to work well.

If that view is correct, and we think it is, two positive developments during the past several years have brought us closer to solving the problem in that they place the authority to plan and act in individuals and bodies with more legitimacy. One is the rise of black political participation, representation, and power, particularly in many of the large cities; the second is the shift toward federal programs (such as revenue sharing and block grants) which place more authority in the hands of cities. These changes should be conducive to achieving more success against the problems in low-income ghettos.

Also conducive to improvement is the presence of an experienced cadre of professionals in and around the ghettos who know what they are doing. Many of these became seasoned in the Community Action Programs and Model Cities Programs of the sixties. And there *are* programs which have achieved a measure of success. Others are now being tried, some under unique experimental conditions. No doubt still others of even more promise will emerge from these experiments and from a finer understanding of some of the problems themselves.

But we do not wish to paint an overly optimistic view. It is one thing to point to factors *conducive* to more effective programs. It is entirely different, and unwarranted, to go on from there to predict substantial progress against the complex problems of the ghetto. None of the problems is easy—crime reduction, raising educational performance, reducing dependency on welfare, improving job prospects. Outside funds, minority political leadership, more experienced professionals and some fully tested ideas will all help, but progress is still apt to be slow. A recent review of the economic history of ethnic groups in the United States points out that it has taken the Irish three generations, and others no less than two, to lift themselves out of poverty, and that in most cases blacks have been in an urban setting for less than two generations.[16] The chances for quick success in overcoming the worst of the problems of the ghetto seem slim against this perspective. On the other hand, the perspective is basically positive, since it does suggest the inevitability of overcoming contemporary problems. The aim of intervention is to speed that day.

* * *

One may easily misread the currents of one's time when they swirl in so many directions, but it is our sense that a period of assessment of the proper and possible reach of government is upon us. This results from a number of trends which have converged in the mid-1970s: widespread disillusionment with government's capacity to deal effectively with social problems generally and with urban distress in particular; and a related resistance to further public spending, in the face of large built-in increases in public spending (e.g., pensions, social security, etc.).

This period of assessment may lead to a more realistic view of what

---

[16] Thomas Sowell, *Race and Economics* (New York, N.Y.: David McKay, 1975), pp. 149-50.

can and cannot be expected of government action as well as to shifts in the boundaries between what is best regulated, financed, and operated by government and what should be left to individual choices and relatively unfettered private markets. It seems to us that a finer shaping of government's role will avert false expectations and over time would be conducive to a more positive relationship between the people and their government.

The Urban Predicament seeks to contribute to this reexamination in general and in the specific urban fields represented by the following chapters.

Chapter 2

Finance

George E. Peterson

> So lavish was the style of our government that we came to depend on it for life itself, forgetting that government was only the result of our industry and not its source. . . . Every interest and group and advocate came to think of the [budget] as a cornucopia, a never ending horn of plenty that could pay for more and more each year.
>
> Now the times of plenty, the days of wine and roses, are over.
>
> Governor Hugh Carey
> Annual Message to the Legislature
> New York State, 1975

> The basic structure of the local revenue base in America does not allow cities, at least the older core cities, to cope with the changing socioeconomic conditions in which we live. Very simply, the matter is slipping out of our hands.
>
> Wallace I. Stecher
> Budget Director, Detroit
> Testimony to Congressional Joint
> Economic Committee, February 1976

The year 1975 will be remembered for its rediscovery of the budget constraint. Where once the budget messages of mayors were crowded with promises of new programs and announcements of pay raises for public employees, in 1975 they carried the more somber theme that resources had given out, leaving no option but retrenchment. The most visible fiscal crisis belonged to New York City. As a condition for staving off bankruptcy, New York was obliged to reduce its labor force by more than 40,000 workers, impose a three-year freeze on the city budget, hand over management of its financial affairs to the State of New York, and ulti-

The author wishes to acknowledge valuable criticism of an earlier draft of this chapter from William Alonso, Thomas Muller, Richard Nathan, Dick Netzer, Francine Rabinovitz, Robert Reischauer, and Louis Winnick. Jean Mecartney, Susan Mick, and Linda Royster provided research assistance.

35

mately seek $2.3 billion of emergency loans from the federal government.

But if New York's was the most severe fiscal distress, other cities had to grapple with nearly commensurate difficulties. Detroit's mayor threatened to lay off as many as one-quarter of the city's employees to balance his budget. The future of several of the old industrial cities was judged so precarious by the financial community that no one could be found to buy their bonds, secured though these were by the full faith and credit of the city government; other cities were forced to pay 9 to 11.5 percent interest rates on their debt—something literally unheard of theretofore in the tax-exempt bond market. With personnel layoffs and budget cuts came reductions in public services. To the residents of Cleveland, the city's budgetary plight may have been best symbolized by the decision to reduce the city's garbage collection to twice monthly.

Of course, the cities' economy measures were taken in a year when the country had fallen upon the hardest times since the Great Depression. When economic activity subsides, it perhaps is to be expected that there will be greater austerity in public expenditures, as in household spending. The budget messages for fiscal 1976 and fiscal 1977 are remarkable not so much for their recognition of the need for immediate belt-tightening as for their bleak assessment of the long-run future. They betray a common conviction that state and local governments may have overextended themselves in the provision of public services. Taken at their word, they portend a prolonged period of adjustment to slower rates of growth in the state and local sector. Governor Carey's statement, quoted at the beginning of this chapter, is representative when it depicts the sudden collision with the budget constraint as signaling a permanent end to the fiscal illusion that had encouraged citizens to ask, and politicians to promise, too much from government.

Whether the present tone of financial stringency will survive economic recovery is difficult to foretell. The mechanisms of state and local finance are constructed in such a way as to exaggerate cyclical swings in the private economy. Unlike the federal government, states and municipalities are prohibited by their state constitutions from incurring budget deficits. In bad times, they have no choice but to raise taxes to help close a budget gap, and when recovery comes, revenues under the stiffened tax structure tend to leap ahead, providing a surplus that invites renewed spending. The budget crunch of 1975 was the bottom point of an extreme version of this cycle. In 1972-73 state and local governments, riding the crest of an inflationary boom in tax revenues, enjoyed unprecedentedly large budget surpluses which reached as high as $10.4 billion per year in the fourth quarter of 1972.[1] These surpluses were used to expand public programs and finance across-the-board tax reductions. The years 1973 and 1974, for example, witnessed the first net reductions in state tax rates since World War II.[2] The heightened level of public sector activity, coupled with a tax base diminished by reform, left the state and local sector highly exposed to the unexpected cyclical turn in the economy that began in 1974. By the first quarter of 1975, state and local governments were wrestling with record *deficits* of $11.5 billion as measured by the national income accounts. At the end of 1975, as this is written, the fiscal cycle has begun anew; taxes have been raised and spending has been reduced. As economic recovery gains speed, the traditional budgetary leverage can be expected to come into play by generating enough additional tax revenue to relieve some of the fiscal pressure now being felt by state and local governments.

The record admonishes caution in looking beyond today's budget difficulties to their longer-run implications. At each extreme of past fiscal cycles, analysts and politicians alike have fallen into the error of predicting that the most recent trend would persist, largely unabated, into the future. In the mid-sixties when the urban financial crisis first attracted public attention, several studies predicted that massive budget gaps would open for local governments in the decade 1965-74.[3] By 1972, with the advent of federal revenue sharing and the emergence of current-year surpluses in state budgets, the American Enterprise Institute and several fiscal experts were forecasting just the reverse, a steady accumulation of excess revenues in the state and local sector.[4] According to one observer writing in 1973, the new circumstances promised "to make fiscal crisis seem a thing of the past" for many state and local governments, though the central

---

[1] The surplus and deficit figures refer to the state and local sector of the national income accounts, after subtraction of the surplus for social insurance funding. See the Department of Commerce, *Survey of Current Business*, National Income and Product Tables, table 15.

[2] Tax Foundation, *State Tax Action in 1973, 1974, 1975* (Washington, D.C.: published in October or November of respective year).

[3] For example, a study prepared for the National League of Cities projected a budget gap of $50 billion per year for the cities by 1975. Robert E. Weintraub, *Options for Meeting the Revenue Needs of City Governments* (Santa Barbara, Calif.: TEMPO, 1967).

[4] David G. Otto, et al., *Nixon, McGovern and the Federal Budget* (Washington, D.C.: American Enterprise Institute, 1972); Tax Foundation, *The Financial Outlook for State-Local Government for 1980: A Summary* (New York, N.Y.: 1973).

cities were excepted from this generally optimistic forecast.[5] In retrospect, predictions like these must seem hurried extrapolations of trends that, although intensely felt at the time, turned out to be far less permanent than they first appeared.

It probably will not become fully clear for several years whether 1975-76 brought an end to the era of exceptionally rapid growth in the local public sector, or merely marked the bottom point of cyclical despondency from which, as before, public sector expansion resumed. However, there are signs that the shift is permanent. Federal aid to the state and local sector has largely stopped growing after a decade of unprecedented increase. Unlike local revenues, intergovernmental assistance is not likely to resume its former expansion once the recession has passed. And for the old central cities of the Northeast and North Central regions, there is the hard reality that the local balance between revenue-raising capacity and expenditures has worsened steadily over the last two decades. For these cities, the budgetary crises of 1975 have compressed the time available to deal with the long-term trends. Some of the options that normally would allow for temporizing (such as borrowing against future revenues) now have been foreclosed or made far more difficult. The tightening of the budget constraint also has thrown into sharper competition the conflicting interests of suburbs and cities, taxpayer-voters and municipal employee unions, and the city's role as an efficient supplier of public services vs. its role as a provider of jobs to the central city market. Because all of the cities' problems gain expression in their budgets, the cities' fiscal predicaments bear witness to just how limited are the cities' resources for coping with the difficulties identified elsewhere in this volume.

I. THE FISCAL STRAIN ON CITIES

Every budget squeeze has as its immediate cause the tendency for spending to outrun revenues. The two sides of the budget, the income side and the expenditure side, therefore afford a natural division for examining fiscal problems.

The Spending Explosion in the State and Local Sector

Over the past quarter century, few parts of the American economy have rivaled the state and local sector for growth. Between 1951 and 1974 state and local spending after deflation for price increases rose by 6.3

---

[5] Dick Netzer, "The Public Economy of the Metropolis," in Eli Ginzberg, ed., *The Future of the Metropolis: People, Jobs, Income* (Salt Lake City: Olympia, 1974), pp. 77-78.

percent per year, or almost twice as fast as the rate of growth of the entire economy. (Through 1975 these relative rates of growth diverge still more dramatically; however, as the bottom year of a deep recession, 1975 distorts longer-term trends.) Table 1 illustrates the steady inroads that state

Table 1

NATIONAL SPENDING SHARES
(Percent of GNP Spent by Respective Sectors) [a]

Year	Private	Federal	State-Local
1951	76.0%	16.8%	7.2%
1952	72.9	19.8	7.3
1953	72.2	20.4	7.4
1954	73.5	18.3	8.2
1955	75.3	16.3	8.2
1956	75.1	16.4	8.5
1957	73.9	17.1	9.0
1958	71.5	18.6	9.8
1959	73.0	17.4	9.7
1960	73.0	17.2	9.8
1961	71.4	18.2	10.4
1962	71.4	18.3	10.3
1963	71.8	17.7	10.5
1964	72.3	17.0	10.7
1965	72.7	16.4	10.9
1966	71.7	17.1	11.2
1967	69.4	18.6	12.0
1968	68.8	18.8	12.4
1969	69.0	18.2	12.8
1970	68.0	18.4	13.6
1971	67.8	18.1	14.1
1972	67.9	17.9	14.2
1973	68.5	17.3	14.2
1974	67.0	18.3	14.7
1975 (first half)	63.6	20.7	15.7

a. Intergovernmental transfers to the state and local sector are treated as final state and local spending.

Sources: 1951-1974, *Economic Report of the President* (1975), Tables C-1, C-67, and C-68; 1975, *Survey of Current Business,* national income and product accounts.

and local government spending has made into national economic activity. It shows that the share of total output spent by the nonfederal public sector climbed from 7.2 percent in 1951 to 14.7 percent in 1974. Over the same span, the share of the private sector in national output fell and the share of the federal government fluctuated without much trend. The growth in the state and local share of total spending has been all the more remarkable because of its consistency; not once in the past 25 years has the state and local share declined by more than one-tenth of a percent, despite the intervention of two wars, inflation, and recession. Some quickening of the pace of substitution of state and local spending for private spending can be observed during the latter part of the sixties, when the Johnson administration's domestic programs were launched, as well as in years (such as 1974-75) when recession blighted private sector growth.

Of all levels of government, it has been the big cities that have witnessed the most rapid gains in expenditures, although obtaining a firm grasp on the spending totals of cities is no easy task. Responsibility for the various urban functions is organized quite differently in different states, and has undergone substantial modification over the last decade. In the majority of states, school districts are operated as independent entities outside of city budgets. On occasion, school district boundaries overlap municipal boundaries in a way that makes the matching of their respective budgets very difficult. Welfare assistance also poses accounting problems. Where such assistance is financed by local governments, responsibility has been assigned primarily to the counties. The fact that some large cities, like New York, Philadelphia, San Francisco, and Baltimore, double as counties, while most other cities do not, can easily distort spending comparisons between city governments.

To side-step problems of definition, spending totals often are examined for those common municipal functions which are provided by all cities. This procedure has the great advantage of rendering spending comparisons compatible with one another, but has the drawback of excluding from spending totals just those services (such as welfare and education) whose financing has been the most frequent object of policy reforms. Welfare and schooling also are the two sectors of the local public economy that have grown most rapidly. Their omission thus can distort studies of expenditure growth over time.

Table 2 provides a basic frame of reference for assessing the growth in city spending. The figures in the last row combine the common expenditures made by city governments and independent school districts for a sample of 28 large cities.[6] Per capita spending in the big cities can be seen to have grown significantly faster than spending by other local governments or spending by the state and local sector as a whole. In evaluating table 2, one should keep in mind that the expenditure totals shown in the first row are the same figures which were used to compute the national sector shares in table 1. Big-city spending, in other words, has been growing relative to a state and local sectoral total which, itself, has gained steadily at the expense of the rest of the economy. Another way of placing city expenditures in perspective is to note that the growth of big-city spending *per capita* during the latter half of the sixties and the early seventies about equalled the rate of total sales growth registered by IBM, one of the premier private market growth companies.[7]

Table 2

GROWTH IN BIG-CITY SPENDING
RELATIVE TO STATE AND LOCAL SECTOR
(1962-72)

Governmental Units	Spending Per Capita		Growth Rate (1962-72)
	1962	1972	
All State and Local Governments	$250.36	$659.02	163%
All Local Governments	176.97	428.89	142%
28 Big Cities a	191.68 b	570.49 b	198% b

a. See footnote 12 for the list of sample cities.

b. City government expenditures plus expenditures of independent school districts, population weighted.

Sources: *Census of Governments, 1962 and 1972,* vol. 4, no. 1, *Finances of School Districts;* vol. 4, no. 4, *Finances of Municipalities and Township Governments;* vol. 4, no. 5, *Compendium of Government Finances;* Washington, D.C.: Bureau of the Census.

In table 3, we have compared per capita spending for cities of different population sizes. The common municipal functions referred to in the first

[6] The sample contains all cities which reached a population of 500,000 or more in either 1960 or 1970, with the exception of Phoenix, where the school districts do not match city boundaries, and Jacksonville and Indianapolis, which consolidated with counties during this period. The cities in the sample are identified in footnote 13. In computing table 2, Atlanta (which reached a population of 497,000 in 1970) also was included.

[7] For example, IBM's revenue growth over the period 1965-73 was 159 percent, compared to an increase of 158 percent in the per capita expenditure of cities having more than 1,000,000 population (see table 3).

Table 3

PUBLIC SPENDING PER CAPITA IN U.S. CITIES
BY POPULATION SIZE [a]

Item	City Size						
	1,000,000 +	500,000 to 999,999	300,000 to 499,999	200,000 to 299,999	100,000 to 199,999	50,000 to 99,999	Less than 50,000
Expenditures for Common Functions	$283	$232	$177	$180	$157	$129	$ 95
Expenditures for All Functions [b]	$681	$427	$328	$325	$280	$229	$158
Growth in Per Capita Expenditures for All Functions (1965-73)	158%	121%	128%	139%	88%	68%	95%

a. Per capita figures are population weighted (i.e., total aggregate spending by the cities in each size class has been divided by total population).

b. City governments only.

Sources: *City Government Finances in 1972-73*, Washington, D.C.: Bureau of the Census.

row include current expenditures on highways, police protection, correction, fire protection, sanitation, parks and recreation, water supply, financial administration, and central control; they exclude current expenditures on public welfare, sewerage, education, and health and hospitals, services which often are provided by other levels of government, as well as all capital outlays. The second line of the table shows total city expenditures, while the last line indicates the rate of growth between 1965 and 1973 in total expenditures. The table demonstrates clearly what most people seem to take for granted: it costs more to operate the public sector in big cities.[8] Large cities not only spend more per capita to perform the same municipal functions but their cost disadvantage has widened over time. Other chapters in this volume suggest that the greater public sector expense of big cities is not compensated for by superior service quality. Although any measure of service quality has its defects, by such standards as crime rates, school achievement scores, or life expectancy, the big cities rank toward the bottom in comparisons of the quality of urban public life. This does not establish that big-city provision of public services is inefficient—many of the conditions that make for higher costs or lower service quality are, after all, beyond governments' control—but it does indicate that the big cities labor under a competitive disadvantage in trying to furnish comparable service quality to their residents.

The Fiscal Dilemma of the "Declining" City

Probably the most salient fact about central cities is that, on balance, people are moving out of them. However familiar this trend may be, its magnitude and rate of acceleration are startling. Between 1960 and 1970 the central cities of U.S. metropolitan areas lost 345,000 persons per year

---

[8] Throughout this chapter, city expenditures and taxable resources are compared on a per capita basis. Such a procedure is not altogether satisfactory, for the larger and older cities tend to house proportionately more nonresidential activity than do the smaller and newer cities. Standardization on a per capita basis implicitly takes the view that public expenses are incurred on behalf of city residents, whereas in fact a good part of budget outlays may be used to provide services to commerce and industry. Per capita figures thus tend to overstate both the expenditures and tax bases of older, larger cities relative to those of newer cities. For some purposes a standardization in terms of daytime population, or some other measure of both the number of city residents and the number of city workers, might be preferable. Note, however, that the *fiscal balance* between expenditures and revenue potential is not disturbed by reducing both figures to per capita terms nor are the trends in spending and fiscal capacity disturbed. The benefit of using per capita data as an intuitively intelligible basis of standardization seems to outweigh the benefits of inventing a new (and inevitably arbitrary) standard to replace per capita comparisons.

through net out-migration; between 1970 and 1975, they lost 1,404,000 persons per year, or more than four times as many.[9] For most of the larger cities, annual net out-migration now exceeds the natural growth caused by an excess of births over deaths. The result is an absolute decline in city population. The image of the "declining" central city has become so firmly embedded in discussions of urban problems that it may be forgotten how recent a development actual population loss is. Of the 60 cities that had populations of 200,000 or more in 1960, only 38 percent declined in size between 1950 and 1960; in the sixties the proportion of such cities losing population rose to 45 percent; by 1970-73, it had reached 73 percent. Cities such as Buffalo, Cleveland, Pittsburgh, and St. Louis lost more than one-fifth of their total net population in the 13 years, 1960-73.

On the surface, the cost comparisons by city size presented in table 3 imply that the population changes now being accomplished by migration should lower the total costs of local public service provision. Households, after all, are moving out of the largest cities, where the costs of public services are highest, and moving into smaller cities and suburbs, where public sector costs are relatively low. In the long run, out-migration from the older cities may have this effect of lowering average service costs. But in the meantime it has been responsible for a good part of the cities' fiscal predicament.

The dilemma confronted by the older cities is that few of the costs associated with urban growth are easily reversible into economies of diminution. Once a city's road, sewer, and water networks have been constructed to serve a given population, the cost of maintaining these networks does not decline significantly when population shrinks. On the contrary, as capital infrastructure ages, it becomes more costly to keep in repair. Cities that are losing population actually spend more, per capita, in capital investment than cities that are gaining population, due largely to the necessity (and difficulty) of replacing their antiquated capital stock. Similarly, when households abandon the central city, the need for police and fire services does not decline in proportion to population. Instead, abandoned homes become foci for vandalism and crime, pose fire hazards, and ultimately must be razed at city expense. The capital infrastructure of a city is like any other productive plant. To run most efficiently it must be operated at or near its designed capacity. Should it become necessary

---

[9] *Mobility of the Population of the United States: March 1970-March 1975* (October, 1975), Washington, D.C.: Bureau of the Census. The data refer to out-migration from central cities as defined by their boundaries in 1970.

to operate the city's stock of housing, factories, public buildings and utility networks at two-thirds capacity or less, the cost per taxpayer rises steeply.

More importantly in terms of budget expense, a city's labor force tends to act as another fixed overhead item, whose cost must be spread over fewer taxpayers once net out-migration commences. It is difficult to reduce public employment under the best of circumstances, but the pressure to retain public sector jobs is doubly great when a city is suffering private-sector job loss, as has been true of most of the cities with serious population declines. Even if current employment could be held in check, other personnel costs would remain as overhead items in the most literal sense. Pension and other retirement benefits now account for a significant part of state and local wages. To city administrators locked in wage disputes with their employees, concessions on pension funding have seemed easier to tolerate than outright wage increases. During the decade 1962-72, negotiated pension benefits in the state and local sector jumped ahead more than 50 percent faster than negotiated wage rates.[10] Under the pay-as-you-go system of pension funding used in most cities, the liabilities incurred under these pension agreements become an overhead debt that future residents of the cities will have to redeem in order to cover the costs of public services consumed by their predecessors.

Much attention has been given to the severe financing problems that plague the Social Security system because the slowdown in national population growth has raised the ratio of Social Security recipients to working taxpayers. The same economic considerations operate with greatly multiplied force in the old central cities. Instead of a slower rate of growth, most cities face the prospect of an absolute decline in the number of employed taxpayers living inside their boundaries. At the same time, the cities must anticipate an acceleration in retirements as the large numbers of persons added to employment rolls in the sixties begin to qualify for the early retirement benefits that they have won in wage negotiations. Projections of New York City's pension obligations, for example, conclude that retirement payments will rise by at least 8 to 9 percent per annum over the foreseeable future, and perhaps much more, no matter what the city does to reduce its current employment levels and wage rates.[11] Ironically, the

---

[10] See, for example, Roy W. Bahl and Bernard Jump, "The Budgetary Implications of Rising Employee Retirement System Costs," *National Tax Journal*, Sept. 1974, pp. 479-90.

[11] Bernard Jump, "Financing Public Employee Retirement Programs in New York City: Trends since 1965 and Projections to 1980," Occasional Paper No. 16 (Metropolitan Studies Program, Maxwell School of Citizenship and Public Affairs, Syracuse University, 1975).

more the city cracks down on current wages, the greater the pension costs it is likely to generate. Many of New York's public workers (like those elsewhere) now have the option of retiring at half pay after 20 years on the job, regardless of age. A freeze on current wages which makes public sector work less attractive is likely to propel large numbers of these employees into accepting their early retirement benefits.

Though the costs of the pension agreements negotiated in the sixties have yet to make themselves fully felt, some cities have been subjected to spectacular increases in employer contributions to retirement funding. Detroit's expenditures for retirement funding increased well over 100 percent between 1969 and 1972 alone, and amounted to 21 percent of the city's total operating budget in 1972-73. The City of Philadelphia was forced to more than triple its annual pension fund payments when the courts ordered it to move toward full funding of its actuarial obligations (i.e., to pay into a special retirement fund the actuarial value of the pension benefits being earned each year by public sector workers). For cities that remain on pay-as-you-go funding (the majority), pension liabilities are not acknowledged in the current budget, but are accumulated as an overhead debt that will be inherited by the future, less numerous and less affluent, residents of the cities.[12]

In sum, because of their physical construction and political orientation, cities have found it unusually difficult to reduce public service expenditures commensurately with declines in the number of users of those services. The simple economics of overhead spreading then dictates that as population falls, the per capita costs associated with city operations must weigh more heavily on the remaining taxpayers.

The population loss of cities also has had a selective character which in at least some instances has raised the costs of producing desired levels of public service outputs. As net out-migration cuts into the city's population base, the remaining population tends to become less well educated, have lower incomes, and be disproportionately nonwhite. Chapters 4 and 5 show that these are population characteristics associated with higher crime

---

[12] One of the most dramatic examples of pension liabilities is afforded by Washington, D.C. At present, pay-as-you-go retirement costs for policemen and firemen total about 40 percent of the wages paid to currently employed personnel. Staff members of the District of Columbia Committee of the U.S. House of Representatives have estimated (under a variety of actuarial assumptions) that by 1990 retirement payments will equal 100 percent of current wages and that the ratio will not peak until the period around 2020, when retirement payments will equal some 130 percent of current wages paid to police and fire department personnel.

rates and lower school achievement scores. They also make it more difficult to produce other types of public services: the incidence of false alarms and housing code violations, for example, is related to the same population characteristics, as is the wear and tear placed on parks and other public facilities. Population loss likewise brings an increase in the share of elderly dependents who need special health and housing services. In economic terms, the socioeconomic characteristics of a population must be considered one part of the "production function" for supplying public services. Population characteristics are crucial in determining public school quality and public safety levels. In other fields population traits, while less decisive, still help to determine how much it will cost to reach any given level of public service quality. A city can maintain any reasonable rate of response to fire alarms or any level of street cleanliness it desires, whatever the composition of the city population, but the expense incurred in doing so will be greater if the majority of residents are poor, less well educated, or without employment.

Just as declining central cities tend to acquire increasingly costly conditions for producing public services as a result of their population losses, growing cities often find service provision made easier and cheaper because in annexing unincorporated suburban areas they are able to acquire low-cost production conditions. The initial capital costs of installing water and sewer networks may be greater in outlying areas (though these costs now are often borne by the users themselves), but they are more than compensated for by savings in police protection, urban renewal, public health and other services where the need for public spending is reduced by low density, modern capital stock, and the socioeconomic characteristics of the annexed population. Overhead spreading also causes population growth to lessen the per capita expenditure burden on city residents.

Spending Comparisons Between "Declining" and "Growing" Cities

To illustrate the effects of demographic and economic decline on cities' spending levels we have constructed a sample of all cities (except Washington, D.C., which also serves the administrative functions of a state) which possessed a population in excess of 500,000 in either 1960 or 1970. There are 28 such cities. These have been divided into growing cities, those which gained population over the entire period, 1960-73; a second class of cities which gained population from 1960-70, but now are losing population; and declining cities, which lost population continuously throughout the period 1960-73.[13] Because of its size and unique financing problems, New York City has been treated separately.

Table 4 compares spending on common municipal functions for the

Table 4

EXPENDITURES PER CAPITA ON COMMON FUNCTIONS[a]

(1973)

Item	Large Growing Cities (n = 7)	Large Cities Growing in Population 1960-70, Now Declining (n = 6)	Large Declining Cities (n = 14)	New York	All Cities between 200,000 and 500,000
Expenditures per Capita, Common Functions	$152	$195	$264	$396	$178
Common Function Municipal Workers per 1000 Residents	8.7	10.5	13.0	13.0	
Average Monthly Wage, Common Function Workers	$812	$912	$958	$1115	

a. The first four columns include all cities, except Washington, D.C., which reached population of 500,000 between 1960 and 1973; the last column includes all cities with a population between 200,000 and 500,000 in 1970. Per capita figures are simple means of individual cities' per capita expenditure and employment levels.

Sources: Derived from data in Bureau of the Census, *City Government Finances in 1972-73,* and in Bureau of the Census, *Local Government Employment in Selected Metropolitan Areas and Large Counties, 1973.*

---

[13] The sample cities are: "Growing"—Honolulu, Houston, Jacksonville, Memphis, Phoenix, San Antonio, and San Diego; "Formerly Growing, Now Declining"—Columbus, Dallas, Denver, Indianapolis, Kansas City, and Los Angeles (of these cities two—Columbus and Denver—gained fewer than 1,000 residents between 1970 and 1973, but are estimated now to be losing population); "Declining"—Baltimore, Boston, Buffalo, Chicago, Cincinnati, Cleveland, Detroit, Milwaukee, New Orleans, Philadelphia, Pittsburgh, St. Louis, San Francisco, and Seattle. New York City has been treated separately.

This sample was constructed in conjunction with my colleague at The Urban Institute, Thomas Muller. For an analysis from a somewhat different perspective, see Thomas Muller, *Growing and Declining Urban Areas: A Fiscal Comparison* (Washington, D.C.: The Urban Institute, 1975).

cities in our sample, as well as for all other cities as a group. Per capita expenditures in the 14 declining cities can be seen to have been more than 70 percent greater in fiscal 1973 than expenditures in the seven large cities that had continuing population gains. Consistent with the pattern, cities that only recently entered into population declines maintained spending levels that were mid-way between the two extremes. In an accounting sense, the greater part of the expenditure difference between declining and growing cities can be explained by differences in the number of public sector workers that the cities employed. The old, declining cities hired more than half again as many workers per thousand residents as did growing cities to perform the same public sector tasks. Wage levels also were higher in the declining cities. In each case, cities that recently began to lose population fit mid-way between the extremes.

When cities' common function outlays are broken out in more detail, it becomes apparent that the cost disadvantage of the old declining cities is greatest in areas like police protection and housing and urban renewal where service costs are particularly sensitive to the characteristics of the resident population and to the age of the city's capital stock (see table 5). Welfare spending, of course, is also far higher in the declining cities, although these costs are frequently borne by higher levels of government. In contrast, services whose cost of provision increases with the land space they occupy may be more expensive in the newer, low-density cities. To a degree, this is true of spending on sewer facilities and parks and recreation.

Table 5

PER CAPITA SERVICE COSTS
BY FUNCTION AND CITY TYPE
(1973)

Service	Growing	Growing to 1970, Declining Thereafter	Declining	New York
Police Protection	27.70	48.50	68.70	67.90
Housing and Urban Renewal	8.75	8.79	20.32	71.43
Fire Protection	17.80	23.40	29.70	31.48
Sewers	14.40	14.20	13.30	29.05
Parks and Recreation	17.50	18.10	16.00	15.18

Source: Derived from data in Bureau of Census, *City Government Finances in 1972-73.* Figures are simple averages of per capita spending in each city.

In expenditure comparisons of this type, it often is difficult to distinguish whether greater per capita outlays reflect the higher costs of providing a given level of service quality or are the result of superior service provision. In the case of police protection, the expenditure difference can be identified unambiguously as reflecting cost differences, for public safety levels are worse in the declining cities, despite much higher per capita expenditures. In other cases there is a strong presumption that the explanation lies in quality differences. The greater expenditures made by growing cities on parks and recreational facilities, for example, almost certainly reflect their more extensive networks of service provision.

Table 6

CHANGES IN CITY EMPLOYMENT LEVELS

City Type	Public Employees per 1000 Residents [a]		Percent Change in Total Employees
	1964 [b]	1973	1973-1975
Growing	22.2	24.0	+11
Growth to 1970, Decline Thereafter	22.5	30.6	+ 4
Declining	25.4	35.8	− 9
New York	35.3	51.6	−13

a. All city employees plus school district employees.

b. 1964 city populations interpolated from 1960 and 1970 data.

Sources: 1964-73, derived from data in Bureau of the Census, *Local Government Employment in Selected Metropolitan Areas and Large Counties, 1964 and 1973;* 1973-75, derived from data in budgets of the individual cities.

Ten years from now, when the mid-seventies can be viewed in historical perspective, it is likely that the period 1974-75 will be perceived as a turning point in municipal spending patterns. As we have seen, up to then the spending, wage, and employment gaps between declining and growing cities had been steadily widening. That process seems now to have been reversed. Under the pressure of financial crisis, the declining cities have been forced to effect sizable reductions in their payrolls and to otherwise curb spending growth. Table 6 compares total public employment by city governments and their associated independent school districts in three different periods. As recently as 1964 there was relatively little difference between the public employment rates of the different types of cities. By far the greater part of the employment gap emerged over the subsequent decade. Though comparable Census figures combining city and school district employment are not yet available for 1975, the budgets of the individual cities suggest that the employment and spending trends of the last decade have been reversed. The third column of table 6 summarizes the recent course of municipal employment for a sample of cities of each type.

The first evidence of a reversal in spending trends also is discernible in the expenditure figures for fiscal 1974. Between 1973 and 1974, the cities in our sample reversed their decade-long ranking by expenditure increase. Total expenditures increased by 5.7 percent in the declining cities, by 8.6 percent in the middle group of formerly growing cities, and by 10.3 percent in presently growing cities.[14] Individual city budgets indicate that since 1974 the reversal in spending trends has become more pronounced. There is nothing inevitable, then, about the more rapid growth of per capita public expenditures in declining cities. Where the fiscal strain is acute enough, even "fixed" costs, such as negotiated pension agreements, have proved to be flexible. By the end of the decade, employment, wage, and per capita spending levels almost certainly will be much more uniform across city types than they were in the mid-seventies. In that perspective, the budgetary experience of the past 15 years may appear little more than an aberrant interval, during which the old cities temporarily refused to accept the fiscal implications of their economic decline.

Local Revenue Capacity

In the aggregate, city revenues must closely match expenditures, as guaranteed by the constitutional prohibitions against deficit spending by local governments. Some year-to-year maneuvering in budget preparation is made possible by the practice of accumulating surpluses in one year and drawing them down in another. Borrowing against the future may also take place in less conspicuous ways, such as underfunding of pension liabilities. But over any extended period of time revenues are obliged to keep pace with expenditures. Once one has identified city expenditure totals, the question to be asked about the revenue side of the budget is not "How much?" but "Where does the money come from?"

If thrown upon their own resources, the declining central cities would have been unable to fund the expenditure growth they experienced during the late sixties and early seventies, except at excruciatingly high tax

---

[14] See Bureau of the Census, *City Government Finances in 1972-73 and 1973-74.* No annual population estimates are available for these cities; however, adjustment for population trends would narrow the difference in per capita spending growth in 1973-74.

rates, well beyond those that city residents in fact have been asked to pay. The property tax traditionally has afforded the principal source of local government revenue. Nationwide, it still accounts for almost two-thirds of all locally collected general revenue and 80 percent of local taxes. The property tax base therefore provides a good indication of the taxable resources that a city can draw upon.

As table 7 illustrates for selected central cities, the property tax has proved a fecund source of revenue for cities with expanding economic and population bases, but in the declining central cities it has lagged far

Table 7

EXPENDITURES AND PROPERTY TAX BASE GROWTH, SELECTED CITIES, 1965-73

	City[a] Expenditure Growth	Assessed Value Growth	True Growth of Taxable Property Value
DECLINING CITIES			
Baltimore	172%	11%	33%
Buffalo	135	[− 1]	21
Cleveland	67	[− 2]	36
Detroit	120	23	14
Newark	135	[−12]	2
Philadelphia	130	29	70
GROWING CITIES			
Houston	118	136	136
Memphis[b]	65	46	76
Phoenix	166	94	251
Portland, Ore.	141	NA[c]	172
San Diego[d]	126	130	167
NEW YORK	186	29	68

a. City government only.

b. All data for Memphis refer to 1967-72.

c. Portland changed its assessment basis over the period.

d. Assessment and property value growth for San Diego refer to 1967-75.

Sources: Expenditure growth derived from data in Bureau of Census, *City Government Finances in 1964-65* and *City Government Finances in 1972-73;* assessed value growth from local assessment records; assessed valuations were converted to true values on the basis of state assessment-sales ratio studies for respective cities, where possible; otherwise aggregate sales ratios as reported in *Census of Governments,* vol. 2 for 1967 and 1972 were used for this purpose.

behind spending totals.[15] In several of the older, eastern cities the assessed valuation of taxable property actually has declined in recent years. To some degree, responsibility for this poor performance can be laid to antiquated assessment systems that fail to keep the assessed valuations of property in line with their market values during periods of inflation. A comparison of the second and third columns of table 7 indicates that the true market value of taxable property has performed much more respectably than has the assessed valuation, which serves as the formal base of the property tax. Cities also have indulged in the expensive generosity of exempting many new buildings from property taxation altogether, in an effort to attract construction into the city, and have been obliged by state laws to grant large numbers of tax exemptions to owners of residential property. As a result, some skepticism is in order whenever municipalities parade a decline in assessments as proof of their fiscal impoverishment.

Qualifications aside, however, there is no blinking the fact that the property tax base in older central cities has failed, by several orders of magnitude, to keep pace with public spending. The downward trend in the taxing capacity of the declining central cities does not appear in quite such a bad light if average income, rather than property valuation, is used as the basis of comparison. There is some irony in the fact that property value differences between growing and declining central cities should be widening more rapidly than income differences, for the property tax commonly is reputed to be an inelastic tax; that is, one whose base grows less than proportionately with income. The most recent inflationary period has upset the conventional wisdom about tax elasticities. As noted in chapter 3, during the last decade housing values, which represent the core of the property tax base, have risen much more rapidly than the prices of other goods or household incomes. Case studies of smaller cities confirm that during the inflationary surge the property tax base did a better job of keeping up with government costs than other local revenue sources, including sales taxes and uniform-rate income taxes.[16]

---

[15] Table 13 (page 76) gives per capita property values for the different cities as of 1971.

[16] *The Fiscal Implications of Inflation: A Study of Six Local Governments* (report prepared by the Metropolitan Studies Program of the Maxwell School, Syracuse University: 1975). This study reported inflation indices for the property

As a tax base for central cities, property values have the drawback of magnifying differences in local economic trends. Population loss and laggard income growth tend to exert multiplier effects on the value of a city's fixed stock of capital. Although some of the declining cities' sluggishness in property value growth is attributable to lower manufacturing and commercial assessments caused by businesses deserting the city, the most important impact of a decline in economic activity is on the demand for housing. No city can withstand population losses of more than 20 percent in the space of 13 years, as has happened in Buffalo, Cleveland, Pittsburgh, and St. Louis, without suffering a decline in demand for the city's standing stock of housing. This is reflected in lower housing prices. The cities in our sample with the worst population declines enjoyed only marginal increases in average housing prices during a period which was, for most of the country, one of rampant housing price inflation.[17] Grow-

and sales tax bases during the period 1971-74 for the six communities studied, as follows:

PERCENTAGE GAIN IN TAX BASE
DUE TO INFLATION, 1971-74

Community	Property Tax Base	Sales Tax Base
New York	+22.1	+17.5
Atlanta, Ga.	+22.3	NA
Lexington, Va.	+17.8	+21.4
Erie County, N.Y. (Buffalo)	+25.5	+18.4
Orange County, Calif.	+21.8	+13.4
Snohomish County, Wash.	+22.8	+18.9

The same source estimated nation-wide tax-base inflation indices for the period 1967-72:

Tax Base	Inflation Index of Base, 1972 (1967 = 100)
Property	142.6
General Sales	129.8
Alcohol	100.1
Tobacco	100.3
Individual Income	139.4
Corporate Income	107.0

[17] Between 1966 and 1971 the average value of single-family houses sold in Buffalo, Cleveland, Pittsburgh, and St. Louis—the four cities to lose more than 20 percent of their population between 1960 and 1973—increased by three-hundredths of one percent. In contrast, in the 13 cities that gained population during the sixties the average sale price of single-family housing increased by 48 percent between 1966 and 1971.

ing cities, on the other hand, have benefited greatly from having their revenues tied to the property tax base. Not only are additions constantly being made to the cities' capital stock, but in-migration generates a vigorous demand for existing housing which drives up market prices. The phenomenon is the same as that accounting for rapid price movements in coal reserves, farmland, or other goods which are in relatively fixed supply. When the supply of a commodity is inelastic, shifts in the demand for it must work large price changes.

To illustrate the sensitivity of the property tax base to underlying economic trends we have estimated tax base elasticities with respect to both city income and population changes. As the footnote shows, over the decade 1961-71 each percentage point difference in a city's rate of population growth (or decline) was associated, on average, with a 1.3 percent difference in the per capita value of the property tax base, while each percentage point difference in a city's rate of per capita income growth was associated with no less than a 2.3 percent difference in per capita property values.[18] These results imply that reliance on the property tax as the principal local revenue source has tended to exaggerate the fiscal consequences of the cities' basic economic trends: declining cities appear to be in even more straitened circumstances when taxable property values are used to gauge their fiscal capacity, while growing cities appear to be even more favorably situated when property valuations are taken as the reference point. It is true that for a time a city may be able to mask the sensitivity of its property tax base to economic growth by refusing to reassess properties in line with value changes.[19] But over the longer term, especially now that many courts have ordered full compliance with state

---

[18] The estimated equations are:

$$Y = 47.0 + 1.27\,X_1 \qquad R^2 = .48$$
$$(4.5)$$
$$Y = -79.1 + 2.31\,X_2 \qquad R^2 = .23$$
$$(2.6)$$

where Y = percentage increase in city property value per capita, 1961-71.
   X_1 = percentage increase in city population, 1960-70.
   X_2 = percentage increase in city per capita income, 1960-70.

The figures in parentheses are t-statistics.

[19] A striking example is provided by New York City, where economic troubles, overbuilding, and rent control laws combined to cause property values to tumble between 1973 and 1975. Assessed valuations, however, remained unchanged. As a result, the assessment–sales ratio for single family homes sold in Manhattan rose from 61.7 percent in 1973 to 76.5 percent in the first half of 1975, while the assessment–sales ratio for elevator apartments rose from 70.6 percent to 93.3 percent (unpublished data collected by the Real Estate Board of New York, Inc.).

constitutional requirements of prompt, even-handed assessment, the erosion of the older cities' property tax bases cannot be hidden.

The slow growth of the property tax base in declining cities has led many of them to try to diversify their revenue sources, albeit without marked success. As of 1972-73, the declining cities in our sample, together with their associated school districts, raised 74 percent of their tax revenue from the property tax, a percentage not greatly different from that of the local sector as a whole. Individual cities, however, did manage to trim their reliance on the property tax.[20]

Whatever tax base is used to measure local revenue-raising capacity, the fact remains that per capita resources in the declining cities are expanding more slowly than they are in growing cities. Actual public expenditures, on the contrary, have risen faster in the old central cities. The juxtaposition of these trends would seem to require that the tax burden on the residents of declining cities should have multiplied greatly in comparison with the tax burden on their peers who have the good fortune to live in growing cities. That is not altogether true. Table 8 shows two comparisons of relative tax burdens. The first two columns compare effective property tax rates in 1967 and 1972 for the different types of cities. Columns three and four attempt to measure the aggregate "tax effort"

Table 8

LOCAL TAX BURDENS

City Type	Mean Effective Property Tax Rate		Total Tax Effort As Percent of Household Income[a]	
	1967	1972	1967	1972
Growing	1.85%	1.33%	3.5%	4.0%
Growing to 1970, Declining Thereafter	1.89	1.98	4.9	6.2
Declining	2.05	2.54	5.1	6.7

a. See text for definition of "tax effort."

Source: Effective property tax rates: computed from data in 1967 *Census of Governments*, vol. 2, *Taxable Property Values* and 1972 *Census of Governments*, vol. 2, Part 2, *Taxable Property Values and Assessment-Sales Price Ratios;* Total tax effort from *Census of Governments* data.

---

[20] For a discussion of cities' efforts at revenue diversification, see Advisory Commission on Intergovernmental Relations, *Local Revenue Diversification* (Washington, D.C.: Oct. 1974).

that payment of all local revenues demands of local taxpayers. Like many of the measures employed in this chapter, an index of the local tax burden is not without its conceptual difficulties. Taxes can be exported beyond city limits, both in the obvious sense that part of a sales or income tax may be paid by suburbanites who shop or work in the central city, but do not live there, and in the more complex sense that the ultimate incidence of a tax may be passed forward to consumers of products or backwards to the suppliers of factors of production in ways that are exceedingly difficult to identify. In table 8 we have chosen to measure tax effort by the ratio of all locally raised general revenue to local household income, after exclusion of the property taxes paid on commercial and industrial property and an estimate of income taxes paid by nonresidents.[21] The incidence assumptions behind these (or any other) burden figures are sufficiently uncertain that less importance should be attached to the exact numbers shown in the table than to the relative standing of the different types of cities and their trends over time.

The table shows that residents of the declining central cities do indeed pay more of their incomes in local taxes than do residents of growing cities. However, the gap between declining and growing cities has not widened as greatly as would be suggested by the expenditure and income trends of the two types of cities, taken separately. The figures in the last column of table 8 indicate that, including school taxes, approximately 6 percent of household income now is paid to local governments in the form of general revenue.

If the comparison of tax burdens is made with respect to effective property tax rates alone, the disparity between growing and declining cities appears to be widening more rapidly. The growing cities in our sample managed to cut their effective property tax rates by more than 25 percent over the five year interval, 1967-72, while the declining cities were obliged to raise their rates by nearly 25 percent. This was the product not so much of a lesser reliance on property taxation in growing cities, but of the strongly divergent trends, emphasized above, in per capita property valuations. Since the locational choices of firms and households are influenced by relative tax rates (which determine the amount of tax that a given house or industrial plant will have to pay), rather than by average tax effort expressed as a fraction of household

---

[21] Thirty percent of city income tax receipts have been assumed to come from nonresidents. This is the average figure estimated by the Advisory Commission on Intergovernmental Relations, based in part on the proportion of commuters to all workers. See ACIR, *Local Revenue Diversification* (Washington, D.C.: 1974).

income, the necessity of continually raising property tax rates to compensate for a declining property value base places the big cities in a constantly worsening competitive position in their efforts to retain commercial-industrial firms or middle-class households. That is to say, while
a calculation like our "total tax effort" best measures local tax burdens,
in the sense of the financial effort that is required of local residents to
pay for the public services they receive, simple tax rate comparisons best
measure the local tax burden in the sense of measuring the competitive
disadvantage which an area faces in competing for future growth.

Intergovernmental Assistance

Spending in the old central cities was able to outdistance local tax
collections over the period 1965-73 because cities were made the beneficiaries of extensive assistance from other levels of government. The
ultimate engine of local public sector expansion during this period was
the federal government, which channeled massive amounts of aid to the
cities both directly and through the intermediation of the states. To be
sure, some of this aid was disbursed erratically, as the targets of federal
concern jumped about from one urban problem to another. But in hind-
sight, the span 1965-73 is likely to appear as the federal system's peak
period of largesse toward the cities.

Interestingly, the period brought forth the expression of two quite
contrary philosophies of federal grants, both of which served to boost
city spending levels. The "Great Society" agenda of the mid-sixties sought
to bring scores of new public services to poor and minority populations.
The programs that were launched under its aegis ranged from early
childhood education to neighborhood health care; from manpower training to legal aid. Many of these programs were of special benefit to the
older cities because the intended recipients largely resided there. Indeed
the entire war on poverty carried a bias toward helping fight "big city"
problems. Local leaders in the old central cities also were the most aggressive in seeking out federal funding. With a modest investment of
local revenue, city officials could mount expensive new programs that
offered numerous job opportunities and at least the prospect of making
valuable services available to the cities' poverty populations. The surge in
federal aid to underwrite Great Society efforts is reflected in the jump in
federal intergovernmental assistance that occurred after 1965 (see table 9).

In its approach to intergovernmental assistance, general revenue sharing differs fundamentally from the Great Society attempt to deliver

Table 9

INTERGOVERNMENTAL GRANTS
(Annual Rates of Increase, Current Dollars)

Item	Period						
	1960-1965	1965-1970	1971	1972	1973	1974	1975
Annual Increase in Federal Aid to State and Local Governments	9.7	14.7	19.6	19.9	25.3	6.6	11.5
Annual Increase in Federal and State Aid to Local Governments	8.5	14.3	16.8	15.1	20.6	14.4	NA

Sources: 1960-72, *1972 Census of Governments,* vol. 6, no. 4; 1973, *Government Finances in 1972-73,* Bureau of the Census; 1974, *Governmental Finances in 1973-74,* Bureau of the Census; 1975, *Budget of the United States Government, Fiscal Year 1977, Special Analyses,* adjusted to conform to Census reporting period.

specified services to specifically targeted groups of recipients. Revenue sharing monies are given to state and local governments, virtually without strings, to be used for the purposes and on behalf of those citizens that the recipient governments judge appropriate. The political negotiations that led to the adoption of revenue sharing made the new program, if not a complete add-on to existing federal funding (as many representatives of local governments thought had been promised), at least a sizable supplement to previous federal expenditures. The 25 percent advance in federal assistance to the state and local sector in 1973 reflects the impact of the first disbursements made under the revenue sharing formula.

The role of intergovernmental assistance in fueling the expenditure growth of old industrial cities scarcely can be exaggerated. Some representative figures on revenue growth over the period 1965-73 are shown in table 10. For the declining cities shown in the table, almost *two-thirds* of all additional revenue received during this period came from state and federal governments, or was borrowed. That is, local taxpayers had to pay for only 35 cents of each dollar of new spending by their city governments. Historically, the split between local and external funding had been almost the reverse. In view of the favorable terms on which intergovernmental aid could be procured after 1965, it is not to be wondered at that city spending should have climbed as rapidly as it did. Studies of

Table 10

SOURCES OF CITIES' REVENUE GROWTH (1965-73)
(Millions of Dollars of Growth and Percentage of Total
Revenue Growth)

	Revenue Source[a]		
	Local Revenue	State and Federal Aid	Net Annual Borrowing
DECLINING CITIES			
Baltimore	165 (29%)	390 (68%)	16 (3%)
Boston	170 (40%)	217 (52%)	32 (8%)
Buffalo	41 (29%)	87 (62%)	13 (9%)
Detroit	260 (44%)	279 (48%)	45 (8%)
Newark	41 (23%)	125 (71%)	9 (6%)
Philadelphia	371 (47%)	349 (45%)	60 (8%)
GROWING CITIES			
Atlanta	132 (56%)	43 (18%)	61 (26%)
Houston	142 (58%)	67 (28%)	34 (14%)
Memphis[b]	42 (48%)	47 (53%)	−1 (−1%)
Portland	51 (54%)	40 (43%)	3 (3%)
San Diego[b]	75 (57%)	54 (41%)	3 (2%)
NEW YORK	2,386 (37%)	3,619 (55%)	508 (8%)

a. City government and school district.

b. 1967-72.

Sources: Bureau of the Census, *City Government Finances in 1964-65, 1972-73.*
School district revenues from local budgets, except Memphis and San
Diego, which are from *Census of Governments,* 1967 and 1972, *Finances
of School Districts.*

specific programs have confirmed that the subsidies written into federal grants in the 1960s were effective at directing local spending to areas where state and federal matching programs were most generous.[22] City expenditures, in other words, responded to the inducements that had been deliberately written into the federal programs. In that sense the high-spending plateau on which the old central cities now find themselves must be viewed as the joint creation of the several partners in the federal system.

If an injection of external aid triggered the rapid growth in city spending over the period 1965-73, the failure of external assistance to grow since that time bears much of the responsibility for the current pressure on city budgets. Table 9 showed the fall-off in federal aid to the state and local sector that began in 1974. From growth rates that had averaged 17 percent per annum for the previous decade, the growth in federal assistance in 1974 fell to 6.6 percent, despite record inflation. In real terms, federal aid to state and local governments barely held its own during fiscal 1974 and 1975. The President's budget called for an even more meager growth in intergovernmental assistance in fiscal 1976, though Congressional resistance and the steep decline in economic activity made that impossible to maintain.[23] The President has proposed a 1.2 percent increase in federal aid to the state and local sector in fiscal 1977.

For some of the declining central cities, the slowdown in external assist-

---

[22] Edward M. Gramlich and Harvey Galper, "State and Local Fiscal Behavior and Federal Grant Policy," *Brookings Papers on Economic Activity,* no. 1, 1973.

[23] The President's budget for fiscal 1976 called for a 3.2 percent increase in federal payments to the state and local sector, after exclusion of energy tax equalization payments. Actual payments, in contrast, are estimated in the 1977 budget to have jumped by 20.2 percent. A little over half of the 1976 increase is directly attributable to Medicaid, temporary employment assistance, public assistance, and other programs related to the cyclical downturn in the economy.

Some explanation may also be in order for the different "federal aid" figures which are cited in official studies. Three different measures of federal assistance are in common use: (a) federal payments to the state and local sector, as given by the Census, (b) federal aid as given in the federal budget (*Special Analysis* "O"), and (c) federal grants-in-aid as given by the Commerce Department. The differences between these definitions are relatively minor and are explained in detail in the *Special Analysis* section of the 1977 federal budget. In addition to these definitional differences, there are reporting period discrepancies. The Census reports of state and local receipts of intergovernmental revenue are based on *state* and *local* fiscal years rather than the federal fiscal year; in particular, they report the sum of intergovernmental transfers received by state and local governments for fiscal years ending at any time in the 12 months prior to June 30.

Tables 1 and 9 in the text are based on state and local receipts of federal aid as reported by Census.

ance actually began earlier. The cities that had been most successful in securing programmatic aid under Great Society auspices discovered that general revenue sharing, with its formula-determined aid allocation, treated them less generously than had their own skills at grantsmanship. Boston, for example, suffered a 20 percent drop in the dollar amount of its federal aid between 1971 and 1975. The growing cities, in contrast, were large gainers from the switch to revenue sharing. Houston's receipt of federal funds leaped ahead 150 percent in 1973 and 30 percent more in 1974, a pattern that was typical of the group, which previously had received relatively little federal assistance of any kind.

The Budget Pressure in Perspective

By now, the nature of the fiscal squeeze on cities should be apparent. The old industrial cities have had their local revenue-raising capacity impaired by slow economic growth and by the misfortune of having their local tax collections tied to a property tax base that exaggerates local growth trends. Up to 1973, most of the declining cities tried to ignore the constraints imposed by their limited local taxing capacity and allowed expenditures to rise at record rates. They were able to do so because most of the additional money they spent was external funding transferred to them through intergovernmental assistance.

From the revenue side, the fiscal crises of 1975 were the product of an unhappy coincidence of timing. The abrupt slowdown in the growth of intergovernmental aid during 1974-75 forced the older cities back upon their own resources at just the moment these resources gave out because of the recession. The necessity of suddenly financing their own expenditure growth (including the wage increases demanded by workers originally hired under federal programs but for whom no more federal assistance was forthcoming) would have strained the cities' fiscal capacity under the best of circumstances. As it was, the simultaneous failure of local and intergovernmental revenue sources precipitated genuine fiscal distress. The newer, growing cities have been spared the worst of this budgetary pressure. Their local revenue sources stood up better during the national recession; they had never embroiled themselves in federal financing to the extent that the old central cities had and thus suffered less from the slowdown in federal aid; and the changeover from programmatic assistance to revenue sharing actually improved their situation.

From the expenditure side of the budget, we have suggested several factors serving to augment spending levels: (1) the difficulties which cities have had in adjusting to population decline, (2) the greater costs of public service provision imposed on cities by changes in the composition of their population, (3) the fact that cities were able to pay for most of their spending increases through intergovernmental assistance rather than locally raised revenue. Needless to say, these are not rival explanations. It is most likely that they mutually reinforce one another. But the discussion to this point has not sorted out the relative importance of the various factors in explaining expenditure growth.

To assay the relative importance of these causes of city expenditure growth, we have fit a regression equation for 24 observations in our big-city sample, all the cities for which comparable data could be obtained. The dependent variable to be explained is the percentage growth in per capita spending by city governments and their associated independent school districts over the period 1967-72. The independent variables are the percentage change in city population, the percentage of total revenue growth during the period that came from other than local sources, and (as a proxy for change in demographic characteristics) the growth in the percentage of nonwhites in city population.

Care must be taken not to claim too much for a regression of this sort. It does not represent a formal test of a particular hypothesis about the causes of big-city expenditure growth. Moreover, the mechanisms by which the variables are translated into expenditure decisions have been left unarticulated. The statistical estimation reported in the footnote is designed only to obtain a rough quantification of the relative importance of the factors which we already have identified as influencing expenditure growth.[24]

[24]

Table 11

FACTORS INFLUENCING CITY EXPENDITURE GROWTH

(Dependent Variable: Percentage Increase in Per Capita Spending 1967-72)

Variable	Regression Coefficient and (t statistic)
Constant	58.9 (7.8)
Percentage Change in Population	−1.30 (3.2)
Percent of Revenue Growth from External Sources	0.41 (2.7)
Change in Percent of City Population Non-White	0.13 (0.5)
	$R^2 = .74$

The factors which we have hypothesized as influencing spending trends turn out to be of statistical significance. The most important effect upon spending growth over the period 1967-72 appears to have been wielded by pure population change. The next most important variable was intergovernmental assistance. Changes in the demographic composition of city population (as measured by the racial proxy) were of far less practical consequence.

From Fiscal Difficulty to Financial Crisis

Long-term fiscal pressure may be a precondition for a financial crisis, but it is by no means a sufficient condition. So far, the only large city to reach the brink of bankruptcy has been New York City, and ironically, until 1975 New York's underlying economic conditions looked relatively favorable compared to those of Cleveland, Detroit, or Buffalo. (Note the tax base growth comparisons in table 7.) The example set by New York has demonstrated that the fiscal problems common to most of the old central cities can degenerate into full-blown crises when local leaders refuse to acknowledge the constraints upon their budgets.

New York's fundamental trouble was that when external assistance to the city faltered, as it did in most other declining cities as well, rather than balance its budget through expenditure reductions or tax increases, it tried to borrow to meet its operating costs, treating the debt it accumulated as if it were merely so much transfer assistance which never would have to be repaid. Table 12 shows the sources of New York's revenue

Table 12

NEW YORK CITY'S SOURCES OF REVENUE GROWTH
(Annual Average Increases in Revenue, in Millions of Dollars,
and Percent of Total Revenue Increase from Each Source)

Period	Local Revenue	State and Federal Aid	Net Annual Borrowing	Unfunded Budget Gap
1965-73	341 (37%)	517 (55%)	73 (8%)	—
1973-75	354 (22%)	125 (8%)	1,130 (70%)	—
Preliminary Budget, 1976	206 (25%)	−7 (−1%)	—	641 (76%)

Sources: 1964-73, table 10; 1973-75, New York City budgets for respective years; 1976, June 1975 projections by the Mayor's office.

growth in three different time periods. Between 1965 and 1973 New York, like other declining cities, relied on external funding for most of its expenditure growth. Beginning in 1973, the traditional sources of external assistance failed. But, as is apparent from the table, instead of shifting to local revenues to replace the lost external support, the city accelerated its net borrowings. In a cash flow sense, the net increase in indebtedness more than compensated for the lost growth in state and federal aid. Between the beginning of fiscal 1973 and the end of fiscal 1975, the city's outstanding general purpose debt jumped from approximately $9.0 billion to $12.4 billion. By 1975 New York probably accounted for 40 percent of all the outstanding short-term debt issued by local jurisdictions in the entire country.[25]

Ostensibly, such massive net borrowing by New York was illegal, for the city's charter required a balanced operating budget. To circumvent the legal restrictions, city officials resorted to a number of budgetary gimmicks. Overdue property taxes, which the city later acknowledged to be uncollectable, were entered on the books as accounts receivable and short term "tax anticipation" notes were issued, purportedly to tide the city over until the late taxes were paid. Since the taxes never were collected, the net effect was to use borrowed funds directly to pay for the city's operating expenditures. Because the city's capital budget could legally be funded by long-term borrowing, the cost of paying many of the city's regular planning and engineering employees was reclassified as a capital expense and the salaries in question were paid from the proceeds of newly issued municipal bonds. Money also was borrowed from the city's pension funds by declaring the rate of interest earned on pension assets to be in excess of statutory requirements and assigning the "excess" portion of pension income to the city's general operating budget. A special state audit later determined that, in all, about $2.5 billion of hidden operating deficits had been accumulated by the city.

The charade of calling loans "income," of borrowing more money each year, and of paying operating expenses with the borrowed cash that came in could continue only as long as creditors were willing to be gulled in

---

[25] As of June 1, 1975 New York City had $5.3 billion outstanding in short-term debt, or 29 percent of the total short-term indebtedness of the state and local sector. According to the *Census of Governments,* approximately one-fourth of all short-term debt outstanding in 1971-72 had been issued by state agencies. If the same proportion held true in 1975, New York's short-term debt would account for just under 40 percent of all short-term debt issued by municipal governments and local authorities.

this fashion. Once New York's banks discovered that they could no longer place the city's notes with investors, and became unwilling to accumulate further inventories of city debt on their own, the financial crisis broke. Without new borrowings, New York was unable to redeem its short-term debt when it became due. First, New York State was forced to intercede by using its own credit to borrow on the city's behalf. Then, the banks and other holders of city debt were persuaded to accept a moratorium on debt repayment as the only alternative to default. Finally, the federal government was obliged to make $2.3 billion of emergency loans to the city in order to avert default by both New York City and New York State.

For other cities, the significance of New York's financial crisis lay in the disruption it caused in municipal financial markets. If nothing else, the experience of 1975 demonstrated the fragile and antiquated nature of the tax-exempt bond market upon which the cities rely for so much of their financing. Traditionally, the greater part of local public capital expenditures have been financed through long-term tax-exempt borrowing. In addition, even the most prudently managed government has had to turn to short-term borrowing to reconcile the erratic inflow of its tax and intergovernmental aid payments with the more regular claims of its payroll and other expenditure items. In principle, the ability to borrow funds on the tax-exempt market should be an important stabilizing force for local governments.

The poor quality of financial information underlying the tax-exempt market not only prevented it from performing this stabilizing function during the budget stress of 1975 but made it have quite the opposite effect. The tax-exempt market threatened to become an instrument of financial contagion by which New York City's default would infect the financial structure of other cities. In contrast to the strict disclosure requirements governing corporate offerings of stock or bonded debt, municipal bond issues, because they are not regulated by the Securities and Exchange Commission, have not had to comply with any generally accepted standards of disclosure. Until 1975, when some local governments began to issue prospectuses describing their financial situation in greater detail in order to insulate themselves from the market resistance bred by New York City's crisis, virtually no information was routinely provided by local authorities to the public regarding the issuing authority's financial condition. Two private bond-rating agencies have performed the only financial analysis generally available to the public; the quality of this analysis can best be described as undistinguished. Moody's bond-rating system did not alert investors to the deteriorating condition of New York State's Urban Development Corporation until three weeks before the latter's default in February, 1975, and then only by downgrading the corporation's bonds from a Baa-1 rating, corresponding to the strongest class of medium grade obligations, to a Baa rating, corresponding to medium quality. Even in the spring of 1975, Moody reaffirmed its "A" rating of New York City bonds. Earlier, during the Lindsay years, both Moody and Standard and Poor had upgraded New York City's bond rating to an "A" position, although it subsequently became clear that at just this time the city began to accelerate its accumulation of hidden budget deficits.

When New York City's crisis broke, the absence of generally available information which would permit lenders to distinguish the true financial situation of different cities, coupled with the apparent unreliability of the standard systems for assessing risk, led investors to apply the simple rule of thumb that it was best to avoid lending to all cities that bore any resemblance to New York. Buffalo, for example, was unable to obtain any offers at all when it tried to issue municipal debt near the height of New York's crisis. Budget directors in other cities, such as Detroit and Philadelphia, claimed that their borrowing costs jumped by 1.5 to 2.0 percentage points because of fears inspired by New York's situation (although their own financial conditions justified investor caution). The lower panel of figure 1 shows the steep fluctuation in tax-exempt interest rates that occurred during 1975. As can be seen, interest rates peaked in September and October, just prior to the decision to render federal assistance to New York City. In the event of actual default by New York, the tax-exempt borrowing market undoubtedly would have become closed altogether to many of the older industrial cities, thereby threatening them with default as well.

The short-term instability of the municipal bond market has to some extent obscured a longer-term erosion in the benefits of tax exemption for local governments. The top panel in figure 1 illustrates the generally upward course in the interest rates faced by state and local governments. Most of this increase can be attributed to a similar increase in the cost of all borrowing. But the savings achieved by tax exemption, as measured by the gap between the taxable and tax-exempt interest curves in both panels of figure 1, also narrowed substantially in 1974-75. Historically,

Figure 1

TAXABLE AND TAX EXEMPT INTEREST RATES

A. LONG-TERM TRENDS

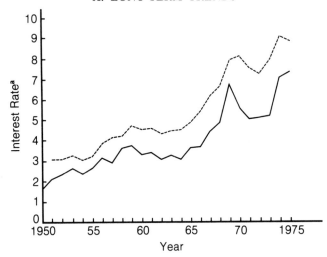

——— Yields on Domestic Municipal Bonds [Bond Buyer 20 bond index]
-------- Yields on Corporate Bonds [Moody's Aa series]
a. Interest Rate as of December of each year; except 1975, which is October

B. SHORT-TERM CYCLE

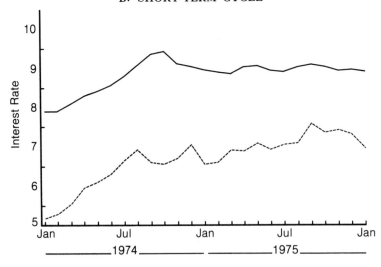

——— Yields on Corporate Bonds
-------- Yields on Tax-Exempt Bonds

tax-exempt interest rates have been some 30-35 percent lower than taxable interest rates, as a consequence of the advantages that tax exemption carries for the investor. In 1975, however, the gap between the two interest rates was closed to as little as 20 percent for part of the year. There are several causes for this weakening of the tax-exempt market beside the uncertainty created by New York's approach to bankruptcy. Commercial banks, which traditionally have been the principal buyers of tax-exempt issues, have found other tax shelters in which to invest their funds and are now less anxious to buy long-term municipal bonds than they once were.[26] This has depressed market demand for tax-exempt securities.

---

[26] The recent withdrawal of commercial banks from the tax-exempt bond market, and their replacement by the household sector as purchasers of local debt, is illustrated by the annual net changes in holdings of municipal securities (in billions of dollars):

Holder	1970	1971	1972	1973	1974	First Two Quarters 1975[a]
Commercial Banks	+10.7	+12.6	+ 7.2	+ 5.7	+ 5.5	+ 4.2
Households	− 0.8	− 0.2	+ 1.0	+ 4.3	+10.0	+11.6
All Other	+ 1.3	+ 5.2	+ 6.2	+ 3.7	+ 1.9	+ 3.7
Total	+11.2	+17.6	+14.4	+13.7	+17.4	+19.5

a. Annual Rate

Source: Congressional Budget Office, *New York City's Fiscal Problem* (October 1975), p. 8 and unpublished Flow of Funds data from Federal Reserve.

For an analysis of the sensitivity of tax-exempt interest rates to the household sector's share of bond purchases, see George E. Peterson and Harvey Galper, "Tax Exempt Financing of Private Industry's Pollution Control Investment," *Public Policy* (Winter, 1975), p. 82-103.

In 1974, the 19 largest commercial banks in the U.S. paid an average U.S. effective tax rate of 2.0 percent on their world-wide income. Obviously, their incentive for further reducing their U.S. tax liability is very small. The average tax burden breaks down as follows, starting with the nominal rate of corporate taxation and subtracting from it the tax advantages enjoyed in 1974 by the sample banks:

Statutory U.S. Tax Rate	48.0%
Tax-Exempt Interest Income (State and Local Debt)	(18.2)
Leasing Activities	
Investment Tax Credit	(0.7)
Accelerated Depreciation	(6.4)
Foreign Credits	
Foreign Income Taxes	(0.2)
Foreign Tax Credit	(17.0)
Excess Loan Loss Provision	(2.5)
Miscellaneous	(1.1)
Average U.S. Tax Rate Paid on Worldwide Income	2.0%

Congress also has allowed private corporations to tap the tax-exempt market to raise capital for investment in pollution-control equipment. Approximately 10-15 percent of all tax-exempt bonds are now issued by private business instead of by state and local governments. The imbalance between a widening supply of tax-exempt issues, on the one hand, and a greater reluctance of traditional buyers to acquire them, on the other, explains the longer-term deterioration of the tax-exempt market.

Quite apart from the measures that can be undertaken to improve the basic fiscal condition of the cities, reforms in the tax-exempt lending market are needed to restore its proper stabilizing influence. The Securities and Exchange Commission, Congress, and the courts all have expressed an interest in improving standards of financial disclosure. During 1975, Congress created a new Municipal Securities Rule-Making Board, which is empowered to establish standards of conduct for municipal bond dealers. Although the legislation continues state and local governments' exemptions from disclosure requirements, it lays the groundwork for court action against underwriters and bond counsel, should it be shown that pertinent information regarding the financial condition of an issuer was not made available to the public.[27] It is difficult to predict whether the outcome of the present debate over disclosure will be the eventual promulgation of federal regulations or the voluntary adoption by state and local governments and bond dealers of clear standards of financial reporting. In either event, it seems certain that the quality of information underpinning the municipal bond market will be vastly improved in the future.

Congress also has indicated renewed interest in the possibility of subsidizing a flat percentage of state and local governments' borrowing costs as an alternative to tax exemption. Under this option (dubbed the taxable bond option) municipalities would have the choice of receiving federal payments variously proposed to equal 30, 40, or 50 percent of their interest costs on newly issued *taxable* bonds, rather than issue tax-exempt securities. The advantages of such an option are several. Each dollar of direct federal subsidy would reduce state and local borrowing costs by considerably more than the indirect subsidy now paid to wealthy investors in the form of tax exemption, since only part of investors' personal tax benefits are passed on to communities as lower interest costs. At present,

---

[27] In January 1976 the Securities and Exchange Commission announced that it was undertaking a formal investigation of the circumstances surrounding the issuance of New York City bonds to determine if pertinent facts about the city's financial condition were culpably withheld from the public.

approximately one-fourth of the costs of tax exemption (or $1.2 billion per year) are captured by upper-income investors as increases in their after-tax income. From an equity standpoint, the taxable bond option would help to close one of the more conspicuous loopholes in current federal tax law. For the cities, the principal advantage of such a proposal is that, besides lowering net borrowing costs somewhat, it would promote stability in the bond market by giving the cities access to large numbers of middle-income buyers who do not pay taxes at a high enough rate to be in the market for tax-exempt securities. The higher interest rates that municipalities would pay also would make their bonds far more appealing to pension funds, which by law do not have to pay taxes on their income and for whom the benefits of tax-exemption thus have no importance. The House Ways and Means Committee has held extensive hearings on the taxable bond option. The prospects for widening the municipal bond markets in this manner are relatively bright.[28]

II. POLICY CHOICES

To this point, we have drawn a profile of the fiscal strain on cities without suggesting, except indirectly, what can be done to alleviate it. The policy options to be weighed fall naturally into three categories. In the short run city governments have no choice but to accept the trend toward parsimony in state and federal aid. They therefore are left with a choice between making expenditure reductions—or at least effecting drastic cut-backs in the rate of expenditure growth—and adopting further tax increases. The evidence points to the fact that taxpayer-consumers, when given the chance to vote on this trade-off directly, favor holding the line on taxes. Austerity in public spending, however, runs against both the interests of organized municipal employees and governments' desire to sustain the central-city job market. Much of the policy maneuvering consequently has involved procedural efforts to strengthen the hand of taxpayer-voters, public employee unions, or other interested parties in the bargaining over future spending levels.

A second group of choices concerns the level and type of external assistance that, over the longer term, will be rendered to the cities. During the past few years many intergovernmental aid programs have under-

---

[28] For further analysis of the taxable bond option, see Harvey Galper and George E. Peterson, "The Equity Effects of a Taxable Municipal Bond Subsidy," *National Tax Journal* (December, 1973), p. 611-24; also Stanley E. Surrey, "Statement on Optional Taxable Bonds," submitted to House Ways and Means Committee (Jan. 1976).

gone basic redesign. A number of states, for example, have changed their methods of assisting local public schooling, while the federal government has adopted general revenue sharing as its principal form of aid to the state and local sector. Federal assumption of welfare costs also remains on the agenda for national consideration. Just as decisions about intergovernmental aid were decisive in shaping the cities' fiscal growth over the past decade, the aid choices to be made now promise to go far toward molding the cities' future fiscal condition.

Before considering measures that may alleviate the cities' fiscal plight, however, we should direct our attention to the third set of policy choices: those which may help to arrest the economic decline that underlies the cities' fiscal predicament.

The Long-Term Choice: Reuniting the City with Its Market Area

Our classification of cities as growing and declining has failed so far to distinguish two quite different causes of population loss which may give rise to different fiscal consequences. To the extent that a city suffers population decline because its metropolitan area is losing out to others in regional economic competition, there is little that can be done to alleviate the trend short of the adoption of a national growth plan. The long-run future of most Northeastern and North Central cities, fiscal as well as economic, must be regarded as bleak because of continuing regional shifts in population and economic activity away from these parts of the country. A greater part of central-city decline, however, stems from the fact that people and jobs are leaving the urban core in favor of other locations within the same metropolitan region. The flexibility of a city's boundaries then becomes an important determinant of its population and fiscal growth. If city boundaries are flexible enough to incorporate within the city some of the new growth that occurs outside the old borders, a jurisdiction can continue to grow in population and tax base, even though any fixed portion of it is suffering declines in both respects. Consider the cities in our sample. As a group, the 13 cities that gained population in the 1960s enlarged their geographical area by 77 percent over the decade as a result of annexation and consolidation.[29] In contrast, none of the declining cities significantly altered its borders. With the single exception

---

[29] Bureau of the Census, *Population and Land Areas of Urbanized Areas 1970 and 1960,* Feb. 1972; also, Bureau of the Census, *Boundary and Annexation Survey,* March 1975.

of Pittsburgh, however, each of the declining cities lies at the heart of a metropolitan area which in its totality gained population during the 1960s. Quite obviously some other definition of city boundaries would have allowed these cities to be classified as growing.

The inflexibility of the boundaries delimiting the old central cities is fundamental to their fiscal dilemma. For years, metropolitan areas in the United States have been thinning out. Decentralization of jobs and population antedates even the development of the automobile, although it appears to have gathered pace since 1920.[30] For the tastes of modern housing consumers and the production methods of modern manufacturers, the old housing stock and factories at the urban core are too densely constructed. As household incomes have risen and transportation systems have improved, firms and families have tended to build their new plants or homes at steadily lower densities. This long-term trend has left its mark on the physical configuration of cities. Cities that grew to maturity in the twentieth century were built at far lower density levels than cities that became populous in the nineteenth century or earlier. The older cities, meanwhile, have moved toward lower densities, though the speed of their adjustment has been limited by the physical constraints placed upon them by an antiquated street network and capital infrastructure, both of which are difficult to replace. Figure 2 illustrates the striking regularity of the relationship that exists between city age, city density, and recent changes in city density levels.

Viewed from the long-term perspective of density trends, the net outmigration of households and firms from the urban core appears to be a natural process. If the legal city could be defined in a way that made it coterminous with the urban market, such a rearrangement of economic activity within the metropolitan area would create no special fiscal hardship. It is the fact that city boundaries have remained fixed in the face of a persistent outward expansion of the urban market area that has isolated the central cities and their tax bases from economic growth. The old city boundaries have been left to encase an aging and underutilized capital stock, whose value is falling in real terms, as well as a declining population that contains a large (and growing) share of economic dependents for whom public service provision is unusually expensive.

---

[30] See, for example, David Harrison, Jr. and John F. Kain, "Cumulative Urban Growth and Urban Density Functions," *Journal of Urban Economics,* no. 1, 1974, pp. 61-98; Edwin S. Mills, *Studies in the Structure of the Urban Economy* (Washington, D.C.: Resources for the Future, 1972), published through Johns Hopkins University Press, Baltimore, Maryland.

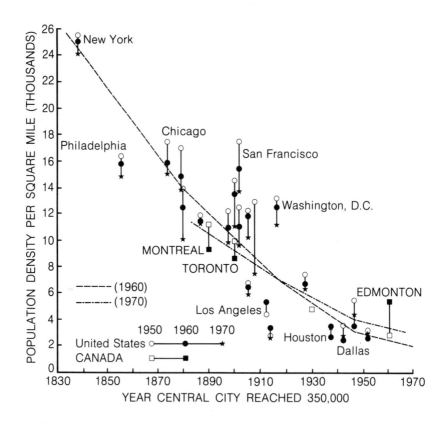

Figure 2

**THE RELATIONSHIP BETWEEN THE AGE OF LARGE
CITIES IN NORTH AMERICA AND THEIR CHANGING
POPULATION DENSITIES IN THE YEARS 1950–1970**

SOURCE: Brian J. L. Berry, *The Human Consequences of Urbanization* (New
York, N.Y.: St. Martin's Press, Inc., 1973), figure 2, p. 37. Reprinted
by permission of the publisher.

A strong element of arbitrariness, even caprice, seems to have gone into the determination of just when the old central cities would stop annexing neighboring areas. For most of the nineteenth century, city boundaries followed hard on the heels of market expansion. When the introduction of street cars caused the Boston metropolitan area to push outward after 1850, the city of Boston annexed the independent townships of Roxbury, West Roxbury, Dorchester, Brighton, and Charlestown in quick succession. But the last expansion of the city of Boston occurred in 1912 with the annexation of Hyde Park. Since that time the economic decentralization of the area has continued—even accelerated—but the legal definition of the city has stayed fixed. New York City took its present form in 1898 when Manhattan, Brooklyn, Staten Island, Queens, and the Bronx (then part of Westchester County) merged into one governmental unit. One can only speculate what the subsequent fiscal history of the area would have been if the five boroughs had remained independent, or if the legal boundaries of "New York City" had followed metropolitan expansion outward beyond Queens to Long Island. The present boundaries of Philadelphia date back even further, to 1858, when the city and county of Philadelphia were consolidated as part of a political reform movement. The Philadelphia standard metropolitan statistical area as defined by Census, the Philadelphia television market area as defined by the Federal Communications Commission, and the Philadelphia commuting radius as defined by the commuting habits of workers, have all continued to expand through the 1970s; but the last 120 years of economic development have left the legal demarcation of the city literally unmoved.

The modern growth of what we have termed growing cities more closely parallels the nineteenth century history of the old industrial towns than it does the latter's present experience. Cities like Houston, Jacksonville, San Diego, and Memphis have been granted generous boundaries to begin with (Jacksonville now encloses the largest incorporated area of any city in the Western Hemisphere), and have further benefited from having their boundaries redefined repeatedly so as to incorporate new metropolitan development within the legal compass of the city. As a result, growing cities have tended to share much more vigorously in the economic expansion of the urban markets they sustain.

Table 13 suggests the effect on tax bases and public expenditures that comes from isolating the central city from the rest of the metropolitan market area. For each of the previously identified 28 large central cities,

Table 13

COMPARISONS OF CENTRAL CITIES AND SURROUNDING METROPOLITAN AREAS

	City Age[a]	Central City Population[b] as Percent of SMSA Population[a]	Central City Density 1970[c]	Annexation or Consolidation 1960-70[d]	Tax Base 1971-72[e]		Costs of Police Protection 1972-73[f]		Percent of Central County Population Receiving Welfare Payments[g]
					Central City Property Value Per Capita	Property Value Per Capita Rest of SMSA	Central City Expenditure Per Capita	Expenditure Per Capita Rest of SMSA	
Declining Cities									
Baltimore	130	41	11,568	No	$ 4,019	$ 9,103	$65	$21	16.8
Boston	120	18	13,936	No	7,346	8,874	83	29	17.0
Buffalo	100	31	11,205	No	8,196	7,435	51	21	4.7
Chicago	110	45	15,126	No	8,577	12,883	68	26	11.2
Cincinnati	120	31	5,794	No	6,696	8,396	56	27	6.4
Cleveland	90	33	9,893	No	6,269	10,311	60	23	9.3
Detroit	90	31	10,953	No	5,968	8,929	72	60	12.8
Milwaukee	90	49	7,548	No	5,655	8,952	56	27	6.9
New Orleans	130	53	3,011	No	6,613	11,456	38	17	11.7
Philadelphia	120	38	15,164	No	5,363	9,004	71	18	16.5
Pittsburgh	90	20	9,422	No	5,574	6,524	44	15	6.8
St. Louis	110	23	10,167	No	6,520	8,223	64	20	15.8
San Francisco	100	22	15,764	No	14,380	13,065	42	33	9.1
Seattle	60	36	6,350	No	12,899	10,361	52	19	4.3
Previously Growing, Now Declining Cities									
Columbus	70	51	4,009	Yes	$ 6,943	$ 8,829	$34	$18	8.1
Dallas[h]	50	33	3,179	No	9,271[h]	7,332[h]	38	19	3.4
Denver	80	39	5,406	Yes	9,407	9,028	39	17	7.4
Indianapolis	80	65	1,963	Yes	7,046	8,051*	27	9	5.1
Kansas City	80	37	1,603	Yes	6,851	9,792	51	22	7.5
Los Angeles	70	39	6,073	No	12,149	11,761	59	49	8.1
Growing Cities									
Honolulu	40	100	3,872	NA	$14,178	—[i]	$37	—[i]	6.4
Houston	50	62	2,841	Yes	10,511[h]	$14,093[h]	24	$22	3.5
Jacksonville	40	82	690	Yes	6,388	—[i]	22	—[i]	4.9
Memphis	70	78	2,868	Yes	6,487	7,076	27	18	10.5
Phoenix	20	60	2,346	Yes	8,973	11,429[h]	46	27	3.1
San Antonio	50	81	3,555	Yes	4,791[h]	6,008	18	12	5.6
San Diego	40	52	2,199	Yes	11,214	10,851	25	28	5.8
New York City	160	77	26,343	No	$10,566	$11,452	$70	$35	12.6

* Error corrected in *Census of Governments* summation of SMSA assessed value total.

Sources and definitions:

a. Years since city reached 100,000 population, *Census of Population, 1960, vol. 1, part 1,* table 28.

b. 1973 central city population/1972 SMSA population as given in *City Government Finances in 1973-74,* table 7, and *Local Government Finances in Selected Metropolitan Areas and Large Counties: 1972-73,* table 3.

c. Persons per square mile, *Statistical Abstract of the United States 1973,* table 23.

d. "Yes" indicates annexation equal to 5 percent or more of city area, Bureau of Census, *Population and Land Area of Urbanized Areas 1971 and 1960.* Population data refer to 1970.

e. Derived from data in *Census of Governments, 1972, vol. 2, part 2.* Aggregate assessment-sales ratios were used to convert assessed values to market-values.

f. Derived from data in Bureau of the Census, *Local Government Finances in Selected Metropolitan Areas and Large Counties: 1972-73,* table 3, (city and SMSA population as in (b) above).

g. Department of Health, Education, and Welfare, "Recipients of Public Assistance Money Payments and Amounts of Such Payments by Program, State, and County," Feb. 1975. (DHEW Pub. No. (SRS) 76-03105, July 1975). Percentages refer to fraction of population receiving payments under Aid to Families with Dependent Children and General Assistance programs.

h. Per capita property values for Texas cities are for central counties and rest-of-SMSA.

i. Honolulu and Jacksonville comprised 100 percent of their SMSAs in 1970.

we have computed the proportion of metropolitan population that lay inside and outside central-city boundaries in 1972, the property tax base per capita of the central city and that of the remainder of the Standard Metropolitan Statistical Area (SMSA), and the respective per capita expenditures on police protection. The last item is included as a proxy for the cost of providing common municipal services. Also indicated is the proportion of welfare recipients in the innermost county of the metropolitan area. The first three columns of the table indicate the age of the city (the number of decades since it reached a population of 100,000), its density as of 1970, and whether or not significant annexation or consolidation occurred during the 1960s.

The pattern that emerges from table 13 is quite consistent. Declining cities are older, and because they were built before the automobile and at a time when average income was much lower than it now is, they tend to be more densely populated than newer cities. In part because of their high starting densities, the old cities suffer from much higher rates of out-migration from the urban core. Yet their boundaries have proven least capable of adjusting to follow the outward migration of economic activity. As a result, the declining cities have been saddled with tax bases that are less valuable than those enjoyed by the rest of their metropolitan areas and with public sector operating expenses that are much higher. Most importantly, the out-migration from the central cities has steadily eroded the existing tax base. In the oldest cities, such as Baltimore and Phila-delphia, the per capita tax base in the central city is now barely half that in the suburbs, despite the historical concentration of commercial-indus-trial property in the cities. In some of the other declining metropolitan areas, such as San Francisco and Seattle, desertion of the urban core has not proceeded far enough to reverse the traditional tax base advantage of the central city, but for all the cities in this group the trend in relative fiscal capacity is downward. For growing cities, current tax base com-parisons are somewhat more mixed and (as we have seen) the trends are more encouraging.

As emphasized throughout this chapter, it is the balance between tax-paying capacity and public sector costs that is decisive in determining a city's fiscal position. The concentration of nonresidential activities in the central city historically has boosted both its expenditure levels (police and fire services are needed to protect factories, offices, and daytime employees as well as residents) and its taxable base, but on balance has benefitted the cities' fiscal position. Today, costs remain far higher in the old central cities, but the tax base advantage formerly conferred by commercial-industrial property has been lost.

Adherence to out-of-date central city boundaries has done more than capriciously allocate urban resources between the central city and the rest of the SMSA in response to the decentralization of private markets. Once in place, the boundaries provide a further *incentive* to out-migration from the central cities. The existence of small, independent suburbs possessing wealthy tax bases and favorable conditions for producing public services creates a purely public-sector motivation for intrametropolitan migration. To escape the tax burden of the central city, its poor schools, or its high crime rate, households can move to independent jurisdictions located elsewhere in the metropolitan area. Separation of the factors contributing to household migration is a difficult undertaking, but there now is a good deal of econometric evidence which indicates that school quality, tax-rate, and other public sector differentials have spurred out-migration from the cities and have exacerbated differences in the characteristics of the populations living inside and outside the central city boundaries.[31]

Actions taken by the suburbs have further strengthened the division of the older metropolis into a relatively impoverished core and a relatively affluent outer ring. (Inner suburbs frequently suffer from the same problems of fixed boundaries, aging capital stock, and selective out-migration as the central cities and are likely to face the next generation of fiscal crises.) In several states, suburbs have effectively resisted central cities' right to annexation. In Florida, for example, suburban pressures caused the state legislature in 1974 to curb the power of annexation enjoyed by central cities. Until 1970, cities in Virginia were able to annex surrounding areas at their own initiative, subject only to a demonstration to the courts that annexation was in the city's economic interest. But when the city of Richmond tried to annex a portion of suburban Chesterfield County under this provision, the state legislature changed the law so that in the future an affirmative vote by affected residents would be required before annexation could proceed.[32] The very contrast which has devel-

---

[31] For example, David F. Bradford and Harry H. Kelejian, "An Econometric Model of the Flight to the Suburbs," *Journal of Political Economy* 81 (May-June 1973); Edwin S. Mills, Bruce Hamilton, and David Puryear, "The Tiebout Hypothesis and Residential Segregation," *Journal of Urban Economics* (1974).

[32] For detailed evaluations of the impact of annexation upon the fiscal situation of Richmond, Virginia, see Thomas Muller and Grace Dawson, *The Impact of Annexation on City Finances: A Case Study in Richmond, Virginia* (The Urban Institute, Washington, D.C.: 1973); and Muller and Dawson, *An Evaluation of the Fiscal Impact of Annexation in Richmond, Virginia* (The Urban Institute: 1975). The legal issues surrounding Richmond's annexation eventually reached the U.S. Supreme Court.

oped between the central city and the rest of the metropolitan area and which, from the cities' perspective, makes imperative a greater flexibility in boundary definition, from the suburbs' perspective has given them a vested interest in retaining present jurisdictional divisions and in curtailing what powers of annexation the central cities still possess.

At this late date, it probably is not feasible to try to restore to old central cities the powers of annexation they have lost. The prospect that the citizens of Nassau County, Long Island, would acquiesce in a merger with New York City, or that the residents of Shaker Heights would accept annexation at the hands of Cleveland, is so difficult to imagine as to suggest that the political obstacles to reuniting the old central cities with their natural market areas, once these have been separated, are insurmountable. The historical lesson more properly can be applied in those states that still grant cities the power to annex territory. Annexation may create short-term conflicts of interest between central city residents and the residents of more affluent suburbs who would prefer to go it alone fiscally, but the area-wide interest—the "public" interest—seems to be served by allowing central cities to share in metropolitan prosperity. Where central cities have not yet been isolated from the growing portion of the metropolitan market, states will do well to resist suburban pressure to restrict the power of central city annexation.[33]

For those cities that surrendered their powers of annexation some time ago, today's policy options are more limited. In special circumstances interjurisdictional cooperation may restore part of the central city's access to growth outside its borders. The Minneapolis-St. Paul area has introduced a well-publicized plan for tax-base sharing among existing independent jurisdictions. It calls for 40 percent of the value of new nonresidential property built in the metropolitan area to be shared among jurisdictions for property tax purposes on an equal per capita basis. Only the remaining 60 percent of assessed valuation is added directly to the tax

---

[33]Recently, the annexation issue has become entangled with disputes over busing and the quality of central city schools. Texas has perhaps the most active history of central-city annexation, a policy which has proved acceptable to the electorate in large part because the state's Municipal Annexation Act calls for the maintenance of independent school districts in annexed areas, rather than their consolidation into the central city school system. A constitutional amendment in Colorado now effectively precludes Denver (alone among Colorado municipalities) from annexing outlying areas. This amendment was adopted in the wake of a busing controversy, apparently as a means of permanently insulating suburban school districts from Denver's busing program. (See also chapter 5 of this volume.)

rolls of the municipality where construction takes place. While this arrangement has lessened the competitive scramble among local governments for new industrial property, and therefore has important implications as a long-term planning tool, its effect on tax bases has been small. During the first three years of the plan, the property tax bases of Minneapolis and St. Paul were increased by two-tenths and four-tenths of one percent respectively, because of the tax-base sharing arrangement.[34] Even if Minneapolis and St. Paul were less prosperous cities, it is not likely that tax-base sharing of this sort would go far to enhance the central cities' revenue-raising capacity. The bulk of the tax base disadvantage under which central cities labor comes from an imbalance in residential property values rather than from an unequal distribution of nonresidential property.

Cities also have tried unilaterally to capture part of the metropolitan tax base by imposing local payroll or other types of commuter taxes, which extract revenue from people who live in the suburbs but work in the central city. The imposition of a commuter tax is an effective way to shift part of the central city tax burden beyond city borders. It thus has an understandable appeal for beleaguered city officials worried about easing the fiscal crunch on city residents. As of 1975, 51 cities had adopted an income or payroll tax on nonresidents.[35] In many areas the issue is a highly explosive one. Oakland, California, for example, adopted its payroll tax only after years of fierce opposition from business and suburban interests, while in Washington, D.C., Congress would grant the city limited home rule only after explicitly barring it from imposing a tax on commuters. For all its one-time benefits, however, a commuter tax cannot slow the long-term deterioration in the central city tax base unless jobs leave the city at a less rapid pace than do households. At best, this is a precarious hope. Although the evidence on job decentralization is somewhat mixed, over extended periods of time jobs and people seem to be deserting the central cities in about equal measure. Thus a tax on downtown jobs is likely to provide no more long-run revenue growth than a tax on downtown property or a tax on downtown retail sales.

Two other strategies sometimes are recommended for combating the fiscal isolation of the central city. First, where jurisdictional competition

---

[34] For a summary of local tax-base changes as a result of the law, see *Citizens League News* (Minneapolis), Jan. 31, 1975.

[35] Municipal Research Bureau of the District of Columbia, *Taxing Non-Resident Income* (Washington, D.C.: 1975).

for fiscal advantage has helped to segregate the metropolitan area into extremes of income and wealth disparity, changes in the rules governing intrametropolitan migration may alleviate some of the burden on central cities. The fiscal maneuvering of independent metropolitan jurisdictions anxious to exclude from their borders households that would pay less in taxes than the cost of the public services they receive has led to the erection of so many zoning and other barriers, such as minimum lot size or minimum square footage housing requirements, that low-income households often find it difficult, if not impossible, to acquire housing outside the central city. In what may turn out to be a precedent-setting case, the Supreme Court of the state of New Jersey recently moved to prevent localities from restricting entry on fiscal grounds. The court's opinion, quoted below, holds suburban zoning restrictions directly responsible for much of the central cities' loss of tax base:

> There cannot be the slightest doubt that the reason for this course of conduct [exclusionary zoning] has been to keep down local taxes on *property*. . . . This policy of land use regulation for a fiscal end derives from New Jersey's tax structure, which has imposed on local real estate most of the cost of municipal and county government. . . . Sizable industrial and commercial ratables are eagerly sought and homes and the lots on which they are situated are required to be large enough, through minimum lot sizes and minimum floor areas, to have substantial value in order to produce greater tax revenues to meet school costs. . . . Almost every [municipality] acts solely in its own selfish and parochial interest and in effect builds a wall around itself to keep out those people or entities not adding favorably to the tax base. . . .
>
> The other end of the spectrum should also be mentioned. . . . Core cities were originally the location of most commerce and industry. Many of these facilities furnished employment for the unskilled and semiskilled. These employees lived relatively near their work, so sections of cities always have housed the majority of people of low and moderate income, generally in old and deteriorating housing. Despite the municipally confined tax structure, commercial and industrial ratables generally used to supply enough revenue to provide and maintain municipal services equal or superior to those furnished in most suburban and rural cases.
>
> The situation has become exactly the opposite since the end of World War II. Much industry and retail business, and even the professions, have left the cities. . . . The economically better situated city residents helped to fill up the miles of sprawling new housing developments. . . . There has been a consequent critical erosion of the city tax base and inability to provide the amount and quality of those governmental services—health, education, police, fire, housing and the like—so necessary to the very existence of safe and decent city life. [*Southern Burlington County N.A.A.C.P. et al. v. Township of Mt. Laurel* (Supreme Court of New Jersey), pp. 21-24 of court's opinion (March, 1975).]

But it may be too sanguine to expect that elimination of zoning barriers can now significantly help the fiscal position of older jurisdictions. Over the near term, individual low-income households stand to benefit more than central-city finances from the dismantling of zoning barriers. Indeed, the sorting out of New Jersey's metropolitan residents by jurisdiction and income grouping probably has proceeded too far to be reversed by a mere relaxation of zoning restrictions. As part of a long-range strategy to reduce metropolitan stratification, however, there is much to be said for elimination of the fiscal zoning that helps to sustain the segregation of wealth and tax bases.

The final set of policy choices goes directly to the problem of outmigration from the central cities. Though private market forces undoubtedly explain the preponderance of this outward population movement, abandonment of the central city has been abetted by several federal policies which have served to hasten urban decentralization. Federal subsidies for new housing construction through VA and FHA mortgage insurance programs and through income tax laws that favor homeownership have lowered the cost of constructing new housing on vacant land at the urban fringe, relative to the cost of preserving or rehabilitating older housing at the urban core. This has accelerated the replacement cycle for metropolitan housing, with a consequent impetus to decentralization.[36] Federal highway programs and grants for the construction of sewer networks likewise have subsidized decentralization by opening up access to suburban land at little or no cost to local taxpayers. The removal of these federal subsidies favoring suburbanization probably would not greatly alter the present pattern of metropolitan development. But in conjunction with other price changes now occurring in the private market—such as the rising costs of suburban land and the increasing expense of automobile commuting—the elimination of the federal subsidies for decentralization could help generate greater demand for central-city residence.[37] Some of the older central cities, such as Boston, Philadelphia, Baltimore, and Washington, D.C., already have experienced a rejuve-

---

[36] For an analysis of the effects of federal tax and subsidy policy on metropolitan growth, see George E. Peterson, *Federal Tax Policy and Urban Development* (forthcoming, The Urban Institute).

[37] In January 1976 the city of Hartford, Connecticut, won a landmark suit which blocked the payment of $4.4 million in federal community development grants to surrounding suburban jurisdictions for construction of roads, sewers, and parks. Hartford argued that the suburban jurisdictions had failed to prepare plans for accommodating low-income households as required to do by law, and that in the absence of such plans the federal grants would merely accelerate the city's loss of middle-income population and businesses to the suburbs.

nation of demand for downtown housing, which has been reflected in higher rates of investment in the standing housing stock and an up-surge in the cities' taxable property bases caused principally by housing price increases. As long as central cities depend on property taxation for most of their local revenue, the quickest way to enhance their fiscal capacity will be to generate demand for the existing stock of downtown housing.

The State and Federal Choice: How Much Aid for the Cities?

Traditionally, the primary means of compensating local governments for the fiscal consequences of their boundary restrictions has been inter-governmental assistance. If a local jurisdiction incurs higher than normal costs to provide common municipal services because of conditions that are beyond its control, or discharges a responsibility on behalf of the state or nation as a whole, it is fitting that some of its costs should be borne by the state or national government. The rub, of course, lies in determining when these conditions for external assistance have been satisfied. Over the last decade federal policy gradually has shifted from regarding the cities' extraordinary public service costs as an index of the greater effort that cities make on society's behalf—and hence as a measure of the special compensation they deserve to receive from higher-level governments—to regarding those costs as a sign of prodigality and inefficient manage-ment, and hence a measure of the greater discipline that is required in local budgeting.

General Budgetary Support from the Federal Government

Federal aid programs no longer are constructed deliberately to stimulate local spending, as was true of many of the federal subsidies adopted during the sixties. If anything, the modest aid increments now proposed by the ad-ministration appear designed to wean local governments from their high-spending habits. The Ford administration has maintained the position that, with the possible exception of a further federal role in income sup-port programs, the entire structure of federal assistance to the state and local sector now is in place. What is required, it is thought, is a sense of permanence in federal funding that will allow state and local govern-ments to set about the task of long-range planning under realistic budget constraints.

The evolution of the general revenue sharing program typifies the shift of focus that has occurred in federal assistance over the last decade. When the revenue sharing idea first was proposed in the early 1960s, it was taken for granted that the state and local sector would—and should—claim a continually increasing share of national output. Early revenue sharing proposals emphasized the desirability of giving state and local governments access to the highly elastic federal tax base. In what became known as the Heller-Pechman plan,[38] the annual amounts to be made available for revenue sharing purposes were specified as a percentage of federal income tax receipts. Since the progressive nature of the federal income tax rate structure ensures that, in times of inflation or real-income growth, tax yields will grow more rapidly than national income, the use of this base would have guaranteed the transfer of a continually increasing share of national income to state and local governments, which could then have increased their spending commitments without having to procure voter approval for higher local tax rates. In the Heller-Pechman proposal, state and local spending was explicitly singled out as warranting spending priority over the two alternative uses for the increased yield foreseen from the federal tax structure. These alternatives were to return money to the private sector by cutting federal tax rates or to increase direct federal spending.

By the time the revenue sharing proposal became actuality in 1972, under a Republican administration, it was designed to be much less stimulative of state and local spending. The sums to be received annually by state and local governments were spelled out in the legislation, rather than made proportional to the federal tax yield. Moreover, the rate of growth scheduled for revenue sharing allocations was quite modest.

The current revenue sharing authorization lapses at the end of 1976. The Ford administration has recommended renewal of the program, but at funding levels that leave little room for future growth. Table 14 shows the actual revenue sharing payments that have been made each year since the program's inception in 1972, as well as the transfers proposed by the administration for the next six years. Payment totals also have been converted to 1972 dollars. For illustrative purposes, a 6 percent per annum rate of inflation has been assumed for years after fiscal 1976. Although this assumed inflation rate is low in comparison with recent experience,

---

[38] So styled because Walter Heller, chairman of the Council of Economic Advisers, and Joseph Pechman, chairman of a task force to study federal-state-local fiscal relations for President Johnson's re-election campaign, urged similar revenue sharing plans in 1964.

Table 14

GENERAL REVENUE SHARING ALLOCATIONS, CURRENT AND CONSTANT DOLLARS
(Billions)

Fiscal Year	Current Dollars[a]	Constant Dollars (1972)[b]
1972	$5.3	$5.3
1973	5.6	5.4
1974	6.0	5.4
1975	6.2	5.0
1976	6.4	4.8
Proposed		
1977	6.5	4.6
1978	6.6	4.4
1979	6.8	4.3
1980	6.9	4.1
1981	7.1	4.0
1982	7.2	3.8

a. Amounts have been rounded.

b. Amounts have been rounded. Fiscal 1973-75 deflated by GNP deflator for December of preceding calendar year; growth in 1975-76 deflated by change in Consumer Price Index for 12 months ending November, 1975; 6 percent inflation assumed for fiscal 1977-82.

Sources: 1972-76, Title I of the General Revenue Sharing Act of 1972; 1977-82, revenue sharing as proposed by Ford administration.

the real value of the proposed revenue sharing allocations can be seen to decline substantially over time.

The revenue sharing debate, then, has turned full circle. Instead of allocations that are designed to increase automatically as a share of national income, so as to make it easier for state and local governments to meet new spending needs, the payments proposed by the administration would decline annually in real purchasing power and, given any growth at all in the national economy, would decline still more precipitously as a share of national income. The most persuasive argument that has been advanced in favor of this tight payment schedule is that, by providing state and local governments with a long-run budget constraint, it will force the state and local sector to practice greater economy in its expenditures, and thus help them to adjust to their new financial realities, while giving them ample time to do so.

In its distributive aspects, the present revenue sharing formula displays a moderate favoritism toward the older central cities. Within states, revenue sharing funds are apportioned to local governments by three criteria: local population, local tax effort, and local income level. The definition of tax effort employed in the revenue sharing formula is especially favorable to the older cities. Tax effort is measured by the ratio of local taxes collected for other than school purpose to local income. Such a measure resembles the tax effort figure shown in table 8 of this chapter, except that it excludes school taxes and includes as part of the local burden all taxes paid on commercial-industrial property as well as taxes on non-residents' incomes. Jurisdictions which are able to export a good share of their tax bill consequently appear to make a greater tax effort than they would under a more careful examination of tax incidence. According to the rankings produced by the revenue sharing formula, the greatest tax effort is made by seasonal resort communities, such as Ocean City, Maryland, or Vail, Colorado, whose year-round residents have rather modest incomes, but which receive ample tax payments from property taxes collected on vacation homes and other seasonal property owned by those living elsewhere.[39] In less dramatic fashion, the older central cities benefit from the fact that they, too, are able to export a higher than average proportion of their tax burden to nonresidents, thus making the comparison between taxes *collected* at the local level and local household income a deceptive basis for measuring tax effort.[40]

The decision not to include school taxes in the measurement of tax effort similarly redounds to the benefit of the old central cities. In suburban communities over half of all taxes are used to pay for school expenditures, while in most of the older cities the proportion of tax revenue spent for school purposes is much less. This difference is explained in part by the lower share of school-age children in the cities' total population and the higher rates of private school enrollment, and in part by the higher costs that cities face in providing noneducational services to their residents. The revenue sharing formula's exclusive consideration of non-school taxes in calculating local tax effort consequently steers more aid

---

[39] Robert Reischauer, "General Revenue Sharing—the Program's Incentives" in Wallace E. Oates, ed., *Financing the New Federalism* (Washington, D.C.: Resources for the Future, 1975).

[40] In the preparation of table 8 it was assumed that all local taxes on commercial-industrial property and 30 percent of local income taxes were exported beyond the borders of the taxing jurisdiction. By this measure, 24 percent of the tax and revenue burden of declining cities was exported in 1971-72, 13 percent in growing cities, and 15 percent in formerly growing cities.

to the cities than would be forthcoming if the entire bundle of local taxes were taken into account.

One factor which limits the revenue sharing assistance received by the cities is the 145 percent ceiling on payments. As the revenue sharing law now is drafted, no country can receive per capita assistance that exceeds 145 percent of the per capita average for the state as a whole, and no locality can receive an amount that exceeds 145 percent of the per capita average for the county in which it is located. This ceiling limitation affects most severely those cities which double as independent counties. For example, it has been calculated that in 1972, St. Louis would have received 78 percent more revenue sharing aid, Baltimore 51 percent more, and Philadelphia 47 percent more had they not been constrained by the ceiling limitation.[41] The National League of Cities/U.S. Conference of Mayors and other urban lobbying groups have urged removal of the ceiling limitations, but care is needed in drafting replacement language, for simple removal of the ceilings would greatly benefit the nation's vacation spots and industrial enclaves, due to the peculiarities of the tax effort formula.

Table 15 summarizes the per capita revenue sharing assistance received in 1972 by selected central cities. As can be seen, the range in per capita aid payments is quite limited, but what difference there is works to the advantage of the older declining cities.

Job Programs and Counter-Cyclical Aid to the Cities

In the last two years, the federal aid which has most strongly favored the cities has come from the job programs financed under the Comprehensive Employment and Training Act (CETA). In its original form, CETA was meant to tie together a series of older manpower programs into a special revenue sharing package in the manpower field (the Nixon administration had proposed, in addition to general revenue sharing, the consolidation of federal grants into defined areas of specialization, such as manpower training, education, and health and welfare; these were termed "special revenue sharing" programs). Among other things, CETA named state and local governments as the administrators of federal job programs. The training focus of CETA is apparent from the legislative language which states that the act's objective is to furnish "unemployed and underemployed persons with transitional employment in jobs providing needed public services in regions of substantial unemployment and,

---

[41]Richard P. Nathan, Allen A. Manvel, Susannah E. Calkins, and associates, *Monitoring Revenue Sharing* (Washington, D.C.: The Brookings Institution, 1975).

wherever possible, related training and manpower services to enable such persons to move into [permanent] employment."

Table 15

PER CAPITA REVENUE SHARING RECEIPTS
SELECTED CITIES (1972)

	Aid Per Capita in City Area	City Aid as Percent of Statewide Average	Aid to Balance of SMSA as Percent of Statewide Average
DECLINING CITIES			
Baltimore	$26.39	145%	90%
Boston	28.05	145	90
Chicago	21.23	129	63
Cleveland	24.82	185	81
Detroit	28.85	171	72
Milwaukee	29.22	146	69
New Orleans	28.83	130	71
Philadelphia	22.77	145	56
Pittsburgh	30.37	193	98
St. Louis	20.32	145	76
San Francisco	24.90	133	79
Seattle	20.84	137	67
FORMERLY GROWING CITIES			
Columbus	15.43	115	60
Dallas	16.14	109	61
Denver	23.06	140	60
Indianapolis	16.41	112	60
Los Angeles	23.34	125	92
GROWING CITIES			
Honolulu	19.05	93	—
Houston	15.66	106	66
Jacksonville	15.26	106	—
Memphis	25.66	153	60
Phoenix	18.48	103	69
San Antonio	16.26	110	36
San Diego	17.24	94	70
NEW YORK CITY	27.13	126	56

Source: Richard P. Nathan, et al., *Monitoring Revenue Sharing,* table 5-3. (Washington, D.C.: The Brookings Institution, 1975).

The swiftness with which the recession struck deflected CETA from its original purpose of manpower training. From Congress' point of view, it became more urgent to provide jobs than to provide skills that could be used in future employment. From the point of view of the state and local governments which administered the CETA program, federally financed jobs seemed to offer a means of continuing to provide basic public services while trimming public sector employees from the local payroll. The desire to create jobs as quickly as possible caused Congress first to augment its funding for CETA, then to drop legislative requirements that the money be used only to provide new services or to help meet previously unsatisfied service needs. This freed federal funds for hiring persons to supply standard local public services. Meanwhile, the executive branch "clarified" the administrative guidelines it had established so as to make the provision of permanent employment opportunities a goal rather than a requirement of the program.

As a result of these modifications, during the recession CETA closely approximated a program of general budgetary support for state and local governments. Local governments used federal funding to pay for services that otherwise would have had to be financed by local taxpayers or eliminated in budget cutbacks. The city of Cleveland, for example, laid off virtually its entire force of sanitation workers and then rehired them with CETA money. During 1975, some 310,000 local public sector employees were financed through CETA, at an annual cost of about $2 billion.

As a program of general budgetary support, CETA has been distinguished from general revenue sharing by the special assistance it renders to areas of high unemployment. The formula for disbursing funds channels aid in approximate proportion to the local unemployment rate.[42] This has augmented the receipts of the old central cities, almost all of which suffer from above average unemployment. By 1975, 12-13 percent of the entire city labor force in cities like Cleveland and Washington, D.C., was being paid by CETA funds.

The future of public employment programs is now one of the most keenly contested areas of disagreement between Congress and the President. Early in 1976 the House approved a measure that would extend CETA's life well into the future, while doubling the number of workers employed under its auspices to 600,000. The President has proposed

---

[42] Under the emergency jobs program, 50 percent of per capita aid was distributed in proportion to the local unemployment rate; 25 percent in proportion to the unemployment rate in excess of 4.5 percent; and 25 percent in proportion to the unemployment rate in excess of 6.5 percent.

terminating federally funded temporary employment at the end of calendar 1976, arguing that the economy will have largely turned around by that time and that permanent employment programs can operate more successfully through the subsidization of private sector jobs.[43] However this dispute is resolved, the dismantling of CETA programs, whether accomplished in 1977 through the termination of 300,000 federally funded public employees or later in the decade with the termination of 600,000 public employees, is bound to create new difficulties for the declining cities, which have come to rely greatly on this indirect form of federal budgetary support.

Congress has made at least one effort to extend to unrestricted budget support the principle of disbursing aid in proportion to the local unemployment rate. The growth of state and local spending has been so great as to make that sector an important factor in the nation's aggregate economic policy. A special study conducted by the Joint Economic Committee in the spring of 1975 estimated that some $8 billion of stimulative force had been removed from the economy by state and local budget adjustments, including expenditure reductions, tax increases, and cancellations of capital projects.[44] This sum was large enough to raise fears in some quarters that the deflationary actions of the state and local sector would jeopardize the stimulus for economic recovery provided by the $22.8 billion federal tax cut which had been approved earlier in the year.

The Joint Economic Committee study revived interest in legislating automatic counter-cyclical aid for the state and local sector which would help the sector combat the fiscal effects of recession. Federal assistance, of course, is most valuable to state and local governments when their own revenue sources fail. Moreover, general economic recovery from recession may be hampered, especially in parts of the country with high unemployment and declining tax receipts, if local governments are unable to maintain accustomed spending levels. For this reason, almost every

[43] The evidence that public sector jobs created under CETA have been a relatively inefficient means of augmenting net long-term employment is convincing. Alan Fechter has shown that every 10 nominal job creations add only 1 to 4 net jobs to public employment rolls, the rest representing a substitution for state and local governments' own hiring. See Alan Fechter, *Public Employment Programs* (Washington, D.C.: American Enterprise Institute for Public Policy Research, 1975).

[44] Joint Economic Committee of Congress, Subcommittee on Urban Affairs, *The Current Fiscal Position of State and Local Governments* (Washington, D.C.: May 1975).

trough in the economic cycle brings with it a proposal to boost federal assistance to state and local governments. Unfortunately, congressional consideration of such proposals invariably has been out of phase with the state of the economy. Proposals for counter-cyclical action typically begin to receive serious attention near the bottom of the economic cycle; by the time they are readied for legislative action, the economy is well on its way to recovery. Congress' recurring tardiness has suggested to some that it would be preferable to install an automatic mechanism for assisting state and local governments in time of recession, rather than wait for Congress to debate specific aid measures each time the economy flags, or to twist other aid programs (such as CETA) into programs of general budgetary support.

The Intergovernmental Anti-Recession Assistance Act of 1975 was designed to provide automatic counter-cyclical aid to state and local governments. Aid was to be initiated automatically whenever the national unemployment rate reached 6 percent; and was to be increased as the unemployment rate rose. As originally drafted, the bill was very generous in its payments; at a national unemployment rate of 8.5 percent, $3.5 billion in special assistance was to be disbursed. In fact, the act would have functioned as an intermediate-term supplement to revenue sharing, since the floor level of 6 percent nationwide unemployment was projected to persist through the 1970s. In its allocation formula, the new proposal adhered closely to the CETA model of distributing funds in rough proportion to the local unemployment rate. The allocation formula would have given the most valuable assistance to the older cities with their high unemployment rates.

In the end, the Anti-Recession Assistance Act suffered the same fate as earlier efforts to assist the state and local sector during recessions. The bill was debated for most of 1975, eventually tacked onto a public works bill in watered down form, and finally approved by Congress at the beginning of 1976, some months after the recession had bottomed out. It was vetoed by the President. As finally drafted, the bill omitted the automatic unemployment trigger, and instead limited assistance to the five quarters beginning April, 1976. It thus was too late to be of assistance in the 1974-75 recession, and without the provisions which would have made it useful in helping state and local governments combat the effects of the next recession. Both Congress and the administration, however, have expressed interest in devising a permanent and automatic policy of counter-cyclical stabilization for the state and local sector. One may hope that, unlike past commitments, this one will bear fruit before the country again finds itself in economic recession.

Federal Takeover of Welfare Costs

From time to time it has been suggested that federal assumption of the entire expense of welfare payments would do more than any other reform to buttress the fiscal position of the central cities. This argument became quite popular during the debate over New York City's financing troubles, since somewhere in the vicinity of $800 million of New York City's locally raised resources go to support welfare expenses.

Table 16

FINANCING OF WELFARE

(Percentage of AFDC Cash Assistance and Medicaid Payments
Borne by Different Levels of Government)

	Year				
	1957	1966	1971	1973	1975 (est.)
Local	15.7	11.4	11.7	8.9	6.3
Federal	44.3	53.1	52.0	58.2	61.6
State	40.0	35.5	36.3	32.9	31.1

Source: 1957-73, compiled by the Advisory Commission on Intergovernmental Relations, as reported in *National Journal Reports* (Feb. 22, 1975), p. 285; 1975 estimates, based on table 17, below.

The hope that federal takeover of welfare will rescue the older cities from their fiscal predicament seems to lose sight of the fact that the bulk of welfare expenditures already has been transferred to either the state or federal level. Table 16 shows the local, state, and federal shares of welfare spending for selected years. Table 17 provides more detail about the composition of welfare expenditures for the principal programs. Together, the tables may help dispel some pervasive misconceptions about the financing of welfare. First, the local share of welfare amounts to $2.0 billion per year or a little more than 2 percent of locally raised general revenues. Almost 40 percent of all local welfare expense is borne by New York City alone. For the average local jurisdiction the "welfare burden" simply is not a factor in its budgetary pressure. Only 21 states require local jurisdictions to contribute to the expense of Medicaid or Aid to Families with Dependent Children (AFDC), and only 15 states require local contributions in excess of one percent of program costs. Thus, while it is true that welfare expenditures have exploded in recent years, it is not fair to ascribe responsibility for the cities' fiscal crises to their welfare burden, except in the case of New York, where responsibility must be shared with numerous other factors. New York City's exceptional budgetary expense for welfare is attributable to a series of special considerations: the fact that New York State has fixed an extremely high standard of welfare and Medicaid payments; the fact that the share of these costs which must be paid at the local level is higher than in any other state in the union; and the fact that because of New York City's special status (each of its boroughs is a separate county) the entire local share of welfare expenses, which normally is a countywide responsibility financed by suburban as well as city residents, falls exclusively upon residents of the city.

Table 17

FINANCING OF WELFARE PROGRAMS
(Billions of Dollars)

Program	Fiscal 1975 Costs	Percent Increase in Costs, Fiscal 1973 to June 1975[a]	Federal Costs	State Costs	Local Costs
Aid to Families with Dependent Children	$ 9.0[b]	28	$ 5.0	$ 3.4	$ 0.6
Medicaid	12.2	67	6.5	4.6	1.1
General Assistance	1.0	57[c]	0	0.7 (est.)	0.3 (est.)
Supplemental Security Income	5.4	NA	4.1	1.3	0
Food Stamps	4.2[d]	186	4.0	0.2	0
Total	$31.8	NA	$19.6	$10.2	$ 2.0

a. Annual Rate as of June 1975.

b. Includes $900 million of administrative costs.

c. Fiscal 1974 to June 1975.

d. Includes $400 million of administrative costs.

Source: Data derived from Joint Economic Committee, *Handbook of Public Income Transfer Programs: 1975;* Department of Health, Education and Welfare, *State Expenditure for Public Assistance Programs;* Department of Health, Education and Welfare, *Public Assistance Statistics,* June 1975.

Public discussion of "welfare" has fastened on the program of Aid to Families with Dependent Children. However, as table 17 shows, Medicaid is a more costly budget item for state and local governments. A number of states suffering from budget deficits have tried to tackle their

Medicaid expenses head-on by tightening up on eligibility requirements, reducing benefits for recipients, or shifting a larger share of program costs to the local level. Some states have attempted to achieve the same type of economies within the AFDC program. In fact, the cities' stake in rationalizing the nation's welfare efforts lies less in the hope that they can substitute federal funds for their own than in the threat that, unless reforms are made, more and more of state budgets will be claimed for welfare purposes, leaving state governments unable to increase (or perhaps even maintain) their present levels of general aid to local governments.

For all the importance of welfare expenditures, however, there is an element of self-deception in state and local projections of what could be accomplished by federal "takeover" of welfare.[45] The proposals for federal income support aim only at replacing AFDC grants and perhaps the food stamp program. It is inconceivable that a federal income assistance program should universalize support levels at anything approaching the payments now made to welfare recipients in New York City or in other jurisdictions with similarly high support levels. Most proposals have envisaged a maximum federal payment in the neighborhood of $3,600 per year for a family of four if the food stamp program is eliminated, and no more than $3,000 per year if the food stamp program is retained. States wanting to continue higher levels of support would have to supplement the federal payment with state and local funds, as at present. A payment of $3,000 per year in New York State, for example, would leave one-third of current support levels to be paid by state and local governments, as compared to the present state and local contribution of approximately 50 percent. Thus it would be a serious mistake to generalize from the magnitude of the welfare item in state and local budgets to the fiscal benefits that could be reaped from any plausible program of federal takeover.

Most importantly, shifting the welfare burden to the federal level would relieve the fiscal squeeze on states only by subjecting the same taxpayers to higher taxes levied by the federal government. A careful examination of the tax burdens borne by New York State residents, before and after adoption of a universal income support program, probably would show them facing a higher tax bill after the changeover, because of the increased federal payments that would have to be made to households in the southern states. The questions surrounding the nation's welfare program are serious enough for any reform proposal to be debated on its

---

[45] As of Jan. 1, 1974, the federal government did take over state administered programs for aid to the blind and disabled.

own merits, not viewed as a roundabout way of transferring fiscal support to state and local governments. In the very few instances where welfare payments create a serious drain on city or county budgets, the short-term remedy lies in persuading state governments to assume fuller responsibility for such payments, as already is done in most states.

Public School Finance

Unlike welfare funding, where the shift of expenditure responsibility to state and federal governments has been virtually completed, the shift in public school finance is still gathering momentum. As table 18 shows, the share of locally raised revenue in school budgets has declined steadily over the last decade. During the mid-1960s the big jump in school support came from the federal government. Since 1971-72, steady progress has been made toward *state* takeover of local school expenses. In fact, the reforms in state aid to education probably mark the most important change in fiscal federalism that has occurred during the 1970s.

Table 18

SOURCES OF PUBLIC SCHOOL REVENUE

Year	Share of Total Elementary and Secondary School Revenue from:		
	Local	State	Federal
1964-65	56.5	39.7	3.8
1965-66	53.0	39.1	7.9
1967-68	52.7	38.5	8.8
1969-70	52.1	39.9	8.0
1971-72	52.8	38.3	8.9
1972-73	51.5	40.6	7.9
1973-74	49.2	42.6	8.2
1974-75	48.6	43.6	7.8

Source: Office of Education and National Education Association as reported in National Education Association, *Estimates of School Statistics, 1974-75* (Washington, D.C.: 1975).

To date, school-finance reforms have focused primarily on eliminating tax base inequalities between school districts. In the context of school finance it is customary to take equal property valuations per public school pupil as the reference point that defines fiscal neutrality. Beginning with the landmark California case of *Serrano v. Priest* in 1971, plaintiffs in court cases have been able to demonstrate in state after state that average property values per pupil are unequally distributed across different school districts. Per pupil valuations commonly vary by ratios as large as five or six to one, and, between unusual districts with concentrations of industrial property or extreme impoverishment, the tax-base disparities may run as high as 50 or 100 to one.[46]

The *Serrano* court argued that as long as local property taxes are used to pay for public schooling, property base differences of this magnitude make a child's ability to obtain quality education dependent upon the average wealth of the school district in which he resides. The court further affirmed that wealth classifications of this sort were inherently suspect under the federal Constitution, especially when tied to the financing of a service like public schooling which is essential to a child's development and therefore should enjoy special protection as a "fundamental interest." In Constitutional law, once a classification that results in different treatment before the law has been judged inherently suspect, or once it has been held that the classification trenches upon a fundamental Constitutional interest, the classifying scheme must be subjected to strict scrutiny by the courts—i.e., it can be sustained only if it is shown that there is an overriding public interest in doing so. The *Serrano* court held that no such overriding public interest required that children should be classified for school finance purposes by the average wealth of the district in which they lived.

The Constitutional grounding for this line of reasoning was removed by the U.S. Supreme Court in *San Antonio School District v. Rodriguez,* when the Court, in considering an appeal on a similar school-finance case from the state of Texas, ruled by a 5-4 majority that education is not a "fundamental interest" under the United States Constitution and that classification by wealth is not inherently suspect. Several state courts, however, have ruled that their state constitutions place more stringent limitations upon inequalities in the financing of schooling than the federal Constitution does, thus interpreted, and have upheld the central thread of the *Serrano* finding for their states. Other courts have ruled that if state constitutions require the state to provide a "thorough and efficient" state-wide system of public education, it is sufficient grounds for overthrowing

---

[46] See John E. Coons, W. Clune, and S. Sugarman, *Private Wealth and Public Education* (Cambridge, Mass.: Harvard University Press, 1970); Betsy Levin, T. Muller, W. Scanlon, and M. Cohen, *Public School Finance: Present Disparities and Fiscal Alternatives* (Washington, D.C.: The Urban Institute, 1972); and Robert Reischauer and R. Hartman, *Reforming School Finance* (Washington, D.C.: The Brookings Institution, 1973).

a school finance system that relies heavily on local property taxation.[47] Even in states where courts have not ruled present school finance arrangements to be illegal, state legislatures sometimes have initiated voluntary reforms in their state aid programs in an attempt to overcome perceived fiscal disparities.

The remedy most frequently adopted has been one originally recommended by the plaintiffs in *Serrano*: statewide equalization of per pupil property tax bases. In educational circles this has come to be known as "district power equalization." Nine of the first 13 states to revise their school financing procedures in the wake of *Serrano* adopted some form of district power equalization.[48] In its purest form, the power equalization principle allows local school districts to continue to set their own school tax rates. For the purpose of computing individual tax bills, the locally selected tax rate is applied to the assessed valuation of property, just as before. However, the revenue per pupil that the school district receives from its school tax levy is determined by applying the tax rate it has chosen to the average property valuation per pupil for the state as a whole. If the tax payments made on local property fall short of the amount a community is entitled to receive by law, the difference is made up by state assistance. Should local tax payments per pupil exceed the statewide average that can be raised from the same tax rate, in theory the excess revenue collected would be turned over to the state to assist below-average districts. In practice, several states have dispensed with the requirement that excess tax collections be delivered to the state. Such programs in effect guarantee all school districts access to the statewide average property tax base, but permit some districts (usually for a limited number of years) to continue to benefit from their above average property wealth. This leveling up explains why power equalization plans generally have required higher overall levels of state assistance.

As a class, the central cities are not greatly benefited by the principle of power equalization. Despite the fact that the cities' per capita property tax bases are low relative to the rest of their metropolitan areas, when

---

[47] For a good review of the legal issues, see David C. Long, "The Property Tax and the Courts: School Finance after Rodriguez," in George E. Peterson, ed., *Property Tax Reform* (Washington, D.C.: The Urban Institute, 1973); also "Future Directions for School Finance Reform," in *Law and Contemporary Problems*, vol. 38, no. 3 (Winter-Spring, 1974). For additional discussion of school finance, also see chapter 5, below.

[48] W. Norton Grubb with Jack Costello, Jr., *New Programs of State School Aid* (Washington, D.C.: National Legislative Conference, 1974).

tax-base comparisons are put on a per pupil footing and are based on the statewide rather than the metropolitan average, the cities look relatively affluent in their taxable property values. The old central cities have fewer—sometimes far fewer—public school pupils per thousand residents than do other school districts. This is a consequence of both the age distribution of city residents and of high private-school enrollment rates. As a result, the cities rank higher, relative to other communities, in property values per pupil than they do in property values per resident. For selected central cities, table 19 illustrates the change in school tax revenues that would have resulted in 1971-72 if the locally selected school tax rate had been applied to the statewide average tax base rather than to the local school district base. As can be seen, without a grandfather clause or some other saving feature in the state-aid formula, most big city school districts would lose out from a straightforward application of the power equalizing principle. For many cities, however, the margin of

Table 19

CHANGE IN SCHOOL REVENUE FROM SUBSTITUTION OF
STATEWIDE AVERAGE TAX BASE FOR LOCAL TAX BASE
(1971-72)

City	Percent Change in Revenue from Statewide Equalization
Baltimore	− 5
Boston[a]	+ 5
Chicago	−23
Cleveland	− 2
Detroit	− 7
New York	−17
Philadelphia	−42
St. Louis	− 6

a. During this period, Boston's assessed valuation was deliberately under-reported to procure additional compensatory state school aid. Correction for this distortion (subsequently ordered by the courts) would show Boston, too, to lose from statewide equalization.

Source: Estimates from Dick Netzer, "State Education Aid and School Tax Efforts in Large Cities," in *Selected Papers in School Finance 1974* (Washington, D.C.: U.S. Department of Health, Education, and Welfare, 1974).

loss is small.[49] Moreover, the deterioration in the relative tax bases of central cities is constantly narrowing the gap between central city and statewide average per pupil valuations. As matters now stand, conversion to a pure power-equalization formula probably would cause a one-time reduction in tax revenues for the majority of central city school districts, but would tie them to more rapidly growing tax bases for the future.

Most states which have implemented power equalization plans have tried to make them more palatable to the cities through special adjustments designed to supplement the aid received by urban districts. One approach is to take explicit account of the cost side of the cities' financing dilemma. In its recent school-finance reform, Florida adopted a weighting system that gives extra importance to handicapped and other children requiring special programs. In computing district property valuations per weighted school pupil, children in special programs may be given weights anywhere from 1.17 to 15.0 times those of regular pupils, depending upon the costliness of the remedial education required. Additional weight also is assigned to pupils with low achievement test scores, low socioeconomic status, and/or low scores in English comprehension. Because big cities have more than their share of special education requirements, these factors help to steer resources to those cities by compensating them for the extra difficulty they face in meeting teaching standards. The Florida legislation additionally adjusts state payments for a regional cost-of-living factor.

Michigan's new school finance program attempts to assist the big cities by another route. It compensates them for "municipal overburden"—i.e., high tax rates borne in financing noneducational municipal services. For each school district in the state, the property tax rate that would be required to finance all local nonschool expenditures is computed. Any school district for which this rate is 125 percent of the statewide average (i.e., any district which has a tax burden, thus defined, that is 25 percent greater than the state average) qualifies for compensatory state educational aid. At present, Detroit is the only district to benefit significantly from this provision of Michigan's law.

Special mechanisms such as these have kept most cities from losing out from statewide adoption of power equalization plans. Table 20 shows

---

[49] For further analysis of how different types of school districts would fare under power equalization, see Betsy Levin, T. Muller, and C. Sandoval, *The High Cost of Education in Cities, 1970-71* (Washington, D.C.: The Urban Institute, 1973); and John Callahan, W. Wilken, and M. Sillerman, *Urban Schools and School Finance Reform: Promise and Reality* (Washington, D.C.: National Urban Coalition, 1973).

how selected cities actually fared from the first round of legislative changes in school finance enacted in the wake of *Serrano*. As can be seen, the results are rather erratic, but, overall, the cities have done better than would be expected on the basis of power equalization alone.

Property Tax Relief

One other innovation in state and local finance that has promised special help for the cities is the use of state revenues to relieve local property tax burdens. Between 1971 and 1974, every state in the union passed a new property tax relief law or amended an old one to make it more generous. By 1974, $1.5 billion in local property tax relief was distributed by the states; in 1975 the figure probably reached $2.0 billion.[50]

Table 20

CHANGES IN STATE AID TO
CITY SCHOOL DISTRICTS AS RESULT OF
SCHOOL FINANCE REFORMS

City School District	Percent Increase in State Aid[a] Per Pupil	Average Increase in State Aid Per Pupil for all Districts in State
Chicago	+ 16%[b]	+ 2%
Cincinnati	.33[c]	1.0[c]
Cleveland	1.99[c]	1.0[c]
Columbus	.95[c]	1.0[c]
Denver	+ 99%	+ 82%
Detroit	+ 16%	+ 11%
Jacksonville	+ 11%	+ 5%
Los Angeles	+ 23%	+ 24%
Miami	+ 16%	+ 5%
Milwaukee	+112%	+ 64%
San Francisco	+ 0%	+ 24%
Wichita	+188%	+138%

a. Refers to first year or first two years after passage of state reform.

b. Per weighted pupil; this understates Chicago's gain because the weighting factor was changed to increase the importance of poverty population.

c. Ohio district increases are expressed as a ratio of the state-wide average increase.

Source: Robert Bothwell, Richard Johnson, Alan Hickrod, "Geographic Adjustments to School Aid Formulae" (processed, National Conference of State Legislators, 1975).

---

[50] Abt Associates Inc., *Property Tax Relief Programs for the Elderly* (report prepared for the Department of Housing and Urban Development, 1975).

Under the most popular form of legislation, called the "circuit-breaker," local taxpayers receive back from the state a fraction—sometimes as high as 100 percent—of the amount by which their property tax payments exceed a "reasonable" share of household income. These circuit-breakers originally were designed to relieve the tax burden on elderly homeowners who were being squeezed between rising property tax bills, on the one hand, and fixed household incomes, on the other. However in several states the circuit-breaker principle now has been extended to grant property tax relief to most of the population, nonelderly as well as elderly, renters as well as homeowners, and middle-income households as well as the poor.

Although the property tax rebates are sent directly to individual taxpayers, their manner of computation makes the payments similar in effect to a subsidy for local governments which maintain high levels of tax effort and have concentrations of low-income populations. In these communities, local authorities can sustain high property tax rates safe in the knowledge that the state will pick up a good part of the tab, especially for those households which have difficulty in making their payments. The old central cities thus are among the main beneficiaries of property tax relief. Preliminary data from the states of Michigan and Wisconsin indicate that the amount of redistribution to city taxpayers from property tax relief is quite large compared, say, to the redistribution achieved by the federal revenue sharing program.

The rush to adopt property tax relief measures has now passed its crest. To a large extent, circuit-breaker laws were the product of the unexpected budget surpluses that states enjoyed in 1972 and 1973. Now that the budget surpluses have disappeared, so has the states' enthusiasm for using their revenues to offset local tax burdens. Two states in 1974 went so far as to rescind previously passed circuit-breaker laws.

Summary

In trying to put intergovernmental assistance to the cities in perspective, it is best to focus on the main features of recent trends. Perhaps the most salient fact is that long-run growth in federal aid to the state and local sector has slowed markedly, although this trend is obscured by the surge in counter-cyclical funding that occurred in 1975. Any prudent projection of future financing must anticipate lesser increases in federal support over the foreseeable future than were enjoyed in the period 1965-73. States, too, have reduced the growth in assistance that they render to local governments. As the bottom rung on the interjurisdictional ladder of transfer payments, local governments feel the repercussions of budgetary restraint in every other part of the federal system. A special study prepared by the National Governors' Conference has identified local government aid as the slowest growing item in state budgets in 1974-75 and as one of the slowest growing items in 1975-76 budgets (up only 4 percent in current dollars over 1974-75).[51] In the hardest pressed states, governors have proposed cutting back on the absolute amounts of assistance to local governments. The prospect that cities will be bailed out of their fiscal difficulties by higher level governments is, in a word, dim.

The Local Choice: Less Spending or More Taxation?

Our review of fiscal options thus far has indicated that the cities are unlikely to be rescued from their fiscal predicament by outside forces. The ultimate choice therefore is a local one: in balancing their budgets the cities must cut back on local spending, raise local taxes, or (what is surely the most probable outcome) adopt a mixture of both strategies.

Many economic discussions of city finances assume that the purpose of the local public sector is to deliver, as efficiently as possible, the public services that taxpayer-consumers demand. If the public sector were in fact operated with only this objective in mind, the choice between less spending and more taxation would be easier to resolve. Local authorities could simply refer the question of spending levels to the electorate for their disposition, either through direct referendum or through a general election where the different candidates endorsed different tax and spending programs. Local taxpayers might feel unhappy about the severity of the budget constraint they faced, but the majority would have no ground for complaint since public spending would be pegged at just the level favored by the majority of voters, given the tax and expenditure possibilities open to them.

In actuality, the interests of taxpayer-voters as consumers of public services have to be balanced in a three-way tug of war against the demands of organized municipal workers and the city's interest in sustaining the downtown job market. In trying to strike a compromise between these competing interests, cities appear to have committed themselves to public expenditure levels that exceed those which taxpayer-consumers would freely choose to support.

Evidence for this proposition takes a variety of forms. First, there are

[51] "State Fiscal Condition," report prepared by the National Governors' Conference, December 1975.

the actual spending levels which cities maintain in states that require different degrees of voter authorization for public expenditures. A good example of stringent requirements is offered by Ohio where, according to the state constitution, every increase in local property tax revenue must be voted on affirmatively by the local electorate. This is true even if the additional revenue results from increases in the assessed valuation of taxable property rather than from rate hikes. In the absence of explicit voter authorization of higher tax collections, the local property tax rate is automatically reduced to offset any growth in yield caused by reassessment of property values. Increases in the local income tax rate likewise must be approved by voter referendum. It is not surprising, then, that Ohio ranks at or very near the bottom in all comparisons of state and local public spending in relation to personal income.

The contrast between spending levels in Cleveland and Detroit illustrates the manner in which voter controls make themselves felt. In 1971 Cleveland employed some 13,000 full-time equivalent municipal workers. In that year the city submitted to the electorate a proposal to increase the city income tax rate by six-tenths of a percentage point to continue existing programs at newly negotiated wage levels. The proposal failed and Cleveland was forced to cut back on its public employment. In November 1974, a second tax-increase proposal was submitted to the voters, this time for a one and one-half percentage point increase in the local income tax rate. The proposal was defeated by nearly a two-to-one margin. Again the city slashed its employment in response. By mid-1975 Cleveland had reduced its work force to under 10,000 full-time equivalents. Table 7 (page 52) showed that even between 1964 and 1973, total city spending in Cleveland climbed at less than half the rate that it did in other declining central cities.

During the same period Detroit's voters rejected a property tax increase and then an income tax which were proposed to pay for the city's budgets. Eventually, the state of Michigan intervened by passing a special law which authorized Detroit, alone among Michigan districts, to enact a 1 percent income tax hike *without* voter approval. The ability to circumvent voter control in this case was a direct prerequisite for continued expenditure expansion.

The effect that voter control has on expenditure levels can be examined in a more formal way. In areas where citizens regularly vote on tax and expenditure levels, as in many states' school districts, it is possible to estimate the public's demand for school spending, either by looking at variations in per pupil expenditures across school districts, or by examining the ballots cast for or against proposed tax increases by individual voters of different characteristics. This type of analysis reveals a consistent picture of taxpayer demand for public school spending which is very similar to household demand for private goods.[52] Desired spending per pupil from local revenue increases with household or community income and with the number of children who stand to benefit from school expenditures; it decreases with the cost to individual households, or to the household sector generally, of raising tax revenues through the local property tax system (this cost is a function of the taxable property wealth in the district). The *shape* of the "demand" curve for public school spending proves to be much the same whether it is estimated for states that decide school expenditure levels by direct voting on school tax referenda or for states that delegate their expenditure decisions to school boards. However, the *level* of school spending is significantly higher in states where there are no direct voting requirements. This is consistent with evidence showing that other types of public outlays also are curbed by the imposition of voter controls. Capital borrowing, for example, has been shown to be significantly lower in areas where bond issues must be authorized by public referendum.[53] To free themselves from voter constraints on borrowing, many state and local governments have resorted to intricate legal devices which allow them to get around the constitutional requirement of prior voter approval for bond issues.[54]

Table 21 shows that voter opposition to tax and borrowing proposals has stiffened since the early 1960s. The figures in column 2 represent the

---

[52] George E. Peterson, "Voter Demand for Public School Expenditure," in John Jackson, ed., *Public Needs and Private Behavior in Metropolitan Areas* (Cambridge, Mass.: Bollingen, 1975).

[53] See, for example, John Cooper, "Institutional Factors Affecting the Outcomes of School-Bond Elections" (unpublished Ph.D. dissertation, Univ. of Virginia: 1972); Frank Marini, "Local Bond Elections in California—the Two-thirds Majority Requirement" (Berkeley: Institute of Government Studies, Univ. of Calif., 1963); George E. Peterson, "Voting Requirements and Public Capital Investment" (unpublished working paper, The Urban Institute: 1975).

[54] The "moral obligation" bond began in New York State as a means of circumventing requirements of voter authorization. By undertaking only a "moral obligation" to repay lenders in the event of program failure, rather than pledging the "full faith and credit" of the government, New York State was able to avoid the requirements of voter authorization of general obligation bonds. Redevelopment authorities in California are excepted from the otherwise general requirement of voter authorization of borrowing. More and more general purpose borrowing has been shifted to the Redevelopment Authorities so as to avoid voter control.

proportion of all school bond elections approved nationwide by voters in each year. Column 3 shows the percentage of school tax proposals that have been approved annually by voters in the state of California, one of the few states to maintain detailed records on school tax elections. The generally declining percentages in both columns indicate a heightened resistance by citizens to growth in public spending. The nadir of support for new borrowing and expenditure was perhaps reached in November 1975 when 93 percent, by value, of all bond proposals submitted to the electorate were rejected by the voters.

Table 21

VOTER SUPPORT OF SCHOOL BONDS
AND TAX PROPOSALS

Year	Percent of School Bond Elections Approved, Nationwide [a]	Percent of Current School Tax Elections Approved, California [b]
1962	72.4	82.0
1963	72.4	84.0
1964	72.5	NA
1965	74.7	NA
1966	72.5	53.0
1967	66.6	48.3
1968	67.6	68.0
1969	56.8	52.1
1970	53.2	47.4
1971	46.7	52.1
1972	47.0	50.3
1973	56.5	51.9
1974	56.4	47.4
1975	51.4 [c]	NA

a. 1962-73, U.S. Department of Health, Education and Welfare, Office of Education, *Bond Sales for Public School Purposes, 1970-71* and *1972-73;* 1974-75, unpublished data collected by Bond Buyer offices.

b. Unpublished data, California State Department of Education (annual data published in Department of Education, *California Public Schools: Selected Statistics).*

c. First 11 months.

Public Employee Unions

The fact that local public expenditures are greater than taxpayer-voters would prefer indicates that something more than consumer sovereignty is at work in fixing spending levels. One influence commonly thought to be working in opposition to taxpayers is that of the public employee unions.

The suspicion that the public unions have used their power to boost public sector wages and employment is bottomed on a few simple observations. During the 1960s, the number of state and local employees per capita grew rapidly. Nationwide, the state and local sector accounted for more than one-fourth of all new jobs in the country between 1965 and 1974.[55] Over the same period public sector wages first caught up with, and then surpassed, earnings in the private sector. The last column of table 22 shows public sector wages as a percentage of private manufacturing wages in each of the years chosen for comparison. An index of 100 indicates parity between the public and private sectors, and an index greater than 100 indicates relatively higher wages in the public sector. Less aggregated comparisons show that wage levels are now skewed most strongly in favor of public employees at lower skill levels.

Table 22

PUBLIC UNION MEMBERSHIP, STRIKES, AND PUBLIC SECTOR WAGES

Year	State and Local Public Employee Union Membership (Thousands) [a]	Man-Days Idle Through Public Sector Work Stoppages (State and Local) (Thousands)	State and Local Public Employee Earnings as Percent of Private Industry Earnings
1955	915	7	91.8
1960	1070	58	95.2
1965	1585	146	98.7
1970	2318	1375	105.0
1973	2460	2299	106.2

a. Data on union membership correspond to the following years: 1956, 1960, 1965, 1970, 1972.

Source: Bureau of Labor Statistics, *Handbook of Labor Statistics, 1975,* Bulletin 1865 (Washington, D.C.: 1975).

Coincidence or not, during the years when public sector employment and wages were climbing there was a boom in public employee union

---

[55] Between 1965 and 1974, a total of 14,848,000 civilian jobs were created in the United States; of these 3,757,000 were in state and local government. See *Statistical Abstract of the United States, 1970,* table no. 316, and *Survey of Current Business,* November 1975.

membership, and strikes by public employees—which once had been a rare event outlawed in every state and fraught with unknown legal implications—became, if not commonplace, at least an ordinary part of life in big cities. The number of person-days lost through public sector work stoppages jumped more than three hundredfold during the years covered in table 22. Over the same period public employee unions emerged as the principal growth sector of the trade union movement.

The parallel pattern of growth rates in union membership, strikes, wages, and public sector jobs has suggested to many that unionization of the public sector has increased the share of national income captured by state and local workers. In particular, the evidence seems consistent with the view that union strength has helped raise public employee wage levels and the number of public sector jobs. At the broadest level, cross-sectional wage comparisons suggest the same relationship. For example, public sector wages are distinctly higher in northern cities, where most public services now are unionized, than in the South where, by and large, public employee unionization has yet to gain hold. The number of public sector employees per thousand residents also is greater in the North.

Despite these broad comparisons, the proposition that union activity is responsible for a significant share of public sector expansion has been an unusually difficult one to establish, since the timing of public sector growth coincides with many other trends besides growth in union membership. We have already seen, for example, that the period 1965-70, during which employment and wage rates climbed most rapidly, was distinguished by a rapid infusion or federal funds into the state and local sector. To determine whether public sector unions have raised wages and employment above what they otherwise would be (and have not merely had the good fortune of being on the scene during a period of high government demand) one must frame tests that adequately control for the influence of these other factors.

A number of such tests and studies have been constructed, mostly involving cross-sectional comparisons of wage rates, and in the last few years a near consensus has emerged as to the magnitude of the effects of unionization. Ashenfelter found evidence that firemen's wages in small cities were approximately 10 percent higher where firemen were organized in unions.[56] Schmenner reported wages for policemen and firemen

---

[56] Orley Ashenfelter, "The Effect of Unions on Wages in the Public Sector: the Case of Fire Fighters," *Industrial and Labor Relations Review,* vol. 24 (Jan. 1971) pp. 191-202.

that were approximately 15 percent higher in all-unionized forces than in forces where there was no union organization.[57] However, probably the clearest evidence of union influence on salary levels exists for public school teachers. Schmenner found that the rate of union membership, the frequency of local work stoppages, and the presence of favorable local collective bargaining laws, all contributed significantly to explaining teacher wage differences. The administrative linkages that establish these wage differences make them easier to understand. The salaries of Detroit's public school teachers, for example, are tied by union contracts to the average level of the three highest-paid suburban jurisdictions in the Detroit metropolitan area, whichever school districts these may happen to be in a given year. The wages of approximately three-fifths of the workers employed by the city of San Francisco were, until 1975, tied by union negotiation to the highest rates granted for comparable jobs in any California city.

Whether wage differences on the order of 10 to 15 percent are judged modest or sizable depends greatly upon one's perspective. Such a difference is of the same order of magnitude as the discrepancy between average employee wages in "declining" and "growing" cities (see table 4). Alone, however, unionization cannot account for more than a modest part of the growth in local public expenditures.

Concern over the influence of public employee unionism may have deflected attention from the central fact about public employment, which is that, however the disparity arose, public sector jobs now are more attractive than comparable private sector jobs. This is more than a matter of wage differences. The civil service principles by which public employment is governed also afford greater job stability. Though public sector workers were laid off in significant numbers for the first time in 1975, Secretary of Labor John Dunlop testified that in March of that year unemployment among state and local employees was only 3.6 percent, at a time when it had reached 11.4 percent in manufacturing and 18.1 percent in construction. The combination of higher wages and lower risk is reflected in the queues of applicants waiting for public positions. The city of Boston, for example, has a waiting list of approximately 3,000 qualified teachers who have passed the city's teacher examination and are seeking full-time employment. In 1975, fewer than 200 persons were hired from that list. Figures such as these are a sure sign that public

---

[57] Roger W. Schmenner, "The Determination of Municipal Employee Wages," *The Review of Economics and Statistics,* vol. 55 (Feb. 1973), pp. 83-90.

sector rewards have become significantly more generous than they need to be to attract qualified personnel.

Any slowdown in the growth of public sector spending is likely to claim as one of its first victims the wage gap between public and private sector employment. Already there are signs that the competitive advantage enjoyed by public sector workers is being eroded. According to the Bureau of Labor Statistics, negotiated wage settlements in the public sector during the first half of 1975 resulted in substantially less than the 12.1 percent average growth in pay that was won by private sector workers. In teaching, where there exists the greatest excess supply of qualified personnel, wage increases for several years have lagged behind the rest of the public sector.[58] The adjustment in teacher wages is likely to presage a similar slowdown in wage increases throughout the public sector as state and local governments begin to take advantage of the fact that they do not have to raise wages to attract or retain qualified workers.

Of late, municipal unions have directed much of their effort to a national lobbying campaign to secure federal legislation requiring state and local governments to enter into collective bargaining with union representatives. At present, states and their political subdivisions, as employers, are specifically exempted from coverage under the National Labor Relations Act, which otherwise regulates collective bargaining in the United States. This has left the individual states free to regulate bargaining between public sector employees and their employers as the states see fit. Municipal employee objectives are well represented in the proposed National Public Employment Relations Act, also known as the Clay-Perkins bill, which has been before Congress for several years. This act would require all public sector employers to bargain exclusively with the employee organization that represents the majority of workers. The bill spells out procedures to be undertaken to resolve bargaining impasses and grants municipal unions the right to decide whether to invoke binding or advisory arbitration of disputes with the employer. In the latter case, public employee unions would specifically reserve the legal right to strike. Passage of the act would considerably alter the present distribution of negotiating power between employers and employees in the public sector and could be expected to strengthen the role of municipal employee unions in setting local public expenditure levels. Some version of the

---

[58] Between 1970 and 1973, while nonschool state and local employee wages rose from 100.5 percent to 103.9 percent of private industry earnings, public education salaries declined from 109.0 percent to 108.1 percent. See Advisory Commission on Intergovernmental Relations, *Trends in Fiscal Federalism, 1954-74* (Washington, D.C.: 1975).

bill originally was expected to pass the 94th Congress. Passage now seems unlikely, in part because of the adverse public reaction to union influence brought about by the budget crises and strikes of 1975.[59]

The conflict between taxpayer-voters and public employees also has led to efforts to strengthen the hand of voters in setting public expenditure levels. After San Francisco's policemen went on strike to force higher wage levels, San Francisco's voters, at the next election, rescinded the charter provision which had enabled the mayor to declare a state of emergency and accede to the police demands over the opposition of the city's legislative branch; at the same time the voters forbade future use of contractual arrangements that automatically tied San Francisco wage levels to the highest levels paid elsewhere in the state. In Seattle, when Mayor Wesley Uhlman was challenged in a recall referendum because of his efforts to reduce personnel and improve productivity in the fire department, the mayor seized the opportunity created by the referendum to generate explicit voter support for his proposed work force reductions. (He won the recall referendum handily.) Some states have begun to move in the direction of more direct voter involvement in public expenditure decisions or more voter voice in the procedures that ultimately determine spending levels. Since 1974, Texas cities have been able to bargain collectively with police and fire departments only if city voters authorize such a procedure by referendum. By mid-1975 voters in Dallas and Houston already had rejected such collective bargaining, though a similar proposal had passed in San Antonio.[60]

Finally, an increased effort has been made to require local public employees to live within the boundaries of the city which employs them. These initiatives frequently have been rationalized on the grounds that the central city needs these workers' taxing capacity. It is also thought that if public employees are obliged to pay their share of public sector costs they will be less aggressive in driving up budget levels. That is, residency requirements strive to make municipal employees view themselves as taxpayers as well as workers. Among the cities in our sample, Los Angeles and New Orleans passed residency requirements in 1973; Baltimore and Washington, D.C., have had similar legislation introduced in

---

[59] Many of the smaller public unions also have opposed the bill, fearful that the requirement that employers bargain exclusively with the union representing the majority of employees would strengthen the position of the largest unions, such as the American Federation of State, County, and Municipal Employees, while injuring other unions. This issue has threatened to dissolve the coalition of public unions within the AFL-CIO.

[60] "Fire/Police Collective Bargaining in Texas," *Texas Town and City* (Sept., 1975).

their city councils; while New York City petitioned the state legislature for a reimposition of its residency requirement, after a lapse of 13 years (as of mid-1975 this proposal had passed the state assembly and was pending before the state senate).[61]

Although part of the present tipping of the scales toward more active voter participation in local spending decisions may be only a temporary concession to fad, it seems likely that the fiscal awareness created by the events of 1974-75 and the public's apparent resolve to resist higher taxes will gain expression in permanently greater voter involvement in expenditure decisions.

City Government as a Supplier of Jobs

One of the most unwelcome consequences of any retrenchment in city spending will be the loss of the public sector as an active, growing employer.

In many of the old central cities, government has been virtually the sole source of new jobs over the last decade. Table 23 shows the change in private sector and public sector jobs for some of the central cities which are also counties, and for which employment data are most readily available. It is obvious that without the jobs supplied by city government, these metropolitan areas would have lost their central city focus

Table 23

CHANGES IN PRIVATE AND PUBLIC SECTOR CENTRAL CITY EMPLOYMENT (1967-72)

City	Change in Number of Jobs 1967-72	
	Private Sector[a]	Public Sector[b]
Baltimore	− 7,000	+ 3,900
New Orleans	+ 7,000	+ 2,500
New York	− 89,400	+57,500
Philadelphia	− 53,000	+18,400
St. Louis	− 26,000	+ 2,300
San Francisco	+ 6,000	+ 5,700
Total, 6 Cities	−162,400	+90,300

a. Jobs covered by Social Security only.
b. City government plus city school district.

Sources: Bureau of the Census, *County Business Patterns, 1967* and *1972;* Bureau of the Census, Census of Governments, *Compendium of Public Employment, 1967* and *1972.*

[61]Note, "Municipal Employee Residency Requirements and Equal Protection," *Yale Law Journal* 84081, July 1975. In March 1976, the Supreme Court upheld the constitutionality of municipal residency requirements.

even more rapidly than they did. In fact, the paucity of private sector employment in central cities has been one of the factors behind the growth in public sector jobs. When there is no other work to be found, citizens naturally put pressure on local governments to solve what is for many of them the most pressing problem of city life, the lack of employment opportunities. With some justice, the hiring of large numbers of teacher aids, community workers, and other paraprofessionals in the late 1960s and early 1970s can be looked upon as a local job program first, and only secondly as a strategy to improve public service delivery.

City governments have become particularly important as employers of minority populations. Under the Equal Employment Opportunity Act, local governments and firms that employ more than 100 persons are now required to file reports on the racial distribution of their employment in different job categories. Unfortunately for analytical understanding of public sector employment, these data reach the public only as private sector employment totals covering entire metropolitan areas.[62] However, the necessity of complying with federal regulations has induced most city governments to adopt a common form of classifying minority employment and has encouraged them to keep far more complete records than in the past. These local records make it possible to examine central city public employment by race.

Table 24 compares the racial composition of public sector jobs in seven

Table 24

RACIAL COMPOSITION OF PUBLIC SECTOR EMPLOYEES

City	Percent Black Population (1970)	Percent Black Public Employees (1974)
Baltimore	46.4	59.6[a]
Boston	16.3	5.9[a]
Chicago	32.7	23.0
Detroit	43.7	45.7
Newark	54.2	68.1
New York	21.2	31.4
Philadelphia	33.6	42.0

a. School System only.

Sources: Unpublished reports of individual cities and school districts.

---

[62] United States Equal Employment Opportunity Commission, *Employment Profiles of Minorities and Women in the SMSA's of 20 Large Cities, 1971* (Research Report No. 43, GPO, Washington, D.C.: July 1974).

cities with the racial composition of the total city population. Although the sample size is slender, the pattern is suggestive. In Detroit, Baltimore, Newark, New York, and Philadelphia, the share of public sector jobs occupied by blacks equals or exceeds the share of blacks in the total population. In contrast, in Chicago and Boston, two cities sharply distinguished for the white ethnic character of their political apparatus, the share of blacks among the total public work force is distinctly lower than the total population share. This suggests that the public sector, as in earlier days, may be parceling out jobs on behalf of a special ethnic clientele. When political conditions change, the racial turnover in the public work force can be quite rapid. Up to 1975, Detroit, for example, was adding approximately 500 minority persons (mostly blacks) to its employment rolls each year, while losing the same number of white workers.

Historically, public sector jobs have been especially important for opening up white-collar positions for ethnic groups having low socioeconomic status. They are now performing that function for racial minorities. The degree to which black professional jobs are concentrated within the local public sector of big cities is illustrated by the pattern of employment in the Baltimore SMSA. The Baltimore city school system alone employs about as many black professionals (4,200) as does the private sector of the entire metropolitan area, even though in total there are eight times as many private sector professional positions. In other cities with large minority populations, the school system accounts for a comparable proportion of white-collar job opportunities for racial minorities.

The cut-backs in city employment levels have struck particularly hard at minority workers. The seniority system established in most contracts between local governments and public employee unions requires that recently hired workers be the first ones laid off in times of budget reductions. As a result of New York City's labor force reductions, between mid-1974 and the beginning of 1976 half of the city's Spanish-speaking workers lost their jobs, as did 40 percent of the black males, and nearly one-third of all female workers employed by the city. By contrast, the overall rate of job attrition was only 13 percent. In several cities the necessity of laying off workers has thrown public employee unions (defenders of the seniority system) and civil rights groups (advocates of minority hiring goals) into open dispute as to the criteria that should be used to identify those who must lose their jobs.

If anything, the effect of the cities' budgetary restraint may be still more severe for minority workers in the private sector. For several years, central-city governments have afforded the most reliable source of demand for minority-owned businesses and minority skilled labor. The *New York Times* has estimated that in 1975 29 percent of all black construction workers employed in the entire country were at work building the Washington, D.C., subway system. Not only does the racial composition of central-city populations give central-city governments a greater incentive to encourage minority enterprise, but the rules governing the use of federal monies require an aggressive policy of equal opportunity employment. Any trimming of central-city budgets will bring an adverse multiplier effect on the demand for minority employment.

Summary

City governments provide public services, offer jobs, and undertake redistributive functions—through selective stimulation of the private sector as well as through direct public-sector payments. These three functions of government are in potential conflict with one another. In the recent past, cities have tilted toward fulfilling their redistributive and job functions. The consequent imbalance between government spending patterns and taxpayer-voter preferences has been reflected in the hardened attitude of taxpayers to new public spending proposals. We seem now to be in a correction of course. The rhetoric of mayors has shifted toward emphasizing basic service provision and acknowledging the practical constraints on further taxation.

Economic hard times have brought forth this policy of financial realism. But there is no blinking its costs. If the central-city government ceases to be an active supplier of downtown jobs and if it no longer can use its purchasing power to stimulate the economic growth of minority population, the burden of the budget constraint will have been shifted largely to the poor, and the city itself will suffer as a job center.

III. WHAT SHOULD BE DONE?

In a chapter on the financing of cities, it is tempting to let one's choice of policy recommendations be guided solely by what would be helpful to city governments and to city taxpayers. However, the days are gone when a proposal stood a plausible chance of adoption by Congress or state legislatures merely because it could be shown to benefit the cities. The severity of the budget constraint now is felt keenly by all levels of government. Coupled with the poor record of past efforts to aid the cities, the current appreciation of government's resource limitations has bred considerable skepticism about the wisdom of pouring more outside funds into the cities. One of the most direct consequences of continued out-migration from the cities, too, has been a shrinking of the urban constituency in Congress and among the public at large. Cities and city problems simply do not carry the political clout they did as recently as a decade ago. To ignore this fact when framing policy recommendations is to prepare the script for an unheeded monologue.

Because the cities no longer form a powerful political constituency on their own, the policies most likely to help them are those which extend, modify, or consolidate existing financial arrangements, rather than those which propose an abrupt break with present custom. Moreover, the cities will have to seek as many allies as possible in their quest for financial assistance. In several states, there would seem to be a harmony of interests between rural and big-city districts, both of which are in position to benefit from any move toward statewide equalization of fiscal resources. Almost everywhere, the inner rings of urban suburbs are beginning to experience the symptoms of "big-city decline," including population and job loss, declining relative incomes, rapid racial turnover, the wearing out of the housing stock, and severe budgetary pressure. While New York City's fiscal distress captured the attention of the national press, its next-door neighbor, Yonkers, came even closer to bankruptcy. Where central city boundaries have been most tightly and rigidly drawn, as in the eastern and north-central industrial states, the first ring of suburbs is, for all practical purposes, largely indistinguishable from the central city in its make-up and fiscal predicament. Yet the cities and inner suburbs have been slow to join in cooperative lobbying before state legislatures.

One important lesson seems to have been learned from the fiscal crises of 1974-76. New York City's distress dramatized to most cities the necessity of calling a halt to the headlong expansion of city budgets. However difficult it may be for the cities to impose spending restraints, and however unfair it may seem to city leaders that their citizens should be singled out to bear the brunt of economic hard times, the example of New York has shown that the problems of the urban public sector are only compounded by trying to ignore the reality of a limited tax base and the fact that demands for public services, in their totality, outrun the cities' capacity for funding. This lesson having been grasped, we seem certain to witness in the next decade a marked slowing down of the local public sector's expansion relative to the rest of the economy. Some of the nation's basic demographic trends—such as the slowdown in the birthrate which has relaxed pressure on the nation's school system—reinforce the prediction that the next decade will see a reduction in the growth of the local public sector.

Some steps can be taken to ease the cities' transition to fiscal restraint. Many states have begun to strengthen the hand of taxpayer-voters by giving them more opportunity to express directly their choice between tax hikes and spending limitations. This procedure has the advantage of relieving some of the pressure on elected officials, by forcing spending interests to argue their case before the public at large. Decision by referendum is no cure-all for fiscal ills, but it is an effective means of taking advantage of the heightened public awareness of fiscal choices which the recent budgetary crises have produced and of giving expression to the apparent public resolve to resist a resumption of past rates of spending increase.

At the other end of the fiscal balance of power, Congress can assist the cities by refraining from strengthening the hand of municipal employee unions through national legislation which would authorize public sector strikes or otherwise dramatically improve the unions' bargaining position. There is nothing to be gained by trying to make public sector unions the scapegoats of the cities' fiscal crises—that interpretation simply is not justified by the evidence. But whatever the benefits may be of overhauling the national legislation controlling public sector union activity, the next two or three years, when cities must adjust to slower long-term growth in spending, are not opportune ones for redefining the balance of local bargaining power by weakening the ability of local public officials to carry out spending controls.

Some solace can be taken from the fact that, though local governments face a difficult job in trying to adjust to slower rates of spending growth, as of late 1975, in any event, the state and local sector, including the big cities, appears to have traversed an extremely severe recession without catastrophe. If a definite end has been put to the prosperous days of 1965-73, when the cities could expand their public sector activities at others' expense, the way has been prepared for a reasonable accommodation to the new necessity of living within the cities' fiscal means.

There remains the fact that from all the evidence presently available, the long-term trend of central city decline persists unabated. Conceivably, this decline may be stemmed in the future, and there are some policies (such as the encouragement of neighborhood rehabilitation and a trimming back on subsidies for new housing construction at the urban fringe) which the federal government could undertake to encourage a return of middle-class households to the cities. As we have seen, there are other fiscal options which might logically be employed to reunite the fiscal base of the cities with the economic base of the metropolitan areas which they sustain; but the political prospects for more vigorous annexation by central cities or widespread tax-base sharing between cities and suburbs must be judged to be somewhere between negligible and nil—and probably closer to the latter.

The most plausible direction in which to seek long-term fiscal aid for the cities is from generalizing the principle of statewide equalization of tax bases which is now incorporated in many states' school-aid programs. The legal justification for court-ordered tax base equalization may be unique to public schooling, but as more and more states adopt such an approach to financing education, even without court pressure to do so, it seems likely that its appeal as an intuitively fair means of paying for part of local public sector expenses will grow.

There are numerous practical advantages to trying to build upon the record of school-finance reform. For one thing, such a strategy points up the harmony of interests between rural, inner suburb, and big-city governments. In most states, all three types of jurisdictions would stand to gain from statewide tax-base equalization, even after correction for local cost-of-living differences. In fact, the distribution of taxable wealth in most states is such that considerably more than half of all taxpayer-citizens could gain from statewide tax base equalization. Tax-base equalization also has the practical advantage of producing only modest immediate benefits for the big cities. Earlier in this chapter, we saw that strict per pupil equalization of taxable property values in most states would actually cause a slight deterioration in the cities' current fiscal position. Equalization on a per capita basis, as would be appropriate for financing other public services, would produce a small gain for most cities. (The difference in effect is attributable to the low ratio of public school pupils to total population in most cities.) But the real benefits to the cities would not lie in improvement of their current fiscal situation, but rather in their ability to arrest the continuing downward spiral in their relative tax bases. Calling a halt to the continuing erosion of the cities' fiscal position is likely to be a more realistic objective than achieving a strong redistribution of present fiscal capacity in favor of the cities.

Chapter 3

Housing

Frank deLeeuw
Anne B. Schnare
Raymond J. Struyk

I. INTRODUCTION

A focal point for every American household is its home, be it a small apartment in the heart of the city, a deteriorating four-family flat in an inner suburb, or a rambling ranch house at the suburban fringes. The dwelling is valued not only for the structural services it provides (such as shelter, warmth, and cooking facilities) but also for its architectural qualities, for the private and public amenities it provides or affords access to, and for the people who live in the neighborhood—in short, for the entire residental environment and, possibly, for the social status it symbolizes. Moreover, housing is financially important since, on the average, it absorbs one-fifth of a family's income and in many cases represents the family's principal form of investment. Because of housing's special importance, it is natural for Americans to take a strong interest in their own housing situations, as well as those of others.

It is difficult, however, given housing's complexity, to evaluate the state of urban housing. Overall, we know that there has been a visible improvement in the structural condition of dwellings in the United States, and many households have also been able to move into the types of neighborhoods they most prefer. Surveys of public attitudes bear out this view of housing. Sixty percent of the respondents to a recent survey, for example,

The excellent comments on an earlier draft from Isabel Sawhill, C. Duncan MacRae, Franklin James, Larry Ozanne, Jack Goodman and Morton Isler are gratefully acknowledged. Sue Marshall provided valuable research assistance.

feel progress has been made in "providing adequate housing for the American people as a whole, both white and nonwhite." [1] Only 44 percent have a comparably optimistic view with respect to the overall problems of the cities, and only 20 percent with respect to combating crime. There is less optimism about housing progress among big city dwellers than among residents of small towns. Interestingly, there is less optimism among the college educated than among those whose education ended with grade school. There is little difference by race. Every group is more optimistic about housing progress than about progress in dealing with crime, drugs, and the economic problems of inflation and unemployment.

While one might expect households to be more content with those aspects of their lives over which they have greater control (like the housing they occupy), the consistency of the feeling of progress is nonetheless impressive. The acceleration in housing costs in the early 1970s, however, seems to have caused some genuine concern that the earlier progress may be eroded. Those on fixed incomes see a rising share of their income devoted to housing; young husband-wife families find house prices moving steadily beyond their grasp; and even middle-aged families are concerned for the future. For these reasons recent cost trends and their implications for various households are examined in some detail in section 2, below.

Quite apart from the housing improvement realized by the average household, two other aspects of housing which are of special interest are the subjects of the final two sections of this chapter. The first is what has been happening to residential racial segregation in the past decade. Segregation has been of continuing and intense interest because it limits minorities in their choice of residence and produces considerable inequality of treatment among households. Poorer quality housing, inferior schools, and higher crime rates often exist inside the urban black enclaves to a degree which cannot be explained by income differences between blacks and whites.

National public opinion surveys conducted intermittently between 1942 and 1968 indicate that there was a meaningful reduction in segregationist views in the 1950s and 1960s. Table 1 summarizes the responses of whites to the question: "If a Negro, with just as much income and education as you have, moved into your block, would it make any difference to you?" In 1942, 62 percent of the respondents answered yes; but by 1968 the percentage which agreed had dropped to 21. This large decline is not the whole story, however, since a sizable proportion

---

[1] Potomac Institute, *Survey of Americans* (Washington, D.C.: 1972).

of whites still prefer not to live with lower-income blacks[2] or to see a large influx of black households into white neighborhoods.[3] Still, a change in white attitudes[4] has occurred; and this change naturally leads to the question of what has happened to actual residential segregation.

Table 1

WHITE AMERICAN ATTITUDES TOWARD RACE AND HOUSING

Answers to the following question: If a Negro, with just as much income and education as you have, moved into your block would it make any difference to you?

Date	Percentage Responding Yes, it would make a difference
June 1942	62
June 1956	46
May 1963	39
December 1963	35
May 1964	36
June 1965	32
April 1968	21

Source: National Opinion Research Center, cited in National Academy of Sciences, *Segregation in Residential Areas* (Washington, D.C.: National Academy of Sciences, 1973).

The second area of special interest is the housing situation of the poor. Americans are concerned about the housing occupied by low-income families; a Harris poll conducted in the early 1970s indicated public support of governmental help for housing the poor by a margin of 68 to

---

[2] William Watts and Lloyd Free report national survey results that 44 percent of white respondents would be unhappy to see black families of lower income and education move into their neighborhood, compared to 24 percent if those black families had the same income and education level as the white residents. For details, see their *State of the Nation,* Potomac Associates, 1973.

[3] In response to the question, "Would you move if colored people tended to live in great numbers in your neighborhood?," 77 percent of a national sample of whites replied "definitely" or "might move" in 1958, compared to 71 percent in 1967. National Academy of Sciences, *Segregation in Residential Areas,* (Washington, D.C.: National Academy of Sciences, 1973).

[4] Among blacks, again according to survey results reported by the National Academy of Sciences, there is a strong preference to reside in integrated neighborhoods, although some of this preference seems to be attributable to the better housing available in white neighborhoods.

12 percent.[5] The quality of housing for the poor (defined to include neighborhood quality) is especially bad when the poor are spatially concentrated, as they are in many of the large metropolitan areas, for it is here that neighborhood conditions and the provision of public services decline to minimal levels. Our discussion centers on these slums—the reasons for their existence, a description of the conditions in them, the forces acting to increase or decrease their size, and the prospects for public policy to improve the broadly defined housing condition of low-income families.

To set the stage for our three topics—trends in housing costs, residential racial segregation, and the housing situation of poor households—we will review the trends in the quality of housing occupied by various households and examine the composition of urban housing markets.

Postwar Trends in Urban Housing

What has been happening to the quality of housing occupied by Americans? Some indications of the structural quality of housing for three income cohorts of households in metropolitan areas over the period 1950-1970 are provided in table 2. These are the rather limited indicators available for individual income groups from the decennial censuses during the period. The trends for owner-occupants and renter households are shown separately. The trend shown in the table is one of unmistakable improvement. In 1950 one poor renter household in five did not have hot running water and exclusive use of toilet or shower; by 1970 it was one in twelve. There was a similar reduction in the incidence of crowded living conditions. By 1970 nearly a quarter of poor households had air-conditioning of some type. Further, in terms of these measures the gap between housing occupied by low-income and other households has narrowed markedly.

While these trends are both dramatic and encouraging, they do not provide a very sharp picture of the type of housing occupied by the urban poor. An improved profile is available from the data in table 3 which are based on a highly detailed 1972 Census Bureau survey of sample dwellings in the Chicago, Memphis, and Portland (Oregon) metropolitan areas. The first panel shows the fraction of dwellings experiencing various kinds of service disruptions, generally over the 3-month

---

[5] The poll results are reported in U.S. Department of Housing and Urban Development, *Housing in the Seventies* (Washington, D.C.: U.S. Government Printing Office, 1975), p. 88. Full results are in a report to HUD, Louis Harris and Associates, Inc., "A Study of Public Attitudes Toward Federal Government Assistance for Housing Low Income and Moderate Income Families."

Table 2

TRENDS IN SELECTED MEASURES OF HOUSING QUALITY
BY TENURE FOR CONSTANT REAL INCOME GROUPS[a]

PROPORTION OF UNITS

Tenure and 1970 income	Mean number of rooms	Lacking some plumb- ing[b]	In dilapi- dated con- dition	Crowd- ed[c]	With Air conditioning		Share of all house- holds owner- occupant
					central	room	
Income under $5,000							
Renters							
1950	3.5	.21	.13	.20	d	d	
1960	d	.19	.08	.15	.01	.05	
1970	3.4	.08	d	.09	.06	.17	
Owner- Occupants							
1950	5.0	.16	.06	.10	d	d	.41
1960	d	.09	.04	.06	.01	.09	.42
1970	5.2	.06	d	.03	.07	.24	.42
Income, $5,000-$10,000							
Renters							
1950	4.0	.07	.04	.17	d	d	
1960	d	.07	.03	.15	.01	.09	
1970	4.2	.03	d	.11	.09	.25	
Owner- Occupants							
1950	5.3	.05	.07	.05	d	d	.53
1960	d	.02	.01	.10	.02	.12	.60
1970	5.6	.02	d	.08	.09	.30	.52
Income over $15,000							
Renters							
1950	4.1	.02	.02	.11	d	d	
1960	d	.03	.01	.10	.03	.17	
1970	4.6	.01	d	.09	.15	.34	
Owner- Occupants							
1950	6.2	.01	.01	.04	d	d	.66
1960	d	.01	*	.06	.05	.19	.77
1970	6.5	.01	d	.06	.21	.31	.75

* = less than .005.

a. Data refer to real incomes in each interval 1950-1970 for households with 1970 incomes in that interval. For example, 1950 and 1960 income equivalents for $5,000 are approximately $3,000 and $4,000, using GNP price deflator, 1967 = 100. Data are only for dwellings in metropolitan areas.

b. Complete plumbing includes exclusive use of toilet and tub or shower, and hot and cold running water.

c. Over one person per room.

d. Data not available for this year.

Source: *1950 Census of Housing*, vol. 2, "Non Farm Housing Characteristics"; *1960 Census of Housing*, vol. 2, "Metropolitan Housing"; *1970 Metropolitan Housing Characteristics*, HC(2)-1.

Table 3

MEASURES OF HOUSING QUALITY IN 1972 BY INCOME OF HOUSEHOLD[a]

	1972 household income		
Indicators of dwelling quality	$0 to $5,000	$5,000 to $10,000	over $10,000
A. Incidence of service disruptions—proportion of dwellings with disruption.			
1. water services[b]	.08	.05	.05
2. sewer services[b]	.06	.06	.02
3. toilet breakdown[b]	.05	.03	.01
4. sink breakdown[b]	.04	.03	.01
5. heating disruption[c]	.01	*	*
B. Incidence of structural defects—proportion of dwellings with defect.			
1. wall sockets not present in all rooms	.09	.06	.03
2. electrical wiring exposed	.08	.06	.05
3. heating outlets not present in all rooms	.09	.06	.03
4. leaky roof	.11	.06	.08
5. plaster chipped or crumbling or paint peeling on: walls	.13	.08	.07
ceiling	.13	.06	.05
6. large holes in the floors	.05	.04	*
C. Expert ratings (100 = excellent[d])—mean value			
1. external condition of sample structure	481	444	371
2. surrounding structures and neighborhood condition	485	440	369
D. Household rating of own unit			
1. distribution			
excellent	.50	.56	.68
satisfactory	.34	.39	.28
poor	.12	.03	.06
very bad	.03	.02	.01
2. mean weighted score[e] (100 = excellent)	168	155	137
E. Sample size	311	218	223

* = less than .005.

a. Tabulations of survey data for Chicago, Memphis, and Portland (Oregon) gathered by U.S. Bureau of the Census in a special survey of five cities under contract to the Department of Housing and Urban Development. For further description, see L. Ozanne and R. Struyk, "Empirical Analyses of Landlords and Owner-Occupants as Suppliers of Housing Services" (Washington, D.C.: The Urban Institute, Working Paper 221-06, 1975).

  b. One or more disruptions in past 90 days.

  c. One or more disruptions during the past winter.

  d. Range of diminishing quality is 100 to 1,000.

  e. Weights used: 100, excellent; 200, satisfactory; 300, poor; 400, very bad.

period preceding the survey—e.g., a toilet malfunctioning. In comparison with households with incomes over $10,000 the differences in the experience of the poor are substantial; frequencies are often 3 or 4 times greater for the poor households. More descriptive are the data in panel B on selected structural defects. One unit in eight occupied by the poor had crumbling plaster or peeling paint over major portions of its walls and ceilings; 5 percent had large holes in the floors; and 11 percent had leaky roofs.

For two reasons, these data tend to understate the condition of the most badly housed poor. First, income here is again current income and a significant number of households with low current income may not be poor by other measures such as their long-term average income or their level of assets. Second, many of the dwellings have a number of these defects, and since we are examining the *means* of individual characteristics, this pyramiding of defects is missed. On the other hand, the average ratings by two teams of expert evaluators of the condition of the neighborhood (as evidenced by the exterior condition of structures, streets, sidewalks and lighting, the presence of abandoned cars and buildings, and similar factors) differ only by about 25 percent between low- and high-income households.

Panel D in the table presents tabulations of occupant responses to a question on the occupant's satisfaction with the dwelling unit.[6] While one must be careful in evaluating these responses because different households have different expectations, it is nevertheless remarkable that some 84 percent of the low income households rate their housing as "satisfactory" or "excellent." If many of these respondents thought that better housing were within their grasp, the number of the satisfied would probably be sharply reduced.

While there has been genuine improvement in the quality of housing for all income classes in the postwar period, it is vital to know whether this is only because families are devoting a greater share of their income to housing. The data in table 4 provide a conclusive answer: the average ratio of housing expense to income in metropolitan areas hardly changed between 1950 and 1970, while housing quality generally improved and the aggregate rate of home ownership (and hence occupancy of units providing relatively more housing services) rose from .50 to .59. Further, nearly all of the types of households shown in the table enjoyed reductions in their housing expenditure to income ratio. Note, though, that three types of households—those with heads over 65,

---

[6] No parallel question about the neighborhood or the entire housing environment was included in the survey.

Table 4

TRENDS IN HOUSING EXPENSE TO INCOME RATIOS, THE RATE OF HOMEOWNERSHIP, AND HOUSEHOLD COMPOSITION (1950-70) [a]

	Housing expense to income ratio			Proportion owner-occupants			Distribution of households by type of household		
	1950	1960	1970	1950	1960	1970	1950	1960	1970
A. All households	.20	.20	.19	.50	.59	.59	1.0	1.0	1.0
B. Husband-wife families									
head under age 45	.19	.17	.17	.45	.60	.60	.41	.38	.34
head age 45-64	.17	.15	.14	.62	.73	.80	.26	.26	.25
head age 65 or over	.23	.21	.21	.66	.73	.74	.06	.08	.08
C. Other families									
male-headed									
head under age 65	b	.18	.19	b	.53	.45	b	.04	.03
head age 65 or over	b	.20	.19	b	.72	.66	b	.01	.01
female-headed									
head under age 65	b	.25	.26	b	.42	.39	b	.07	.09
head age 65 or over	b	.25	.20	b	.67	.66	b	.02	.02
D. Single individuals									
under age 65	b	.29	.23	b	.26	.28	b	.09	.11
age 65 or older	b	.51	.38	b	.44	.47	b	.05	.07
E. All elderly-headed households	.29	.29	.27	.60	.63	.62	.13	.16	.18

a. Data are for households in metropolitan areas only. Values converted to rents using rent-value ratio of .008.

b. In 1950 data for single individuals cannot be separated from non-husband/wife family data.

Source: *1950 Census of Housing*, vol. 2, "Non-Farm Housing Characteristics"; *1960 Census of Housing*, vol. 2, "Metropolitan Housing"; *1970 Metropolitan Housing Characteristics*, HC(2)-1.

families headed by females, and single individuals—devote a larger share of their incomes to housing than do other households, and that the overall mix of households has been shifting pervasively toward higher proportions in these three household types in recent years. For example, elderly-headed households accounted for 18 percent of all urban households in 1970 compared to 13 percent in 1950 (see panel E of the table). For this reason, the average expenditure-income ratio of all households has remained virtually unchanged while the ratios of most household *types* have declined.

In summary, there has been marked and continuous improvement in the quality of housing in urban areas during the postwar period. However, a substantial number of households still occupy dwellings well below the minimum standard generally accepted by society. Over the same period there has been little change in the fraction of income the average household devotes to housing, but there has been an important shift in household composition away from traditional husband-wife households in the prime working ages to female-headed, single-individual, and elderly-headed households—that is to households that devote a greater share of their incomes to housing expenditures.

The Web of Urban Housing

Even the casual observer is struck by the variation both between and within cities in the cost of equivalent housing. Why is it that even after controlling for regional price differences housing is cheaper in some cities than others? Why are there conspicuous differences by race in the cost of equivalent structures within the same city? Why is there abandonment of housing in one city but not in another when both cities are in many respects similar?

The answers to these questions have to do with the characteristics of housing itself and with the dynamic forces within housing markets, i.e. within the area (usually an entire metropolitan area) in which households compete for the same structures. The two characteristics which distinguish housing from most other goods are its durability and the association of a set of neighborhood characteristics with each dwelling unit. "Durability" means not only that a structure lasts a long time—usually 50 years or more—but that it is also comparatively "inflexible," or difficult and costly to modify, once it has been built. An important consequence of this inflexibility is the relatively slow and quantitatively small increase in housing services produced by suppliers in response to increased housing demand.

Among the neighborhood characteristics are the race and social status of the inhabitants, the condition of other dwellings, the presence of amenities like parks, and the quality of public services, especially schools. It is clearly difficult for an individual to influence the environment of a neighborhood. At the same time, however, households definitely prefer certain types of dwellings and neighborhoods in which to live, and they prefer them strongly enough to pay premiums for the "housing bundle" they want.

Because of this durability and these strong household preferences, a series of closely related yet distinct housing submarkets develop within the metropolitan housing market. Stated differently, because dwellings and neighborhoods are not easily or quickly changed, households confine their search to existing housing bundles which closely match their preferences; and they continue to search until they discover they cannot afford their most preferred bundle. Thus it is possible for identical structures to rent or sell for different amounts in different neighborhoods within the same metropolitan area. More precisely, the price per unit of housing service can vary—where "services" are measured in theory by an index of all the things which a dwelling provides and on which people place a value. This segmentation or splitting of the market may help to answer the questions we have posed above.

An example may help to clarify the origin of these price differences. Imagine a market in which there are only two kinds of housing, modest houses providing 100 units of service a month (as measured by some index) and luxury houses providing 200 units of service a month. Suppose furthermore that the initial distribution of family incomes is such that the proportion of families choosing luxury houses over modest houses is just the right proportion to keep the price of a luxury house at twice the price of a modest house—that is, to keep the prices per unit of service in these two types of dwellings equal.

With the passage of time, however, suppose that incomes in the community grow and cause the demand for luxury houses to grow and, hence, the demand for modest houses to fall. In the short run the market would respond to this shift in demand by a rise in the price of luxury houses relative to modest houses. Eventually construction of new luxury houses and withdrawal of modest houses from the stock (through abandonment, for example) when they could no longer meet operating expenses could restore price parity; but in the interim families occupying modest houses would be getting a bargain in the price they pay per unit of housing services.

Rising incomes, then, can lead to price benefits for occupants of low-quality dwellings, but it is easy to imagine other changes which would leave consumers of modest houses worse off. For example, migration of a sizable number of low-income families into a housing market might raise the demand for low-quality housing sufficiently to cause it to sell at a premium. Again, there are forces at work tending to restore price parity per unit of services in different kinds of houses; but the forces moving prices *away* from parity can be stronger than the forces moving them *toward* it for extended periods of time, due in large measure to the inflexibility of existing housing. Starting from a parity situation, an increase in demand for low-quality dwellings raises special problems. Price parity cannot be restored until more dwellings become available to the low-income market. But in most cities and suburbs of the United States the quality of newly built dwellings is fairly stringently regulated, so that increased supply through (nonsubsidized) construction of new dwellings for poor people is effectively prohibited. The only remaining source of increased supply—the depreciation of higher quality existing dwellings—can be a very lengthy process.

One way to demonstrate some of the forces at work is to examine the changes in four widely diverse metropolitan areas over the 1960-70 period. Table 5 presents data on two slow growing (Chicago and Pittsburgh) and two fast growing (Austin and Washington) areas. In each of the four areas the percentage change in households (line 1) and the per-

Table 5

INDICATORS OF DEMAND AND SUPPLY FOR DWELLING UNITS IN SELECTED METROPOLITAN AREAS

	Metropolitan Area			
Indicator	Chicago	Pittsburgh	Austin	Washington
Percentage change, 1960-70, in number of				
households	15.0	6.9	56.5	52.1
dwelling units	15.3	7.0	53.6	47.1
Percentage of 1970 units built 1960-70 / Percentage change in households 1960-70	1.40	2.11	.83	.72
Percentage change 1960-70 in the number of households with incomes under $4,000	−19	−20	−9	−13

Source: U.S. Bureau of the Census, *Metropolitan Housing Characteristics,* 1960 and 1970 Census of Housing (Washington, D.C.: U.S. Government Printing Office, 1962 and 1972).

centage change in the net number of dwellings (line 2) are comparable. In the slow growing areas, however, there were substantially more new units built than new households formed; and there were major declines in the number of poorest households. Since households moving into newly constructed dwellings vacate their former dwellings, the supply of moderate quality housing rises sharply relative to demand; and this works to decrease the prices of these dwellings. The lower prices would allow lower income households to occupy these units while vacating their own. This process may continue until the worst quality housing is permanently vacated, but competition still may be such as to keep prices depressed. Of course, the extent to which prices drop will vary according to neighborhood conditions, including racial mix, access to employment, and public service factors.

In Washington and Austin, on the other hand, new construction did not keep pace with household formation, which in turn produced a reduction in vacancies and the conversion of buildings into more dwelling units (e.g., the subdivision of a single-unit structure into several units). This circumstance, combined with smaller reductions in the number of poorest households (due to higher rates of immigration), presumably produces an excess demand and high prices at all quality levels. These prices do not necessarily imply excessive profits, however, because revenues must be sufficient to cover the costs of converting and upgrading the dwelling units.

Thus, these forces, in conjunction with strong household preferences and temporarily limited supplies of certain dwelling-plus-neighborhood bundles, continually act in the direction of creating discounted prices or premium prices in particular neighborhoods or for particular types of structures. There is no reason to expect the distribution of price premiums and discounts to follow the same pattern in every city, and this largely explains why households of equivalent incomes within the same city and between cities occupy different quality units, quite aside from regional cost differences.

The critical role played by the price per unit of service of newly constructed dwellings can now be appreciated. During extended periods of relatively low interest rates and building material costs, new dwellings are competitive in price with many existing dwellings; as households select new dwellings, their former units become available for other, less affluent households. Whether these lower-income households end up with better housing at a lower price depends, of course, on a host of other factors including the extent to which households of different income classes migrate into the market and the rate at which the vacated units depreciate. On the other hand, a rise in the price per unit of services of new dwellings causes the flow of dwellings to lower-income households to be sharply reduced, even in areas like Pittsburgh and Chicago, because higher-income households are more likely to remain in their current residences. This situation can lead to market-wide increases in the price of housing and even absolute shortages for the lowest-income households. Thus these indirect market effects of higher new construction costs can far outweigh the direct consequences felt by potential purchasers of new homes.

Variation in the price per unit of housing service of existing dwellings and shifts in the price of new dwellings may also influence the costs and degree of residential racial segregation. Given the lower average income of black relative to white households in urban areas, the presence of deep price discounts for spatially concentrated lower quality dwellings will contribute strongly to racial segregation, quite aside from the desire of many households to live with others of their own race. If the discounts are deeper for lower quality units, then the cost to the household of moving into better housing or a superior neighborhood will be greater than if no discounts existed. A low price per unit of service for new units facilitates residential mobility by blacks (and the poor generally) by increasing the supply of available units and thus narrowing the cost difference between low-quality dwellings and good housing.

When the black population in an urban area grows, it usually acquires more housing through the expansion of black enclaves at their borders, with little change occurring in the degree of segregation. In some markets but not all, the increase in the housing choices made available through enclave expansion may improve the welfare of black households significantly. The main point, however, is that the housing prices which low-income (often black) households pay are sensitive to demand and supply conditions in the overall market. Indeed, the various quality submarkets ranging from luxurious new units to slum level housing are all joined through a web of dynamic interactions.

Several points from this discussion will come up again in the remainder of the chapter. The diversity of metropolitan areas in terms of the availability of dwellings and the price of housing faced by low and lower-middle income households is one of them. It follows that public policies designed to improve the quality of housing occupied by these households must be flexible enough to apply under the full range of market conditions. The future of the central city housing stock depends importantly on how costly the alternative of new suburban housing will be. In the same vein, the association between poverty or minority status and housing abandonment varies widely, depending on the strength of market forces.

II. THE COST OF HOUSING

In 1964 the price of the average new one-family home in this country was slightly over $20,000. In 1974, the average was within a few hundred dollars of $40,000 and then crossed that mark in 1975. Thus, there has been a doubling of price in 11 years. Even this doubling understates the rise in monthly costs for the purchaser of a new house, for it does not include the rise in interest rates on mortgages. Mortgage interest rates were less than 6 percent 10 or 12 years ago. In early 1975 they were in the neighborhood of 9 percent.

By themselves, these figures do not tell very much, however. The prices of almost everything else have been going up too, as have wages and income from other sources. Housing costs need to be compared to these other changes before we can say whether the "typical" household can afford more housing or less housing now than in the past. Another problem is that the average price figures do not adjust for changes in the "quality" of the average house: they do not tell whether the house of 1975 is bigger or smaller, has more or fewer built-in appliances, and so on, than its 1964 counterpart.

A further, ostensible limitation of the cost figures referred to above is that they apply to new housing, which is occupied by only a small part of the population. We will, nevertheless, focus the immediate discussion on the costs of new housing because they eventually dominate costs throughout the market. As noted earlier, new units are directly cost competitive with a large segment of the existing stock, and as such the cost of new units provides an effective ceiling above which the costs of existing units cannot rise. Hence, higher costs for new units permit higher costs for existing dwellings, although in the latter case they may be associated with more housing services. Further, the cost of new units indirectly affects the cost of existing units through its effect on the total supply of dwellings relative to the number of households. For these reasons, we view new-unit costs as the weathervane for the costs of existing housing as well.[7] To make it a useful weathervane, however, it

---

[7] It is very difficult to obtain accurate information in this area, but it seems to be true that, over long periods, cost trends for widely available existing dwellings follow trends roughly parallel to cost trends for widely available new dwellings.

is important to be clear on what it is that we want to know about housing costs.

What Do We Want to Know?

The facts about housing costs can be viewed in many ways, and the different ways will answer different questions—questions about housing prices versus other prices, about the changing "quality" of the average house, about trends in the monthly cost of occupying a house in comparison to trends in the structure price, and so on. The procedure chosen here—one which brings a great many concerns together in one comparison—is to take a new, "standard" middle-quality house, trace its monthly cost over time, and then ask how this cost compares with some measure of average family income. Does it require a larger or a smaller fraction of income to buy this standard house now than it used to? If larger, then the average family must either accept the added burden on its income or suffer a decline in housing standards. If the fraction is smaller, the average family can enjoy rising housing standards without any increase in the share of income devoted to housing.[8]

The house taken as the standard of comparison is a one-story, one-and-a-half bathroom, suburban dwelling of about 1,200 square feet with a garage but without basement—a modest new dwelling of the kind built in large numbers in the late 1950s. Even in the late 1950s this house was slightly below the average new dwelling in quality. It is possible to piece together indicators of the cost of this standard house, year by year, and they suggest that its price rose from $17,500 at the end of the 1950s to $31,000 in 1974.[9] (Note that our standard dwelling is distinct from the "average" unit referred to earlier.)

Our concern, however, is not simply with the purchase price of the dwelling but rather with the average monthly cost of occupying it. Due

---

[8] The housing-to-income ratio described here differs from the one discussed earlier in that we are talking about the fraction of income needed to buy a house of specified quality, whereas previously we were reporting the fraction of income actually spent on housing.

[9] For a general description of the derivation of this price index, see "Revised Deflators of New Construction, 1947-73," *Survey of Current Business*, vol. 54, no. 8 (1974), pp. 18-27, where the index used for 1947-62 is given in table 1. The index for the more recent years is described in U.S. Department of Commerce, *Price Index of New One-Family Houses Sold* (Washington, D.C.: U.S. Government Printing Office, Report C27-73-2, Nov. 1973). The indices in the two sources differ in their treatment of the value of the site, but this does not materially affect the trend.

to data limitations, this cost, over a period extending back to the early fifties, is best approximated by the monthly mortgage payment, which reflects changes both in the purchase price and in mortgage interest rates.[10] (More comprehensive data including operating costs for recent years are discussed later.) To derive this figure for a given year a typical 25-year mortgage covering 85 percent of the purchase price is assumed, and it is combined with the dwelling price and interest rate applicable for each year.[11]

This is probably the most reliable cost measure for housing of all types that can be developed over an extended period. It does, as noted, have several possibly offsetting defects. The cost of the new standard dwelling is compared to median family income, as reported by the Bureau of the Census. This measure, like the others available, is not perfect for our purposes.[12] However, since the intention is to focus on broad trends in the movement of the ratio of costs of new dwellings to household income, the shortcomings of the series employed should not materially affect the results.

Costs, Incomes, and Housing Standards

The basic trends at work since 1950 are plotted in the two panels of figure 1. The top panel shows that the monthly cost of a mortgage on a

---

[10] This measure assumes that other costs of occupying the new dwelling do not vary enough to alter the results. One problem with this is that dwellings of this sort have probably been located farther away from metropolitan centers and work places in recent years than in early postwar years. Precise information is not available but this factor leads to some understatement of the overall increase in cost over time, since there is an increase in travel cost (and time) not taken account of. A second factor working in the same direction is that the cost measure omits property taxes and maintenance costs, both of which have increased rapidly during the last two decades. On the other hand, a factor working in the opposite direction is that the particular kind of dwelling we are pricing—a moderate-quality new single-family home—is one whose cost has probably gone up faster than the cost of other dwellings. Statistics on monthly rents, for example, suggest that the cost of older central city houses and apartments have gone up less than the cost of our standard house.

[11] The mortgage rates for years prior to 1963 are a weighted average of those on mortgages insured by the Federal Housing Administration and rates charged by lending sources which were collected by the Federal Home Loan Bank Board. Since 1963 a more comprehensive index based on Bank Board collected data has been used; these rates are reported in "Business Statistics," the biannual supplement to the *Survey of Current Business.*

[12] These data are reported in U.S. Bureau of the Census, *Current Population Reports,* Series P-60 (Washington, D.C.: U.S. Government Printing Office, various issues). It is known that these reported figures understate the level of actual family income; but there is no particular reason to suspect that the degree of understatement has grown larger or smaller over time, and it is the trend over time in which we are mainly interested. Median income also has a defect, in that it tells us only about the average family, not about the wealthy, the poor, or single individuals.

Figure 1
NEW HOUSING COSTS AND FAMILY INCOME

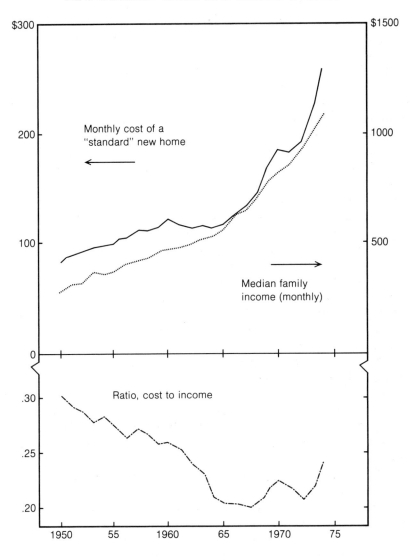

Sources: Table 1 in "Revised Deflators of New Construction, 1947–73," *Survey of Current Business*, vol. 54. no. 8 (1974), pp. 18–27; U.S. Department of Commerce, *Price Index of New One-Family Houses Sold* (Washington, D.C.: Government Printing Office, Report Series C27, various issues); U.S. Bureau of the Census, *Current Population Reports*, Series P-60 (Washington, D.C.: Government Printing Office, various issues.

"standard" house has tripled, from $83 a month in 1950 to $256 a month in 1974, but that median family income has nearly quadrupled, from $3,300 in 1950 to $13,000 in 1974 (or, on a monthly basis, from $275 to $1,083). It follows that the fraction of median income required for mortgage payments on a standard house has fallen. In 1950 that fraction was 30 percent, while in 1974 it had dropped to 24 percent. The bottom panel of the chart shows, year by year, the fraction of median income required to buy the standard new house.

While the basic trend from 1950 to 1974 in the bottom panel is downward, the panel makes it clear that progress has not been smooth. From 1950 to 1965, income was rising faster than cost and the required fraction of income was falling, reaching a 15-year low of 20 percent at the end of that period. In the more recent period, however, the rise in costs has exceeded the rise in income, and the fraction of income required has been fluctuating around an upward trend.

The emergence of rising housing costs as an issue stems basically from this interruption or reversal of a favorable rate of progress. For a few years in the mid-1960s, 20 percent of median family income could buy the standard suburban new house of our example, a considerable improvement from the early postwar situation. Since then the required fraction has risen and there is less optimism that housing standards can be improved at "reasonable" costs. Furthermore, while median family income has continued to grow in money terms, the growth in "real" median income after correcting for increased prices has been meager in recent years (even before the recent recession) compared to the long growth period of the 1960s.

The major shift in the ratio of new housing costs to income in the latter part of the 1960s raises two related issues. The first is whether the shift is merely an aberration from a long term trend. The second is whether quality adjustments in new units have been made in response to the higher costs of new dwellings. Adjustments in quality would be an indication of the widespread interpretation that a fundamental shift has occurred.

The very fact that the upward trend in the ratio of new housing costs to income has persisted for six to seven years argues against viewing the trend as a transitional deviation. A quick look at the components of the increase in housing costs is also consistent with this position. Figure 2 plots the rise in capital and operating costs as well as in the aggregate consumer price index for the 1963-74 period.

Total purchase price data and mortgage interest rates for new homes

Figure 2
TRENDS IN THE PRICES OF HOUSING
COMPONENTS, 1963–1974

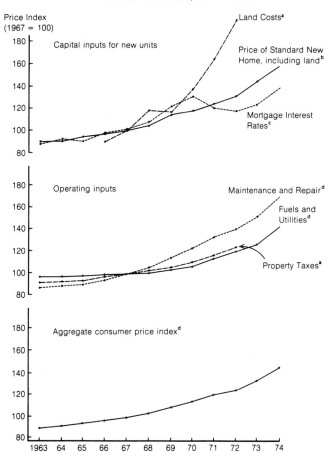

a. Land cost and property tax indices based on data in *FHA Homes 1967*. (FHA Division of Research and Statistics, 1969). Both indices stop in 1972 because after that date the combination of mortgage value restrictions and competition from private mortgage insurers caused a great reduction in the number of units insured and the composition of units insured which makes the data for 1973 and 1974 incomparable with that for earlier years. The land cost index is the price per square foot of the site as estimated by the FHA's data, first reported in this form in 1966. In general the FHA data has the deficiency of changing in composition by location and housing quality from year to year. No adjustment for these changes have been made here; the data used are average values for all new units insured under the Section 203(b) program.

b. Based on "Revised Deflators of New Construction, 1947–73," *Survey of Current Business,* vol. 54, no. 8 (1974); and U.S. Department of Commerce, *Price Index of New One-Family Houses Sold* (Washington, D.C.: U.S. Government Printing Office, 1973).

c. Based on Bank Board collected data reported in "Business Statistics," biannual supplement to *Survey of Current Business.*

d. Data are from the Consumer Price Index as compiled by the Bureau of Labor Statistics in U.S. Bureau of the Census, *Statistical Abstract of the United States, 1973* (Washington, D.C.: Government Printing Office, 1973), p. 354. The data for maintenance and repairs and fuels and utilities apply to both new and existing dwellings, but we believe that this introduces little bias into the cost trends for new dwellings.

are the components of the housing cost curve in the first panel; the land cost data are based on properties insured by the Federal Housing Administration and are one component of the aggregate cost of a new house. Since payments for mortgage interest and principal account for roughly two-thirds of the total monthly costs for homeowners,[13] trends in house prices and interest rates are of paramount importance. The prices of new houses have accelerated since 1970. Given that sales prices are probably beginning to incorporate expected future capital gains on the property, as well as the sharply rising material and labor costs, it seems likely that some time will pass before there is any sustained reduction in the rate of increase in house prices. Interest rates, on the other hand, have fluctuated quite a bit since the mid-1960s; but on balance they have clearly increased. While it is very doubtful that they will go much higher in the near future, they probably will not return to their prior, lower level. The major rise in the interest paid on 4 to 6 year certificates of deposit by savings and loan associations—the most important source of residential loan funds—makes this point emphatically. (Interest rates are discussed more fully below.)

Acceleration is also apparent in two of the three categories of operating expenses shown in figure 2.[14] Maintenance and repair cost increases are being driven upward by the rise in charges for labor services.[15] Fuel and utility costs, which together accounted for 17 percent of monthly expenses in 1967, jumped in 1972-74 and can be expected to mitigate their price rise somewhat if the economy remains soft and if oil prices stabilize. On the other hand, property taxes have been increasing less

---

[13] This is consistent with data on properties insured under the FHA Section 203(b) program and the weights used in the consumer price index. The FHA data are reported in U.S. Department of Housing and Urban Development *FHA Homes 1967* (Washington, D.C.: FHA Division of Research and Statistics, RR: 250 Book, HUD SOR-3, 1969); and U.S. Bureau of Labor Statistics, *Relative Importance of Components in the Consumer Price Index 1967-68* (Washington, D.C.: U.S. Government Printing Office, 1970).

For rental properties, however, the share of total costs accounted for by debt service and return on capital is somewhat less according to data of M. Stegman for Baltimore and G. Sternlieb for New York City. The comparison is not perfect, though, since both the FHA and BLS data for homeowners are for recent purchases whereas the Stegman and Sternlieb data are for the stock of rental housing. See M. Stegman, *Housing Investment in the Inner City* (Cambridge, Mass.: MIT Press, 1963); and G. Sternlieb, *The Urban Housing Dilemma* (New York: New York City Department of Rent and Housing Maintenance, 1970).

[14] Not shown are charges for hazard and home mortgage insurance which together account for 7 percent of total monthly housing expense.

[15] The service charges are based on the costs of five specific tasks, e.g., repainting living and dining rooms, re-siding a house, replacing a sink.

rapidly, and even the payments made may overstate the actual burden due to widespread property tax rebates to elderly households in recent years. This one bright spot, however, is a small offset to the other factors. On balance, it seems clear that in the early 1970s housing costs increased more than most other goods and services; further, it is likely that the relatively higher cost of housing will remain at its new level for at least several years.

While there is much uncertainty about the rate of household income growth in the years immediately ahead, one point is clear—that as long as the effects of the recent economic recession persist, the average growth in real household income will not be great.[16] Based on the projection of a slow, anti-inflationary recovery, no decline in the housing expense to income ratio for most of the 1970s can be safely predicted. This means that nearly a decade of increasingly burdensome housing costs is in prospect.

With the price of new dwellings rising faster than incomes, it follows logically that unless Americans have been willing to devote a greater share of their incomes to housing, the amount of "housing" built into each new dwelling should, on average, be declining. There has, indeed, been a decline in the quality of the average new home, not in the sense of inferior workmanship but in the sense of less space—fewer garages or bathrooms—and other economy moves. In 1963, for example, 64 percent of all new single-family homes came equipped with garages. The percentage rose to 75 percent between 1963 and 1968. But in the period since 1968—the period of rising housing costs—the percentage has fallen back to 68 percent. Similarly the proportion of new one-family homes with more than 2 bathrooms rose from 12 percent in 1963 to 26 percent in 1968 then fell back to 17 percent by 1972. Not all housing characteristics went through this cycle; the proportion of homes with central air conditioning, for example, has continued to increase since 1968. But enough housing attributes did follow the cycle for the index of the average quality of new single-family homes from 1965 to 1974 to show a distinct break in trend, rising until 1968 and fluctuating around a declining trend since then.[17] (See figure 3.)

---

[16] An exposition of several scenarios consistent with this general outcome are given in chapter 2 of B. M. Blechman, E. M. Gramlich, and R. W. Hartman, *Setting National Priorities: the 1976 Budget* (Washington, D.C.: The Brookings Institution, 1975).

[17] These data are taken from various issues of *Price Index of New One-Family Houses Sold,* op. cit.

Figure 3
"QUALITY" OF NEW ONE-FAMILY HOMES

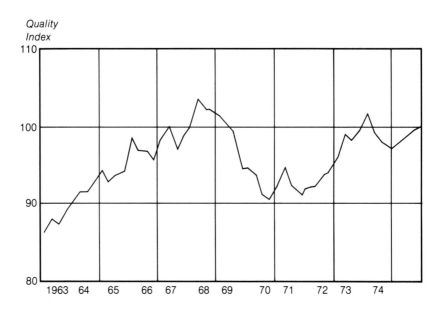

The quality index was derived as follows. Both (a) the price of a new unit of fixed quality and (b) the price of new dwellings of the actual average quality for each year 1963–1974 are given in the Department of Commerce, *Price Index of New One-Family Houses Sold* (Washington, D.C.: U.S. Government Printing Office, 1973). Since the former is a price index, any difference between the two prices for a given year must be due to quality differences between the base of the constant-quality index and average, actual quality. Hence the ratio (b)/(a) yields an index of housing quality.

The rise of mobile homes is another economy move in housing, though it is much more important in small towns and rural areas than metropolitan areas. By 1973 mobile home shipments were equal to half of the number of single-family dwellings constructed by traditional methods.[18] The total cost of a typical mobile home is much less than our standard home. The cost per square foot, however, is only modestly lower; and the *monthly* cost per square foot is probably not lower at all, allowing for the relatively high interest rates on mobile home financing and for the site rents which must be added to the cost of the mobile home itself. The appeal of the mobile home is not its low monthly cost per square foot but rather the opportunity it affords to buy a smaller "package" of housing services than the traditional single-family home.

The growing importance of multifamily apartments is another approach to economizing on housing. New buildings containing five or more dwellings accounted for about 30 percent of all housing starts in the mid-1960s and then rose to nearly 40 percent by the early 1970s (the fraction has fallen in the precipitate housing decline of 1974-1975, but that may well be temporary).[19] The appeal of the multifamily unit is partly the smaller "package" of housing services it affords, especially to childless couples and individuals, and partly the cost savings due to economies in the use of land and of fuel. The trend has also been strengthened by the ability of households that prefer multi-unit structures to realize the tax advantages of homeownership via condominiums.

Overall, then, private markets have reacted to the rise in new housing costs in a variety of ways which make economic sense. There is, however, one response which may make economic sense but which, so far at least, is absent from the list. This is the rehabilitation of inner city housing. In some older cities, the conservation of present existing stock by reversing the flight from the central city and calling a halt to abandonment could be a sensible response to high construction costs. This depends, of course, on the attractiveness of the entire housing bundle—structure, neighborhood amenities, and location—and how the attractiveness of central city units is changing compared to that of suburban dwellings. Suburbia apparently still holds an advantage. Apart from isolated instances there does not seem to be any evidence of a general return to the inner city. Net migration out of the central city, as a later section of this chapter will document, does not as yet appear to be slowing down.

---

[18] U.S. Bureau of the Census, *Housing Starts* (Washington, D.C.: U.S. Government Printing Office, C20 Series, 1975), table 8.

[19] *Housing Starts,* op. cit., table 6.

Policies toward High Costs

Should there be public policies designed to reduce the high cost of housing? It is not obvious that the answer is yes. If low cost can be achieved only at the expense of higher taxes, for example, it is possible that the cure is worse than the disease. Rising costs can be an important signal to consumers that an increasing input of scarce resources is required to produce housing services. Economizing in the use of housing services in response to that signal may be entirely appropriate.

This classic argument for leaving market prices alone does not, however, fit all cases and in the case of housing it is worth at least asking some questions about the recent rise in costs. The first has to do with land prices, an important component of the recent increase in costs:[20] *Does this rise reflect a growing scarcity of land and is it hence a legitimate signal to economize on residential land use?* The second is a somewhat similar inquiry with respect to interest rates, a major source of high housing prices: *Is the rise in this case a signal of scarcity or of other economic forces?* The third has to do with the gainers and losers from higher housing prices: *Do the losers include any group which is especially disadvantaged and in need of assistance?*

With respect to the first question, surely the rise in land prices *is,* in some degree, a legitimate indication of scarcity. Rising population density means greater scarcity of land; and countries with high population densities, such as the countries of Western Europe, tend to have especially high land costs. The United States, however, is certainly far from experiencing any absolute shortage of urban land, even though rising food prices and speculation may have increased the price of undeveloped land outside of urban areas. The sharp rise in land prices more probably results from increased competition for more centralized locations consistent with changing preferences—a competition fed by higher energy costs and shifts in household composition. Thus while land costs for new units have increased, site values in already urbanized areas have probably accelerated more.[21]

One land-use policy currently under active discussion is to increase the

---

[20] According to FHA data cited earlier, land costs constitute about 20 percent of the purchase price of housing. With purchase plus mortgage expense accounting for about two-thirds of total monthly housing expenditures for homeowners, land costs account for about 13 percent of housing expenditures. Moreover, the FHA data suggest that this fraction is increasing.

[21] Unfortunately there is no readily available data series with which this hypothesis can be tested, although the trends in construction of multi-unit structures and household composition certainly provide logical support.

control of land use by states or other broad jurisdictions. Other policies often advocated are to increase taxes on the value of land and on capital gains on land, although usually on grounds having to do with the distribution of wealth rather than the reduction of housing costs.

In fact, it is not at all clear that either these or other proposed land policies would reduce residential land costs. Land-use controls by states would probably raise rather than lower the consumer's costs. Taxation charges could bring down the price of land per acre; but it is doubtful that they would do much to reduce the monthly cost of housing. In the case of a land value tax, in particular, reduced purchase payments for land would be offset by increased tax payments. Likewise, in the case of increased land capital gains taxation, it is at least possible that reduced land prices per se would be offset by higher prices required to support the tax payments, so the price to consumers would be unchanged. All in all, it is hard to make out a strong case for public policies toward land on the grounds that they would reduce housing costs, so the case must rest on other grounds.

Our second question concerned the reasons for the rise in interest rates. Here, two related sets of causal forces appear to be at work. One set, consisting of inflationary pressures, has moved mortgage interest rates upward, thus keeping real interest rates more or less constant. The second set involves sharper competition for funds on the part of savings institutions, a result, at least in part, of the growing sophistication of individual investors. The latter may be especially important to savings and loan associations which are trying to protect themselves from the recurrence of fund squeezes of the type experienced in recent years. These institutions are particularly vulnerable to such squeezes because their mortgage loans are long term while their savings deposits are short term.[22]

While some shift in interest rates among different institutions may be occurring, interest rates have been driven primarily by the first of the two forces mentioned, inflation. It is possible to argue that in a world of perfect rationality and perfect foresight, high interest rates due to inflation would not cause anyone to reduce his demand for housing. High monthly payments by owner-occupants, the argument runs, would be offset by the expectation of large capital gains, and these same expected capital gains

---

[22] For a discussion of the vulnerability of these institutions see William E. Gibson, "Deposit Demand, 'Hot Money', and the Viability of Thrift Institutions," *Brookings Papers on Economic Activity*, no. 3, 1974, pp. 593-636. An analysis of the flow of credit to various sectors in recent years can be found in A. Diamond, *Credit Flows and Interest Costs*, a study prepared for the Joint Economic Committee of the Congress of the United States (Washington, D.C.: U.S. Government Printing Office, 1975).

would cause landlords in competition with one another to charge lower rents or at least to offset the higher rents due to high interest payments.

It is doubtful, however, that actual housing markets follow this competitive, rational, perfect-foresight model. Under the conventional mortgage the same dollar amount is required monthly for the life of the mortgage; and under inflationary conditions this means that the sacrifice in terms of other goods and services is much larger in the first month than it is in subsequent months and years. It is very likely that this high initial burden affects both the level of housing demand and the kinds of housing —particularly multifamily versus single-family housing—that are being produced.[23]

One possible policy response to the burden of high interest rates is to modify the traditional level-payment mortgage. The aim is to develop a mortgage under which payments in current dollar terms are smaller in the initial month than in later months, so the burden of payments in "real" terms is evenly distributed over time. But there are problems with a mortgage of this kind, one of which is that the borrower does not know how much he will have to pay next month or next year. Another is that since payments in the initial months might be too small to cover the full monthly interest costs of the mortgage, the owner's equity in the property would actually fall during the initial period of the mortgage. Some experimentation with alternative mortgage instruments is in fact taking place. Any new instrument acceptable to both borrowers and lenders should surely be encouraged, so that an alternative to the traditional level-payment mortgage is available.

The final question with respect to policies about costs for new housing is whether some groups are especially harmed by higher costs and whether they include disadvantaged persons in special need of protection against the decline of their purchasing power. The immediate losers from the high cost of new housing are probably concentrated among young families trying to buy their first home.[24] Over a longer period, the losers probably include a much larger group of households at a wide range of income

---

[23] While it is true that the monthly payment will decline over time in real terms, it should also be noted that there is no necessary gain to the household. If the interest rate on the mortgage accurately reflects inflation which is to occur over the life of the mortgage, then the household pays back the loan in constant dollars.

[24] One way to help these households during inflationary periods was embodied in an early version of the Emergency Housing Act of 1975. It was to offer a lower interest rate for the first several years of the mortgage, a period long enough for the inflation to subside and for the incomes of the households to increase. A somewhat higher interest rate, sufficient to pay back the first years' subsidy, would then apply for the duration of the mortgage.

levels. The reason for this diffused effect is that, as noted earlier (pages 127-32), prices in different sectors of the housing market tend to move up and down together; if they do not, households take advantage of bargains and so drive up prices in the bargain sectors until a normal price structure is restored. Thus high costs for new suburban housing eventually mean high costs for city as well as suburban housing and old as well as new housing.

The eventual losers from high housing costs thus may include not only young families but also many low-income or otherwise disadvantaged households. Society may well wish to help the poor, although it does not follow that the best means of doing so is to lower their housing costs. This issue will be taken up in the final section of this chapter.

III. RESIDENTIAL SEGREGATION BY RACE

Residential segregation by race is an inescapable fact of life in the majority of U.S. cities. Although ethnic and socioeconomic stratification also exists in the urban areas of most other countries of the world, racial segregation has received special attention in the United States because blacks tend to be more segregated than other readily identifiable groups and because segregation by race may reflect discriminatory treatment of the black minority.

In this section we review the changes in the extent of residential racial segregation which occurred during the 1960s. Relatively little is known about these trends, in part because analysis of the spatial ordering of households requires information for small geographic areas (data which are available for many cities only in the decennial Census), and in part because extensive computations are involved. Even with the additional calculations made for this presentation, the evidence will not be definitive. It is nonetheless valuable to ask what appears to have happened between 1960 and 1970 and then to document as far as possible the changes that actually did occur.

As noted at the beginning of the chapter, public opinion surveys indicate that during the 1960s whites were more willing to have black neighbors than they were immediately after World War II. In addition, several reforms to end overt discrimination in real estate transactions, effected through legislation or executive action, were implemented during the 1960s. In mid-decade FHA abandoned its requirement that neighborhoods in which it insured properties had to be "economically sound," a criterion that had long been used to deny mortgage insurance in mixed or transitional areas. Shortly thereafter, Title VIII of the 1968 Civil

Rights Act barred discrimination by race, religion, or national origin in both owner-occupied and rental housing. While this legislation did exempt certain types of dwellings, they were soon covered under a 1968 U.S. Supreme Court ruling (*Jones v. Alfred H. Mayer Co.*), which reinterpreted the 1866 Civil Rights Act as prohibiting racial discrimination in all types of housing. There are, in brief, grounds for thinking that some reduction in segregation occurred during the sixties.

The Evidence

The most extensive analysis of residential segregation to date is by Karl and Alma Taeuber.[25] Their index of segregation ranges from a minimum of zero (perfect integration) to a maximum of 100 (absolute segregation). With perfect integration, each neighborhood in the market has the same proportion of blacks; and with absolute segregation, all neighborhoods are either all white or all black. Values of the index between the two extremes represent the minimum percentage of either whites or blacks that would have to be moved in order to produce a uniform distribution by race in all neighborhoods.

Below are listed the average values of the Taeuber index over a thirty year period for 109 central cities for which it has been compiled using census tract data.

Year	Average value of Taeuber index
1940	85.2
1950	87.3
1960	86.1
1970	80.0

While 1960-70 is the first period to achieve a decline in the average value of the index below its 1940 level, and while the reduction applied to 80 percent of the sample cities, the magnitude of the decrease is certainly modest.

The change reflected in the Taeuber figures is difficult to interpret because it refers only to events in the central cities, not entire metropolitan areas. For this reason, and because we are interested in determining

---

[25] Karl E. and Alma F. Taeuber, *Negroes in Cities* (Chicago: Aldine, 1965). This work is extended in Annemette Sorensen, Karl E. Taeuber, and Leslie J. Hollingsworth, Jr., "Indexes of Racial Residential Segregation for 109 Cities in the United States, 1940 to 1970," (Madison: The Institute for Research on Poverty, University of Wisconsin, February 1974).

whether the changes shown by the index measure true integration instead of a change in the size or spatial configuration of black areas, we have examined racial patterns in 24 metropolitan areas in 1960 and 1970 in considerable detail. The areas were drawn from only four states—California, Georgia, Ohio, and Texas—to facilitate the computations; and the restricted sample may limit the applicability of our results to all metropolitan areas.

The exploration begins with an examination of changes that occurred in households' exposure to members of a different racial group. The concept of "exposure" is identical to that employed in the chapter on education. For each black, it represents the proportion of his neighbors who are white; and for each white, the proportion of his neighbors who are black. Group exposure rates refer to the average exposure experienced by members of the race in question.[26]

Exposure rates, like the segregation index, are a fairly direct measure of the physical isolation of households. By themselves, however, they do not reveal the degree of potential integration, which depends on the racial composition of the city. Later, therefore, segregation indices are presented. The exposure rates have an advantage over the segregation index, however, in that they can be used to detect changes in the pattern of the growth and development of black areas. It is this use which provides especially interesting findings.

Table 6 presents average exposure rates of blacks and whites (actually, all non-blacks) for the metropolitan areas in each of the four states.[27] For all calculations, neighborhoods were assumed to coincide with census tracts—geographic groupings of about 1,500 households on average, whose boundaries are determined by local boards on the basis of homogeneity of housing and other criteria. To help distinguish trends occurring in dif-

---

[26] Thus, if an area contains n neighborhoods, black exposure to whites is defined by:

$$BX = (1/B) \sum_{i=1}^{n} B_i w_i$$

where B_i is the number of blacks in the ith neighborhood; w_i is that neighborhood's fraction of whites; and B is the area's total number of blacks ($B = \sum_{i=1}^{n} B_i$).

White exposure to blacks (WX) has an analogous definition. Indeed, for a given set of neighborhoods, the ratio of the two rates of exposure (WX/BX) is equal to the overall ratio of blacks to whites. This correspondence is not surprising since the two measures are simply alternate ways of describing the same basic phenomenon.

[27] Similar data for the individual areas is given in the Appendix, table A-1.

ferent sectors of the market, tracts were divided into two groups based on their median family income. "High" income tracts had average incomes that were above the median for an SMSA as a whole; "low" income tracts had incomes that were below the SMSA-wide median. Black and white exposure rates were calculated for each of these two neighborhood types, and for the SMSA as a whole.

Table 6 reveals several distinct patterns that are persistent over time and across cities. Perhaps the most striking is the enormous difference between the exposure rates of whites to blacks in the two neighborhood types. In low-income neighborhoods white exposure averages about .12, implying that a "representative" white resident lives in an area which is 12 percent black. In neighborhoods with incomes above the area-wide median, the average white exposure is closer to .02.

Poor white households are attracted to racially transitional neighbor-

Table 6

AVERAGE RACIAL EXPOSURE RATES FOR SMSAs IN SELECTED STATES (1960 AND 1970) [a]

Exposure Rates	Georgia	California	Texas	Ohio
A. White Exposure to Blacks [b]				
1. SMSA average				
1960	.14	.03	.07	.05
1970	.12	.03	.06	.04
2. Low-income neighborhoods				
1960	.30	.05	.15	.10
1970	.27	.06	.14	.08
3. High-income neighborhoods				
1960	.06	.01	.02	.01
1970	.05	.01	.02	.01
B. Black Exposure to Whites				
1. SMSA average				
1960	.31	.64	.37	.42
1970	.29	.58	.35	.39
2. Low-income neighborhoods				
1960	.25	.62	.32	.39
1970	.22	.56	.32	.36
3. High-income neighborhoods				
1960	.78	.87	.82	.89
1970	.75	.80	.78	.76
C. Number of SMSAs	3	5	7	9

a. See text, footnote 26, for definition of exposure rate.

b. Whites include a small proportion of Orientals and Indians.

hoods by the cheaper, although lower quality, housing frequently available there and by the frequently still lower rents which black-averse whites are willing to offer other whites.

Another pattern is the relatively high level of black exposure to whites —about 78 percent in the high-income neighborhoods and 37 percent in the low. Of course, the large difference between black and white exposure rates is to be expected since blacks are the minority. Black exposure to whites is distinctly higher in neighborhoods with incomes above the area-wide median. But since the overwhelming majority of blacks (74 to 98 percent in these SMSAs) live in low-income areas, the relatively high rates of exposure in high-income tracts refer to a handful of blacks in prosperous white neighborhoods.

A third general pattern is the higher rate of exposure of whites to blacks in the metropolitan areas in the two southern states and the lower rates of exposure of blacks to whites in the same states. The very high rates of exposure of blacks to whites in California SMSAs is also noteworthy. Finally, the exposure of blacks to whites declined on a widespread basis over the decade; all of the state averages fell, for SMSAs as a whole as well as for the different types of neighborhoods. The changes in white exposure rates are less consistent; but general declines appeared in Georgia and Texas, while an increase occurred in all neighborhood types on average in California.

Before trying to explain these differences in exposure rates, it is useful to consider how these rates would change over time in a metropolitan area undergoing a typical expansion of the black residential sector. For the purpose of understanding the basic logic involved, assume that blacks live in one centrally located all-black area surrounded by an integrated border or transitional zone. Assume further that any growth in the number of blacks is accommodated by peripheral expansion of the area. Under these conditions, black exposure to whites will decline, since the perimeter of a circle or square grows less rapidly than its area.

This highly simplified example suggests that exposure rates may vary across cities and over time with little or no variation in the general spatial ordering of households. If black neighborhoods simply fill in and expand outward as the black population grows, the *average* black will be exposed to a smaller fraction of whites. Declining exposure rates over time could, therefore, signal the preservation of established racial patterns, rather than a deterioration in the level of actual integration. By the same logic, growth in the black population accompanied by an increase in black exposure to whites should indicate a change in the overall ordering of households—either wider transitional areas around established black neighborhoods or an increase in the dispersion of blacks throughout the metropolitan area.

To examine the relation between size of the black population and black exposure rates, separate exposure rates were calculated for the sample cities grouped under three categories according to the size of the black population. The results, shown in table 7, confirm our expectations: black exposure to whites declines as an area's number of blacks rises, both for the SMSA as a whole and for the two neighborhood types. This implies that a significant proportion of the observed variation in black exposure to whites reflects differences in the size of the black population, rather than differences in the general spatial ordering of households.[28]

Table 7

AVERAGE 1960 AND 1970 BLACK EXPOSURE RATES BY
SIZE OF BLACK POPULATION FOR 24 SAMPLE SMSAs[a]

| | Size of Black Population[b] | | |
	Small	Medium	Large
SMSA total	.60	.37	.29
Low-income neighborhoods	.62	.30	.28
High-income neighborhoods	.92	.81	.70

a. Each cell based on 16 observations, 8 for 1960 and 8 for 1970.
b. Range of black population in each size group is:
      small 4,200–45,000
      medium 45,000–90,000
      large 90,000–750,000.

The inverse relationship between black exposure rates and the size of the black population may have two additional implications. One, which is generally confirmed by the data, is that growth in the number of blacks is typically accompanied by a decline in blacks' exposure to whites. The second, which we are unable to test with these data, is that the relationship partly explains differences in exposure rates between high- and low-income neighborhoods within a metropolitan area.

By contrast, the variation in white exposure rates (shown in table 6 and Appendix table A-1) demonstrates less consistency, aside from the

---

[28] A statistical analysis of the relationship shown in table 7, presented in Appendix table A-2, indicates that population differentials alone explain from 50 to 60 percent of the total variance in exposure rates.

regional variations already noted. Interestingly, there is little pattern in the direction of change in white exposure rates over time, compared to the direction of change in black exposure rates. One consistency which does emerge, however, is that those areas which began the decade with an unusually high rate of white exposure experienced a decline in the exposure rates of whites.[29] The cause for the initially high exposure rate seems usually to have been an extraordinarily high ratio of blacks to whites in the metropolitan area, rather than greater spatial dispersion of blacks. Also, in most areas where white exposure declined, the white population grew faster than the black, both overall and in each neighborhood type. The sample cities characterized by an initially high ratio of blacks to whites and relative growth in the white population over the decade are located largely in the South.

In summary, four general points emerge from our examination of exposure rates. First, blacks' exposure to whites is lower in metropolitan areas where there are more blacks, due to the strong historical tendency for the black enclave to expand peripherally. Second, for the same reason, black exposure rates tended to decline during the 1960s in individual urban areas where the black population increased. Third, white exposure to blacks in 1960 was higher in metropolitan areas where blacks were relatively more numerous, and over the decade these rates declined in southern cities where white population growth exceeded that of blacks. Finally, there is no obvious systematic relationship between changes in the exposure of blacks to whites and whites to blacks.[30]

To synthesize this information into some judgment on the overall change in "residential segregation" raises knotty problems with definitions

---

[29] In high-income neighborhoods 10 of the 11 areas registering a decline in white exposure had an initial value that was greater than one percent, the approximate median in 1960; in low-income neighborhoods, the figures are 11 out of 13, with a median of 9 percent.

[30] One source of additional information regarding national trends in the exposure rates of blacks and whites is the series of sample surveys conducted by the Institute of Social Research of the University of Michigan. In these surveys individuals are asked whether the neighborhood in which they live is all white, largely white, mixed, largely black, or all black. It is possible using these figures and some supplementary data to calculate very crude "exposure" rates nation-wide for whites and blacks. In the ten years from 1964 to 1974 the answers to the survey questions suggest a considerable increase in white exposure both before and after 1970. However with respect to black exposure, the figures suggest a smaller increase, and one which is largely confined to the period before 1970. Since this latter trend is different from the one which we observed, these nation-wide rates of exposure seem to imply that our sample of 24 cities may not depict trends that are occurring in all parts of the country, but exact comparisons are really not possible.

and concepts. Until now, we have examined exposure rates in absolute rather than relative terms. However, as noted earlier, in devising a measure of segregation one must consider the maximum rates that are possible, given the size of the two racial groups. Obviously, a city which is 50 percent black can achieve very different exposure rates from a city which is virtually all white; and it has been necessary to devise a measure which somehow takes these possibilities into account.

Table 8

INDICES OF RESIDENTIAL SEGREGATION FOR
METROPOLITAN AREAS IN SELECTED STATES
(1960 AND 1970)[a]

	Georgia	California	Texas	Ohio
For SMSAs based on Exposure Rates				
1960	50.0	33.9	56.2	53.9
1970	59.9	38.6	58.8	56.7
For SMSAs using the Taeuber Index				
1960	63.3	76.3	73.6	75.8
1970	70.6	69.9	77.4	77.6

a. See Appendix B for definitions.

The results of computing a segregation index based on the exposure indices are presented in table 8.[31] The entries are once again average values of the indices for the metropolitan areas in each of four states. Like the Taeuber indices, which we have recomputed for whole metropolitan areas and included in the table for reference, the segregation index based on the exposure rate also ranges from zero (complete integration) to 100 (complete segregation). According to both sets of indices when computed for entire metropolitan areas, segregation generally increased over the decade.[32] The patterns of decreasing black exposure with increasing

[31] Definitions of the exposure-rate segregation index and the Taeuber segregation index are presented in Appendix B. Segregation indices for each of the 24 cities appear in Appendix table A-3.

[32] For individual SMSA's, the index based on exposure rates shows increased segregation in 17 areas, and decreased segregation in 7. The 7 areas which registered declines were the same areas which recorded an overall increase in blacks' exposure to whites. In contrast, the Taeuber index shows decreased segregation in 12 of the 24 areas. Nine of those areas experienced a rise in white exposure to blacks, while only 4 registered an increase in the exposure rate of blacks.

black population is probably an important determinant of this pattern. But how does one explain the paradox of a racially more tolerant society becoming more segregated?

Factors Inhibiting Change

One possible explanation is that the open housing legislation of the late 1960s had been in effect for only a short period of time before the initiation of the 1970 Census. Since established racial patterns will undoubtedly be slow to change, the lack of any immediate major change was to be expected.

There is also evidence of continued discrimination in the real estate industry, although the form of that discrimination is considerably more subtle than the tactics which were once employed. For example, recent studies have documented the prevalence of "redlining," a practice whereby conventional lenders avoid loans in racially mixed or transitional neighborhoods on the ground that such areas are high credit risks; others have noted the tendency among real estate brokers to steer prospective black buyers away from predominantly white neighborhoods, thereby preserving established racial patterns. While allegations regarding these more sophisticated kinds of discrimination are difficult to substantiate, scattered evidence indicates that discrimination in housing has far from vanished from the American scene.

The main explanation for the continuance of a high level of residential segregation by race, however, is probably one stressed by Thomas Schelling.[33] Schelling has shown that in some plausible but very simple hypothetical situations, rather mild feelings about racial preferences can easily lead to an extreme degree of racial segregation. As a simple example, suppose that every white and every black were perfectly willing to live with members of the other race, provided that his own race constituted more than 50 percent of his neighborhood. In comparison to common attitudes in this country, these would have to be rated as fairly mild feelings about racial segregation. Nevertheless, it is easy to see that the only "equilibrium" outcome in this instance is completely segregated neighborhoods. Every neighborhood has to have (except for temporary coincidences) a majority of one race or the other; and if the dissatisfied minority tends to move away, then any initial pattern of racial settlement will keep changing until completely segregated neighborhoods are reached.

---

[33] See Thomas Schelling, "On the Ecology of Micromotives," *The Public Interest,* no. 25 (Fall 1971) pp. 61-98.

Applied broadly to the U.S. experience, this argument suggests that the very strong feelings of discrimination in the past were much more than was necessary to produce a high degree of racial segregation. The overt discrimination in real estate transactions easily observable in past years was also beyond the degree required for considerable segregation. In sum, the change in attitudes in recent years and the public policies limiting overt discrimination have reduced the strength of discriminatory forces; but even the remaining forces are sufficient to cause highly segregated residential patterns.

Policies toward Residential Segregation

The policy implications of the preceding analysis are somewhat fatalistic. As long as families are free to move to neighborhoods of their choice, even slight feelings of discrimination can produce a high degree of segregation. To prevent overt discrimination in real estate transactions may well have only a limited impact on the results. Probably the same is true of judicial rulings with respect to zoning or to other land-use restrictions which have unequal racial impacts.

This is not to say that action on fair housing or land use is completely futile. Doubtless it does increase the housing opportunities of minorities in a few cases, and these cases may be symbolically important in indicating national commitment, or lack of commitment, to equal opportunity goals. In addition, even when opening up a neighborhood leads to only temporary integration, it may relieve price pressures within all-black sections of the urban area. Reduction in housing premiums paid by blacks, which were documented in some metropolitan areas during the 1960s,[34] would clearly improve the welfare of blacks.

It is always possible, furthermore, that attitudes toward race will soften to the point where free choice of neighborhoods alone would produce only a mild rather than a high degree of segregation. Under these conditions, fair housing laws and zoning regulations could have a much more significant impact on segregation than they appear to have had so far.

Apart from equal opportunity laws and rulings, it seems likely that policies with a low profile, aiming at moderate increases in racial integration together with other goals, have a greater chance of success than

---

[34] For a review of this evidence, including the statistical problems involved in isolating racial premiums, see A. Schnare and R. Struyk, "An Analysis of Ghetto Housing Prices Over Time" (New York: National Bureau of Economic Research, forthcoming).

policies which attack segregation frontally by moving a large number of minority families into a majority neighborhood. The latter approach seems all too likely, given present racial attitudes, to lead to integration only temporarily, with resegregation the final outcome.

An example of a low-profile approach is the leasing of existing housing under the public housing program (formerly a part of the Section 23 Leasing Program and currently a part of the Section 8 Program). Under this program housing authorities rent apartments or houses of moderate but decent quality and sublet them to low-income tenants, with a federal subsidy for the difference between what the tenants can afford to pay and the full rent. One analysis of that program suggests that it probably has had the effect of moving black participants in the program from all-black neighborhoods to somewhat more integrated neighborhoods—that is, of increasing white exposure to black participants.[35] The main goal of the program, however, was to find decent housing for low-income families, and the program was generally run in a way that avoided community confrontations. In the present situation, public policy may be able to contribute toward residential integration through programs of this kind which are not dramatic enough to provoke widespread attention and neighborhood flight.

IV. SLUMS AND THE INNER CITY

The single most significant feature of slums is the poverty of their inhabitants. For the employable, low income is due to the lack of formal education and skills; for the unemployable, it is due to disabilities. Low incomes, in turn, account for the minimal rents which slum residents can afford. But there is more to slums than low incomes and bad housing. The spatial concentration of such households and dwellings is one aspect; the social problems of the residents—broken homes, personal and property crime, severe unemployment, drug addiction—are others.

The total problem of slums is clearly too broad and complex for adequate treatment in the confines of a single chapter; the fact that much of this volume is concerned, indirectly at least, with slums illustrates the pervasiveness of the issue. We therefore restrict our attention fairly narrowly to the housing aspects of slums, although more general issues do necessarily enter the picture. Thus, in very broad terms, we will first

---

[35] Frank de Leeuw and Sam Leaman, "The Section 23 Program," in U.S. Congress, Joint Economic Committee, *The Economics of Federal Subsidy Programs*, 1972, pp. 542-91.

examine the household demand and the market conditions which combine to produce slum housing, together with the trends in these factors
during the period following World War II. We will then discuss alternative policies for improving the housing situations of the urban poor and
try to assess their implications for the future of slums

Slums: Why, Where, and How Large?

Prominent aspects of slums are the intense spatial concentration of poor
households and miserable living conditions, living conditions exacerbated
by the massing together of households. Why such concentrations? There
are three related reasons. One is that slums contain the oldest, and frequently the most obsolete, portion of the available housing stock and thus
are located in the oldest parts of most cities;[36] often there are several such
locations in a metropolitan area, since the metropolis has grown to encompass once-independent towns. Second, certain sections of the central
city have traditionally been the reception area for impoverished immigrants, both from abroad and from other regions within the country. And
third, racial and ethnic segregation has been strong and persistent; with
income growth, forced ethnic segregation has nearly vanished, but, as
demonstrated earlier, racial segregation remains virulent.[37]

The archetypical slum is in the heart of a northern central city, but
there are numerous exceptions. In some southern cities the postbellum
black enclaves were on the periphery of the developed city; and in the
Southwest a similar pattern, imitative of South America, developed with
poor Mexicans and Indians housed outside of the main city. Wherever
begun, however, the clusters of poor tended to expand at their perimeters
as their numbers increased; but interestingly, as described later, little
contraction has accompanied a decline in their numbers.

In the economic sense the poor demand very low quality housing because that is all they can afford without devoting an unreasonable share

---

[36] This is obviously not a universal rule. It is, however, very difficult to document the age of dwellings in various parts of a metropolis from readily available
data, since the census simply categorizes the oldest dwellings as being built before
1939.

[37] The literature documenting these patterns is extensive. For the Pittsburgh area
as an example, Florette Henri, *Black Migration: Movement North 1900-1920*
(New York: Doubleday-Anchor Press, 1975); Abram Epstein, *The Negro Migrant
in Pittsburgh* (New York: *New York Times* and Arno Press, 1969, reprinting of
1918 original publication); Roy Lubove, *Twentieth Century Pittsburgh: Government, Business, and Environmental Change* (New York: John Wiley and Sons,
1969).

of their income to housing. One way to determine how poor they are is to compare those households in what the Bureau of the Census has defined as poverty areas in 1970—groups of contiguous census tracts in which at least one-fifth of the households had incomes below a poverty income level—with all households in the metropolitan area. Table 9 displays the average income distributions of poverty area residents and all metropolitan area residents by race for twenty large metropolitan areas. The lower incomes of white poverty area residents and the low income of blacks, in general, stand out sharply. On average, poverty area residents are disproportionately black (58 percent), more often live in households headed by women (nearly a third), and constitute about one-fourth of the central city population.

The progress made in raising the average incomes of the poorest fifth of the households in individual metropolitan areas has been a struggle between two forces. On the one side are poor households whose roots in an area are deep and long established—especially where the head of the house was born in the area. The incomes of these households have tended to increase over time. On the other side is the influx of even poorer and more broadly disadvantaged households into these cities. Since 1945 the

Table 9

INCOME DISTRIBUTION OF FAMILIES IN ENTIRE METROPOLITAN AREAS[a] AND POVERTY AREAS WITHIN THESE METROPOLITAN AREAS IN 1970, BY RACE[b]

| Income | Location and Race | | | |
| | White families | | Black families | |
	poverty areas	entire SMSA	poverty areas	entire SMSA
Under $5,000	.30	.13	.38	.32
$5,000 to $10,000	.37	.30	.34	.36
Over $10,000	.31	.57	.25	.34

a. Included metropolitan areas are: Atlanta, Baltimore, Boston, Buffalo, Chicago, Cincinnati, Cleveland, Dallas, Detroit, Houston, Los Angeles, Milwaukee, Minneapolis-St. Paul, Newark, Philadelphia, Pittsburgh, San Francisco, St. Louis, Washington, D.C.

b. Figures are the arithmetic averages of the distributions of the individual areas, and for this reason may not sum to 1.00.

Sources: U.S. Bureau of the Census, Census of Population: *1970 Employment Profiles of Selected Low Income Areas*, PHC(3) Series (Washington, D.C.: U.S. Government Printing Office, 1971) and 1970 vol. 1, *Characteristics of the Population* (U.S. Government Printing Office, 1973).

incomes of both white and black families have increased dramatically on average (see Appendix table A-4), but the same period has also witnessed tremendous interregional migration. Table 10 shows only the net migration of individuals between the very large census regions in 1950, 1960, and 1970, and hence greatly understates total population movement. The numbers are still enormous.

Table 10

NET LIFETIME MIGRATION AMONG U.S. REGIONS
(1950-70)
(Numbers in thousands)

	Born in the specified region but living in some other region		Living in the specified region but born in some other region	
	whites	blacks	whites	blacks
1950				
Northeast	3,347	88	1,522	1,016
North Central	6,800	117	3,629	1,269
South	4,818	2,593	3,307	108
West	780	36	7,288	440
1960				
Northeast	4,754	129	1,958	1,221
North Central	6,606	177	4,824	1,559
South	6,687	3,256	4,954	160
West	1,247	61	9,558	683
1970				
Northeast	6,143	184	2,410	1,245
North Central	9,784	233	5,529	1,576
South	7,376	3,410	6,859	221
West	1,983	62	10,488	846

Sources: U.S. Bureau of the Census, 1950, 1960, and 1970, Special Reports, *State of Birth,* P-E no. 40, PC(2)-2A and PC(2)-2A (Washington, D.C.: U.S. Government Printing Office, 1953, 1963, 1973).

Further, many immigrants to metropolitan areas have been comparatively ill-equipped to make a livelihood in urban society. This point is illustrated in table 11 which gives the distribution of schooling for males and females over age 25 in 1970 living in northern metropolitan areas, stratified by Census region of birth—north, south, or west. There is an obvious disparity between the number of years of school completed by

Table 11

EDUCATIONAL ATTAINMENT OF PERSONS 25 YEARS OF
AGE AND OLDER LIVING IN NORTHERN METROPOLITAN
STATISTICAL AREAS IN 1970, BY REGION OF
BIRTH, BY SEX, AND BY RACE
(Percent distribution)

| Years of School Completed | Race, Sex, and Region of Birth | | | | | |
| | white males | | | black males | | |
	north	west	south	north	west	south
8 or fewer	20	10	33	27	20	43
9–11	20	11	20	29	27	26
12	32	25	24	31	29	22
13–15	11	16	8	8	15	6
16 or more	17	39	14	5	10	4
	white females			black females		
	north	west	south	north	west	south
8 or fewer	17	7	24	20	14	36
9–11	24	21	25	38	28	33
12	39	32	31	32	28	20
13–15	12	21	10	8	14	7
16 or more	8	18	9	3	14	4
Total number of persons (000's)	34,035	351	2,306	1,951	11	1,987

Source: Tables 23 and 29 in U.S. Bureau of the Census, Census of Population:
1970 Subject Reports, Final Report PC(2)-2B, *Mobility for States and the Nation* (Washington, D.C.: U.S. Government Printing Office, 1973).

whites and blacks born in the South compared to those born in other
regions. Over 40 percent of southern-born black males had 8 or fewer
years of school, more than twice the rate of northern-born whites. Also
note that the number of southern-born blacks living in northern SMSAs
is roughly equivalent to the number born in the north, but that the number of white migrants from the South is greater than the comparable
number of blacks.[38]

A fourth and final point on the housing demand by migrants is that
there are indications of the rate of migration having abated. Gross black

---

[38] For an excellent discussion of the characteristics of southerners migrating up
to 1960, see J. F. Kain and J. J. Persky, "The North's Stake in Rural Southern
Poverty," in U.S. Department of Agriculture, *Rural Poverty in the United States:
A Report by the President's National Advisory Committee on Rural Poverty*
(Washington, D.C.: U.S. Government Printing Office, 1968), pp. 288-308.

migration from the South averaged nearly 150 thousand persons annually between 1950 and 1970, but it declined to 60 thousand between 1970 and 1974 and there may have been a net immigration of blacks into the South for the first time since the war.[39]

These statistics obviously mask radical differences between individual urban areas, although two general points do emerge. One is that the demand for low quality housing, often by blacks and available only in segregated neighborhoods, has been swelled by a continuous wave of regional migration sweeping along large numbers of poorly educated individuals. The other is that since the tidal wave has in all likelihood passed, the growth in demand for slum quality housing will be stunted and probably reduced absolutely as the immigrating households and their children become assimilated into the economic mainstream.

But what about the supply of slum quality housing? In general, as noted earlier, peripheral expansion of the areas of worst housing has been the rule, due to economic and racial segregation. This type of growth has meant that before the poor could afford higher quality housing it had to be converted into more housing units, or else maintenance and other services had to be greatly reduced. If the total rent available from the converted structures was not enough to provide a profit after all costs, including those of conversion, the slum boundary would not move outward, at least in that locale. At times, strong resistance to such expansion has produced more doubling up within the slums and more rapid deterioration of the housing stock, until price pressures once again become sufficient to permit expansion.

While the interplay of demand and supply at the slum boundary are clearly important for the growth of slums, several other supply-side considerations are also critical. One is the strength of the desire of middle- and upper-income whites not to live near the poor or the blacks. The stronger this preference the more rapidly the boundary shifts, other things being the same. It is interesting to note that the resistance of ethnic communities to invasion by the poor or blacks has gone quite beyond the point at which other middle-class households begin to move away. In these cases the attractiveness of the community more than offsets the aversion.

The second factor governing the rate at which additional neighborhoods are converted to low quality housing is the availability of alternative suit-

---

[39] Social and Economic Statistics Administration, U.S. Bureau of the Census, *The Social and Economic Status of the Black Population in the United States,* 1971 and 1974, Series P-23, nos. 42 and 54 (Washington, D.C.: U.S. Government Printing Office, 1972 and 1974).

able housing for the original residents of these neighborhoods. In the post-war era several circumstances made relocation relatively attractive to such households. As we have shown earlier, increases in the cost of new housing were low relative to income growth. Additionally, the low-interest, long-term mortgage loan guarantees of the Federal Housing Administration (enacted during the Depression but effectively utilized only after the war) increased the possibility of homeownership for moderate-income households and hence fueled suburban demand. Finally, the national highways program initiated in the mid-1950s enormously improved the accessibility of locations further from the city center.[40]

These circumstances, including racial preferences, encouraged households to leave the central cities. Table 12 shows the systematic reduction in the relative importance of the white population in central cities from 1950 to 1973. In addition, the data in Appendix table A-5 highlight the composition of shifts in the black and white populations within the fifteen largest metropolitan areas during the 1960s. They show that whites migrated from the central cities in all but one SMSA, and that the net migration exceeded 15 percent of the base year population in all but two instances.[41]

Such outmigration might be construed as a healthy sign, not in terms of attaining a socially desirable mix of households but in terms of transferring housing resources to where they are most needed *if* there is sufficient demand for lower quality housing to occupy the stock made available. During the 1950s and the early 1960s when migration rates were high, little comment about potential housing abandonment was heard, but beginning in the late sixties conditions changed. The outward flight of whites continued but the rate of migration, especially from the South, was abating; in addition, incomes were growing at unusually high rates for all households. These factors combined to produce significant excess supplies of low quality central city housing in a number of areas.

The effect of these forces has been partly in the form of price move-

---

[40] For a general discussion of the effects of transportation improvements on household location see chap. 2 of R. F. Muth, *Cities and Housing* (Chicago: University of Chicago Press, 1969) and Part I of J. R. Meyer, J. F. Kain, and M. Wohl, *The Urban Transportation Problem* (Cambridge: Harvard University Press, 1965). For a discussion of the effects of FHA insurance on homeownership, see chap. 5 of Henry Aaron, *Shelter and Subsidies* (Washington, D.C.: The Brookings Institution, 1972).

[41] A more detailed presentation of these trends is in L. H. Long, "How the Racial Composition of Cities Changes," *Land Economics*, vol. 51, Aug. 1975, pp. 258-67.

ments and partly in the form of changes in the housing stock. On the price side there is fairly convincing evidence that rents and housing costs have risen less rapidly in the older portions of central cities than in the rest of the metropolitan areas. The figures in table 13 compare 1960-70 increases in rents and values for Census-drawn samples of metropolitan dwelling units which *did not* undergo major changes—conversion, demolition, or merger—over the decade. Increases for central city dwellings are far smaller than increases for suburban dwellings.

Some reduction in occupied dwellings is almost inevitable under the conditions outlined here. The specific form of reduction—vacancy, conversion to nonresidential use, or abandonment—is much less prede-

Table 12

POPULATION BY METROPOLITAN AND
NONMETROPOLITAN RESIDENCE AND RACE:
PERCENT DISTRIBUTION (1950-73)

Total Population	1950	1960	1970	1973
Total	100	100	100	100
Metropolitan Residence	63	67	69	68
Inside Central Cities	36	34	31	30
Outside Central Cities	27	33	38	38
Nonmetropolitan Residence	37	33	31	32
Whites				
Total	100	100	100	100
Metropolitan Residence	63	67	68	67
Inside Central Cities	35	32	28	26
Outside Central Cities	28	35	40	41
Nonmetropolitan Residence	37	33	32	33
Blacks				
Total	100	100	100	100
Metropolitan Residence	59	68	74	76
Inside Central Cities	44	53	58	60
Outside Central Cities	15	15	16	17
Nonmetropolitan Residence	41	32	26	24

Sources: 1950 data based on National League of Cities, *State of the Cities, 1974,* p. 12. 1960 and 1970 data from U.S. Census Bureau, *General Demographic Trends for Metropolitan Areas, 1960 to 1970,* report PHC(2)-1, pp. 1-23. 1973 figures based on *Current Population Survey Mobility Estimates, 1970 to 1973* (report P-20, no. 262), table 3. All figures refer to a construct sample of SMSAs but are not adjusted for central city boundary changes. 1973 figures are subject to wider margins of error than those for earlier years.

Table 13

VALUES AND RENTS OF IDENTICAL DWELLINGS
(1960 AND 1970)[a]

	Central Cities	Suburbs (rest of metropolitan areas)
1. Values of Owner-Occupied Dwellings		
Median value, 1960	$12,800	$14,800
Median value, 1970	16,600	20,500
1960-70 change	+3,800	+5,700
Percent below $20,000, 1960	85	77
Percent below $20,000, 1970	66	48
1960-70 change	−19	−29
2. Gross Monthly Rents of Rented Dwellings		
Median gross rent, 1960	$ 74	$ 83
Median gross rent, 1970	98	113
1960-70 change	+24	+30
Percent below $100, 1960	81	74
Percent below $100, 1970	53	39
1960-70 change	−28	−35

a. Figures in the table are based on tables S4 and S6 in U.S. 1970 Census of Housing, *Components of Inventory Change,* HC(4)-1, U.S. Bureau of the Census, 1973. They refer to identical samples of dwellings for the two years, omitting not only new, demolished, or converted dwellings but also omitting dwellings which changed tenure during the decade.

termined. Abandonment, in which an owner abandons any legal claim to his property and attempts to escape any financial obligations related to the property in the form of taxes or mortgage payments, is a product of specific legal institutions and of the racial, social, and demographic developments in a neighborhood.[42]

A point worth repeating is that the experiences of individual metropolitan areas can differ radically. At the same time, the forces causing households to leave cities are pervasive, and areas with quite different records of immigration may be undergoing similar changes. To make this

[42] Only sporadic attempts have been made to collect data on housing abandonment. A compendium of the relevant studies is included in G. Sternlieb, R. W. Burchell, J. W. Hughes, and F. J. James, "Housing Abandonment in the Urban Core," *Journal of the American Institute of Planners,* vol. 40, Sept. 1974, pp. 321-32.

more concrete, we will look at selected events in the Pittsburgh and Boston metropolitan areas over the 1950-70 period—two areas for which detailed prior analysis has been done.[43] These areas are alike in a number of respects: they are older northeastern areas and have comparable populations; both have fairly small black populations, generally concentrated in the central cities; and both have had a rate of white outmigration from the central city of around 15 percent for each of the two decades in the period. Also, as shown in the top part of table 14, both areas went from extremely low vacancy rates in 1950 to a moderate vacancy situation in 1970. They differ sharply, though, in the rate of growth of their black populations. Pittsburgh had an 18 percent growth rate in the fifties and a 5 percent rate in the sixties. For Boston, by contrast, the comparable figures were 51 and 62 percent. Finally, the real incomes of black and white families rose by 27 percent in Pittsburgh during the sixties versus only 12 percent for black Boston families and 28 percent for white Boston families.

The figures in the lower panel of table 14 paint a rough picture of the housing situation in the black neighborhoods of Boston and Pittsburgh in 1950, 1960, and 1970. The focus on black neighborhoods clearly limits the analysis, since there are substantial numbers of poor whites in these same markets; but the conclusions are nevertheless highly relevant. Three clear patterns are evident in these numbers. First, the black neighborhoods became more solidly black during the period. Second, the quality of housing —as measured by the presence of central heat and complete plumbing facilities or by occupancy of a single-unit structure—rose dramatically over the period, consistent with the growth in real incomes since 1950 and the general housing improvement experienced by low-income households, as noted in the introductory section of this chapter. Finally, and somewhat surprisingly, in both areas the vacancy rate in black neighborhoods had risen to 9 percent in 1970.

In Pittsburgh this outcome is understandable given the low growth of both black and white populations coupled with substantial new construction (see table 5). This is similar to the pattern documented for St. Louis.[44] The outcome for Boston, though, was less expected. Closer examination of the Boston black neighborhood situation reveals that the vacancy rate in tracts near the boundary with dominantly white neigh-

---

[43] A. B. Schnare and R. Struyk, "An Analysis of Ghetto Housing Prices Over Time," op. cit.

[44] Institute for Urban and Regional Studies, *The Contemporary Neighborhood Succession Process: Lessons in the Dynamics from the St. Louis Experience* (New York: Praeger, forthcoming).

borhoods is less than the SMSA average; the high rates are in the heart of the black enclave.

The consistency of these findings strongly suggests a general process. Even with a sufficient number of dwellings available in the black area, the boundary continues to move outward, pulled in part by white flight and the depressed rents and property values, pushed in part by the demand for better housing—especially improved neighborhood conditions—by blacks. The latter, in turn, has been fed by income growth. Note that just as higher-income whites prefer to live away from poor whites (aside from certain tight ethnic communities), higher-income blacks may prefer to live away from poor blacks, so that this push-pull model may be fairly generally applicable, although the evidence on desire of higher-income whites to avoid poor whites is totally undeveloped.

Left in the wake of this outward movement are extremely depressed housing prices, along with unmaintained deteriorating structures in which the most destitute seek refuge in neighborhoods where other, abandoned structures attract perpetrators of property and personal crime. These adverse neighborhood conditions are a prime factor in keeping investors from improving the dwellings that are already available to the poor to satisfy the demand for housing which accompanies income growth.

Again, the situation in many metropolitan areas does not approach the bleakness of the abandonment problem in the worst cases, such as St. Louis and some other major cities. There is little doubt, however, that much housing which can still be serviceable is being wasted in the pattern of neglect and decay seen developing in many cities. The challenge which *is* being met in some places, is to take advantage of the reduction in the demand for low quality housing relative to its supply to limit or halt the growth of slums.

Before turning to a discussion of public policies, it is worth asking what the possibilities are that the market will correct the imbalances we have noted. Most of the declining neighborhoods are centrally located; and, although the singular importance of the central business district has clearly diminished, access to central locations is still prized. Further, the increased cost of new construction and the jump in the price of energy make the existing central city housing stock a more attractive investment than it was only a few years ago. It is probably too early to see what effect these inducements might have on the viability of the central city, although by 1973 no change in the rate of outmigration from the central cities was evident (table 12). Nevertheless, the ultimate hope for regaining a balance in the orderly development of the blighted central city probably rests on

Table 14

SELECTED CHARACTERISTICS OF THE BOSTON AND
PITTSBURGH METROPOLITAN AREAS (1950-70)

A. General Characteristics

Characteristics	Pittsburgh			Boston		
	1950	1960	1970	1950	1960	1970
Population						
Metropolitan area, total (000's)	2,213	2,405	2,401	2,370	2,589	2,754
Proportion blacks:						
Metropolitan area	.062	.067	.071	.022	.030	.046
Central city	.122	.167	.202	.050	.091	.163
Suburbs	.035	.034	.035	.007	.008	.011
Vacancy Rates						
Metropolitan area, total	.01	.02	.02	.01	.02	.02
Central City	.01	.03	.04	.01	.04	.05
Suburbs	.01	.02	.02	.01	.02	.02
Median Family Income, in 1967 dollars[a]						
All families	4,632	6,579	8,365	5,059	7,731	9,811
Families headed by whites	NA	6,724	8,560	NA	7,812	9,990
Families headed by blacks	NA	4,269	5,448	NA	5,141	5,727
Source of change in the black population 1960-1970						
Natural increase (000's)	NA	NA	13	NA	NA	21
Net migration (000's)	NA	NA	−6	NA	NA	26

B. Characteristics of Black Neighborhoods [b]

Characteristic	Pittsburgh			Boston		
	1950	1960	1970	1950	1960	1970
Percent of population black	52	61	72	55	55	68
Mean real family income, in 1967 dollars [a]	2,300	4,800	7,600	2,900	5,700	6,300
Percent of dwellings vacant	1	4	9	1	6	9
Percent of dwellings						
With complete plumbing facilities [c]	44	80	92	66	79	85
With central heat	55	60	76	61	81	78
In single unit structures	32	50	49	6	10	19

a. Income of families and unrelated individuals in 1950; for 1960 and 1970, income of families.

b. Black neighborhoods were defined as those groups of contiguous census tracts each with at least 20 (30) percent of the population black in Boston (Pittsburgh). These limits were determined on the basis of the fraction black at which tracts became extremely unlikely to stabilize their racial mix, based on the 1960-70 experience. A single black neighborhood was defined for Boston, 4 for Pittsburgh.

c. Includes piped hot and cold water and exclusive use of toilet and tub or shower.

Source: Tables 3, 4, and 7 of A. Schnare and R. Struyk, "An Analysis of Ghetto Housing Prices over Time," op. cit., and U.S. Bureau of the Census, *The Social and Economic Status of the Black Population in the United States, 1971* (Washington, D.C.: U.S. Government Printing Office, 1972).

broad market forces, including further changes in household preferences concerning their neighborhoods, rather than on specific public action.

Improving the Housing Conditions of the Poor

Conceptually, at least, the housing of low-income families can be divided into structural and neighborhood components, where the latter includes all of the nonstructural services associated with a dwelling—public services, protection against crime, cleanliness of the block, and so on. Were the poor not spatially concentrated, policies for improving their housing situation could be focused largely on the structural issue. But even with the segregation of many low-income families, focusing on the comparatively straightforward structural aspects offers a convenient starting point.

The central theme of a policy discussion on how to improve the structural housing condition of the urban poor should be the proposition that, as a first approximation, bad housing is due to low income. A subsidiary theme is that the widely varying housing conditions existing in individual metropolitan areas make it imperative to tailor the mix of income subsidies and other, more direct housing programs to specific metropolitan housing situations.

One elementary consequence of the basic proposition is that the current public policies which most importantly affect the housing of poor people are income policies rather than government policies specifically related to housing. The term "housing policies" suggests to most people subsidies for new construction, mortgage market regulations, and other measures dealing with housing market. But social security, welfare payments, and other programs affecting how much money people have available to spend on housing have far more effect on the housing consumption of most low-income households. In the absence of such programs the housing conditions of the poor would be appreciably worse than they are at present.

The specific housing market programs used in the past in this country placed heavy emphasis on new construction subsidies, in effect lowering the price per unit of housing services to households with qualifying incomes. Some of them, like conventional public housing, have directly provided new dwellings for occupancy by low-income families. Others, like the Section 235 and Section 236 programs of the 1968 Housing Act, have provided direct subsidies for moderate-income families, on the assumption that by removing moderate-income families from competition for existing housing the supply available to the poor would be increased. Similarly, the insurance activities of the Federal Housing Administration, while not providing any overall subsidy, had the effect of stimulating construction via the demand for single-family dwellings. According to the evidence, this so-called "filtering" strategy has been successful in increasing the supply of dwellings to low-income households, but, as argued earlier, the current desirability of this strategy is open to question.

While acknowledging the indirect effects of such programs, it is nevertheless instructive to look at the income distribution of households participating in some of these programs as shown in table 15. The salient point to emerge from these data is that only a small fraction of the eligible households are served by the programs, and this feature creates major inequities among households of the same income. In fact, in 1972 only about 60 percent of the $2.4 billion expended for the programs listed in the table directly benefited households with 1972 incomes under $5,000.

Table 15

DISTRIBUTION OF HOUSEHOLDS SERVED BY MAJOR
HOUSING PROGRAMS AS OF DECEMBER 1972[a]

Gross Income (1972)	Households Served (000)	Total Households (000)	Households Served as Percent of Total Households	Income Distribution of Households Served (percent)
$0–999	29	1,800	2	1.6
1,000–1,999	320	3,800	8	17.8
2,000–2,999	293	4,300	7	16.3
3,000–3,999	244	4,999	5	13.6
4,000–4,999	230	3,800	6	12.8
5,000–5,999	230	3,800	6	12.8
6,000–6,999	198	3,600	5	11.0
7,000–9,999	227	11,200	2	12.6
$10,000 or more	25	32,300	b	1.4
Total	1,795	68,500	3	100.0

a. Programs included are: low rent public housing, rent supplement, and Sections 235, 236, 502 Interest Credit, and 504 of the National Housing Act as amended.

b. Less than .05.

Source: Table 9 of U.S. Department of Housing and Urban Development, *Housing in the Seventies* (Washington, D.C.: U.S. Government Printing Office, 1974).

Moderate-income households received the rest, and this causes inequities in income redistribution between households of different income classes in addition to inequities between households within each class.[45]

The direct programs have also been flawed by not being tuned to specific market conditions. In markets characterized by a surplus of low quality units, and hence lower prices per unit of housing service for low quality dwellings than for higher quality and new units, subsidies for new construction are a very costly way to provide minimum standard housing, compared to upgrading the existing stock. On the other hand, in markets where low quality housing is in short supply relative to the demand for it, new units make economic sense.[46]

Spurred in part by dissatisfaction with features of the existing programs, there has recently been considerable discussion and some action related to giving housing subsidies directly to consumers. These subsidies basically increase the amount of money people have to spend on housing. Unlike most housing programs, they are not linked to new construction, and unlike most other income transfer programs, they try to channel a big share of the subsidy into housing rather than leave the housing proportion up to recipients. These subsidies thus fall somewhere between income transfers on the one hand and construction subsidies on the other. Experimental "housing allowance" programs are underway at a dozen or so sites across the country.[47] In addition, the Section 8 phase of the public housing pro-

---

[45] The data in the table woefully understate the benefits to households from non-program sources, especially the provisions of the Internal Revenue Code. Renter households pay lower rents due to the allowance of accelerated depreciation, and owner-occupants are able to deduct tax and mortgage interest payments and to not report imputed rental income from the structure. While there are no reliable estimates of the benefits to renters, Aaron (op. cit., chap. 4) estimates that the benefits to homeowners were at least $7 billion in 1967, and much of this amount accrues to higher-income households. A more recent but less comprehensive estimate ascribes nearly $12 billion to homeowners in fiscal 1976; see *Special Analyses, Budget of the United States Government, Fiscal Year 1976* (Washington, D.C.: U.S. Government Printing Office, 1975) pp. 108-9.

[46] For some estimates of the cash equivalents required to achieve household satisfaction equal to that of some of the direct programs, see chap. 4 of U.S. Department of Housing and Urban Development, *Housing in the Seventies* (Washington, D.C.: U.S. Government Printing Office, 1974). A comparison of the efficacy of new construction programs under differing market conditions is provided in chapter 6 of F. de Leeuw and R. Struyk, *The Web of Urban Housing* (Washington, D.C.: The Urban Institute, 1975).

[47] For an overview description of these experiments, see U.S. Department of Housing and Urban Development, *Experimental Housing Allowance Program: Initial Impressions and Findings* (Washington, D.C.: HUD, Office of Policy Development and Research, 1975).

gram, under which local housing authorities lease dwellings in the private market and then sublet them at a discount to low-income tenants, resembles in many ways an earmarked income subsidy.

There is a continuing policy debate about how to provide better housing to the poor and about the strengths and weaknesses of these alternative approaches and the best way to combine them. The remainder of this section discusses these questions, but does not discuss the question of *how much* assistance to transfer from the well-off to the poor. This question may be even more important than the question of alternative approaches, but its answer lies beyond the analytical tools of social scientists, in the values society holds and the political accommodations it develops. Rather, we evaluate the approaches in terms of conceptual economic criteria, administrative feasibility, political acceptability, and effects on slums.

Among alternative approaches, income transfers have three strong advantages over construction subsidies or subsidies to households earmarked for housing. One is that a general income subsidy tends to be much simpler to administer than subsidies channeled through a particular market or earmarked for a particular kind of consumption. The second is that a general income approach is much less likely than a specific market program to create unintended and adverse side effects such as price inflation in a particular market or excessively high tax rates at some income levels resulting from the pyramiding of the income tax rates and the rates at which program benefits are reduced as income increases. The third is that the recipients of a general subsidy have more freedom in choosing what to buy than do recipients of earmarked subsidies or occupants of subsidized low-rent dwellings; and recipients therefore value unrestricted dollars more than restricted cash grants or in-kind transfers. As a broad strategy for reducing poverty, general income assistance is probably preferable to housing assistance.

On the other side, an argument for an approach specifically focused on housing is the fact that neither the public nor the Congress necessarily face a choice between the income approach and a housing approach. There are times when there is strong interest-group support for housing programs buttressed by feelings on the part of some that housing is a "merit good" deserving more attention than other forms of consumption. There are also times when there is a legislative impasse with respect to general income assistance programs but some willingness to try other kinds of assistance programs. Finally, the cost of a comprehensive income maintenance program is high, possibly double or triple that of a housing allowance and much greater than all direct federal expenditures on housing.[48] In these situations the choice is not between a housing program and a general income transfer program but between a housing program and some other method of using or redistributing national resources. Housing programs, either in the form of dwelling subsidies or of earmarked demand subsidies, may then be the preferred choice.

In addition to the "political" arguments for housing programs of some kind, there are several economic arguments for subsidies to suppliers. The first, related to the nature of the supply of existing housing, is that if there is a large-scale increase in the demand for housing by poor people because of either a housing allowance or a direct income subsidy, the prices which families in the low or moderate quality sector of the housing market have to face might rise significantly. Higher demand in these sectors must be met either by upgrading the existing low quality dwellings, which is often a very expensive process, or through the depreciation of higher quality dwellings. If serious inflation is induced by either an earmarked or a general income subsidy, part of the subsidy will be a transfer to landlords or to the persons they pay rather than to low-income families. If some subsidy to suppliers to produce additional housing or to upgrade their dwellings more quickly accompanies earmarked subsidies to the consumer, it may serve to limit this leakage of the subsidy to landlords.

An argument against a comprehensive program of cash grants to households, on the other hand, is that they could have unintended consequences for property owners. One can readily imagine a substantial wave of household relocations as recipients try to improve their housing-neighborhood situations. Thus, owners of properties the recipients no longer wanted to live in, or of properties in undesirable neighborhoods, or even of properties into which recipients move, in neighborhoods where socioeconomic conditions were superior before the program was implemented —all could suffer significant capital losses. Others would enjoy windfall profits. Supplier targeted subsidies may not be the answer in this instance either; still, such side effects need to be considered in assessing cash transfers.

A few other broad points seem warranted. One is that subsidizing the construction of new housing for low-income families in markets where there is an oversupply of low quality dwellings will merely worsen the

---

[48] Estimated costs of universal negative income tax are from table 7-12 in B. M. Blechman, E. M. Gramlich, and R. W. Hartman, *Setting the National Priorities: The 1975 Budget* (Washington, D.C.: The Brookings Institution, 1975); the cost of a national housing allowance program is based on analysis done with the Transfer Income Model (TRIM) at The Urban Institute, the same model used to estimate costs of the negative tax program.

basic situation. More generally, a national housing policy—some particular intervention to be applied in a fixed manner in all metropolitan areas—is a simplistic notion which must be replaced with program mixes designed for individual areas. Where abandonment is occurring, sharp actions should be taken to destroy the abandoned units, particularly where whole neighborhoods are involved. At best, the destruction would improve the possibility of other investment occurring on the sites; and at minimum it would remove hazardous physical structures. In this regard it might be noted that cities with aggressive urban renewal projects in the 1960s, which destroyed thousands of the worst dwellings, have (rather accidentally) mitigated the abandonment problem in the present decade.

We have said nothing thus far about programs like Model Cities which are designed to improve the general conditions in neighborhoods, to create a heightened sense of community, and hence to help stabilize housing and families. Such programs are not generally viewed as having achieved their goals. It is easy to understand the problems that have beset such attempts: the poverty in the areas involved made various community-action associations look like luxuries; the instability of households worked against any neighborhood cohesion; and, in some areas, the deterioration of neighborhood conditions defeated any steps toward preservation or improvement. If one removes the impediment of poverty or at least attains adequate structural housing for those who are presently slum residents, greater success will still be debatable unless some greater stability is achieved. The major stabilizing forces have already been noted, but it is possible to improve the condition of streets, parks, and lighting and other public services—trash collection, street cleaning, and so on—to produce a positive effect on the attitudes of residents and producers of housing services. For these purposes, the funds made available under the Housing and Community Development Act of 1974—which allows localities considerable latitude in housing-related expenditures—may prove instrumental.

While the challenge of improving the overall housing situation of the poor should not be underestimated, enormous progress has been made, and more is possible. Indeed, the continued growth of family income, combined with reductions in migration rates, makes further progress likely. Furthermore the continuing changes in the attitudes of households about the socioeconomic status of their neighbors may also facilitate improvement. The main role of a national government in reducing slums is largely indirect. It can aid by providing the resources to attain minimal structural housing quality for all households, but public intervention must be carefully designed for the conditions in each metropolitan area.

APPENDIX A

Table A-1

RACIAL EXPOSURE IN SELECTED METROPOLITAN AREAS (1960 AND 1970)

	White "Exposure"[a]						Black "Exposure"					
	Average SMSA		Low-income neighborhoods		High-income neighborhoods		Average SMSA		Low-income neighborhoods		High-income neighborhoods	
	1960	1970	1960	1970	1960	1970	1960	1970	1960	1970	1960	1970
Akron	.043	.040	.075	.077	.0168	.0106	.498	.458	.451	.419	.805	.929
Atlanta	.080	.061	.183	.144	.0259	.0268	.273	.215	.233	.166	.727	.584
Austin	.073	.058	.119	.095	.0363	.0219	.501	.475	.431	.426	.868	.942
Beaumont	.082	.084	.337	.263	.0197	.0108	.270	.303	.231	.284	.869	.877
Canton	.034	.030	.073	.085	.0039	.0043	.598	.570	.581	.553	.975	.977
Cincinnati	.046	.050	.107	.090	.0140	.0271	.277	.333	.236	.266	.896	.637
Cleveland	.034	.035	.080	.082	.0054	.0120	.205	.186	.191	.158	.651	.457
Columbus	.055	.048	.116	.097	.0041	.0106	.423	.360	.413	.339	.988	.623
Dallas	.048	.039	.097	.083	.0120	.0084	.281	.212	.254	.193	.727	.629
Dayton	.034	.029	.090	.040	.0042	.0210	.227	.239	.213	.178	.965	.499
Fort Worth	.032	.032	.060	.060	.0095	.0134	.266	.268	.233	.226	.904	.668
Galveston	.121	.102	.265	.234	.0507	.0228	.447	.417	.376	.387	.880	.808
Houston	.068	.075	.139	.167	.0227	.0200	.274	.314	.239	.287	.635	.611
Los Angeles	.026	.034	.051	.059	.0035	.0121	.352	.280	.337	.247	.841	.644
Macon	.191	.173	.363	.318	.0887	.0750	.381	.424	.311	.360	.830	.845
Sacramento	.031	.036	.054	.053	.0085	.0198	.756	.738	.740	.700	.875	.880
San Antonio	.040	.034	.056	.055	.0228	.0106	.564	.469	.502	.433	.822	.941
San Diego	.024	.023	.046	.042	.0049	.0075	.621	.520	.602	.506	.845	.606
San Francisco	.046	.051	.086	.103	.0077	.0125	.484	.430	.466	.398	.835	.901
San Jose	.006	.016	.010	.025	.0030	.0071	.962	.943	.966	.942	.968	.979
Savannah	.145	.111	.367	.352	.0791	.0612	.281	.220	.192	.137	.777	.808
Springfield	.068	.051	.132	.101	.0262	.0111	.659	.555	.613	.525	.878	.948
Toledo	.034	.038	.069	.073	.0063	.0059	.329	.355	.306	.335	.906	.908
Youngstown	.069	.049	.139	.108	.0049	.0088	.521	.468	.512	.442	.961	.897

a. The category "white" includes a small proportion of Orientals and Indians.

Table A-2

REGRESSIONS OF BLACK EXPOSURE ON THE NUMBER OF BLACKS

Dependent Variable	Ln (Black Exposure)		
Sample	SMSA	High-income tracts	Low-income tracts
Independent Variables			
Constant	1.80	.879	1.79
	(4.21) a	(6.03)	(3.54)
Ln (Number of black)	−.250	−.129	−.260
	(6.59)	(7.68)	(5.82)
State Dummy (1 = California/	.390	.026	.468
0 = others)	(2.68)	(0.39)	(2.65)
R²	.58	.58	.53
Number of Observations	48	48	48

a. t-statistics in parentheses.

Table A-3

INDICES OF RESIDENTIAL SEGREGATION FOR SELECTED METROPOLITAN AREAS (1960 AND 1970)

	Index Based on "Exposure Rates"		"Taeuber" Index of Dissimilarity	
	1960	1970	1960	1970
Akron	45.9	50.3	78.1	77.0
Atlanta	64.7	72.5	76.6	80.9
Austin	42.6	46.7	63.3	71.3
Beaumont	64.8	61.3	66.6	77.7
Canton	37.0	39.5	74.6	76.8
Cincinnati	67.7	61.8	72.7	69.0
Cleveland	76.1	77.9	90.4	87.8
Columbus	52.1	59.3	75.3	79.1
Dallas	67.2	74.9	80.3	84.3
Dayton	74.0	73.2	96.8	86.8
Fort Worth	70.2	70.0	84.3	87.0
Galveston	43.2	48.1	64.3	71.4
Houston	65.8	61.1	80.0	77.6
Los Angeles	62.2	68.6	88.2	87.0
Macon	42.8	40.3	44.0	56.0
Sacramento	21.3	22.7	71.5	63.5
San Antonio	39.7	49.8	76.7	72.4
San Diego	35.5	45.6	77.9	72.3
San Francisco	47.0	51.9	78.1	74.9
San Jose	3.5	4.3	65.6	51.8
Savannah	57.4	66.9	69.4	75.1
Springfield	27.3	39.4	60.9	68.1
Toledo	63.8	60.7	82.9	75.1
Youngstown	41.0	48.5	50.5	78.6

Table A-4

TRENDS IN FAMILY INCOME BY RACE (1947-1972)
IN CONSTANT 1972 DOLLARS
(Percent distribution)

Income	Year			
distribution	1947	1960	1970	1972
All families				
Under $5,000	42.3	27.0	17.3	16.6
$5,000 to $10,000	41.2	39.3	28.7	27.0
Over $10,000	16.5	33.7	54.0	56.4
White families				
Under $5,000	38.9	23.9	15.3	14.5
$5,000 to $10,000	43.1	40.2	28.3	26.4
Over $10,000	18.0	35.9	56.4	59.1
Black and other races				
Under $5,000	75.5	54.5	34.3	35.2
$5,000 to $10,000	19.3	32.1	33.7	31.1
Over $10,000	5.2	13.4	29.0	33.7

Source: Social and Economic Statistics Administration, U.S. Buureau of the
Census, *Consumer Income,* Current Population Reports, Series P-60,
no. 87, June 1973.

Table A-5

RATES OF NATURAL INCREASE AND NET MIGRATION
BY RACE (1960 TO 1970)
(percentages)

Standard Metropolitan Statistical Areas by Rank, 1970	White		Negro and Other Races	
	Natural Increase	Net Migration	Natural Increase	Net Migration
New York, N.Y.	6.6	− 6.1	23.6	37.7
Inside central city	5.1	−14.4	23.4	38.2
Outside central city	10.1	13.9	25.3	33.7
Los Angeles-Long Beach, Calif.	10.5	− 0.4	28.3	47.0
Inside central cities	7.5	− 2.8	26.0	29.6
Outside central cities	12.9	1.5	34.9	96.3
Chicago, Ill.	9.8	− 2.6	25.2	16.2
Inside central city	5.2	−23.8	24.9	13.5
Outside central city	14.5	19.6	28.9	45.8
Philadelphia, Pa.-Camden, N.J.	8.4	− 0.6	18.0	9.9
Inside central cities	3.9	−16.8	17.8	7.4
Outside central cities	11.4	10.2	18.6	19.3

Table A-5 continued

Standard Metropolitan Statistical Areas by Rank, 1970	White		Negro and Other Races	
	Natural Increase	Net Migration	Natural Increase	Net Migration
Detroit, Mich.	12.0	— 4.9	18.2	19.3
Inside central city	3.6	−32.7	18.0	20.0
Outside central city	16.9	11.4	19.2	14.8
San Francisco-Oakland, Calif.	8.6	2.5	23.9	38.2
Inside central cities	0.5	−17.7	22.6	28.7
Outside central cities	13.5	14.7	27.4	62.4
Washington, D.C.-Md.-Va.	17.3	19.3	22.3	23.0
Inside central cities	0.7	−40.1	21.5	9.2
Outside central cities	21.9	35.9	27.6	117.9
Boston, Mass. (state economic area)	8.7	— 1.8	29.4	39.1
Inside central cities	4.8	−17.5	31.2	38.7
Outside central cities	10.2	4.2	21.9	41.0
Pittsburgh, Pa.	6.4	— 7.2	12.4	— 2.5
Inside central city	1.7	−19.7	12.3	— 6.3
Outside central city	7.7	— 3.7	12.6	6.1
St. Louis, Mo.-East St. Louis, Ill.	10.1	— 0.7	20.2	9.7
Inside central cities	2.4	−34.0	19.5	— 0.4
Outside central cities	13.3	13.3	22.0	37.2
Baltimore, Md.	9.9	1.3	19.3	9.1
Inside central city	3.1	−24.5	20.0	9.7
Outside central city	15.0	20.6	14.8	5.2
Cleveland, Ohio	9.3	— 4.7	17.6	12.9
Inside central city	6.7	−33.1	16.8	— 1.1
Outside central city	11.0	12.5	56.9	658.0
Houston, Texas	16.7	22.7	23.7	18.6
Inside central city	16.2	9.3	25.3	25.6
Outside central city	17.6	45.7	18.3	— 5.5
Newark, N.J.	6.7	— 4.2	26.9	32.4
Inside central city	3.4	−40.1	31.0	22.6
Outside central city	7.4	3.7	19.8	48.9
Minneapolis-St. Paul, Minn.	15.5	6.2	32.9	54.3
Inside central cities	8.8	−17.0	33.0	46.4
Outside central cities	23.1	32.5	30.6	150.9

Source: Table 12 in U.S. Bureau of the Census, Census of Population and Housing: 1970, *General Demographic Trends for Metropolitan Areas, 1960-1970*, Final Report PHC(2)-1 (Washington, D.C.: U.S. Government Printing Office, 1971).

Appendix B
DEFINITIONS OF SEGREGATION INDICES

A measure of segregation which is related to the exposure rates defined in the text compares the actual exposure rate of blacks to whites (BX) to the exposure rate that would arise if blacks were distributed evenly throughout the metropolitan area. The latter, of course, is equal to the fraction of the area's population that is white (1-m). Segregation is then defined by:

$$I_s = \left[1 - BX/(1\text{-}m) \right] \cdot 100$$

or, alternatively, by:

$$I_s = \left[1 - WX/m \right] \cdot 100$$

where WX is white exposure to blacks and m is area's proportion of blacks. Because the ratio of white to black exposure (WX/BX) is equal to the ratio of blacks to whites, m/(1-m), the two measures are equivalent.

They are also equivalent to a third measure, which compares the average interracial exposure rates of all households to the overall exposure that is possible:

$$I_s = \left[1 - \frac{mBX + (1\text{-}m)WX}{2m(1\text{-}m)} \right] \cdot 100$$

From the above formulation, it is obvious that our proposed index of segregation weights the exposure rate of each group by the relative size of its population.

An alternative measure of segregation is the well-known Taeuber index of dissimilarity, defined by:

$$D = 100 \cdot \left[1/2\Sigma_i (B_i/B - W_i/W) \right]$$

where B_i and W_i are the tract's number of blacks and whites, respectively, and where B and W are the corresponding metropolitan-wide population totals. Both the Taeuber index and the "exposure" index range from a minimum of zero to a maximum of 100, with 100 depicting an area where tracts are either all white or all black and with zero representing an equalized distribution of households. For other locational patterns the two indices typically differ and over time can display markedly different trends. In general, the Taeuber index appears to give greater weight to movements in the exposure rates of whites.

Chapter 4
Crime

James Q. Wilson
Barbara Boland

The high and rising levels of crime during a decade of widespread and generally increasing prosperity have given a greater plausibility and even urgency to efforts to deal with crime, not by eliminating its causes but by increasing the security of potential victims and by improving the effectiveness of the criminal justice system. Citizens, of course, have long been taking measures to make their homes and persons more secure, and the police and others have long argued for changes in the way we handle arrested offenders. But now scholars and public officials, having discovered that in the short run it is difficult if not impossible to alter those social conditions that stimulate crime, are displaying a greater interest in various protective and deterrent techniques.

To understand how great a change this is, one has only to recall that a decade ago (or less), many writers were arguing that the increase in crime then being reported was either nonexistent or highly questionable owing to defects in the methods by which crime statistics are collected and reported. The Uniform Crime Reports of the FBI are still gathered in about the same way as they were ten years ago, but now scarcely anyone denies that they show a genuine increase in crime. In part this is because so many citizens have been victimized that fewer are inclined to doubt the generality of crime. But there are also reasonable factual grounds for accepting this view. In 1966, the National Opinion Research Center, under contract to the President's Commission on Law Enforcement and Administration of Justice, conducted a survey of ten thousand households to find out how many had been victimized by crime. It found that just under 32 out of every thousand households had been burglarized in the preceding year. In 1973, the Bureau of the Census, acting under the direction of the Law Enforcement Assistance Administration, again conducted a victimization survey of a larger but somewhat differently drawn sample of households. The Census Bureau found that 94 out of every thousand households had been burglarized, suggesting that the burglary rate had increased by 195 percent during the seven-year period, 1966-1973. (Interestingly enough, the FBI Uniform Crime Reports gave the increase as 108 percent.) [1]

During this period, median personal income, in real dollars, was rising, the proportion of families living below the poverty line was declining, the quality of the housing stock was improving, and expenditures on police protection were growing. A cynic could find in these facts grounds for asserting that efforts to eliminate the presumed causes of crime—poverty, poor housing, etc.—and efforts to upgrade the quality of law enforcement have produced, not a decline in crime, but an increase.

Indeed, such a view may not be cynical at all, as there are plausible grounds for expecting this relationship to exist. Improved material standards may in the short run stimulate consumer expectations faster than they can be satisfied, leading some, especially the young, to steal more in order to keep pace with those who can afford to buy more. Some have argued that putting more policemen on the street may conceivably induce people to report crime more frequently.

In the long term, it may well be that the apparent positive relationship between rising incomes and rising crime will not hold, for several reasons. In the first place, higher income communities have on the whole less crime than those with lower income, and in the long run a lasting increase in the level of affluence and amenity in a community should contribute to a reduction in crime. But, of course, it is not income alone that affects crime. We know that middle-class communities produce less predatory crime than do lower-class communities, but "class," insofar as it is related to crime, is not simply a product of income. Middle-class communities also are more likely than lower-class ones to have intact families, a high level of achievement motivation, a concern for the good will and respect of others, and a stronger set of internalized rules and norms about

---

[1] Comparing the results of the 1966 and the 1973 surveys is difficult. We deal with some of the issues in the Appendix. See also, "Criminal Victimization in the United States," 1973 Advance Report, May 1975, U.S. Department of Justice, Law Enforcement Assistance Administration; Philip H. Ennis, *Criminal Victimization in the United States*, a report of the National Opinion Research Center to the President's Commission on Law Enforcement and Administration of Justice, May 1967; Federal Bureau of Investigation, *Uniform Crime Reports, 1973.*

traditionally acceptable behavior. Decent incomes and steady employment may be necessary conditions for the development of such attitudes (though in some cases even that is not clear), but they are far from being wholly responsible for them.

Furthermore, the effect of prosperity on crime has been confounded by the operation of other important social forces. The prosperity of the 1960s was accompanied, unlike some previous periods of prosperity, by a great increase in the youthful (that is, the crime-prone) component of the population and, though the changed age distribution cannot explain all (or even most) of the crime increase, it does explain some of it. The past decade has also witnessed a vast increase in the level of drug abuse, with an unmeasured but probably substantial effect on crime, especially theft. Finally, there was a sharp increase in the proportion of broken homes (i.e., of families with one parent absent).[2]

Whether or not economic and social policies that lead to improvements in housing, education, and job opportunities in high crime areas will yield large reductions in the crime rate is not an issue here. Good housing, education, and employment opportunities are desirable for their own sake. As a rough generalization, all of them are less available in high crime areas than elsewhere. To the extent that public policy can promote better housing, education and jobs in such areas, it should do so. But whatever the effects of crime rates on economic and social progress, they take a long time to be felt, and they will surely be more effective in an environment where the positive rewards of social behavior are reinforced by the expectation of fairly assessed penalties for antisocial behavior. For the present, therefore, we must deal with crime by selecting those variables that are subject to change at an acceptable cost and that if changed will significantly alter the rate at which crimes are committed. These variables, it turns out, are those that relate to the personal protection of the citizen, to the physical conditions that prevail in his neighborhood or community, and to the operation of the criminal justice system. They are to a large degree "mechanical"—that is, they involve constructing facilities, deploying equipment, or making decisions between feasible alternatives. We believe that there is no incompatibility between employing useful crime-reduction techniques, however mechanical, and addressing, by other means, larger social questions of employment, income distribution, family structure, and education. Indeed, we put the matter

[2] For a discussion of single-parent homes and juvenile delinquency, see H. L. Ross and I. V. Sawhill, *Time of Transition* (Washington, D.C.: The Urban Institute, 1975), pp. 133 ff.

more strongly: it is hard to imagine how many programs designed to improve education or employment can succeed when certain forms of crime disrupt the operation of schools and offer attractive alternatives to legitimate jobs.

Every survey in recent years has shown that the public ranks crime as a matter of great personal concern. Further, most people believe that the main reason why some persons become criminals has to do with some failing in their home life—a belief that is quite consistent with much, though not all, criminological research.[3] But as we shall point out later in this chapter, it is far from clear what society can do about weak or disorganized families that will reduce their contribution to criminal careers. Most citizens, black and white, believe the police are doing a good job, though young black males are quite critical of them.[4] Most citizens also believe the courts are "too lenient" in dealing with offenders.[5] But when asked to what kinds of prisons judges should send offenders, the vast majority—84 percent—believe that prisons should emphasize "rehabilitation." Interestingly, the higher one's education, the more one is likely to believe in rehabilitation, and whites are much more likely to believe in it than blacks. Citizens are not convinced that prisons have been very successful in rehabilitating offenders (only 5 percent think they do) but seem quite optimistic that it can be done.[6] As we shall see, there is little evidence to support that optimism.

It is not surprising that the public's views should be accurate on matters which immediately affect them and are salient to their deepest interests, while on matters, however important, that are more remote from their experience their beliefs should be inconsistent. Thus, it is no wonder that in the early 1960s citizens were well ahead of politicians and social scientists in recognizing the sharp increase in crime rates but were no better than politicians and social scientists in devising remedies for the problem.

I. PREDATORY CRIME

For our analysis of crime, we must first make some distinctions. We shall be concerned, as most citizens are concerned, not with all crime,

---

[3] Joint Commission on Correctional Manpower and Training, *The Public Looks at Crime and Corrections* (Washington, D.C., 1968), p. 5.

[4] James Q. Wilson, *Thinking about Crime,* (New York: Basic Books, 1975), chap. 6.

[5] Joint Commission, *The Public Looks at Crime and Corrections,* p. 6.

[6] Ibid., pp. 7-8.

but with predatory crime against innocent victims, usually for financial gain. For the most part we shall look at only one such type of predatory crime: robbery. Among the frightening crimes, it is quite common, and it often involves violence. In 1973 about 382,680 robberies were reported to police, two-thirds of them in cities of over 250,000 population.[7] For purposes of analysis robbery is an interesting crime because the characteristics of the offender as well as of the victim are usually known, whereas with crimes of stealth they are not.

Some may question why we emphasize one crime to the neglect of crime in general. To us, talking about crime "in general" is what requires justification. Crimes differ greatly in their incidence, costs, risks, and prevention, and measures intended to reduce one may have no effect whatsoever on another. Even the crime of robbery is too general a category; one must distinguish between residential robbery (often the unintended result of a burglar finding his victims at home), personal robbery on the street (muggings, holdups, and the like), and commercial robbery. Burglary affects four times as many citizens as robbery, and the financial loss in a typical burglary is greater than in a personal street robbery. We will, accordingly, devote some attention to burglary. But robbery is what most citizens have in mind when they speak of "crime in the street"—it occurs to a person, not to an unoccupied house; it involves force or the threat of force; and injuries can result, sometimes serious ones. It is mostly fear of robbery that induces many citizens to stay home at night and to avoid the streets, thereby diminishing the sense of community and increasing the freedom with which crimes may be committed on the streets. These psychic and communal costs of robbery, impossible to measure, are, we believe, so great as to make it the most costly of all common crimes.

Our measures of the number of robberies and of the characteristics of victims and assailants are taken from the household victimization surveys carried out by the U.S. Bureau of the Census for the Law Enforcement Assistance Administration. These surveys were conducted during late 1972, early 1973, and early 1974 in 26 cities.[8] In each household, the respondent was asked to list every crime committed against any and

---

[7] Federal Bureau of Investigation, *Uniform Crime Reports, 1973,* (Washington, D.C.: U.S. Government Printing Office), pp. 15-17.

[8] Atlanta, Baltimore, Boston, Buffalo, Chicago, Cincinnati, Cleveland, Dallas, Denver, Detroit, Houston, Los Angeles, Miami, Milwaukee, Minneapolis, Newark, New Orleans, New York, Oakland, Philadelphia, Pittsburgh, Portland (Oregon), St. Louis, San Diego, San Francisco, and Washington, D.C.

every member of that household aged 12 and over during the preceding year. (There were also surveys of commercial establishments, but they do not concern us here.)

These surveys employed the following definition of robbery: "Theft and attempted theft, directly from a person or commercial establishment, of property or cash by force or threat of force, with or without a weapon." Excluded from this definition are thefts from a person that involve no force or threat of force, such as purse snatching and pocket picking.

According to the citizens involved, about half of all the robberies reported to the Census Bureau had also been reported to the police. The robberies not reported tended to be the less serious ones: that is, attempted but unsuccessful robberies, robberies without injuries, or robberies involving minor degrees of assault. The proportion of all robberies said to have been reported to the police ranged from a low of 44 percent in Denver and San Francisco to a high of 65 percent in Miami.[9]

Persons who had been victimized by a robber were asked about the criminal's identity—sex, race, and whether there was one perpetrator or several. In about 95 percent of the robberies, information about the perpetrator was obtained. The vast majority of offenders were described as strangers; in about two-thirds of the cases there was more than one perpetrator; almost all offenders were identified as males. The racial identity varied greatly from city to city, reflecting, among other things, the number of blacks living in a city.

Two rates were calculated from these data. The *victimization rate* is the number of victimizations per thousand population aged 12 and over, as of the survey date. When more than one person was victimized in a single incident, each person counts as a separate victimization. Various age-, sex-, and race-specific victimization rates were also calculated: for example, the number of victimizations of black females per thousand black females living in the city. For the 26 cities, 17 per thousand whites and 26 per thousand nonwhites were victimized by robberies.[10]

The *offense rate* is the number of victimizations committed by persons with a particular characteristic (age, sex, race) per thousand per-

---

[9] These and other statistics relating to the victimization surveys were derived from unpublished census tabulations made available to us by the Law Enforcement Assistance Administration of the U.S. Department of Justice.

[10] It should be mentioned that the count of robbery victims in the LEAA victimization survey is different from the count of robberies in the FBI's *Uniform Crime Reports*. A single robbery incident involving three victims would be counted as one robbery by the *UCR*, but as three victimizations by the LEAA survey.

sons with that characteristic in the city. For example, the white offense rate for robbery is the number of victimizations committed by persons observed to be white per thousand white persons in the city. For the 26 cities, 76 percent of the robberies were reported as having been committed by nonwhites. The offense rate was 4.8 robberies per thousand whites and 58.6 per thousand nonwhites.

Not all robberies are of equal seriousness. A thirteen-year-old boy might be set upon by two bigger boys on the way to school and have his lunch money taken away. A sixty-five-year-old widow might be threatened with a gun and have the entire proceeds of her Social Security check taken. As we shall see, in some communities where robberies are comparatively rare, the lunch money episode might be reported to the police and recalled for the Census interviewers, while in another city where robberies are quite common, such an episode will be neither reported nor recalled. We attempt to control for the seriousness of the crime in certain calculations by using a rate of "serious robberies," which we define as those in which more than $10 is taken.

Victimization rates for robbery vary enormously by place, race, age, sex, and income. In general, the risk of being robbed is greater for blacks than for whites, for the young than for the old, for males than for females, and for the poor man than for the rich. The riskiest of the 26 cities is Detroit (31 robberies per thousand), the least risky is Miami (9 robberies per thousand). In Detroit, a nonwhite male under the age of 15 has about 9 chances in 100 of being robbed during a given year, which is more than five times the rate at which elderly white females are robbed in that city (1.8 chances per hundred for those over 65).

There are some exceptions to these patterns. In New York City, for example, whites earning over $25,000 a year are just as likely to be robbed as those earning under $3,000, and nonwhites in the upper-income brackets are *more* likely to be robbed than those in the lower ones. This probably reflects the fact that in New York, as opposed to many other cities, a disproportionate number of affluent persons, white and black, choose to live in the high-risk central city areas (i.e., Manhattan), whereas in other cities they would live in the lower-risk periphery.

In general, people in southern cities are less likely to be robbed than those in northern ones, even allowing for differences in the social composition of the city. Atlanta is 54 percent nonwhite and Dallas 26 percent, yet the robbery victimization rate in these cities is less than half what it is in Detroit (47 percent nonwhite) or Philadelphia (32 percent nonwhite).

If we take into account robberies in places of business, the risk rises substantially. Commercial establishments were robbed at the rate of 95 out of every thousand; among only retail establishments, the rate was 189 per thousand. (Adding burglary to the list of offenses increases the risk substantially. During the year preceding the survey, there were 45 robberies or burglaries for every 100 commercial establishments.)

The rates of personal victimization are for a single year only and may be higher or lower in earlier or later years. Assuming, however, that the chances of being robbed remain constant every year for persons in a given group, and assuming that no one is robbed before reaching the age of 12 and lives to age 65, one can calculate the lifetime probability of being robbed. For a black male in New York City, it is 84 chances in one hundred; for a black male in Detroit, it is 92 chances in one hundred.[11]

II. SELF-DEFENSE

The policy implications of the foregoing are not especially encouraging. A young, poor, black male in Detroit would be well advised to get older, become a woman, turn white, earn a high salary, and move to Miami. How he might go about following that advice is not clear.

And that is the difficulty. Many of the factors most dramatically associated with high victimization rates—age, sex, race—are not subject to planned change, and a major factor that *can* be altered—location—cannot be changed for large numbers of people without defeating the purposes of the change. Any given person moving from Detroit to Miami will experience a two-thirds reduction in his chances of being robbed, but if everyone in Detroit moved, Miami might well acquire Detroit's robbery rate.

Relocation

If movement from city to city is a practical approach to risk-reduction for only a part of the population, what about movement within a city?

---

[11] The probability of being a victim of at least one crime between the ages of 12 and 65 is approximately $1 - e^{-54a}$ where a is the age-specific victimization rate of a given area. For a mathematical derivation see Benjamin Avi-Itzhak and Reuel Shinnar, "Quantitative Models in Crime Control," *Journal of Criminal Justice*, vol. 1, 1973. Such calculations assume that each victimization in a given year occurs to a different individual. To the extent that victimizations are redundant, these calculations overstate the average risk to the entire population. On the other hand, ignoring redundant victimization understates the frequency of victimization of those who are affected.

Everyone is aware, of course, that in any city there seem to be "high crime" areas and many persons move to peripheral or suburban locations to avoid those areas. Studies many decades ago by the "Chicago school" of sociology suggested that crime and delinquency rates were at their highest in the innermost parts of a city, decreasing more or less steadily as one moved outward. On the other hand, public attention has recently been directed to the rapid apparent increase in suburban crime rates, leading some to suppose that no metropolitan location is any longer safe.

A crude answer to the question can be obtained from the crime rates calculated by the FBI for cities grouped by size and by urban or suburban location. As table 1 shows, the reported robbery rates are strongly correlated with city size while the burglary and breaking-and-entering rates are only weakly correlated with size. Robbery rates for cities of 250,000 to 500,000 population are only about half what they are for cities over 1 million population; burglary rates, on the other hand, are slightly higher for the middle-sized cities than for the very large ones. Burglary rates begin to decline with population for cities smaller than 250,000 but not nearly as steeply as do the robbery rates.

Table 1

RATES OF ROBBERY AND BURGLARY REPORTED TO THE
POLICE, BY URBAN POPULATION GROUPS (1973)
(per hundred thousand population)

Population group	Robbery rate	Burglary rate
6 cities over 1 million pop.	756.2	1850.4
21 cities, 500,000 to 1 million pop.	457.6	1964.1
31 cities, 250,000 to 500,000 pop.	396.9	2101.9
101 cities, 100,000 to 250,000 pop.	236.9	1807.1
264 cities, 50,000 to 100,000 pop.	145.2	1342.4
505 cities, 25,000 to 50,000 pop.	109.3	1138.3
1,271 cities, 10,000 to 25,000 pop.	60.9	965.5

Source: FBI, *Uniform Crime Reports 1973* (Washington, D.C.: U.S. Government Printing Office), pp. 104-5.

Among suburban cities (table 2), the robbery rate also declines with decreases in population—cities under 10,000 have only half the robbery rate of those 25,000 to 50,000. The burglary rate, on the other hand, seems about the same for all suburban cities whatever their size.

Table 2

RATES OF ROBBERY AND BURGLARY REPORTED TO THE
POLICE FOR SUBURBAN CITIES, BY POPULATION SIZE (1973)
(per hundred thousand population)

Population group	Robbery rate	Burglary rate
300 cities, 25,000 to 50,000 pop.	117.3	1102.8
833 cities, 10,000 to 25,000 pop.	64.7	992.6
1,526 cities under 10,000 pop.	51.4	935.5

Source: FBI, *Uniform Crime Reports 1973* (Washington, D.C.: U.S. Government
Printing Office), p. 106.

These aggregate totals conceal, however, a good deal of variation within cities. Reppetto, in his detailed analysis of residential burglary and
robbery in Boston, compiled crime reports for 39 "Reporting Areas"—
the smallest unit within the city by which police data are collected.
(There are 824 such areas in Boston.) To check the validity of police
reports, a victimization survey was conducted in 18 of these areas.
Reppetto concluded that the average annual burglary rate (per thousand dwelling units) was 39 in the innermost part of the city but only
12 in the outlying parts. However, there was also a good deal of variation
in the burglary rates between adjacent Reporting Areas, suggesting that
other factors than proximity to the core are also important. Among these
are the kinds of dwelling units (whether well-guarded, high-rise apartments or unguarded detached or duplex houses), the presence of valuable targets (the fashionable Back Bay was more heavily burgled than
adjacent, less affluent areas), and the existence of a strong community
organization (the Italian North End, highly cohesive, was less frequently
burgled than more disorganized areas with the same housing and income levels).[12]

In short, residential relocation within a metropolitan area can make a
substantial difference in the risk of robbery, even when measured by
the most aggregate statistics, and can also make a difference in the risk
of burglary, provided one chooses the neighborhood with great care.

Relocating oneself within a metropolitan area is obviously a more
practical matter than moving across the country. Even so, there are
limits to that policy. If everyone moves, there are few if any gains in

---

[12] Thomas A. Reppetto, *Residential Crime* (Cambridge, Mass.: Ballinger, 1974),
pp. 34-35, 47-78, 132-33.

safety; furthermore, some persons—blacks, for example—experience great difficulty in moving to a safer area. Either the costs of moving into such an area are high (in terms of community resistance, housing prices, or restrictive real estate practices) or the benefits to be obtained are rather low (if many crime-prone individuals of the population follow the pioneer black families into a new neighborhood, thereby increasing the crime rate). It is harder for law-abiding black families to put enough distance between themselves and non-law-abiding blacks than it is for law-abiding whites to separate themselves from criminal whites. Increasing numbers are managing to do it, however, and thus for them, as for most people, intrametropolitan relocation remains the best available means of reducing the risk of robbery; highly selective relocation may also reduce the risk of burglary, but not as much.

This is obvious to the average citizen and millions of Americans have acted on this knowledge. The problem for those concerned with public actions to reduce crime is to find less obvious and perhaps less costly means for further reducing the risk of victimization, especially for those who cannot or will not relocate. The list of alternatives is discouragingly small.

Hardening the Target

One form of personal risk reduction is to "harden the target"—that is, to increase the costs of committing a crime at the point where the crime is apt to occur, by making an object harder to steal, a building harder to enter, or an alarm summoning the police more likely to be triggered.

Since a large proportion of all burglaries are committed by unskilled persons who often act opportunistically rather than by careful plan, devices that ward against illicit entry into a building can often prevent the crime. (There are few, if any, devices that will defeat a determined professional thief.)

While some methods of hardening the target may reduce the occupant's risk of crime, they may also result in displacing the crime to unhardened targets nearby. For example, if I place deadbolt locks on all my doors, the chances that my less cautious neighbor will be victimized may go up. We can find no well-designed studies that test either the security or displacement effects of locks and alarms. Arlington, Virginia, amended its county code in December 1971 to require deadbolt locks on all apartment doors and special latches on all first-floor windows. By the end of 1973, all but 2 percent of the apartments were reported to be in compliance with the law. Apartment burglaries dropped sharply in February 1972 and remained well below 1971 levels throughout the year. Complete data from 1973 are not available, but apartment burglaries were starting to rise again in early 1973. Burglaries of houses, not covered by the law, rose during 1972.[13] Some of this house burglary may reflect displacement from apartments.

Burglar alarms have not been comprehensively evaluated. One California study found that one-half of the burglaries of sites equipped with alarms were not detected because the burglars defeated the alarms; furthermore, the false-alarm rate was very high.[14] It is possible, however, that even with many false and nullified alarms, the proportion of burglars caught entering alarm-equipped spaces is higher than the proportion caught entering spaces without alarms. The best study of this we can find was carried out in Cedar Rapids, Iowa, beginning in 1969. Silent alarms connected to the police station were placed in over one hundred locations, and these sites were matched to a control group consisting of an equal number of buildings without alarms. During 1970-1971, the burglary rate in the places with alarms was as high as the rate in places without them—about one-fourth of the locations in each group were burgled. But in the sites with alarms, arrests of burglars on the scene were four times as frequent as on-scene arrests at sites without alarms.[15]

Street lighting is popularly supposed to be an effective deterrent to street robberies. Most of the studies on which these suppositions rest are of little value since they rely on only short-term observation of changes in the crime rates on lighted streets. They do not take into account the possible displacement of crime or determine whether the effects are long-lasting, and they do not specify control areas to measure the effects of other changes not related to lighting. One of the few studies attempting to surmount these limitations was carried out in Kansas City, Missouri, in 1971-1972. Bright new lights were placed on about 500 city blocks. Analysts from the University of Michigan compared changes in reported crime rates in 129 of these blocks before and after the relighting and also compared the after-lighting results on these blocks with crimes reported in a sample of similar blocks that were not relighted. Nighttime, on-the-street crimes of violence—assault and battery

---

[13] Thomas W. White, et al., *Police Department Programs for Burglary Prevention* (Washington, D.C.: The Urban Institute, 1975), pp. 24-25, 54.

[14] Ibid., p. 33.

[15] Ibid., pp. 71-72.

—decreased by 48 percent after the blocks were relighted. On the un-relighted control blocks, these crimes decreased by only 7 percent. As a further check, the authors looked at crimes being commited during the day or indoors in the relighted blocks and found that neither of these categories of crime showed any decrease during the study. They could not directly measure the amount of street crime displaced to nearby unrelighted streets, but they estimated that about one-fourth of the nighttime drop in crime on relighted streets had been so dis-placed. In short, the analysts concluded that a genuine reduction in street robberies and assaults at night occurred in the relighted blocks, although there was no statistically significant reduction in burglaries or larcenies.[16]

A good deal of attention has been given to the possibility of reducing personal risk by technological means—equipping citizens with alarms, whistles, mace, guns, and even bullet-proof vests to permit them to resist robbery, summon help, or frighten off the robber. There is no in-formation of which we are aware that indicates whether any of these measures work but there is a great deal of data showing that the vast majority of citizens do not use them. In the victimization survey, re-spondents were asked whether they took any self-protective measures at the time they were robbed or assaulted. About half said they did, but in most cases this consisted of hitting the attacker with the bare hand or running away. Scarcely anyone used a weapon and, interestingly enough, only a small minority yelled for help. The likelihood of fighting or run-ning was greatest, not surprisingly, for the younger victims; older vic-tims were more likely merely to yell, if indeed they did anything. It is possible that equipping those who cannot fight or run with more effective ways of yelling—an alarm, for example—might help them avoid losses, but it seems unlikely that any government program to do this would attract much interest. Various alarms are on the market now, yet few use them. Citizens who refuse to use seat belts in their cars are not likely to tote around robbery alarms, especially since no one knows whether the alarms will make matters better or worse.

Though it is unrealistic to expect citizens to protect themselves in ways that are either costly or risk-enhancing, it may be more realistic to devise ways to protect the areas in which citizens move. In 1971, two major studies were published addressed to the problem of achieving

---

[16] Roger Wright, et al., *The Impact of Street Lighting on Street Crime,* a report to the National Institute of Law Enforcement and Criminal Justice, U.S. Depart-ment of Justice, mimeographed, May 1974.

"defensible space," one by Oscar Newman, and the other by William Fairley and Michael Liechenstein. The Newman study is concerned with how best to design housing projects so that their features will discourage criminals *from* using, and encouraging residents *to* use, public spaces in and around buildings.[17] IIis data, and data from the New York City Housing Authority, suggest that the rate of robberies and burglaries in housing projects increases as the height of the building increases from about five to about thirteen stories; the crime rate is unaffected by height below five stories or above thirteen. Furthermore, robberies and other crimes against persons are most likely to occur in low-visibility public spaces: elevators, stairwells, walled-in lobbies, and corridors with frequent turns. Finally, projects with many dwelling units have higher crime rates than those with few units, independent of building height.

Fairley and Liechenstein, on the other hand, take the existing design of a building as given and estimate the effectiveness of various security systems—locks, alarms, guards, surveillance equipment, and so forth. Like Newman, they carried out no experiment that involved making and evaluating the changes; furthermore, the data employed are frequently rough estimates. Their conclusions are, not surprisingly, that security systems do make a difference in victimization, both for robbery and for burglary occurring in buildings, but that the effectiveness of these systems is closely related to their cost. The cheapest system—locking the lobby door and having an intercom with which visitors announce themselves—is the least effective; the most expensive system—locks plus a full-time guard in the lobby, surveillance by closed-circuit television, and individual alarm systems in each apartment—was the most effective.[18]

Newman's proposal is helpful to those planning new buildings but of little value to those occupying existing ones. For an existing building, the cost of adopting the most effective security system would necessitate an increase of 37.7 percent in the monthly rent per tenant. Affluent tenants can and do pay these costs; poor tenants cannot.

Whether citizens should be expected to absorb the full cost of design and security features intended to reduce crime or whether some or all of these features are public goods properly eligible for public financing is an interesting and complex question. Clearly, low-rise, low-density public housing projects with ample security systems are much more expensive

---

[17] Oscar Newman, *Defensible Space* (New York: MacMillan, 1972).

[18] William Fairley and Michael Liechenstein, *Improving Public Safety in Urban Apartment Dwellings* (New York: Rand Institute, 1971).

than conventional projects; just as clearly, public expenditures on such projects are now set sufficiently low to discourage extensive use of "defensible space" concepts.

III. PUBLIC DEFENSE

The crime-reduction measures thus far considered have one thing in common: they by and large involve self-protection measures that require the active participation of the would-be victims of crime. Some measures, such as residential relocation, offer any given individual the opportunity to substantially reduce the risk of victimization. No direct public outlays would be required for this "policy" but neither can such a policy be useful for more than a fraction of potential victims. Furthermore, the gains to the individual would be greater with respect to robbery than with respect to burglary. Other self-protection measures (as far as we can tell from very sketchy data) either offer little gain to the individual (as with personal self-protection measures) or require joint action by many individuals, which entails substantial shared or public expenses (as with building security projects).

We now turn to crime-reduction measures that involve policies aimed at actual and prospective criminals. To oversimplify, such policies may seek to change the preferences of actual or potential offenders, to change the behavior of potential offenders by altering the perceived costs and benefits of acting on the basis of unchanged preferences, or to prevent the predatory behavior of offenders by physically restraining them from acting on the basis of whatever preferences and whatever benefits.

When we change the preferences of potential criminals by increasing their attachment to law-abiding norms or by decreasing their taste for risk, we are engaged in *reducing the recruitment of criminals;* when we succeed in doing the same thing with persons who have already engaged in criminal acts, we say we have *rehabilitated* the offender. When we change the behavior of offenders by increasing the net costs of crime above the net benefits without altering the offender's attachment to law-abiding norms or his preference for risk, we can say we have *deterred* criminals. When we physically restrain offenders, usually by confining them in jails, we say we have *incapacitated* them.

Prevention and Rehabilitation

In recent years, grave doubts have been raised about the efficacy of known methods for either reducing the recruitment of criminals or rehabilitating existing ones. As for the latter strategy, the evidence to date seems fairly clear: no methods that have thus far been carefully evaluated give us any reason to believe that large numbers of convicted offenders can be rehabilitated in the sense that their future propensity to break the law is materially reduced as a result of deliberate third-party intervention.[19] This is not to say "Once a criminal, always a criminal": a large number of offenders do not become repeaters, whatever society may or may not do. Nor does it mean that society can do nothing of value to an offender when it has him in its clutches: illiterates can be taught to read, health problems can be remedied, job training can be provided, and all of these may be helpful to the inmate and perhaps even useful to society, although such programs, so far as present evidence suggests, do not significantly alter the chances that the offender will be a repeater.

The evaluation of rehabilitation programs has been the subject of a number of major studies, and their findings—almost without exception, negative—need not be reviewed here. Because important segments of public opinion as well as many judges and correctional officers believe that rehabilitation is possible, it is important to make it crystal clear that there is at present very little factual or scientific support for that belief. And it is not for want of trying: well over two hundred serious efforts have been made to discover whether rehabilitation works, many by persons who wanted it to work, but these efforts so far have come to little.

No such categorical judgment can be made about efforts to reduce the recruitment of first-time offenders. The fact that most young persons do not commit a serious crime while growing up suggests that *something* operates in our society, and in all societies, to induce conformity to law-abiding norms or the avoidance of the risk and stigma of arrest. Familial and peer group processes make most of us conform to most laws most of the time and to some laws all of the time. But these are processes that go on under private, not public, auspices and in ways that no government program has managed to duplicate. There has always been a substantial relationship between growing up in a disorganized, loveless family and getting in trouble with the law and

---

[19] Robert Martinson, "What Works?—Questions and Answers about Prison Reform," *The Public Interest*, no. 35, pp. 22 ff., 1974; and Wilson, *Thinking About Crime*, op. cit.

there is no reason to assume that that relationship—which we suspect is causal—will change.[20]

But the difficulty with any planned effort to reduce the recruitment of new offenders is that we do not know how to organize disorganized families or bring affection into loveless ones. And even if we knew how to do these things, we would either have to direct such programs to a very large number of persons—perhaps all persons—or we would have to devise a means of predicting who is likely to become a criminal and aim those programs at these few. The first approach is likely to be ruinously expensive, or—to put it more precisely—quite inefficient, for many resources would of necessity be spent on persons who, if left to their own devices, would become quite law-abiding anyway. The second approach may well lead us to stigmatize "problem" families by predicting for their offspring a criminal career—not a serious problem, perhaps, if our predictions are very reliable, but quite a problem if we score many "false positives" (i.e., if we wrongly predict that someone will become criminal). Our wrong predictions may become self-fulfilling prophecies. Furthermore, by the time we have enough information about a young person or his family to be reasonably sure that, without our intervention, he will head for a life of crime, he may have aged beyond the point where any preventive program can change him.

These statements should not be interpreted as conclusive arguments against any effort to prevent the recruitment of a new criminal. Rather, the intent is only to suggest how unlikely it is that we shall have many successes or even that we shall know whether or not we have succeeded. We continue to try, nonetheless, through the school system, counselling programs, and various forms of individual and group therapy, but factual evidence about the success of these programs in diverting persons from crime who otherwise would be disposed toward it is thus far fragmentary and unconvincing.

Nothing in this chapter should be read as an argument against improving the incomes and opportunities of citizens. It would be a mistake, however, to suppose that reducing poverty, improving housing, or equalizing educational opportunities will, of themselves and in the short run, contribute substantially to a reduction in predatory crime. Indeed, as stated at the outset of this chapter, the experience of the last decade

---

[20] See Thomas P. Monahan, "Family Status and the Delinquent Child," *Social Forces,* vol. 35, 1957, pp. 250-58; Urie Bronfenbrenner, "The Origins of Alienation," *Scientific American,* vol. 231, August 1974, pp. 53-61; Wilson, *Thinking About Crime,* op. cit.

is consistent with (but does not prove) the opposite view. The case for
public measures to improve the quality of life should therefore be based
on grounds other than the short-term impact of such improvements on
crime rates. Further, to the extent that crime does increase, at least
in the short run, during periods of prosperity, special effort should be
made to control it so that "rising crime" does not become a pretext for
discrediting other social policies and is not allowed to shift the costs
of social change onto those (the poor, the elderly) least able to afford
them.

It is, indeed, precisely the uncertain relationship between social progress
and crime, as well as the difficulties attendant on efforts to produce
social progress, that leads us in this chapter to emphasize those manage-
able institutional changes that may reduce crime or slow down its rate of
increase.

Disarming the Criminal

One often-suggested way to reduce murders, robberies, and other crimes
is to disarm criminals. But while there may be good arguments for gun
control with respect to some types of crime, it is not clear that it would
affect the robbery rate, and there is some chance that gun control, if
effective, would actually increase the number of persons injured in
robberies.

The most persuasive arguments for denying citizens access to hand
guns is that in a large number of assaults and murders the availability of
a gun can make the difference between a serious or fatal injury on the
one hand and a minor injury or none on the other. A fight between
friends, husband and wife, or relatives can become murder if, in the
heat of the moment, one party or both can lay hands on a gun even
though no one planned to use a weapon because no one had planned
to fight. The kind of gun also makes a difference: the larger its caliber
the greater the chances of a fatal injury.[21] Whether legislation could
be designed and implemented to remove a significant number of such
guns from the premises of those most likely to engage in deadly quarrels
is another matter, given the very large number of handguns in private
ownership, the unwillingness of people to surrender them voluntarily,
and the restrictions on police powers to search for and seize contraband.

All these difficulties are much greater in the case of robbery, for here

---

[21] Franklin E. Zimring and Gordon Hawkins, *Deterrence* (Chicago: University
of Chicago Press, 1973).

we are attempting to reduce, not the casual availability of a weapon, but the extent to which criminals planning a robbery can obtain and use one. Preventing a determined robber from finding a weapon seems much harder than preventing an irascible citizen from coming upon a weapon during a quarrel. On the other hand, we have not sufficiently explored the deterrent possibilities of making sentences for persons arrested for assault or robbery depend on whether or not a weapon was used. If assaulters and robbers knew that they would face a much higher penalty if caught with a weapon, they might be apt to use weapons less frequently.[22] Unfortunately, there have been few if any studies of this possibility and there is good reason to suspect that the courts do not act on this principle. In the case of assault, if friends or acquaintances are involved, the case is typically dropped without prosecution if the "victim" so wishes, whether or not a weapon was employed. In the case of street crimes, the police report great difficulty in finding judges who will impose penalties for illegal possession of weapons. Massachusetts now has on the books a law mandating a one year jail sentence for anyone caught with an unregistered gun, but experience with the law is too brief to permit an assessment of its effect.

But there is an even larger problem. Every study we can find shows that there is a *greater* chance of injury resulting from unarmed than from armed robberies.[23] The reason is simple: displaying a weapon makes the verbal threat of the robber credible to the victim. An unarmed robber must often use force instead of merely threatening it, and so the victim is struck. On the other hand, the greater cost of obtaining a gun may induce some would-be robbers (especially those of slight stature!) to forsake robbery for crimes not requiring force. Whether the reduction in total robberies would offset the increase in injuries from the greater proportion of unarmed robberies is an interesting problem in cost-benefit analysis; we know of no data with which to address it.

Deterrence

If prevention, rehabilitation, and disarmament are of uncertain value, and if we are not willing to lock ourselves indoors and thereby abandon

---

[22] Ibid.

[23] See Lynn A. Curtis, *Criminal Violence* (Lexington, Mass.: D. C. Heath, 1974), p. 115; Reppetto, *Residential Crime,* op. cit.; John Conklin, *Robbery and the Criminal Justice System* (Philadelphia: Lippincott, 1972); A. Normandeau, "Trends and Patterns in Crimes of Robbery," unpublished Ph.D. dissertation, University of Pennsylvania, 1968.

the streets to the criminal, it becomes important to look carefully at the deterrent effect of the criminal justice system. The renewed interest of late in deterrence reflects, in part, the belief, still under investigation, that we can more easily develop effective techniques in these areas than in those that require changing human attitudes; in part, the recognition that programs directed at known offenders may prove less costly than programs aimed at all potential offenders; and in part, the desire to avoid some of the unjust implications of the prevention and rehabilitation strategies (e.g., allowing prison terms to be affected by an inmate's prospects for rehabilitation rather than by the nature of his offense, or wrongly stigmatizing potential offenders).

Most deterrence theories are based on the assumption that would-be offenders are rational and take into account, however imprecisely, the costs and benefits of alternative courses of action. This assumption may be unwarranted for so-called "crimes of passion" (there are many who stoutly deny even this) but there is a growing body of evidence to suggest that it *is* at least warranted for crimes committed for material profit. Such theories also recognize that offenders may differ greatly from the law abiding population in their taste for risk and in how they value both the costs and benefits of crime, but that like everyone else they respond to incentives. That is, if the costs of crime are increased or the benefits drop, there will be some criminals for whom the benefits no longer outweigh the costs and there will be fewer crimes. These theories, however, tell us only that there should be some effect and nothing about the magnitude of the response that will be observed. The latter must be determined by empirical estimation.

Most empirical studies of deterrence do not test all aspects of the rational-actor model. The earliest and still the most numerous examples of these studies consider only the probability of imprisonment (the "certainty" of punishment) and the average length of a prison term (the "severity" of punishment), sometimes controlling for various population characteristics, such as race or region. The measure of certainty is the number of known offenses (say, robberies) divided into the number of persons sent to prison for that offense in a given year. The larger the ratio of sentences to offenses, the more "certain" the punishment. The measure of severity is the average time served in state prisons by persons convicted of a given offense. In general, these studies—summarized by Tittle and Logan and also by Tullock [24]—support the proposition that as the certainty of punishment for a given offense increases, the rate at which

---

[24] Charles R. Tittle and Allan R. Rowe, "Certainty of Arrest and Crime Rates," *Social Forces,* vol. 52, pp. 455-67, June 1974; and Gordon Tullock, "Does Punishment Deter Crime?" *The Public Interest,* no. 36, Summer 1974, pp. 103-11.

that offense is committed goes down. Results with respect to the severity of punishment are somewhat less consistent, but a number of researchers do report a negative relationship between crime rates and the average lengths of prison terms across jurisdictions. When an attempt is made to determine the relative importance of the two variables, the usual conclusion is that the frequency of punishment has a greater effect than the length of punishment.

Unfortunately, the "certainty" variable, primarily because of data constraints, neglects the fact that the probability of arrest for a given offense may or may not vary independent of the probability of being sentenced. Ideally, one would like to know the relative deterrent effect of each variable, since what deters may be the chance of being arrested rather than the chance of being imprisoned. This is no small matter, for only a small proportion of those arrested for a felony are imprisoned for one. We want to know whether it is better to invest more heavily in police resources or in court resources and prison space.

More sophisticated studies of deterrence generally use the same measures of certainty and severity but have the advantage of taking into account the benefits of legitimate alternatives to crime as well as the costs of crime. Ehrlich, for example, considers the would-be offender to be choosing between licit and illicit activities, each of which generates payoffs proportional to the time spent on them.[25] Participation in illicit activities (i.e., the crime rate in a given state) thus depends on the extent to which net returns from crime exceed the net returns from legitimate activity. The value of illicit and licit opportunities are measured by median family income and the proportion of families with incomes less than half the median, respectively, while the costs of crime are measured by the usual "certainty" and "severity" measures described above. Other studies, which do not include criminal justice variables but do attempt to estimate how the availability of legitimate opportunities affects crime, measure opportunities by using the mean family income of the second lowest quartile of the income distribution, the unemployment rate,[26] or the labor force participation rate.[27]

These studies have more or less consistent findings. Fleisher finds that as unemployment increases over time and across jurisdictions, juvenile arrest rates go up (and presumably the actual rate of juvenile delinquency

[25] Isaac Ehrlich, "Participation in Illegitimate Activities," *Journal of Political Economy,* vol. 81, 1973, pp. 521 ff.; and Isaac Ehrlich, "The Deterrent Effect of Criminal Law Enforcement," *Journal of Legal Studies,* vol. 1, 1972, pp. 259-76.

[26] Belton Fleisher, *The Economics of Delinquency* (Chicago: Quadrangle Books, 1966).

[27] Llad Phillips, Harold L. Votey, and Darold Maxwell, "Crime, Youth, and the Labor Market," *Journal of Political Economy,* May-June 1972, pp. 491-504.

goes up as well). He also finds a consistent negative relationship between low levels of income and arrest rates in several cross-sectional samples of various types of communities. Ehrlich finds that the rates of burglary, larceny, robbery, and auto theft go up as median income rises and as the proportion of families earning less than half the median goes up. He also finds that, independent of changes in the economic variables, the rate of crime goes down with an increase in the probability and severity of imprisonment. The work of Phillips, Votey, and Maxwell suggests that crime rates of 18- to 19-year-old males for burglary, robbery, larceny, and auto theft were highly sensitive over several years to labor market conditions. They argue, further, that labor force participation is a more important explanatory variable than unemployment with respect to changes in property crime for this age group. Unemployment rates measure only short-run experiences with job-hunting and, since a large fraction of young people are outside the labor force at any given time, fluctuations in unemployment affect a relatively small fraction of all youth.

In sum, there is a good deal of evidence, employing a variety of techniques, that is consistent with (but does not prove) the theory that property crime rates will decline as the availability and value of legitimate opportunities increase, the benefits of crime drop, and the costs of punishment are increased. Indeed, an even more specific statement can be made: there are not, to our knowledge, any studies which suggest that the rate of reported property crime is insensitive to the probability of imprisonment.

The existing studies, however, suffer from some problems of measurement. Most rely on the FBI Uniform Crime Reports (which fail to measure crime that is not reported to the local police or that *is* known to the police but not reported to the FBI). Most use crime statistics for entire states which combine into a single figure the very different experiences and reporting practices of urban, suburban, and rural areas.

One way, therefore, to either strengthen or weaken our confidence in the alleged deterrent effect of the criminal justice system is to use measures of crime derived from victimization surveys rather than official police reports and to look at the data only for large cities (where the crime problem is especially acute) rather than for whole states. Our measure of deterrence is arrest rather than imprisonment rates. Although our procedure is also open to criticism, it has the virtue of being independent of the estimates of deterrence now available; thus, if our findings are consistent with those estimates, our confidence in both will be increased.

We want to know whether differences in the rate at which individuals (not business establishments) report having been robbed in 26 large American cities are related to differences in the rate at which robbers are arrested by the police, and whether this relationship is independent of the effect of other factors—primarily, the racial, economic, and population characteristics of the various cities. The robberies with which we will be concerned are those in which $10 or more was taken. The probability of arrest is the total number of robbery arrests made by the police divided by the total number of robberies reported in the victimization surveys during (approximately) the same year. For all 26 cities, about 14 percent of the robberies result in an arrest but the variation among cities is great—the Washington, D.C., police have an arrest rate that is six times higher than the arrest rate in Portland, Oregon, or Houston, Texas.

The result of our statistical analysis, the details and limitations of which are fully reported in Appendix B, can be simply stated: the higher the rate at which robbers are arrested, the lower the rate at which citizens are the victims of robbery. This is true after one has taken into account the racial, economic, and population differences among the cities. If our analysis is correct, a 10 percent increase in the probability of being arrested will result, other things being equal, in a 5 percent reduction in the rate of serious robberies.

The policy implications of this finding are not entirely clear. It is possible that our results measure, not what the police do, but what is done by the community, the courts, or the correctional system. High arrest rates, and thus low robbery rates, may be due to more effective police tactics, or to greater levels of citizen cooperation with the police in identifying suspects and testifying against them, or to court sentences that take arrested robbers off the street. We know, for example, that arrests usually result, not from clever detective work, but from information supplied by victims and eyewitnesses to the patrolman on the scene. Arrest rates may also differ because prosecutors themselves differ in their willingness to bring charges against arrested robbery suspects. Certainly courts differ in their willingness to sentence convicted robbers to prison. Whatever the mechanisms that account for our results, however, there appear to be strong grounds for believing that the criminal justice system makes a difference in a citizen's chances of being the victim of a robbery.

Incapacitation

Two separate lines of inquiry—one using police reports of crime aggregated by states and cities and the other using victim reports of crime aggregated by cities—suggest that when economic "need" and criminal opportunities are held constant, differing degrees of activity in the criminal justice system will produce different rates of crime. Just what this "criminal justice activity" may be and how it affects crime rates, however, is not clear. Deterrence theory rests on the assumption that would-be offenders observe and act on differences in the risk of apprehension or imprisonment. Available data are consistent with the hypothesis that they do act on these perceived differences, but unless a controlled experiment is conducted, the differences that we attribute to deterrence might, in fact, be due to incapacitation. A deterrent effect may be operating, but whether the deterrence is the result of arrest rates, conviction rates, imprisonment rates, length of prison term, or some combination of all of thése is uncertain. Therefore deterrence research to date offers little guidance about the point in the system at which the investment of more resources will be most promising. (It is also possible that the association we observe between the criminal justice system and crime represents neither deterrence nor incapacitation but rather represents an inverse causal relationship, is the result of variables we have not considered, or is due to measurement error. We think this unlikely, but it cannot be ruled out.)

Some, but not all, of these problems are avoided by examining the effect on crime of incapacitating the convicted offender by jail or prison. For example, to examine the effects of incapacitation there is no need to make assumptions about the perceptions of offenders, since a person confined in an institution cannot victimize persons outside that institution.

The percentage of those convicted on felony charges who are sent to some kind of institution (jail, work camp, prison) seems to vary considerably between jurisdictions and over time. In California in 1970, of those convicted of robbery, 32 percent went to prison (meaning they received a sentence of one year or more in confinement), 8 percent went to jail (and thus were confined for periods less than one year), 29 percent were given a sentence combining jail and probation. The remainder were fined, placed on probation, sent to the Youth Authority as minors (what disposition the Youth Authority made is unknown), or civilly committed because of drug abuse. Within the state, however, there was considerable variation in sentencing. Only 24 percent of those convicted of robbery in Los Angeles were sentenced to prison (what proportion went to jail is unknown). Only 37 percent of those convicted of robbery with a prior prison record were sentenced to prison.[28] This

---

[28] Peter W. Greenwood, et al., *Prosecution of Adult Felony Defendants in Los Angeles County* (Santa Monica, Calif.: Rand Institute, 1973), pp. 109-10.

last figure means that 63 percent of those convicted of robbery, who had a prior prison record, were either not confined or were confined for a period of less than a year.

In Washington, D.C., by contrast, the court in 1971 found 420 persons guilty of robbery; 84 percent were imprisoned, almost all for periods in excess of one year.[29]

Further complicating this matter is the fact that the time actually served in prison is typically much less than the time to which persons are sentenced. For example, persons convicted of robbery who were released from federal prisons in 1970 had served, on the average, only 41 percent of the sentence imposed by the judge. Though the typical sentences imposed by federal judges have been increasing in severity for the past decade or so, the percent of the sentence actually served has been declining just as rapidly, with the result that over this period the average time served in prison has remained about the same.[30] Data from state court systems suggest that the probability of going to prison has been declining there, while average time served has been roughly constant.[31] Overall, the prison population of the United States dropped during the 1960s despite a sharp upsurge in the amount of crime being committed.

During the 1960s, there was a decrease, nationally, in both the proportion of all reported crimes that resulted in arrests and in the proportion of all arrests that resulted in imprisonment. In 1960, there were 24 arrests for every 100 "Index" crimes;[32] in 1970, there were only 16 arrests for every 100 Index crimes. In 1960, 24 persons went to state prisons for every 100 arrests for Index crimes; in 1970, only 13 persons

---

[29] Administrative Office of the U.S. Courts, *Federal Offenders in the United States District Courts, 1971* (Washington, D.C.: Government Printing Office, Oct. 1973), p. 77.

[30] Michael J. Hindelang, et al., eds., *Sourcebook of Criminal Statistics, 1973* (Washington, D.C.: National Criminal Justice Information and Statistics Services, U.S. Department of Justice), pp. 416-18.

[31] There is some indication that even though aggregate time served has remained constant, the distribution of prisoners by crime type has shifted toward the more serious crimes—suggesting a decline in time served by crime type. In 1960 six percent of the prisoners in New York State were serving time for the crime of murder; in 1970 the percentage was 17 percent. See Reuel Shinnar and Shlomo Shinnar, "The Effects of the Criminal Justice System on the Control of Crime," *Law and Society Review,* vol. 9, Summer 1975, pp. 581-612.

[32] Federal Bureau of Investigation, *Uniform Crime Reports, 1970* (Washington, D.C.: U.S. Government Printing Office). "Index" crimes are those on which the FBI collects data, and consist of murder, rape, aggravated assault, burglary, larceny, and automobile theft.

went to prison for every 100 Index crime arrests.[33] This means that the combined probability of imprisonment for every 100 Index crimes dropped from 6 per hundred to 2 per hundred.[34]

Some persons arrested for an Index crime might be sent to a local jail rather than to a state prison. If the proportion sent to jail rather than prison rose substantially during the 1960s, the rates in the preceding paragraph might be misleading. Jail populations did increase in the 1960s, but by less (9,510) than the prison population decrease (16,230).[35] Furthermore, only 21 percent of the jail population at any given moment is serving a sentence for something more serious than drunkenness, traffic offenses, or nonsupport.[36] Adding this 21 percent to the figures on imprisonment given earlier does not materially change the results: for every 100 Index arrests, 35 persons went to jail or prison in 1960 but only 19 in 1970, a 47 percent decline.[37]

Clearly, a much larger proportion of convicted persons could be sent to prison (if facilities were available) than is now the case. There are, of course, many forms of confinement short of prison—local jails, work camps, and so forth. Whatever the form or the degree of amenity of the confinement, the problem in evaluating its effectiveness is to estimate how much crime would be prevented if a larger proportion of convicted persons were confined in institutions (instead of granting them probation or suspended sentences or fining them). This estimate, even if reliable— and, as we shall see, there are many reasons to doubt that at this stage we can produce a reliable estimate—should not be used by itself as a decisive argument either for or against a policy of greater incarceration. In selecting an appropriate penalty for any offense, one must take into

---

[33] United States Department of Commerce, *Statistical Abstract of the United States, 1972* (Washington, D.C.: U.S. Government Printing Office), p. 160.

[34] If the ratio of reported to actual number of crimes committed changes over time, the real change in arrest and imprisonment probabilities may be distorted. This argument does not apply, however, to the conditional probability of imprisonment given arrest, which itself declined considerably during the years 1960-70.

[35] United States Department of Commerce, U.S. Bureau of the Census, "Persons in Institutions and Other Group Quarters," 1960, 1970 (Washington, D.C.: U.S. Government Printing Office).

[36] United States Department of Justice, Law Enforcement Assistance Administration, "Survey of Inmates of Local Jails, Advance Report" (Washington, D.C.: National Criminal Justice Information and Statistics Services, U.S. Government Printing Office, 1974).

[37] The 21 percent figure is strictly accurate for 1970 only. But even if one makes the restrictive assumption that no Index arrests resulted in commitments to jail in 1960, the decline in the probability of imprisonment is still 33 percent.

account other factors in addition to the crime-reduction potential of the penalty, particularly its moral appropriateness. A ten-year sentence might reduce the auto theft rate, but society might well conclude that it is far too severe given the nature of the offense. Similarly, a five-year term might produce all the reduction in the murder rate that is attainable by imprisonment, but society could well decide that such a penalty would unreasonably cheapen the value we attach to human life.

To carry out this analysis, one must have data on the following variables:

- The size of the criminal population.

- The number of crimes committed by any given criminal per year (more accurately, we want to know the frequency distribution of all crimes of a given type over the criminal population).

- The probability that a person is arrested, given the commitment of a crime.

- The probability that a given arrested person is convicted.

- The probability that a given convicted person is sentenced to prison.

- The time served by the average criminal sentenced to prison.

Thus far, our ability to construct mathematical models of the crime reduction effects of incapacitation is substantially greater than our ability to obtain reliable estimates of the key variables. Some, such as the probability of arrest, conviction, and sentencing, are known approximately and, happily, do not fluctuate much from year to year. The length of the average sentence is discoverable in principle, but almost no jurisdiction in the country actually compiles these data. We skirt the problem somewhat by calculating the *marginal* crime reduction achieved by additional increments of time in prison. The size of the "criminal" population, or even the population of robbers, is unknown and perhaps unknowable. In our first use of the model, we simply assume that this population, whatever its size, is constant—i.e., that a new robber does not immediately appear to replace a robber sent to prison.

But the crucial variable is the average number of crimes per criminal per year (defined in the model as *lambda*): crucial because the results are highly sensitive to this value and because we know of no accurate way to measure it. It clearly will make an enormous difference in the robbery rate whether the imprisoned robber has committed many or few robberies. For example, a city may experience 1,000 robberies either because 1,000 persons commit one robbery each, or because ten persons commit 100 robberies each, or some combination in between. In the former case, locking up one robber for one year would spare the city only one robbery per year; in the latter case, locking up one robber would spare it 100 robberies each year. We cope with the problem of estimating *lambda* by giving estimates of the crime reduction potential of incapacitation for various assumed values of *lambda*.

Our guess as to the true value of *lambda* and our data on the time now served in prison by offenders are for adult offenders only. This is an important limitation, since a large fraction of all crimes—and especially of such crimes as robbery, larceny, and auto theft—is committed by juveniles. Unfortunately, we can find no information on the average time served in some secure facility by juveniles. We suspect that in many states, juveniles are less likely to be incarcerated than adults committing the same offense and, if they are incarcerated, are likely to serve shorter terms than adults. If this is true, the estimates of the crime reduction potential of the sentencing policies in table 4 would be smaller. How much smaller depends on the actual difference in juvenile sentencing practices and the share of crime that they commit. Obviously, we might wish to avoid punishing some juveniles, especially very young ones or first offenders, even at the cost of some increase in crime.

To our knowledge, the first effort to develop a rigorously derived model such as this was made by Benjamin Avi-Itzhak and Reuel Shinnar of The City College of New York.[38] A somewhat simplified version of their model was subsequently developed by Reuel and Shlomo Shinnar and was presented along with empirical estimates to support the basic underlying assumptions.[39] The calculations we present are derived from the simplified version reported by Shinnar and Shinnar. The principal results are given in tables 3 and 4. Table 3 shows the percentage reduction in the crime rate that would occur if everyone arrested and convicted of a crime were given sentences ranging in length from 0.2 years (about two and half months) to 5.0 years, under varying assumptions as to the average number of crimes committed per criminal and the probability of being caught and imprisoned, given commitment of a crime. These percentages reflect the *total* reduction in crime from what would occur if *no* convicted offender were confined at all. For example, if the average

---

[38] Benjamin Avi-Itzhak and Reuel Shinnar, "Quantitative Models in Crime Control," *Journal of Criminal Justice*, vol. 1 (1973).

[39] Reuel Shinnar and Shlomo Shinnar, "The Effects of the Criminal Justice System on the Control of Crime," *Law and Society Review*, vol. 9 (Summer 1975), pp. 581-612.

criminal commits ten crimes per year and has a 10 percent chance of being caught and convicted, then sentencing all such convicted criminals to one year in prison would lower the crime rate by 50 percent below what it would be if no one went to prison.

Table 3

PERCENT REDUCTION IN EXPECTED CRIME RATE PRODUCED BY PRISON SENTENCES UNDER VARYING CONDITIONS OF CRIMINAL CAREER AND PROBABILITY OF IMPRISONMENT[a]

Crimes per offender	Prob. of imprison-ment	Length of total sentence (years)					
		0.2	0.5	1.0	2.0	3.0	5.0
5	.05	4.8%	11.1%	20.0%	33.3%	42.9%	55.6%
	.10	9.1	20.0	33.3	50.0	60.0	71.4
	.20	16.7	33.3	50.0	66.7	75.0	83.3
10	.05	9.1	20.0	33.3	50.0	60.0	71.4
	.10	16.7	33.3	50.0	66.7	75.0	83.3
	.20	28.6	50.0	66.7	80.0	85.7	90.9
20	.05	16.7	33.3	50.0	66.7	75.0	83.3
	.10	28.6	50.0	66.7	80.0	85.7	90.9
	.20	44.4	66.7	80.0	88.9	92.3	95.2
50	.05	33.3	55.6	71.4	83.3	88.2	92.6
	.10	50.0	71.4	83.3	90.9	93.7	96.2
	.20	66.7	83.3	90.9	95.2	96.8	98.0

(Assumes criminal population is of constant size and that all caught and convicted offenders receive same sentence. We are grateful to Ann Young for preparing this table.)

---

[a] The figures of Tables 3 and 4 are derived from the following expression:

$$A/P = \frac{1}{1 + \lambda(qJS)}$$

Where:

P = potential number of crimes an average criminal will commit over his criminal career if the criminal justice system incapacitates no one.

A = actual number of crimes an average criminal will commit over his criminal career under a system with incapacitation.

q = probability of arrest per crime committed.

J = given arrest, probability of conviction and imprisonment.

S = average length of a prison term.

λ = annual number of crimes committed by the average criminal.

Source: Reuel Shinnar and Shlomo Shinnar, "The Effects of the Criminal Justice System on the Control of Crime," *Law and Society Review,* vol. 9 (Summer 1975).

Table 4

PERCENTAGE REDUCTION IN EXPECTED CRIME RATE
DUE TO INCREASES IN PROBABILITY OF IMPRISONMENT
AND AVERAGE TIME SERVED FROM CURRENT VALUES
(i.e., .03, 2) FOR TWO VALUES OF LAMBDA

Average no. years served	Lambda = 2				Lambda = 10			
	2.0	2.5	3.0	4.0	2.0	2.5	3.0	4.0
Probability of imprisonment								
.03	—	2.6	5.1	9.7	—	8.6	15.8	27.2
.04	3.4	6.7	9.7	15.2	11.1	20.0	27.3	38.5
.05	6.7	10.4	13.8	20.0	20.0	28.9	36.0	46.7
.06	9.7	13.8	17.6	24.3	27.3	36.0	42.9	53.0
.07	12.5	17.0	21.1	28.2	33.3	41.8	48.3	58.9
.08	15.2	20.0	24.3	31.7	38.5	46.7	53.0	62.0
.09	17.6	22.8	27.3	34.9	42.9	50.8	56.8	65.2

(Probability of imprisonment and average time served based on 1970 state prison population figures, 1970 adult Index crimes [estimated], and assume 21 percent of jail population is serving a one-year sentence for an Index crime.)

Obviously, some criminals are already being given prison sentences; what we wish to know, therefore, is the marginal reduction in crime that would result from increasing either the probability of being sentenced to prison or the length of time spent in prison, or both. Furthermore, it is important to make some reasonable estimate of the number of crimes committed by each offender per year (*lambda*). Table 4 attempts to show the effect on the crime rate that would result both from increasing the probability of being imprisoned (qJ) beyond its present value (about three chances for every 100 Index crimes that are reported) and from increasing the amount of time served in prison (S) beyond its present average of about two years. These calculations are shown separately for two values of *lambda*—two and ten.

For example, if the average criminal commits two serious (i.e., "Index") crimes per year, doubling the chances of all such offenders going to prison for the average stay of two years from three chances in a hundred to six in a hundred would decrease the rate of serious crime by a little over 9 percent. If, on the other hand, one left the chances of being imprisoned the same but increased the average time served from two to three years, crime would be reduced by a little over 5 percent. Finally, if one followed both policies simultaneously—twice as great a chance of imprisonment and three-year rather than two-year terms—serious crime would be reduced by over 17 percent.

If it turns out that the average offender commits more than two serious crimes a year, the crime-reduction potential of greater incapacitation will clearly be much larger. If, for example, a criminal commits ten crimes a year, then lengthening the average sentence from two to three years would result in nearly a 16 percent drop in crime; doubling the chances of being imprisoned, while leaving the prison term at two years, would result in a 27 percent decrease in crime.

It is not yet possible to give a reliable estimate of the number of crimes per offender. Shinnar and Shinnar assume that the number is greater than five and may be as high as twenty.[40] Greenberg, using very different procedures, has estimated that this number is closer to two.[41] Both estimates are open to question since in neither case were they based on a direct count of the number of offenses committed by known offenders. We are presently exploring ways of developing a more reliable estimate. Simply knowing how many times a year a person is arrested for a crime is, of course, not enough—it is almost certain that the average offender will commit many crimes for which he is not arrested and that he will be innocent of some fraction (we think a small one) of those charges on which he is arrested.

Nor is it clear from our data which method for increasing the incapacitation of offenders would be most feasible. Even if we assume that the police cannot increase the chances of an offender getting arrested, and even if the courts do not change the chances of being convicted, there remain substantial opportunities to alter both the proportion of those convicted who are imprisoned and the length of that prison sentence. A careful study by the Vera Institute of persons arrested on felony charges in New York City shows that, of those convicted, less than half go to prison, and of those who go to prison nearly 80 percent are given sentences of less than one year. Stated another way, of those convicted only 10 percent are sentenced to prison for more than one year and of those, of course, most will actually serve much less than one year.[42] A policy of mandatory minimum sentences would presumably increase

---

[40] Ibid., pp. 597, 604.

[41] David F. Greenberg, "The Incapacitative Effects of Imprisonment: Some Estimates," *Law and Society Review,* vol. 9 (Summer 1975), pp. 541-80.

[42] "A Criminal Justice System under Stress: A Study of the Disposition of Felony Arrests in New York City," Vera Institute of Justice (New York: August 15, 1975).

the proportion of convicted offenders imprisoned but it might lead to a reduction in the proportion of arrested offenders convicted. (Some judges may refuse to convict if they believe the accused must go to prison; some prosecutors may for the same reason refuse to prosecute or, if they do prosecute, may reduce the charge to one for which no mandatory minimum exists.) Without a careful experiment we are not likely to know whether the theoretically-possible crime reduction shown in table 4 can in fact be attained by the application of any likely set of laws (such as mandatory minimum sentences) to the existing pattern of discretion found in the criminal justice system.

But if we assume that such gains are feasible, we must still consider their costs. Were we successfully to double the proportion of convicted offenders sentenced to prison, we would have to double our use of prison space unless we simultaneously reduce the maximum time a person may spend in prison and restrict the kinds of offenses for which prison is appropriate. If, for example, 20 percent of our prison space is now being used by persons who spend twenty years in prison and we were to reduce the maximum time anybody could spend in prison to five years with the average sentence two years, we would obtain a 10 percent increase in available prison space without any new construction. Similarly, if 20 percent of our detention facilities are occupied by chronic alcoholics who are sentenced for public drunkenness, finding noncustodial alternatives for these persons would increase our detention capacity by 20 percent. Had we accurate data on the kinds of offenses and the time in confinement for all prisoners, we might calculate how large the actual gains would be from altering the present mix of offenders and sentences, but such data do not exist.

Nonetheless, it seems likely that a substantially greater reliance on a deterrence and incapacitation strategy, coupled with the need, expressed by many prison authorities, for rebuilding those facilities that are outdated, in disrepair, or too large, will necessitate the construction of new facilities—not simply conventional prisons, but also jails, work camps, prison farms, community institutions providing some degree of custodial control, and so forth.

Figures from the U.S. Bureau of Prisons on the per inmate capital and operating costs of their facilities—which are generally superior in amenity and design to many state facilities—are shown in table 5.

We do not attempt a cost-benefit analysis of increased facilities because the hard-to-measure psychic and communal costs of crime are perhaps the most important of all the costs; inevitably their calculations will be made, implicitly if not explicitly, by the political process.

Table 5

FEDERAL PRISON SYSTEM PER CAPITA
OPERATING AND CAPITAL COSTS

Fiscal Year	Per Capita Operating Costs	Per Capita Capital Costs a	Per Capita Total Costs
1969	$3220	$ 47	$3627
1970	3676	164	3840
1971	4200	135	4335
1972	4790	142	4932
1973	5302	143	5445
1974	6007 est.	137 est.	6144 est.
1975	7118 est.	137 est.	7255 est.

a. It may be argued that these per capita capital costs understate the "true" cost of providing "adequate" facilities since many of the prisons within the federal system are quite old and have been fully depreciated for a number of years. Therefore, an alternative estimate of capital costs has been derived using cost figures for the recently constructed federal correctional facility in Pleasanton, California. This facility was designed to house 250 young adults between the ages of 18 and 25 under conditions of low security; its initial cost was $6.6 million. Employing National Bureau of Prisons accounting rules, straight line depreciation over an average life of 50 years yields an estimate of annual per capita costs of $528.

Source: The Budget of the United States Government, Appendix, U.S. Government Printing Office, appropriate years.

It is worth noting, however, that the United States has not been willing, during the last decade or so, to increase its use of prison despite the enormous increase in crime. There were 212,957 prisoners at the end of 1960 but only 196,429 at the end of 1970, a decline from 118.6 per 100,000 population in 1960 to 96.7 per 100,000 in 1970.[43] The number of persons entering prison fell from 88,575 in 1960 to 79,351 in 1970. The decline in the use of prisons was especially marked in some states. New York, for example, experienced a decline in its year-end prison population from 17,207 in 1960 to 12,059 in 1970.[44]

There are no doubt a number of reasons why the use of prisons has been declining. Judges, believing that prisons ought to rehabilitate and noting (correctly) that they do not, may put offenders back on the street lest they be corrupted by prison. Or judges may erroneously believe that prison cannot reduce the crime rate either by deterrence or incapacitation. We hope that judges who read our findings will reconsider these views.

[43] Department of Commerce, *Statistical Abstract*, op. cit., p. 160.
[44] Ibid., p. 161.

One important rejoinder to this line of argument is that, to the extent that prisons are "schools of crime" which increase the recidivism rate of those confined in them, increasing the proportion of convicted offenders sent to prison, or lengthening their terms, would produce ex-convicts who upon their release commit crimes at a greater rate than they would had they not been imprisoned at all. This gain in recidivism, attributable to prison, might nullify most or all of the crime reduction achieved by deterrence and incapacitation.

The evidence on the "schools of crime" hypothesis is not all in. Such evidence as we have been able to find does not, however, strongly support it. Obviously prisons differ greatly in their inner life—some may have a reasonable level of amenity and privacy, others may so brutalize the convict as to embitter him. And prisoners differ as well. Some may be so relieved to get out that nothing can induce them to risk reimprisonment (and, in fact, most ex-convicts are not reimprisoned during their first few years out of prison), while others might set about applying the criminal skills they learned while inside.

David Greenberg, in reviewing studies comparing recidivism rates of released prisoners and matched groups of probationers, concluded that "there is no compelling evidence that imprisonment substantially increases (or decreases) the likelihood of subsequent criminal involvement."[45] This was the conclusion as well of studies by Wilkins; Hammond; Babst and Mannering; Shoham; and Lamb and Goertzel.[46] One of the best known studies was of youthful offenders in California sent randomly to community probation programs and to regular juvenile institutions. After two years, there was no significant difference in the recidivism rate of the two groups—suggesting both that the community-based probation system was no better at rehabilitating offenders and that juvenile institutions were no worse at inculcating criminal skills and desires.[47]

Another objection to increasing the use of incapacitation is that our courts and correctional systems will be crushed under the increased workload, partly because more persons will be imprisoned and partly because

---

[45] Greenberg, "The Incapacitative Effects of Imprisonment," op. cit., p. 23.

[46] See Leslie T. Wilkins, "A Small Comparative Study of the Results of Probation," *British Journal of Delinquency,* vol. 8, 1958, pp. 201ff.; W. H. Hammond, *The Sentence of the Court* (London: Her Majesty's Stationery Office, 1969); D. V. Babst and J. W. Mannering, "Probation versus Imprisonment for Similar Types of Offenders," *Journal of Research in Crime and Delinquency,* vol. 2, 1965, pp. 53-61; Shlomo Shoham, *Crime and Social Deviance* (Chicago: Regnery, 1966); and H. R. Lamb and Victor Goertzel, "Ellsworth House: A Community Alternative," *American Journal of Psychiatry,* vol. 131, 1974, pp. 64ff.

[47] Paul Lerman, *Community Treatment and Social Control: A Critical Analysis of Juvenile Correctional Policy* (Chicago: University of Chicago Press, 1975).

a higher proportion of those charged will ask for time-consuming trials rather than plead guilty. The policy we suggest does imply that more resources should be devoted to courts and corrections, especially the latter. Only estimates of workloads based on alternative sentencing rules will suggest how great these resources must be, and since we propose no specific sentencing policy we make no estimates. The objection based on cost is, we suspect, a disguised form of an objection based on principle: just as those who do not like programs for income redistribution, job creation, or more schooling object to their cost, so also do persons who do not like prisons object to their cost. We prefer that the issue of principle should be faced and debated first so we can be clear about the benefits, if any; then we should decide what we are willing to pay for these benefits. If citizens were asked to vote on programs that would reduce predatory crime by some significant fraction, we suspect they would approve any reasonable expenditure.

The court workload variant of this objection is more tantalizing. At one level, it suggests an objection to the idea of trials and not-guilty pleas —strange preferences coming from those who on other issues are strongly committed to constitutional guarantees. If more accused persons plead not guilty—which is their privilege in any event—we should not sacrifice community protection to lighten court workloads. Furthermore, if the chances of imprisonment are increased, there ought to be more trials to insure that the more certain prospect of punishment does not result in innocent persons going to jail.

Studies we have seen suggest, however, that in many jurisdictions there is already a good deal of slack in the court system and that more cases could be heard, and for longer periods, without major new investments. Feeley found, in his study of Connecticut criminal courts, that what made the difference between busy and not-so-busy courts was not to be found in their sentences but in the fact that in busy courts, the judges work longer hours than in the not-so-busy ones.[48] Similarly, Gillespie's studies of circuit courts in Illinois and the federal court system suggest that, on average, excess capacity exists in both of these court systems.[49]

Though there is slack in the existing court system, it would be wrong

---

[48] Malcolm M. Feeley, "The Importance of Heavy Caseloads," Yale Law School, January 1975, mimeographed.

[49] See Robert W. Gillespie, "Judicial Productivity and Court Delay: A Statistical Analysis of the Federal District Courts," typescript, submitted to National Institute of Law Enforcement and Criminal Justice, Law Enforcement Assistance Administration, U.S. Department of Justice, March 5, 1975, and "A Supply and Demand Analysis of the Judicial Services Provided by the Trial Courts of Illinois," Department of Economics, University of Illinois, September 15, 1973, mimeographed.

to suppose that this unused capacity is adequate to handle the workload that would result if, as a result of new sentencing laws, trials became more frequent. There are indications that trials have significantly increased in frequency as a consequence of the adoption by New York State of laws mandating minimum sentences—in some cases, quite severe ones—for certain kinds of offenders. Since 1971, New York City has more than doubled the number of judges sitting each day in order to keep up with the increased workload, especially the increased proportion of cases handled by trial. Even so, the number of judges is only about 110—scarcely an unmanageable number. Nor would comparable increases be necessary everywhere—after all, New York in 1973 reported having nearly one-fifth of all the known robberies in the entire United States.

IV. SOME CONCLUSIONS

Designing a rational approach to crime control—or even to the more modest goal of controlling urban robbery rates—is exceptionally difficult. A policy maker wishing to make the best possible decisions in this area would want to know how one could maximize crime reduction for a given level of expenditures or minimize the expenditures necessary to maintain a given level of crime control. But it is impossible even to know how much is now being spent on all phases of crime control (public expenditures directly on the criminal justice system are known, but private expenditures on security are unknown and both public and private expenditures on social programs that may have some crime control value are probably unknowable). We cannot compare the value, in terms of crime reduction, of spending the marginal dollar on programs to alleviate poverty, provide jobs, light streets, further schooling, hire police officers, or build jails. We do not even know with much accuracy the gains in public safety that result from expenditures on specific police strategies, to say nothing of the gains from simply spending more money on the police generally. Indeed, we are inclined to agree with those who have found no relationship at all between how much we spend on the police and how much crime there is.[50]

But this is not surprising, nor should it be discouraging. There is virtually no significant government objective about which we can make strictly rational decisions—in this sense, crime control is no different from the problem of improving education, strengthening the family, or pre-

---

[50] Thomas F. Pogue, "Effect of Police Expenditures on Crime Rates," *Public Finance Quarterly*, vol. 3, January 1975, pp. 14-44.

paring for war. And even if a thoroughly rational decision were possible, no policy maker would ever be in a situation to make it. The fragmentation and localism of the crime control apparatus in this country will defeat any effort at comprehensive planning.

We believe the way to proceed in situations of this sort is to make careful, experimental modifications in the existing array of policies, evaluate them rigorously, and extend them where the evidence warrants. We also believe that these experiments should involve relatively simple techniques aimed at clear but modest objectives and undertaken in a frankly questioning frame of mind.

This is not the way public policy is ordinarily made. Typically, a "war" or "crusade" against crime is proclaimed, vague or utopian objectives are sought ("revitalize the family," "strengthen religious values," "end racial hostility"), large sums of money are spent on existing practices and personnel, and little effort is made to discover whether anything has changed.

From our review of the available evidence, we offer some guidelines for a different approach.

First, the primary responsibility for public safety will fall on the citizen. He will have to select those living places, take those precautions, and install those devices that in a happier world would be unnecessary and in this world are irritating, but for which there is no substitute. Government programs should make it easier, not harder, for people to move to communities of their choice and assert and maintain a decent style of life. When the government builds housing or subsidizes the building by others, it should define and enforce reasonable standards of security. Streets should be brightly lit and alarm systems more systematically tested.

Second, the police must continue to define and test alternative deployment strategies such as "decoy" patrol techniques and selective investigative methods. This is not easy. What is easy is to let officers on patrol ride about in marked cars waiting for a radio call, to put officers on foot in whichever communities are able to generate sufficient political demand, and to assign officers to duty in accordance with habit or union contracts rather than on the basis of community needs. Still, we are impressed with how relatively open to experiment the police are, compared to prosecutors and judges, though we remain depressed by the frequent disinclination of the police to secure independent evaluations of their programs. The apparent benefits of a higher arrest rate are supported by the data. What remains to be discovered is what police strategies in various cities produce those gains.

Third, we must find out what is happening to persons after they are arrested. We were continually frustrated in our efforts to write this chapter by the absence of reliable information on who, of those arrested, gets charged, and for what; on how pleas are heard and acted upon; on what sentences are imposed; and on how long and in what way people serve out those sentences. The explorations by ourselves and others of the possible effects on crime of pursuing more explicitly and rigorously a deterrence and incapacitation strategy are suggestive but we cannot say on the basis of available information how big a difference in crime would be made by a radical shift in our sentencing practices. Indeed, we cannot even say with certainty what those practices are today.

Fourth, we believe that of the strategies aimed at crime control available to a free society, those involving sentencing and correctional policies offer the greatest potential for gain. Making some form of custodial or closely-supervised disposition more likely as a consequence of a conviction should, unless our analyses are seriously in error, lead to some reductions in crime. With better data and more refined models, we might be able to state more precisely what "some" reduction means.

Some of our colleagues do not like this conclusion and are (properly) critical of the estimates on which it is based. Better studies of the existing system may help answer their questions, but we think that a careful evaluation of a *changed* system would produce even more reliable knowledge. Several states, as well as the federal government, are now considering various ways of increasing the probability of custodial sentence, either through the use of mandatory minimum sentences or the development and required use of fairly specific sentencing guidelines. A major effort should be devoted to evaluating these policies if they are enacted.

At the same time, the reader should not infer from our data that merely passing a law requiring a different sentencing policy will produce the results we have indicated. Such a mechanistic interpretation of our results fails to take into account the realities of the criminal justice system. The central reality is that the various persons in it—police, prosecutors, defense counsel, judges—who have discretion will struggle to maintain it. If we reduce that discretion in one place it will expand in another. Some discretion is inevitable and desirable, though we believe the present levels are unacceptably great. If we wish to reduce discretion to achieve certain ends, we must build into the system incentives that make those who run the system want to attain those ends. For example, it would be a mistake to find ways to enable the police to make more valid arrests if doing so required them to spend additional hours waiting to appear in court, filling out papers, and losing sleep, all with the result of the offender going free for want of adequate correctional facilities. Similarly, we cannot expect custodial sentences to be more frequently employed unless we design a set of custodial institutions that satisfy the moral and political standards of the sentencing authorities. We may try to force judges to send more convicted robbers to jail, but if all the jails are old, crowded, and abusive they will find ways not to do it. (Of course, a few judges will send prisoners to such places precisely because they *are* degrading, but we think these jurists are the exception.) This means that custodial facilities must keep pace, in quality and variety, with the level of expected amenity in society as a whole, differing from society primarily in that inside those facilities liberty is lost. Or more exactly: prisons must deprive people of their liberty to such an extent that people will prefer to stay out of them and that the community will be protected by them, but prisons should not deprive the offender of his liberty in a fashion that offends the standards of a humane judge.

Fifth, there will be changes in the crime rate—both increases and decreases—over which society can exercise almost no control. Crime began going up in the late 1950s and early 1960s in almost every industrial society for which records are available. This increase reflected powerful but hard-to-specify forces that were operating on a world-wide basis, involving, at their root, important changes in values which modern government may have encouraged—by enlarging the scope of personal freedom and stimulating the commitment to general consumer affluence—but which it is all but powerless to reverse. Crime is not a disease of the American character and the rate of increase has been no greater here than in, say, England.

Some forces will abate. The baby boom has been replaced by the baby bust, and by the early to mid-1980s, the number of persons in the crime-prone younger age group will be proportionately smaller than it is today. Crime, therefore, ought to decline. But offsetting that trend is another, more ominous one: the probability that any given young person will commit a crime has been steadily rising for the past dozen years or so. Given today's much higher crime rate, it takes fewer young people—perhaps only half as many as were alive in 1960—to produce the same level of crime we had in 1960. Unless there are additional, unforeseeable changes in values, we should not expect the lower birth rate, by itself, to bring crime down to the rates we enjoyed in the 1940s and early 1950s.

Sixth, we think public opinion has been generally ahead of elite and official opinion on the crime issue. The public recognized the crime wave before our leaders did and they have been more willing to support measures to deal with it than have our officials. It is not the public that resists hiring more judges, revising the penal code, reducing the backlog in the courts, making penalties more certain or more severe, or keeping repeat offenders off the streets. It is *the government* that has resisted these things. Nor has the public expressed its concern for crime at the expense of its support for social programs. To a remarkable degree, the public has been willing to endorse increased expenditures for health, education, and income maintenance (at least of certain kinds). We are astonished and pleased at how forebearing public opinion has been but we should not rely on that forebearance indefinitely. Without more effective and more just public policies on crime, there will be increased support for extreme (and probably unrealistic) measures. We note, for example, that a majority of the residents of the District of Columbia, including a majority of the black residents, now favor the death penalty—almost certainly a major change in attitude, perhaps an unprecedented one.

Finally, whatever one may conclude about police efficiency, judicial sentences, or correctional policies, the test of a good criminal justice system cannot be only its capacity to reduce crime. It must also be a *just* system, by which we mean both that it must be fair to those it accuses and satisfying to those whom it serves. We have not considered the gains in crime control that might come from reducing individual rights. There might well be such gains (though we know of no good evidence one way or another on this score), but we are not certain such gains would be worth the cost. In any event, we believe that a society wishing to preserve the liberties of those *accused* of a crime should be especially concerned with greater effectiveness in dealing with those *convicted* of a crime. Failure to do so would increase the pressure for a reduction in the rights of the accused.

At the same time, justice, and not merely crime control, should be served by the courts in sentencing those it convicts. The most powerful argument against unconstrained judicial discretion, wide disparities in sentences, and the opportunity for some serious offenders to escape punishment is not that these outcomes increase the crime rate but that they are wrong— unfair to those sentenced to longer terms than others convicted of the same crime and unjust to society and to the victims of a crime who have a right to see "justice done." Even if a particular punishment deterred no one and caused no reduction in crime, that punishment—provided it met standards of reasonableness—would still be necessary if our laws are to continue to bear an appropriate relationship to the prevailing moral order and to our sense of fairness.

Appendix A.

COMPARISON OF NATIONAL OPINION RESEARCH CENTER
(NORC) AND NATIONAL CRIME SURVEY (NCS)
CRIME RATE ESTIMATES

While both the NORC and NCS crime rate estimates are based on household victimization surveys of a representative sample of the national population, there are a number of differences in the technical methodologies which may bias comparisons between the two. For the type of comparison we are making (i.e., an estimate of the increase in crime rates between 1966 and 1973) the most important differences to be accounted for are those that would spuriously inflate an estimate of any observed increase. Several such differences do exist.

1. In the NORC initial screen questionnaire one person was asked to identify all crimes, personal and household, that occurred to all members of that household. Individual household members were then asked detailed questions about the personal crimes that happened to them and the household respondent answered detailed questions about household crimes. The NCS asks initial screen questions and detailed questions of all household members over 14 for personal crimes but of only one member for household crimes. It is possible that this difference may result in a substantial underestimate of the number of personal crimes in the NORC survey. For this reason we have limited our comparison in the text to the household crime of burglary.

2. The NORC survey used a 12-month reference period, while the NCS has a reference period of only 6 months. The 1966 survey asked persons to recall all crimes that occurred to them over the preceding year, but the 1973 survey asks persons to recall only crimes that occurred within the past 6 months. The NCS (national sample) is a quarterly survey with a rotating sample so the Census Bureau is able to construct annual crime rate estimates with only a 6-month reference period (the NCS city samples use a 12-month reference period, however). If a longer reference period significantly increases the proportion of victimizations that persons forget to report to an interviewer, then again the NORC estimates could be biased downward. Preliminary comparisons prepared by the Census Bureau between city sample data for New York City and national sample data for New York City (the size of NYC allows it to be separately identified in the national sample data) suggest that the discrepancies in the estimates of crime between the two different surveys are quite small. This does not prove that variation in reference periods has no effect on survey

estimates of crime, as there are several other differences between the city and national data, but it does suggest that survey estimates of crime may be relatively insensitive to some dissimilarity in survey methodology.

3. The NORC survey imposed a limit of two incident reports per household, while the NCS allows nine per person or 25 per household. It is possible but seems unlikely that the lower NORC limit would result in an underestimate of burglaries in 1966. Of all *households* reporting at least one victimization of any type in 1966 only 10 percent reported three or more for all *household members* combined. In addition, interviewers were instructed to exclude less serious crimes when multiple victimization was a problem.

4. In general the NCS questionnaire is a more precise, thorough, and carefully worded questionnaire than the one used in the earlier NORC survey. For example, the NCS burglary screen question includes illegal entry into home/apartment, garage, or other building on the respondent's property, while the NORC question is limited to home/apartment. Also, the NCS questionnaire includes a number of specific questions about the exact nature of the incident. The responses to these questions are the basis of an elaborate coding scheme that is used to determine if a burglary really did occur. The NORC survey asks only one open-ended question, about the details of the incident, which was hand coded to determine if a burglary or some other crime occurred. It is very difficult to judge the magnitude of these general differences on the NORC/NCS estimates. However, given the size of the apparent increase in burglary rates (i.e., by a factor of three) observed between the two surveys, it seems reasonable to conclude that a substantial increase in "real" crime rates did occur and that all of the increase cannot be dismissed as an artifact of the underlying methodologies.

Appendix B.

STATISTICAL ESTIMATION OF DETERRENT EFFECT
OF POLICE ACTIVITY ON ROBBERY RATES

Virtually all previous studies of deterrence suffer from problems of measurement and data accuracy. Most of them use the FBI Uniform Crime Report statistics of crime for entire states, reports which almost certainly vary enormously in quality. Indeed, most authors note the discouragingly poor quality of these data and numerous discussions on the subject appear in the literature.[51] Differences in crime rates that are

---

[51] See Michael J. Hindelang, "The Uniform Crime Reports Revisited," *The Journal of Criminal Justice,* vol. 2, no. 1, Spring 1974.

observed across jurisdictions may represent—in addition to differences in the behavior of criminals—differences in the proportion of victims who decide to report crimes to the police and/or differences in the methods and skill with which local police departments record and report crimes to the FBI.

We can deal with at least one aspect of the data problem by estimating the effect, if any, of the criminal justice system on crime rates derived from victimization surveys, rather than from the official FBI police reports, with the data aggregated by cities rather than by states, and employing a different measure of deterrence. Though our method is also open to criticism, it has the virtue of being empirically independent of the estimates now available and thus, should it provide findings consistent with those estimates, would tend to increase our confidence in them.

We shall attempt to see whether differences in the rate at which persons (not business establishments) are victimized by robbers in 26 large American cities are related to the level of police activity. We shall use as our dependent variable the rate per thousand persons over the age of 12 at which individuals were victimized by "serious robberies," defined as robberies in which $10 or more was taken. The measure of police activity is the total arrest rate for robbery: that is, the total arrests for robbery that occurred in a city in a given year as reported to the FBI by local police departments[52] divided by the total number of robberies reported in the victimization survey for that city during a roughly comparable time period.[53]

Our focus on personal robbery is dictated partly by a priori value judgments about the type of crime citizens find most fearsome and partly by data constraints. Robberies occur with sufficient frequency to allow detailed analysis and, by definition, they involve personal contact and the use of force. Also, the typical robbery is committed in open public spaces by person(s) unknown to the victim(s)—in our sample of 26 cities approximately 90 percent involved strangers and about 65 percent occurred in the street. (Commercial robberies have been excluded because of unreliability due to sampling problems.) We use the serious robbery rate rather than the total robbery rate because, as noted earlier, persons frequently victimized may not recall and report "minor" robberies, even

---

[52] Unpublished arrest data for the 26 cities were made available to us by the Uniform Crime Reporting section of the FBI.

[53] Our measure of police activity, based on *total* arrests for robbery and *total* robberies, is not strictly comparable to the dependent variable which measures only robberies where $10 or more was taken. This was necessary because FBI arrest data is not collected by amount stolen. The estimated coefficient will be biased only to the extent that the distribution of arrests by amount relative to the distribution of robberies by amount varies significantly across cities.

to Census interviewers, as reliably as persons less frequently victimized. Relying on the total robbery rate, we believe, may lead to a bias in our equations resulting from understating the rate of victimization among poor, black, or otherwise frequently victimized populations.

We have already seen that the robbery rate varies considerably among the cities; so also does the probability of arrest. For the latter the mean is 0.143, the range from a low of 0.057 (in Portland and Houston) to a high of 0.318 (in Washington, D.C.). We have chosen the probability of arrest to represent the degree of risk associated with robbery, not because we think the police are more important than other elements of the criminal justice system, but rather because measures of these other elements (i.e., courts and prisons) are virtually impossible to obtain at the city level.

Obviously, more than the criminal justice system will affect the crime rate. For our model, in addition to the arrest rate for robbery, we select one variable (rate of participation in the labor force in 1970 for men of ages 16 to 34 living in central city low-income areas) as a measure of the extent to which the population is engaged in legitimate alternatives to crime by working or actively seeking work, one variable (percent of the population that is nonwhite) that summarizes a combination of social factors relating to the level of need and the opportunity to participate in the larger society,[54] and one variable (1970 population density per square mile) that estimates the ease or frequency with which a robber comes into contact with a potential victim. The hypothesis is that the robbery rate will increase as participation in the labor force and the risk of apprehension decline and as population density and the proportion nonwhite increase. When persons perceive that they have few legitimate opportunities for earning money, observe that the chances of being caught for any given robbery are low, and live in a city whose density affords many opportunities for robbing with some anonymity, the victimization rate for robbery will be higher than when any or all of these conditions are reversed.

The results of the full equation (estimated by ordinary least squares assuming a linear model) are given in table B-1. We shall interpret it and then deal with the qualifications and problems it presents.

---

[54] The correlation between the nonwhite proportion of the population and the crime rate is frequently observed. The reasons for this correlation are complex and poorly understood. We include the variable here because it is highly significant; we do not make claims about what underlying social factors it represents.

Table B-1

REGRESSION ON SERIOUS ROBBERY RATE OF PROBABILITY
OF ARREST AND THREE SOCIOECONOMIC VARIABLES
FOR 26 CITIES

Variable	Coefficient	t-statistic	Elasticity
Arrest probability	−25.98983	−4.0642	−0.46487
Percent nonwhite	0.12998	5.0671	0.48999
Labor force participation	0.01931	0.23067	0.19064
Density	0.00037	4.4167	0.43242

Constant = 2.842; corrected R^2 = .74; F = 18.959

Data Sources:
Serious Robbery Rate
  Central city population: LEAA victimization surveys.
  Serious robberies: unpublished data from the LEAA victimization surveys provided by the National Criminal Justice Information and Statistics Service.
Probability of Arrest
  Total robberies: LEAA victimization surveys.
  Robbery arrests: unpublished city arrests for robbery provided by the Uniform Crime Reporting section of the FBI.
Percent Nonwhite: LEAA victimization surveys.
Labor Force Participation Rate (of men ages 16-34 living in low-income areas): Employment Profiles of Selected Low-Income Areas, U.S. Census 1970.
Density: 1972 Statistical Abstract, based on 1970 population.

The signs of three of the independent variables are as predicted and the total explanatory power of the equation is quite high (R^2 = .74). Three of the four independent variables are statistically significant. Most interesting, the elasticity of the probability of arrest suggests that a 10 percent increase in the robbery arrest rate is associated with a nearly 5 percent decrease in the rate of serious robberies.

We are not certain whether the labor force participation rate in fact has no significant influence on the robbery rate or whether its effect is masked by other variables. When density is omitted from the equation, labor force participation is significantly and negatively related to the serious robbery rate. However, population density and labor force participation are highly correlated (the densest cities have, on the whole, the lowest rates of participation in the labor force), and thus when density is entered, labor force participation becomes an insignificant variable.

Nor are we certain how to interpret the density variable. There are three obvious possibilities. One, our original hypothesis might be called the "opportunity" theory: the denser the population, the more frequently and easily a robber can find a victim. Robbers are not highly mobile—much less mobile, for example, than burglars.[55] Other things being equal, it is easier to find victims in downtown Manhattan than in downtown Portland. The second is the "subculture" theory: dense cities should, as predicted by Wolfgang and Ferracuti, make it easier for like-minded individuals to find and associate with each other under conditions of weak communal control and so, by their interaction, intensify any proclivities they may have for criminal activity. The third is the "regional" theory: certain regions by their history, traditions, and patterns of settlement have long records of high urban crime rates—the older, industrial cities of the Northeast have always had higher robbery rates than the cities of the Far West and especially the Northwest, while blacks living in southern cities tend to have lower rates of property crime than blacks living in northern ones. We do not choose between these interpretations of the density variable; indeed, all may be true in varying degrees.

The apparent effect of police arrest rates on robbery is a controversial finding. At the methodological level, there is a question as to how to interpret the direction of causality. A high arrest rate may, by its deterrent effect, cause a low robbery rate or, conversely, a high robbery rate may produce a low arrest rate. The latter could be the case if, for example, the effect of a large number of robberies was to strain the resources available to the police system and reduce its efficiency. In addition, when the ratio of arrests to robberies is used to measure the arrest rate, robberies appear in the numerator of the dependent variable and the denominator of the independent variable. If there are errors of measurement in the number of robberies, spurious negative correlation between the robbery rate and the arrest rate may result.[56]

We can cope with these problems by deriving an estimate of police activity which is theoretically independent of police resources and statistically independent of the number of robberies—but which past research suggests is associated with high arrest rates. In a 1960 study of 146 middle-size cities, Wilson was able to show that arrest rates were sensitive to the degree to which a city's administration was highly professionalized: in communities with council-manager, nonpartisan regimes run by highly professional city managers, the arrest rates for various offenses were much higher than in communities where the regimes were partisan and the ad-

---

[55] Thomas A. Reppetto, *Residential Crime* (Cambridge, Mass.: Ballinger, 1974).
[56] This and other problems of measurement in the probability of arrest variable are discussed below.

ministration nonprofessional. The explanation offered—consistent with other findings about the production of urban services—is that professionalized "good government" regimes will select police chiefs and develop policies that lead to a "professional" style which produces high arrest rates for certain offenses.[57]

We asked three expert and knowledgeable observers of urban police forces to rate independently each of the 26 cities in our sample as having either professional, aggressive departments or relatively nonprofessional, lax departments. There was a correlation between these expert ratings and the arrest rate of each department. Of the nine departments rated "professional," eight were above the mean in robbery arrest rates; of the fourteen cities rated "nonprofessional," ten were below the mean in arrests. (Three were not rated for lack of knowledge.) [58]

---

[57] Economists' studies of police behavior assume that quantitative resources play a key role in determining the level of police activity as measured by the probability of arrest. Thus, when crime rates rise, the probability of arrest may fall, due to "strained resources," or community demand for more police may lead to an increase in police expenditures and a rise in the probability of arrest. In either case, attempts to measure empirically the deterrent effect of arrests on crime are hampered by a statistical identification problem. That is, it is difficult to determine what part of the empirically-observed association between crime rates and the probability of arrest is due to the behavior of criminals responding to the sanctions of the police system and what part is due to the response of the police system to higher crime rates. Sophisticated econometric techniques exist to handle such problems and they have been applied in econometric studies of deterrence.

Our view of police behavior is that expenditures are much less a determinant of high arrest rates than the policies of the police administrator aimed at controlling the officers' use of discretion in making arrests. In highly professionalized departments the police chief influences the behavior of patrolmen by developing policies that emphasize the law enforcement aspect of patrol work. When infractions of the law are observed, even minor ones, an officer is *expected* to invoke the formal process of the law. In contrast, administrators in nonprofessional departments develop policies that allow the patrolman to overlook a number of situations that technically could be handled by making an arrest. The police administrator's decision and success in developing either of these styles of police behavior is a function, we think, not of expenditures or explicit community choice (such as the demand to do something about rising crime rates) but of the general organizational and political environment as crudely measured by the form of city government.

In the future we hope to focus directly on the ability of these competing hypotheses to explain differences in police activity as measured by the probability of arrest. (The nature of the relationship between the political/organizational environment, police chief policies, and patrol officers' use of discretion is developed in James Q. Wilson, *Varieties of Police Behavior* [Cambridge, Mass.: Harvard University Press, 1968].)

[58] Professional departments are Cincinnati, Dallas, Los Angeles, New York, Oakland, Portland (Oregon), St. Louis, San Diego, and Washington, D.C. Buffalo, Minneapolis, and New Orleans were not rated.

If we use the expert ratings as a dummy variable in our estimation equation in lieu of arrest rates, we obtain the results shown in table B-2. The R² is .68 and the three variables found significant in the previous equation remain significant with the same signs though somewhat changed values. The coefficient of the "police efficiency" dummy variable is 2.373, suggesting that cities with "professional" departments have 2.4 fewer serious robberies per thousand population than those without them. (The mean number of serious robberies in the sample is 8 per 1,000 population.)

Table B-2

REGRESSION ON SERIOUS ROBBERY RATE OF ESTIMATE
OF POLICE EFFICIENCY AND THREE SOCIOECONOMIC
VARIABLES FOR 23 CITIES

Variable	Coefficient	t-statistic	Elasticity
Police efficiency (0,1)	−2.37306	− 2.5967	
Percent nonwhite	0.06234	2.2598	0.28657
Labor force participation	0.01652	0.1431	0.16067
Density	0.00040	3.5974	0.48416

Constant = 1.887; corrected R^2 = .68; F = 13.529

On a substantive level, this finding may seem to contradict the various studies, such as the Kansas City patrol experiment, suggesting that police make no difference in crime rates.[59] In fact there is no contradiction. The Kansas City experiment tested the efficacy of random preventive patrol in marked police cars and found that this strategy made little difference in crime rates. There has been no published experiment, comparable in quality and evaluation, of other police strategies aimed at crime. Non-experimental police data suggest that certain strategies (e.g., "decoy" units) produce much higher arrest rates than either patrol or follow-up investigation but there is as yet no information on the relationship between those strategies and crime rates.[60]

Though no set of controlled experiments either denies or confirms the crime reduction potential of the police, our finding that police behavior makes a difference is consistent with other recent studies employing the same techniques with police reports of crime (as opposed to victimization

---

[59] These studies are reviewed in Wilson, *Thinking About Crime,* op. cit., chap. 5.
[60] Abt Associates, "Exploratory Project Validation Report: New York City Anti-Crime Patrol," typescript submitted to National Institute of Law Enforcement and Criminal Justice, U.S. Department of Justice, Nov. 11, 1974.

surveys). Tittle and Rowe analyzed crime and arrest rates for cities and counties in Florida using partial correlation techniques and found that, above a certain threshold level of arrests, high arrest probabilities were associated with low rates of serious reported crimes.[61] Sjoquist, using ordinary least squares estimation techniques, found that high arrest probabilities are significantly associated with decreases in the rates of robberies, burglaries, and larcenies over $50 in value.[62] Both these studies used the customary controls for socioeconomic variables.

Another methodological issue concerns the specification of the model. It is possible that selecting different variables would eliminate the effect of the police variable or increase the significance of (changeable) socioeconomic variables. We have experimented with other variables, and find none significant. If the proportion of persons with incomes below half the median is substituted for the proportion nonwhite, it is significant, but entering both variables simultaneously eliminates the effect of income. In short, race dominates income for reasons we do not fully understand. We do know that this is consistent with the findings of other studies. In their study of a cohort of ten thousand Philadelphia boys, Wolfgang, Figlio, and Sellin found that the probability of being arrested for an offense was higher for nonwhites than for whites at all socioeconomic levels; indeed, the probability of being arrested was higher for high status nonwhites than for low status whites.[63] The conditions under which nonwhite children grow up are so profoundly different from those under which white ones are reared that they cannot be captured merely by measuring income differences.

Nor are measures of income inequality (Gini ratios) significantly related to robbery rates when other factors are controlled, though in a simple correlation, the Gini ratio is *negatively* associated with robbery (that is, the greater the degree of income inequality, the lower the robbery rate). This may reflect the disproportionately low robbery rates in many southern cities where income inequalities are high.

City size is related to robbery rates—the bigger cities have higher rates—but that relationship disappears when density is controlled. Density is a much more powerful explanatory factor, at least for this sample of cities.

---

[61] Charles R. Tittle and Alan R. Rowe, "Certainty of Arrest and Crime Rates," *Social Forces,* vol. 52, June 1974, pp. 455-67.

[62] David Lawrence Sjoquist, "Property Crime and Economic Behavior: Some Empirical Results," *American Economic Review,* vol. 63, June 1973, pp. 439-46.

[63] Marvin E. Wolfgang, Robert M. Figlio, and Thorsten Sellin, *Delinquency in a Birth Cohort* (Chicago: University of Chicago Press, 1972), p. 301.

The age structure of the population has no identifiable effect on the robbery rate, probably because there is relatively little variation in age structure among these cities (except for Miami with many older persons, and Boston with a large youthful, probably student, population). Furthermore, cities with low crime rates are more likely to retain families with children within their boundaries than are cities with high crime rates, and this fact would confound the predicted effect of youth on crime.

In sum, our initial hypothesis is partially confirmed: low density cities with high arrests and low proportions of nonwhites will have fewer serious robberies than cities with any or all of the opposite characteristics —though we acknowledge our uncertainty as to the exact causal significance of "density" and "arrest." Our measure of the availability of legitimate economic alternatives to crime did not prove to be significant at the city level, though studies using national, statewide, and sub-city data have indicated its importance. These other studies indicate that increasing the employment of young males is of value in reducing crime; our study adds support to the view that increased levels of criminal justice activity can also reduce serious robberies.

Probability of Arrest Measurement Error

Our first measure of police activity is derived by dividing the number of robbery arrests in each city as reported by city police departments to the FBI (*Uniform Crime Reports,* appropriate years) by the number of robberies in that city as measured by the robberies reported by residents to the victimization survey. Both because of the way this variable is constructed and because of measurement problems in the number of arrests and the number of robberies, it seems likely that it is to some extent a biased measure of police activity. In the section above, we dealt with this problem by developing an alternative measure of police activity. Here we deal with these measurement problems directly.

The most serious source of bias results from the fact that the independent variable (probability of arrest) and the dependent variable (the crime rate) are both ratios with the number of robberies in the numerator of the dependent variable and in the denominator of the independent variable. If the number of robberies is over- or under-estimated in some (not all) cities in the sample, the measured relationship between the independent and dependent variable includes spurious negative correlation. Since the theoretically predicted relationship between these two variables is negative, it is impossible to judge if a true negative relationship exists without an alternative measure of police activity—unless the magnitude of the measurement error can be estimated.

Careful analysis of the robbery victimization data suggests that data for certain cities in the sample of 26 may indeed represent an underestimate of the true number of robberies. The rate of trivial robberies (i.e., robberies where no injury occurs, no weapon is used, and the amount stolen is less than $10) is almost three times higher in a low crime city like Portland than in a high crime city like Detroit. Thus, one suspects that persons in Detroit exclude such minor incidents from account in the survey interviews, resulting in a smaller proportion of the true robbery rate being measured in Detroit than in Portland.

If the nature of this underreporting could be more precisely determined it would be possible to estimate the size of the bias mathematically and subsequently derive an unbiased estimate of the probability of arrest coefficient. In the absence of such precise estimates, we must rely on the statistical significance of our alternative measure of police activity as an indication that a true negative relationship exists.

A second source of measurement error arises from the fact that the victimization survey interviews only residents of a city, whereas the police report arrests for all crimes that occur within a city whether the victim was a resident or a nonresident. The probability of arrest coefficient will be biased to the extent that the distribution of arrests for robberies against residents and nonresidents of the city is nonproportional across cities. It seems reasonable to assume that the proportion of arrests for robberies committed against nonresidents will be greater in those cities where the ratio of the transient population to the resident population is highest. Thus, in cities with relatively large transient populations the overstatement of the measure of arrests relative to the measure of crimes will be greater, and the probability of arrest will be a more biased (upward) estimate of the true probability of arrest.

If the overstatement occurs where crime is low, then the negative correlation we are observing between crime and the probability of arrest may simply be spurious correlation resulting from this bias. If the overstatement occurs where crime is high, the bias would tend to result in positive spurious correlation between crime and the probability of arrest. In this case, the negative correlation we are observing would be an underestimate of the true negative relationship. If the overstatement of the probability of arrest is not at all related to the level of crime, then the bias has the effect of obscuring any true relationship and the correlation and regression coefficients are biased toward zero. Again, in this case, the observed negative relationship would be an underestimate of the true negative relationship.

We have used the proportion of the total SMSA population residing in the central city (CC/SMSA) as a crude measure of the relative extent to which nonresident populations move into and out of the central city. The lower the proportion living inside the central city the higher the ratio of the transient population to the resident population. Thus, cities with a low CC/SMSA are those where we would expect the probability of arrest to be overstated—i.e., where a higher proportion of robbery arrests would be for robberies committed against nonresidents. So we want to know if CC/SMSA for our 26 cities is positively, negatively, or not at all related to the robbery rate. The correlation coefficient between CC/SMSA and the total robbery rate for 22 of the cities (Oakland, San Francisco, Minneapolis, and Dallas were excluded because of dual central cities) is $-.053$, suggesting no relationship.

Assuming CC/SMSA is an adequate measure of the overstatement of the probability of arrest, we can conclude that the data are consistent with the hypothesis that the bias in our estimate of the probability of arrest (due to the inclusion of arrest for robberies committed against nonresidents) results in an underestimate of the true negative relationship between crime rates and the probability of arrest.

A third source of measurement error could arise from the fact that we count as robberies only personal victimizations but we use for arrest data police reports of *total* (personal and commercial) robbery arrests. There is no way to break down police arrest data by type of robbery committed. We have found no way to correct for this error and thus we cannot estimate whether the effect of counting reported robberies and arrested robberies differently tends to strengthen or weaken the observed negative relationship. The reader will have to bear in mind this source of uncertainty.

Chapter 5

Education

James S. Coleman
Sara D. Kelly

I. AUTHORITY OVER EDUCATION

Educational policy in the United States is in a state of disorganization and confusion, a disorganization and confusion that has particular impact on education in the cities. The past two decades, and especially the decade of 1965-1975, have marked a change more fundamental than that of the content of educational policy. The change over this period has been in the very agencies of educational policy, and it is the uncompleted character of this change that produces the current state of disorganization and confusion.

In 1954, before the historic Supreme Court decision in the *Brown v. Board of Education* case, authority over educational policy was well established and generally accepted by the various interested parties. The distribution of authority differed somewhat in different cities and states, but it could be described without serious error in this way: Constitutional authority over education rested with the states. However, the states had, from the very beginning of public education, delegated to the localities nearly full control over educational matters, along with responsibility for financing schools in those localities. There was good reason for this, since localities differed widely in their demand for education, in their affluence, and in the costs of education. Thus, although education was to be free and public (not class stratified, as in Europe), it was not to be uniform, but dependent on the demand of local communities and on their capacity to pay for it.

Education was, accordingly, financed by property taxes levied by the locality and was governed by a school board elected by or appointed for that locality. The locality was a city or town, a township, a county (primarily in the South), or in some cases a special taxation district distinct from other political jurisdictions. The school board made some educational policy decisions and left many others to the school superintendent. There was little further delegation, and school principals and teachers were essentially subject to the policies of the superintendent's office. However, authority on questions of discipline and maintenance of order in the schools was generally exercised by the principal.

Thus school policy was divided between three parties, and authority over students primarily held by one party. A few policies were established at the state level (such as age of compulsory education, the length of the school year, some curriculum requirements, etc.); more policies were established by the local school board; and most were established by the local superintendent. Finally, the principal had authority over student behavior in his school. There were significant variations between large city school districts, which were only minimally subject to state authority, and districts in smaller cities and towns, which both used state services more fully and were more subject to state authority. In some states, such as New York, the state superintendent's office exercised more authority than in others. But in general, the states exercised little authority.

From this early pattern, there had been slow changes involving a drift of authority to the state level. The drift occurred because of increasing social and economic interdependence among localities, and it was manifested both by state assumption of responsibility for supplementary financing of education, and state assumption of authority over a greater range of matters. These included accreditation of schools for state aid, with state-established criteria for minimally-acceptable educational programs and facilities, and, in some states, selection of textbooks.

This was the way matters stood when the educational turmoil of the 1960s began. The present state of control of schools, after more than a decade of that turmoil, is one of chaos. Many schools are operating under court orders which dictate the distribution of pupils and staff among schools, school budgets, and some policies within schools. Others are operating under a "plan" deemed acceptable by the U.S. Department of Health, Education, and Welfare, involving the same administrative activities. For all school districts, the allocation of funds among schools within a district, and among expenditure categories within schools, is now subject to federal government jurisdiction, following federal entry into school financing with the 1965 Elementary and Secondary Education Act. In response to the clamor for neighborhood control, local school boards in several large cities have formed "community school boards" with broader powers over the subdistrict (e.g., hiring and firing of principals) than ever before existed. Teachers, through unionization and collective bargaining, have in some places not only greatly increased their control of budget allocation but have also gained a voice in textbook selection and other program-related policies.[1] State legislatures have enacted laws about transfer policies from one district to another, or one school to another within a district, and have begun to reassume responsibility for equality of educational opportunity within the state. State courts and the U.S. Supreme Court have ruled on the constitutionality of particular forms of state supplementation of school financing, leading to great confusion about how schools should be financed, and about who has the authority to determine it.[2]

Along with these challenges to control over school policies, the principal's authority over students within the school has been sharply reduced with the emergence of students' rights, most often won through court cases. Clearly, the present state of authority over school policy is not a stable one. It could lead to any of a number of different stable states.

In this chapter we will examine, in addition to the issue of control discussed above, three general issues that have been at the center of education controversy in American cities. They are racial integration in the schools, school financing, and the internal functioning of the school. The aim will be to examine the issues and then to give some ideas both about possible stabilization in the structure and functioning of schools and possible resolutions of the issues themselves.

While these upheavals in policy surrounding and within the schools have been taking place, cohorts of children have passed through the

---

[1]Unionization of teachers has been extraordinary during a period in which unionization elsewhere was increasing little or none outside the public employee sector. Between May 1965 and May 1974, the American Federation of Teachers' membership increased from 110,552 to 414,854. Teachers' strikes also began during this decade. Before 1966, there had never been more than 9 work stoppages by teachers (as recorded by the Bureau of Labor Statistics); since 1966, the number has grown from 30 in 1966 to 117 in 1973. By 1973, educational employees, teachers, and support personnel were on strike more frequently than any other category of government employees, and their strikes comprised 83 percent of total idleness by government employees.

[2]A major issue has been whether education is a "fundamental interest" under the Constitution; if so, the federal courts have the authority to judge how schools should be financed, in protection of that fundamental interest. If not, state legislatures have this authority. The U.S. Supreme Court has in *San Antonio Independent School District v. Rodriguez* ruled that it is not a fundamental interest, thus throwing the issue back to the state legislatures.

schools, experiencing whatever policies are in effect, and by their demands as well shaping the functioning of the schools. During the past ten years, over 80 million Americans, or nearly 2 out of every 5 Americans living today, have experienced at least one year of elementary or secondary school.

Consequently, it is important to gain some sense not only of these struggles involving the schools, but also of the outcomes of schooling. A major one of these outcomes is achievement as measured by standard tests. This achievement outcome of schooling has itself been part of the controversies over school policy, being used to justify one or another policy position. Furthermore, a controversy that has gone to the heart of schooling itself has centered around achievement in school. In the 1960's research began to be used for the first time on a wide scale to examine the effects of variations in schooling on achievement. The results of these analyses have not only been important elements in the school desegregation fights, but have led to arguments that schools have no effects or minimal effects on achievement.

In order to gain some knowledge of how achievement has changed over the past few years, we will attempt to piece together some results of achievement testing in several school systems over years for which data can be obtained. This will not be a comprehensive picture of trends in achievement outcomes, but insofar as consistent trends may be found in different systems, some idea of trends throughout the country can be gained.

II. DESEGREGATION[3]

Since the Supreme Court decision of 1954 which outlawed dual school systems for blacks and whites in the United States, various policies have been instituted to bring about desegregation of schools. The first policies, adopted in many school systems in border states immediately after the decision, eliminated the dual systems in compliance with the Court decision by having all children from the same geographically-defined area attend the same school—in some cases accompanied by adjustments of boundaries to insure acceptance by whites. Beginning in 1966, however, and slowly at first, the executive branch of the federal

[3]Much of the material in this section is drawn from *Trends in School Segregation, 1968-73*, by James S. Coleman, Sara D. Kelly and John A. Moore (Washington, D.C.: The Urban Institute, 1975). That paper includes a more extensive analysis of the changes in segregation during the period 1968-73.

government, armed with the Civil Rights Act of 1964 and school aid funds from the Elementary and Secondary Education Act of 1965, began to impose demands for more complete desegregation on those districts that had not eliminated the dual system. In some cases the demands required those districts to institute affirmative integration when residential patterns would lead to a high degree of racial imbalance if nothing were done beyond elimination of the dual system. In addition, a number of anti-segregation court cases were instituted (primarily by the Legal Defense Fund of the NAACP). As a general rule, the later the compliance of the district with a court order or with an approved HEW plan of desegregation, the more extensive the desegregation required. For example, border cities like Baltimore and Washington, which desegregated shortly after the 1954 decision, did so by eliminating their dual school zoning pattern, and were thus in compliance (though standards imposed later have often declared such systems out of compliance). Cities in the deep South which desegregated in the late 60's or in 1970, in contrast, were required to initiate action to increase integration beyond that which arose from abolition of dual attendance zones.

This is one of the major trends in school segregation over the past ten years: an increase in "segregation" simply through an expansion of what is defined to be segregated. Thus a shifting ideal has increased the disparity between the ideal and the actual in school integration.

In more recent years, court suits have been instituted in a few northern districts which had never maintained dual systems. The general pattern of these suits (the best-publicized of which were Denver, Detroit, and Boston) followed those of the more recent and aggressive suits in the South, charging that specific actions of the school board or administration (such as location of new buildings or drawing of school assignment boundaries) were designed to increase or had the effect of increasing the racial segregation within the system. The remedies imposed by the courts ranged from specific actions designed to undo the effect of earlier segregating policies to the achievement of system-wide racial balance through busing of students, and in one case, Detroit, to the achievement of integration through busing children across system boundaries between city and suburbs (a remedy overturned by the Supreme Court). The precedent followed in most recent cases has been one in which the remedy required is the achievement of system-wide racial balance through busing of students.

This brief description of policies on racial segregation in this country is intended merely as an introduction to a series of questions about the actual state of racial integration in schools, and recent trends in that state.

For actions taken by one branch of government and at one level of government interact with actions taken by individuals and by other branches and levels of government. The actual state of school integration is a result of this interaction. It is different from what it would be in the absence of the policies designed to bring about integration; but it is more than a simple consequence of the policies. It is especially important in the case of school desegregation to examine this interaction, because many of the actions taken by individuals, and some of those taken by their local government bodies, have precisely the opposite effect on school desegregation to that intended by federal government policy. (Indeed, there are numerous examples of government policy in which the result of the interaction between policy and response is precisely the opposite of the result intended by those who initiated the policy.) The most obvious such individual action, of course, is a move of residence to flee school integration.

There is only one set of data that allows a systematic examination of trends in school desegregation. Beginning in 1968 and continuing to the present, the Office for Civil Rights of the Department of Health, Education, and Welfare has obtained data from school systems throughout the United States showing the racial composition of each school in the district, the racial composition of teaching staffs, and related information. The data for the years 1968-73 are available and allow a detailed statistical analysis of the desegregation status and trends among schools throughout the United States although they do not show the racial mix in classrooms within the school. They are unique in this, and in the opportunity they provide for examining what has actually occurred throughout a period during which numerous policies related to school desegregation have been initiated at local, state, and federal levels, in courts and legislatures, and in the executive and administrative branches of government. Most of these policies have been aimed at bringing about desegregation, though in a few cases, such as antibusing actions in Congress, they have been aimed at preventing certain kinds of desegregation.

In the following examination, we do not intend to imply that the policy aim of eliminating all segregation among schools within a system is the "correct" one, or that other policies which would either go less far (such as eliminating only that school segregation not due to residence) or further (such as eliminating all segregation among classes within a school) are not correct.[4] Rather, the analysis is simply descriptive, showing

---

[4] What the "correct" policy is depends not only on the implicitly aimed-for social consequences, but also upon the scope of authority legitimately exercised by the government units applying the policy. This in turn depends on just which individ-

the result of government desegregation actions and individual segregating actions taken together, and allowing some assessment of the effects of each. In this way, the result suggests the limits of government policy, or at least the limits of policies carried out in the conflict mode that has characterized school desegregation policy.

We will begin by examining the state of racial integration among schools within districts in 1968, and then examine the changes that occurred over the period 1968-73. What will be of special interest is the differential changes that occurred over that period of time in different kinds of school settings: in different regions of the country, in school districts of different sizes, and in particular in large cities, giving rise to very divergent trends.

For much of the analysis of trends, two separate data series must be used. The even years, 1968, 1970, and 1972, constitute a census of U.S. school districts, covering all but a few small districts and over 90 percent of the children in school.[5] The odd years include only a sample of school systems, primarily the districts in which most minority pupils are found. When we examine trends over time in individual districts the odd-numbered years can be safely included, because each district is either included as a whole or excluded. But for national averages and averages across regions, across states, and across metropolitan areas, the odd years cannot be included, and the series must end with 1972.

---

ual rights citizens have vested in their government for collective use, through the Constitution and legislative acts. For example, for the policy aim of eliminating all segregation among schools, whatever its source, the most effective implementation would be federally-specified pupil assignment to schools to create precise racial balance, disregarding school district and state lines. However, such a policy would use collectively certain rights that individuals have retained to themselves or vested in a more local level of government. As another example, citizens have vested certain authority in the court, such as constitutional protection, but have vested a wider range of authority in elected legislatures. Thus certain policy aims, such as the elimination of segregation among schools whatever its source, may be appropriate for legislative action if it achieves certain desired consequences, but not appropriate for court action, which must be directed, not toward achieving desirable social goals, but toward insuring constitutional protection for all citizens. It is useful also to point out that data such as these which show the indirect and unintended consequences of school desegregation actions may be relevant for certain desegregation decisions, but not for others. They are relevant for an executive or legislative body which is attempting in its action to achieve a desirable social consequence. They are not relevant for a court decision which is acting to insure equal protection under the 14th Amendment.

[To us this seems too rigid a view of the division of authority among the branches.—Eds.]

[5] See Appendix A of Coleman, Kelly, and Moore, op. cit., for sampling plan.

For a school system, a statistical measure directly relevant to the question of school segregation is the proportion of white children in the same school with the "average" black child. This gives a measure of the experience of the "average" black child with whites in that school district. A similar measure can be calculated for the proportion of children of each racial group in the school attended by the average child from each racial group.[6]

This measure, however, is affected not only by the degree of segregation between two racial groups in different schools in the system, but also by the system-wide proportion of children in each group. If there are few white children in the system, for example, then whether or not each school has the same proportion of whites, there will still be few whites in the average black child's school. Because of this, it is valuable also to have a measure of just how far from an even distribution across the schools the actual distribution is, that is, a measure that is standardized for the number of whites in the system. Such a measure can be constructed, having a value of 1.0 if segregation is complete, and 0 if there is complete racial balance.[7]

---

[6] The Office of Civil Rights surveys measure enrollments of the following categories: Negroes, American Indians, Orientals, Spanish Surnamed Americans, and Others. White nonminority and undesignated minority groups are included in the category "Other."

The measure of interracial school contact may be constructed as follows: if we number the schools in the system $1, \ldots k, \ldots n$, and consider the first school, there is a given proportion of whites in this school. Call this p_{1w}. There are a certain number of blacks in the school. Call this n_{1b}. Then for this number of blacks, the proportion of whites in their school is p_{1w}. If we average this proportion over all schools, weighting by the number of blacks, we obtain the desired measure, which we may call s_{bw}, the proportion of white children in the school of the average black child (or more generally, labeling the group i and j for generality):

$$s_{bw} = \frac{\sum_k n_{kb} p_{kw}}{\sum_k n_{kb}} \tag{1}$$

or for any groups i and j

$$s_{ij} = \frac{\sum_k n_{ki} p_{kj}}{\sum_k n_{ki}} \tag{2}$$

[7] The standardized measure of segregation is constructed as follows. If the same proportion of children from group j were in each school, then s_{ij} (see preceding footnote for notation) would be equal to p_j. If the children of group j were all in schools by themselves, totally isolated from children of group i, s_{ij} would be 0. Thus a measure of how far s_{ij} is from p_j is $(p_j - s_{ij})/p_j$. This we

Segregation in 1968

In 1968 in the United States, 15 percent of the children in public schools (grades 1-12) were black, 6 percent were of other minorities, and 79 percent were majority whites. But the average black child in the U.S. schools went to a school which had 74 percent black children in it, only 22 percent white children, and 4 percent other minorities. Meanwhile, the average majority white child was in a school which was 93 percent white, only 4 percent black, and 3 percent other minorities.

These numbers show that the interracial contact in American schools in 1968 was quite low. Black children had more contact with whites than whites had with blacks, due to the disparity in overall numbers; but the separation was quite marked. This separation is composed of two parts: segregation among schools within the same school district, and segregation due to blacks and whites living in different school districts. Using the measure in which complete segregation has a value of 1.0, as described above, we obtain a segregation index of .63 for average within-district segregation, weighted according to the number of blacks in the district for the United States in 1968. The average, weighted according to the number of whites in the district, is only .23. This means that the average white child, living in a smaller district in a suburb, attends school in a less racially segregated district than does the average black child. In the following analysis where average within-district segregation is used, the average is weighted by the number of blacks.

Variation by Region

The degree of school segregation differed considerably from one part of the country to the other in 1968. Table 1 shows the contact of blacks and whites, and the segregation, in each of the Bureau of Census geographic regions.[8]

---

will call r_{ij}, which may be thought of as a measure of the degree of segregation, or the degree to which segregation between schools is responsible for the value of s_{ij}. The formula is

$$r_{ij} = \frac{p_j - s_{ij}}{p_j} \qquad (3)$$

[8] Two regions have been subdivided because the character of racial segregation has differed within the region. Hawaii and Alaska have been separated as "outlying" states from the Pacific region; and the South Atlantic and East South Central regions have been combined and redivided into Border (Delaware, Maryland, West Virginia, Kentucky) and Southeast (all others in these two regions). In all tabulations the outlying states, Hawaii and Alaska, are dropped because there is no black-white segregation in their schools, and the number of blacks in those states is very small.

If we compare columns 1 and 3, the table shows the disparity between the proportion white in each region and the proportion white among the average black's schoolmates. Although the proportion white ranges from .69 to .93, in no region does the average black have a majority of white schoolmates, and only in New England does the proportion even approach a majority. A comparison of columns 2 and 4 shows a similar disparity for whites: although the proportion black reaches .29 in one region, in no region does the average white have more than 7 percent black schoolmates.

Table 1

BLACK-WHITE CONTACT AND SCHOOL SEGREGATION IN 1968 BY REGION

| | Proportion | | Schoolmates | | Average black-white segregation within district (5) |
	White (1)	Black (2)	Whites for average black (3)	Blacks for average white (4)	
U.S.	.79	.15	.22	.04	.63
New England	.93	.05	.49	.03	.35
Middle Atlantic	.81	.14	.31	.05	.43
Border	.79	.21	.26	.07	.49
Southeast	.69	.29	.16	.07	.75
West South Central	.78	.16	.18	.04	.69
East North Central	.87	.12	.29	.04	.58
West North Central	.90	.09	.28	.03	.61
Mountain	.81	.03	.37	.01	.49
Pacific	.78	.08	.26	.02	.56

Source: James S. Coleman, Sara D. Kelly, and John A. Moore, *Trends in School Segregation 1968-73* (Washington, D.C.: The Urban Institute, 1975), table 2, revised.

These disparities reflect the overall separation of black and white children in each region, partly as a result of separation into different districts in the region, partly as a result of attendance at different schools within the same district. The measure of segregation for the latter, the within-district segregation, is shown in column 5. The Southeast shows the highest level of within-district segregation with the West South Central region showing the second-highest level and other regions following closely after it.

Variation by Size of District

Policies of desegregation, as well as individual responses to it, also vary greatly by district size. The process of desegregation in an urban area is very different from that in a small district in a rural area. Thus, just as it is important to examine regional variations because of historical differences and because of the different desegregation policies applied in the North and South, it is also important to examine variations by district size. Since district boundaries most often coincide with central city boundaries, variations in district size are largely coincident with variation in city size.

Table 2 shows the 1968 interracial contact and segregation by district size. The columns, numbered 1–5, have the same meaning as columns 1–5 of table 1. First, columns 1 and 2 show the sharp racial differences by district size: the smaller the district, the greater the proportion white and the smaller the proportion black. One result of this is shown in columns 3 and 4: the average black child has an increasing proportion of white schoolmates as district size decreases, and the average white has a decreasing proportion of black schoolmates as district size decreases.

Table 2

BLACK-WHITE CONTACT AND SCHOOL SEGREGATION IN 1968 BY DISTRICT SIZE[a]

| | Proportion of all blacks in districts of this size | Proportion | | Schoolmates | | Black-white segregation within district (5) |
		White (1)	Black (2)	Whites for average black (3)	Blacks for average white (4)	
U.S.	1.00	.79	.15	.22	.07	.63
DISTRICT SIZE						
More than 100,000	.35	.52	.38	.12	.09	.71
25-100,000	.23	.73	.20	.22	.06	.66
10-25,000	.14	.83	.11	.30	.04	.54
5-10,000	.13	.86	.11	.28	.04	.59
2.5-5,000	.09	.88	.09	.30	.03	.56
Less than 2,500	.06	.90	.06	.35	.02	.44

a. The size classification for districts was carried out only once, for comparability across years. Sizes are based on 1972 enrollments.

Source: Coleman, Kelly, and Moore, *Trends in School Desegregation*, table 3, revised.

Column 5 shows that, given the racial distributions in the districts, the average segregation is greatest within the largest districts, and declines somewhat as district size decreases. Thus not all the increase in the proportion of white schoolmates for the average black child in smaller districts is due to the greater proportion of whites in those districts. Part is due to less segregation in the smaller districts.

This lesser segregation in smaller districts is even more pronounced in most regions of the country than is shown in table 2. Only in the Southeast and West South Central states is segregation in smaller districts in 1968 rather high (though not as high as in the larger districts). Segregation declines sharply in the other regions as district size decreases; segregation in the largest districts is as high as segregation in the South, but for the smaller districts in nonsouthern regions it is much less.

Segregation in the 22 Largest Central City Districts

As table 2 showed, segregation is most pronounced in the largest school districts, which tend to be located in the largest cities. Table 3, in the same format as table 2, shows for twenty-two of the twenty-three largest central city districts the proportion of schoolmates of the other race in columns 3 and 4 and the measure of segregation in column 5.[9] The first seventeen of these cities have enrollments of over 100,000 (the largest size category in table 2); the last five are in the 25-100,000 class. In only four cities (Columbus, Boston, San Diego, and San Francisco) did the average black child have more than a quarter of his schoolmates white, and in only six cities (Philadelphia, Detroit, Baltimore, New Orleans, New York, and San Francisco, excluding Washington, D.C., which is an aberrant case, almost racially homogeneous) did the average white child have more than 15 percent of his schoolmates black. This low degree of contact is reflected by the segregation measures, eight of which are .80 or above, and only three of which are below .60. These figures reemphasize what was suggested earlier: that segregation in large cities in 1968 was not concentrated in any region of the country, but appeared to a similar and high degree in cities of all regions.

It is clear from these data that by 1968 desegregation of schools was far from an accomplished task in cities and towns of all sizes in the South; but that in the largest cities it was equally high in many places where dual school systems had never existed. But this was the picture in 1968, before the major thrust of desegregation in schools had occurred.

---

9. These central city school districts are classified according to 1972 enrollment and an Office of Education metropolitan status classification. Of the 23 largest central city districts, Albuquerque (the 22nd largest) has been excluded because it is not among the largest 50 cities in total population.

The next four years show extensive desegregation. It is these trends to which we now turn.

Table 3

BLACK-WHITE CONTACT AND SCHOOL SEGREGATION
IN 1968 FOR 22 LARGEST CENTRAL CITY SCHOOL DISTRICTS
(Districts ranked by 1972 Enrollment)

| | Proportion | | Schoolmates | | Segrega-tion within district (5) |
	White (1)	Black (2)	Whites for average black (3)	Blacks for average white (4)	
1. New York	.44	.32	.23	.17	.47
2. Los Angeles	.54	.23	.08	.03	.86
3. Chicago	.38	.53	.05	.08	.86
4. Philadelphia	.39	.59	.14	.21	.64
5. Detroit	.39	.59	.13	.20	.66
6. Houston	.53	.33	.06	.04	.89
7. Baltimore	.35	.65	.10	.19	.71
8. Dallas	.61	.31	.06	.03	.91
9. Cleveland	.42	.56	.07	.09	.85
10. Washington, D.C.	.06	.93	.03	.44	.53
11. Memphis	.46	.54	.04	.04	.92
12. Milwaukee	.73	.24	.18	.06	.76
13. San Diego	.76	.12	.26	.04	.66
14. Columbus	.74	.26	.30	.10	.60
15. Tampa	.74	.19	.16	.04	.78
16. St. Louis	.36	.64	.07	.12	.82
17. New Orleans	.31	.67	.09	.19	.72
18. Indianapolis	.66	.34	.22	.11	.67
19. Boston	.68	.27	.27	.11	.60
20. Atlanta	.38	.62	.06	.09	.85
21. Denver	.66	.14	.20	.04	.69
22. San Francisco	.41	.28	.26	.17	.38

Source: Coleman, Kelly, and Moore, *Trends in School Segregation,* table 6, revised.

Trends in Within-District Segregation

Between 1968 and 1972, black-white segregation in the United States was sharply reduced. In 1972, 16 percent of public school children were black and 77 percent were white. The average black child in 1972 went to a school that was 61 percent black (compared to 74 percent in 1968) and 34 percent white, and the average white child was in a school which

was 89 percent white and 7 percent black. The following comparison
shows the change from 1968 to 1972:

| | Proportion | | Schoolmates | | Black-white segregation within district |
	White	Black	Whites for average black	Blacks for average white	
1968	.79	.15	.22	.04	.63
1972	.77	.16	.34	.07	.37

The change from 1968 to 1972 is substantial. Indeed, the average
within-district segregation in 1972 between blacks and whites may be no
greater than that between some pairs of white ethnic groups. But the
change from 1968 to 1972 consists of very different changes in different
locales. Figure 1 shows the trends in average segregation within school
districts (comparable to column 5 of table 1) in each region over the
three points in time, 1968, 1970, and 1972. There is a radical drop in
the Southeast, from highest at .75 in 1968 to lowest at .19 in 1972, and
there are rather large declines in the West South Central, Mountain,
and Pacific regions. In the New England, Middle Atlantic, and East North
Central regions, there has been virtually no change in segregation. These
trends show that school desegregation during this period (during which
most desegregation took place) was almost wholly a southern affair, with
the far West being the only exception. As we have seen, this concentration in the South was largely the consequence of federal requirements,
supported by legal decisions in the courts, aimed at eliminating segregation where dual school systems remained. The figure suggests, however,
that the segregation eliminated was not only that due to dual systems;
it was also that due to patterns of individual residential location within
districts that in the North have led to within-district segregation of between .35 and .60.

But apart from having occurred primarily in the South and to a lesser
extent in the far West, how did desegregation proceed in districts of
different sizes? Figure 2 shows the changes in average segregation within
districts of various sizes over this four-year period. The results are striking.
Districts greater than 100,000 in size changed very little; and the amount
of change increased steadily as the district size decreased. Among districts
10,000 or below in size, segregation is small indeed, less than .15 in 1972.
The figure thus shows that desegregation policies were very effective in
the smaller districts (though we have not yet examined the effects on
total segregation), and much less effective in the largest districts.

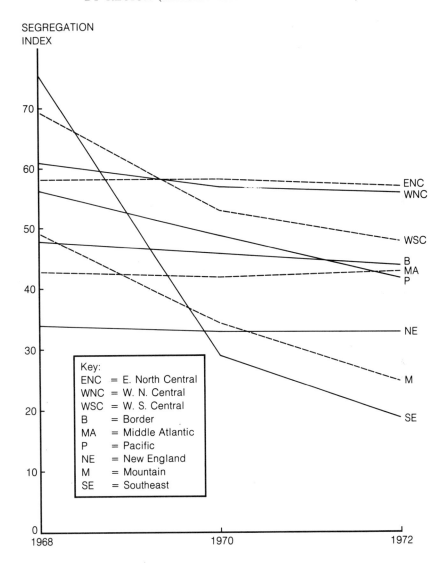

Figure 1
AVERAGE WITHIN-DISTRICT SEGREGATION, 1968–1972,
BY REGION (ALASKA AND HAWAII OMITTED)

SOURCE: James S. Coleman, Sara D. Kelly, and John A. Moore, *Trends in School Segregation 1968–73* (Washington, D.C.: The Urban Institute, 1975), table 2, revised.

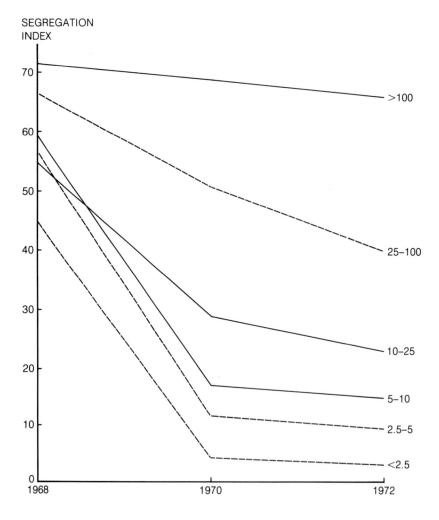

Figure 2
AVERAGE WITHIN-DISTRICT SEGREGATION, 1968–1972,
BY DISTRICT SIZE (IN THOUSANDS)

SOURCE: James S. Coleman, Sara D. Kelly, and John A. Moore, *Trends in School
Segregation 1968–73* (Washington, D.C.: The Urban Institute, 1975), table
3, revised.

But these changes in segregation by size of district do not give the complete picture because desegregation policy was focused primarily in the South. Moreover, most of the blacks in smaller districts were located in the South, so great amounts of desegregation did take place in small districts in those regions (the Southeast and West South Central states) where small-district segregation had existed. As a result, by 1972 the Southeast not only had, overall, the least segregation, as figure 1 indicated, but it had less segregation than most other regions in all size districts. During the period 1968-72, and primarily during the two-year period 1968-70, school districts of all sizes in the Southeast changed from being the most segregated in the nation to being among the least segregated.

Change in 22 Largest Central City Districts

Finally, what changes in within-district segregation were occurring in the 22 largest central city districts? The left side of table 4 shows the segregation of each in 1968 and 1973, together with the change, in column 3. The table reveals the dramatic reduction in some southern cities, in Indianapolis among the northern cities, and in Denver and San Francisco among western cities. It shows, however, an increase in five northern cities and one border city, indicating that even during this period of major desegregation, and even within the city boundaries themselves, there were residential movements increasing the segregation. In fact, the number of northern cities in which segregation increased was as great as the number in which it was reduced.

But this does not tell the whole story, even apart from the question of segregation between districts. There have been substantial population shifts in some of these cities, and we can ask, given these population shifts, to what extent does the decrease in segregation (where it occurs) increase the proportion of white schoolmates for the average black? The right-hand side of table 4 answers that question by comparing the proportion of white schoolmates for the average black in each of these districts in 1968 with the proportion in 1973. Although segregation decreased between 1968 and 1973 in 16 of the 22 cities, the proportion of white schoolmates for the average black increased in only ten of those sixteen. In three it decreased, and it remained unchanged in three. Thus although segregation was reduced in most of the 22 cities, the contact of the average black with white schoolmates has increased in less than half of them. Only in those cities where desegregation was great did the contact increase substantially—and even in Atlanta, where segregation decreased

Table 4

BLACK-WHITE CONTACT AND SCHOOL SEGREGATION FOR
22 LARGEST CENTRAL CITY SCHOOL DISTRICTS (1968-73)
(Districts ranked by 1972 Enrollment)

	Segregation Measures			Proportion white schoolmates for average black		
	1968 (1)	1973 (2)	change (1973−1968) (3)	1968 (4)	1973 (5)	change (1973−1968) (6)
1. New York	.47	.50	+.03	.23	.17	−.06
2. Los Angeles	.86	.79	−.07	.08	.09	+.01
3. Chicago	.86	.88	+.02	.05	.04	−.01
4. Philadelphia	.64	.72	+.08	.14	.10	−.04
5. Detroit	.66	.62	−.04	.13	.11	−.02
6. Houston	.89	.73	−.16	.06	.11	+.05
7. Baltimore	.71	.69	−.02	.10	.09	−.01
8. Dallas	.91	.69	−.22	.06	.15	+.09
9. Cleveland	.85	.87	+.02	.07	.05	−.02
10. Wash., D.C.	.53	.49	−.04	.03	.02	−.01
11. Memphis	.92	.31	−.61	.04	.22	+.18
12. Milwaukee	.76	.73	−.03	.18	.18	.00
13. San Diego	.66	.53	−.13	.26	.34	+.08
14. Columbus	.60	.57	−.03	.30	.30	.00
15. Tampa	.78	.04	−.74	.16	.72	+.56
16. St. Louis	.82	.85	+.03	.07	.05	−.02
17. New Orleans	.72	.57	−.15	.09	.09	.00
18. Indianapolis	.67	.39	−.28	.22	.35	+.13
19. Boston	.60	.63	+.03	.27	.21	−.06
20. Atlanta	.85	.48	−.37	.06	.09	+.03
21. Denver	.69	.31	−.38	.20	.39	+.19
22. San Francisco	.38	.07	−.31	.26	.28	+.02

Source: Coleman, Kelly, and Moore, *Trends in School Segregation*, op. cit., table
10, revised.

markedly, from .85 to .48, the proportion of white schoolmates for the average black child increased only .03—from .06 to .09—because the white school population dropped 62 percent between 1968 and 1973.

This last result leads directly to a set of further questions about the larger effects of school desegregation over this period. Desegregation policies have been confined wholly to within-district desegregation, but, as has been evident in earlier examination, there was, especially in the North, substantial segregation because blacks and whites lived in different districts—in particular, there were larger proportions of blacks in large districts and larger proportions of whites in small districts. We can ask, then, what change there has been in segregation between districts during this period. Has it increased, as appears likely, and if so, to what extent? Finally, we can ask just how desegregation within districts has affected the movement of whites from districts with high proportions of blacks and low segregation to districts with smaller proportions of blacks.

These questions are important because the distribution of children by race in schools is not merely the result of court orders and the policies of federal, state, and local governments—it is also the result of individual decisions about where to live and whether to send one's children to public or nonpublic schools. As incomes increase, more families have these options open to them, though residential options for black families are more restricted, due to lower average incomes and residential discrimination. Thus the distribution of children among schools is the result of interaction between the collective decisions by governmental units and the decisions of individual families. In economic policy, governments have come to recognize that final outcomes depend not merely on the direct effects of a policy but also upon the indirect effects. In other areas of social policy, the indirect effects have usually been ignored, as if the policy directly controlled all of the final outcomes.

Racial segregation among schools can show well these indirect effects, because much of the indirect effect is to modify the distribution of white and black children among districts, and thus to change the between-district segregation. In contrast, the direct effects of government policy have consisted of changes in the distribution of white and black children among schools within a district. Having examined the latter effects, we will now turn to between-district segregation, which has not been the object of governmental policy.

Changes in Segregation between Districts

The increase in segregation between districts has partially counterbalanced the decreases in segregation within districts. This can be seen in table 5, which presents figures on within- and between-district segregation in 1968 and 1972 for each geographic region.[10] Within-district segre-

---

[10] The between-district segregation is calculated just as in equations (2) and (3), except that the units over which interracial contact is calculated in equation (2) are not schools, but school districts. It should be noted that the total segregation is not the sum of within-district (which is an average over districts, weighted by the proportion black in each district) and between-district segregation. Total segregation in a region is calculated over the whole region, as if there were no school districts. (It would be the sum of within- and between-district segregation if the average for the former were weighted in a different way.)

Table 5

CHANGES IN WITHIN-DISTRICT AND BETWEEN-DISTRICT
SEGREGATION IN 1968 AND 1972 IN EACH REGION

	Within district			Between district		
	1968 (1)	1972 (2)	Change (3)	1968 (4)	1972 (5)	Change (6)
United States	.63	.37	−.26	.32	.36	+.04
New England	.35	.33	−.02	.25	.31	+.06
Middle Atlantic	.43	.43	.00	.38	.44	+.06
Border	.49	.44	−.05	.48	.48	.00
Southeast	.75	.19	−.56	.19	.22	+.03
West South Central	.69	.48	−.21	.32	.37	+.05
East North Central	.58	.57	−.01	.30	.32	+.02
West North Central	.61	.56	−.05	.35	.39	+.04
Mountain	.49	.25	−.24	.15	.17	+.02
Pacific	.56	.42	−.14	.30	.34	+.04

Source: Coleman, Kelly, and Moore, *Trends in School Segregation*, op. cit., table 11, revised.

gation has declined in every region except the Middle Atlantic, where it remained constant, while between-district segregation has increased in every region except Border, where it remained constant. In 1968, within-district segregation was greater than between-district segregation in every region; by 1972 between-district segregation was greater in three of the nine regions. Thus, segregation that reflects residential separation into different school districts shows a steady increase throughout the country.

Segregation within and between Districts in Metropolitan Areas

Another way of seeing what's happening in school segregation in the largest urban areas is to examine trends in the segregation between different school districts in the same metropolitan area. Most large cities have a separate school district from that of the surrounding suburbs (although many districts in the South are countywide), and just as there is racial segregation because blacks and whites attend different schools in the same district, there is also racial segregation because blacks and whites live in different districts in the metropolitan area. Although within-district segregation has been reduced in a number of cities (especially in the South), between-district segregation has been increasing in each of the metropolitan areas containing the 22 largest central city districts, except Washington, D.C.

Table 6 compares the within-district segregation in each of the 22 largest central city districts and the between-district segregation in their metropolitan areas in 1968 and 1972.[11] In addition, the trends in between-district segregation exhibited from 1968 to 1972 are projected forward to 1976 in a simple linear projection. The data show that already in 1972, the between-district segregation is substantial in many of these metropolitan areas, for example, greater than .40 in nine of them. In Washington, D.C., and San Francisco, it exceeds the segregation within the central city itself. Furthermore, the projections of these trends to 1976 show that it may be expected to grow substantially in many metropolitan areas. And in two metropolitan areas in addition to Washington and San Francisco—Detroit and Atlanta—it will exceed the within-district segregation of these cities (assuming that the latter does not change).[12] Thus future segregation in metropolitan areas is as much a matter of segregation between districts as it is a matter of segregation within districts.

The Washington, D.C., metropolitan area, as the only one in which between-district school segregation is decreasing, illustrates the kind of process that may ultimately be expected to occur in many metropolitan areas as an outgrowth that is partly, or sometimes heavily, fueled by present patterns of within-district school desegregation, and by continuing patterns of residential change in major cities with large black populations. Washington schools became almost completely nonwhite (6 percent white in 1968, and 3 percent in 1973), with between-district segregation of whites and blacks increasing before 1968, when it was highest of all the 22 cities. Finally, the between-district segregation had nowhere to go but down, and in 1972 Washington, though still highest, had dropped from 66 to 59 percent. In this pattern, of course, the central city schools first turn nearly all black before there is reduction of the city-suburb segregation by expansion of the black ghetto to the suburbs.

All the changes described so far suggest a strong response on the part of families to school desegregation, especially where desegregation has

---

[11] Data are available, as in other tables, for 1973 for these central cities, but cover only some of the noncentral city districts in 1973. Thus 1972 comparisons must be used. Unfortunately, 1974 data, which will soon be available, is on an even more restricted sample.

[12] Of course, desegregation within Boston in 1974 and in Detroit in 1976 reduces sharply the within-district segregation in those cities.

Table 6

BLACK-WHITE SCHOOL SEGREGATION WITHIN THE
CENTRAL CITY DISTRICT, AND BETWEEN DISTRICTS
IN THE METROPOLITAN AREA

	1968		1972		Projected* 1976
	Within Central City	Between Districts	Within Central City	Between Districts	Between Districts
New York	.47	.28	.48	.34	.41
Los Angeles	.86	.25	.80	.28	.31
Chicago	.86	.40	.87	.48	.55
Philadelphia	.64	.39	.70	.44	.48
Detroit	.66	.47	.64	.57	.67
Houston	.89	.15	.74	.26	.37
Baltimore	.71	.38	.69	.42	.46
Dallas	.91	.16	.72	.26	.36
Cleveland	.85	.43	.87	.47	.51
Washington, D.C.	.53	.66	.47	.59	.52
Memphis	.92	.04	.79	.05	.06
Milwaukee	.75	.15	.76	.21	.27
San Diego	.66	.06	.55	.07	.07
Columbus, Ohio	.60	.12	.58	.14	.16
Tampa	.78	.01	.03	.01	.01
St. Louis	.82	.47	.84	.54	.61
New Orleans	.72	.24	.61	.32	.41
Indianapolis	.67	.19	.57	.25	.31
Boston	.60	.21	.64	.28	.34
Atlanta	.85	.36	.63	.51	.65
Denver	.69	.21	.33	.26	.31
San Francisco	.38	.40	.08	.45	.52

* Projections are simple linear projections which, over small ranges and in the absence of sharp actions such as large-scale desegregation over the whole metropolitan area, are sufficient for rough projections.

been great. Direct evidence, however, lies in the loss of white children from districts undergoing desegregation, which shows the effect of desegregation on the composition of central city schools. Analysis of these effects, using the same data, is reported elsewhere,[13] and it is sufficient here to summarize some of the results.

There is a sizable acceleration of the general loss of whites from the

---

[13]Coleman, Kelly, Moore, *Trends in School Segregation 1968-73,* op. cit.

central city school district when substantial desegregation occurs within that system. The acceleration is less in cities smaller than the 22 we have discussed, and it appears to occur principally in the year in which desegregation takes place. The loss rates in subsequent years may return to prior rates, or they may be somewhat higher. The loss of white students when desegregation takes place differs considerably among cities, increasing as the proportion of blacks in the city increases and as the availability of predominantly white suburbs outside the central city district is greater.

Apart from the loss of white students resulting from desegregation, there is a continuing loss of white children from city schools which increases as the proportion of blacks in the city school district increases. Thus, the blacker the central city, the greater the loss of whites, with or without desegregation.

Policy Implications

Thus, the growing problem in school segregation is the problem of segregation between a black central city and white suburbs. In addition, the means by which schools are being desegregated are intensifying the problem rather than reducing it. The loss of whites is intensified by extensive school desegregation in central cities, but in cities with high proportions of blacks and predominantly white suburbs, it proceeds at a relatively rapid rate without desegregation.

This change in the character of school segregation raises the question of policy alternatives with regard to the school segregation issue, and what their likely effect might be. These alternatives are, of course, not mutually exclusive nor purely theoretical. Some may be combined, either simultaneously or as stages in a sequence, and some are currently in practice.

1. One of these alternatives is to carry out full-scale desegregation (i.e., racial balance) within central cities, using court orders, following the precedent that the remedy for any official act which fosters segregation is to eliminate all segregation in the system. This is the policy which current legal precedent follows in many of those cities in which court cases are brought. A similar policy is in force in HEW approval of desegregation plans, where the threat for noncompliance is a cutoff of federal funds. Virtually no districts are voluntarily instituting such plans, although a few small districts (such as Evanston, Illinois, and Berkeley, California) have done so in the past.

   According to our earlier analysis this policy will eliminate within-district segregation but it will not address the increasing segregation between districts, and will, in the larger cities, worsen the between-district segregation, hastening the time when the city schools become nearly all black and the suburbs nearly all white.

2. A second alternative is to eliminate school segregation within central cities only to the extent that it is directly attributable to official actions designed to segregate schools, but not to eliminate school segregation due to residential segregation. This alternative entails such measures as redrawing school district lines, but does not include compulsory busing. Such a policy will reduce segregation, but will not have much effect in the larger cities with extensive racially homogenous neighborhoods. It will also not address the segregation between districts and will increase the flow of whites to the suburbs, although by a smaller amount than the first alternative.

3. A third alternative is to institute metropolitan area busing—which, while initiated in a few localities, cannot by current legal precedent be imposed by the courts. Where there is public support for such a policy and where distances are short enough to make busing feasible, it will probably produce a stable pattern of low segregation. But where the proportion of lower class blacks is high, where the metropolitan area is large, or where the public is antagonistic, this policy may lead to disruption of the educational system and the increased enrollment of students, especially white but black as well, in private schools.

4. A fourth alternative is to aim at increasing residential integration. This would include opening up suburbs to blacks, as well as making the cities more attractive to whites, particularly by reducing crime. Crime reduction, of course, is a goal rather than a policy, but its continuing increase in large central cities may well be one reason for the 1968 to 1972 increase in residential segregation by race between the large central cities and their suburbs.

   Policies of this sort will not have striking or immediate effects in reducing school segregation, but will ultimately produce the most stable form of racial integration in the schools.

5. A fifth alternative is to open up suburban schools to black children through provision of the right for any child to attend any school in the metropolitan area (as long as it does not have a higher proportion of his own race than his local school). Such a policy—without veto power from the suburbs but with a limitation on the proportion of out-of-district students—can be instituted at the state or fed-

eral level.[14] This policy would reduce the growing between-district segregation, and if accompanied by a moratorium on policies of within-district racial balancing (alternative 1), would probably reduce the rate of loss of whites from central city schools.

The Relevance of Desegregation Policy to Educational Outcomes

So far, we have not examined the relevance of desegregation policies to educational outcomes. As long as desegregation policy was focused on the eradication of dual school districts, this omission was appropriate. But as the policies have moved toward affirmative integration, the issue is no longer Constitutional protection but how to promote beneficial educational and social outcomes. Apart from demographic stability, discussed in the above policy options, these outcomes include school achievement, years of school attended, and attitudes (such as racial attitudes and attitudes about oneself). Evidence on these latter outcomes is not as good as it might be, since it is based on scattered and only partially comparable studies of school desegregation in particular localities. But, although the results are not conclusive, there are certain consistencies: first, integration does not, generally, reduce achievement among whites nor, according to available studies, does it greatly improve achievement among blacks.[15] Some studies find no increase in black achievement, others slight increases. Perhaps the longest study and one of the most thorough, covering six years of desegregation in Riverside, California, shows no achievement effects at all.[16] The attitudinal consequences of desegregation are similarly inconclusive, although the available data suggest that we must revise the simple notion that desegregation has a generally beneficial effect on interracial attitudes and self-concepts. The sociopsychological effects appear somewhat more complex and less beneficial to blacks, at least over the short run.[17]

These results indicate that desegregation is not an educational panacea, since it is now clear that desegregation does not, by itself, produce important educational benefits, despite indications from earlier research.[18]

---

[14] A bill introduced by Representative Richardson Preyer in the U.S. House of Representatives carries this provision.

[15] See Nancy St. John, *School Desegregation* (New York: Wiley, 1975).

[16] Harold B. Gerard and Norman Miller, *Desegregation: a Longitudinal Study* (Plenum Press, 1975).

[17] Ibid. See also St. John, op. cit.

[18] One research report which was widely used to infer probable benefits was J. S. Coleman, et al., *Equality of Educational Opportunity* (Washington: Government Printing Office, 1966).

III. EDUCATIONAL FINANCE

Several major issues in the financing of education [19] have come to the fore in recent years. One is the increasing cost of schooling (both in dollars and in relation to other costs), coupled with the increased unwillingness of taxpayers to vote for additional school funding. A second issue centers on the equity of school financing, which has been challenged in recent years, principally in the courts. The long-term context for both of these issues is the slow and steady shift in the relative proportions of school revenues supplied from federal, state, and local sources.

In table 7, covering over half a century, one can see the continuous

Table 7

PUBLIC ELEMENTARY AND SECONDARY SCHOOL REVENUE
RECEIPTS FROM FEDERAL, STATE, AND LOCAL SOURCES:
UNITED STATES (1919-20 TO 1972-73)

School Year	Federal	State	Local [a] (including intermediate)
1919-20	0.3%	16.5%	83.2%
1929-30	0.4	16.9	82.7
1939-40	1.8	30.3	68.0
1941-42	1.4	31.5	67.1
1943-44	1.4	33.0	65.6
1945-46	1.4	34.7	63.8
1947-48	2.8	38.9	58.3
1949-50	2.9	39.8	57.3
1951-52	3.5	38.6	57.8
1953-54	4.5	37.4	58.1
1955-56	4.6	39.5	55.9
1957-58	4.0	39.4	56.6
1959-60	4.4	39.1	56.5
1961-62	4.3	38.7	56.9
1963-64	4.4	39.3	56.3
1965-66	7.9	39.1	53.0
1967-68	8.8	38.5	52.7
1969-70	8.0	39.9	52.1
1970-71	8.4	39.4	52.1
1971-72	8.9	38.3	52.8
1972-73	8.7	40.0	51.3

a.   Includes, a relatively minor amount from other sources (gifts, tuition, and transportation fees from patrons), which accounted for 0.4 percent of total revenue receipts in 1967-68.

Source: U.S. Department of Health, Education, and Welfare, Office of Education, *Digest of Educational Statistics,* 1974 Edition, table 71, p. 60.

---

[19] This section may be supplemented by a reading of the section on public school finance in chapter 2.

decline in what was once an almost complete reliance on local sources (primarily the property tax) for financing public schools.[20] Thus, between the school years beginning in 1919 and 1972, the local share of school funding dropped by 32 percentage points, pursuing a fairly even downward plane except for a sharp drop in the 1930s, the decade of the Great Depression. Meanwhile there was a corresponding rise in the state share, which began at 16.5 percent of the total, jumped over 13 percentage points in the depression decade, and from 1947 has continued, with only minor vacillation, in the vicinity of 40 percent. With the state share relatively static after 1947, the federal share moved upward to 4.4 percent of the total in the school year 1963-64, jumped 3.5 percentage points in 1965-66, the year of the first Elementary and Secondary Education Act, and then stabilized at around 8.5 percent. The net results of these shifts is that where localities once assumed by far the major portion of the school financing burden, at present about half is borne by state and federal sources.

Level of Financing

Despite the shifting proportions of school revenue supplied by the local, state, and federal sources, the principal decision (as well as half the financial burden) about how much will be spent on education in any locality lies at the local level. Thus, it is at the local level, at the polls and in the city councils, that the conflict over the level of educational expenditure has taken place.

The costs of education have grown enormously in recent years, due in small part to an increase in the number of students, and in large part to an increase in the expenditures per pupil. The combined effect of the two has increased the total U.S. expenditure on elementary and secondary education 164 percent, from $21.3 billion in 1964 to $56.3 billion in 1974 (see table 8). This absolute increase is also an increase in proportion of GNP: expenditures in 1974 were a higher percentage of GNP than in 1964. The largest portion of the increase in total expenditure is due to a 142 percent increase in expenditure per pupil (from $460 per pupil per year in 1964 to $1,116 per pupil per year in 1974). The remaining portion of the increase is due to an increase in the number of pupils.

Overall and per pupil expenditures have been increasing at a substantial rate each year. This increase is partly because schooling is labor intensive and its costs rise primarily with the wage scale rather than

---

[20] Table 7 shows minor differences from a comparable table (for the later years of the series) in chapter 2 on financing the city. This is due to different data sources, which involve slightly different classifications.

merely with the cost of living (thus rising more rapidly than most other goods and services), partly because of the increased power of teachers in wage negotiations, and partly because of other factors.[21] Whatever the reasons for rapidly rising costs, they have been accompanied by an increased unwillingness of voters to acquiesce in the increase. Over the past decade, voters have shown a greater resistance to school tax rate increases and bond issues. Table 8 shows both the rising expenditures for education from 1962 to 1974, and the declining rate of approval of school bonds by voters to 1973. The decline is from 72.4 percent in 1962 to a low of 46.7 percent in 1971. There is, however, an increase since 1973, which indicates an increase in willingness to fund education since the low point of 1971 and 1972.

Table 8

RESULTS OF SCHOOL BOND ELECTIONS, 1962-73, COMPARED TO PER PUPIL EXPENDITURES, 1962-74

School Year Ending Spring:	Estimated Expenditures U.S. Elementary & Secondary Public Schools (billions)	Expenditures Per Pupil	Bond Elections % Approved
1962	$18.4	$ 419	72.4
1963			72.4
1964	21.3	460	72.5
1965			74.7
1966	26.2	537	72.5
1967			66.6
1968	33.2	658	67.6
1969			56.8
1970	41.0	816	53.2
1971		858	46.7
1972	49.8	934	47.0
1973	52.1	1,026	56.5
1974	56.3	1,116	56.2

Sources: U.S. Department of Health, Education, and Welfare, Office of Education, *Digest of Educational Statistics, 1973,* and *1974,* and *Bond Sales for Public School Purposes, 1970-71* and *1972-73.*

[21] One is willful destruction of school property by students. This is a minor factor for the nation as a whole, but is important in some city districts. The total cost was estimated at $0.5 billion for 1973 by the President of the Association of School Security Directors ("Our Nation's Schools—A Report Card: 'A' in School Violence and Vandalism," report of Committee on the Judiciary, United States Senate, April 1975).

The decline in bond approval is probably not wholly a consequence of the increased costs of schooling but is probably also due to a general decline in satisfaction with the schools, as evidenced in opinion polls, which reported very high levels of satisfaction in the 1940s and 50s and somewhat lower levels in the 1960s and 70s. Simultaneously, polls have also shown a general decline in satisfaction with a wide range of institutions of society, suggesting that the increased dissatisfaction with schools might possibly be linked to a more general trend. In any case, the dissatisfaction has increased, and the bond approvals have decreased, with only a very recent reversal (since 1973) to suggest a possible change in the long-term trend.

It is not apparent just how the conflict between rising educational costs and rising voter resistance will be resolved. One resolution, of course, is for the costs to continue to rise at current rates, and to be covered through state or federal taxes. Another resolution is for the increase in costs to diminish. The change from an increasing student population to a decreasing one (brought about by a decline in the birth rate) has already had some effect in that direction; but as the figures already presented show, 92 percent of the increase has been in per pupil expenditure, and that component shows no signs of decline. Still a third resolution lies in a renewed willingness of citizens to vote increased local property taxes for schooling. That may now be beginning, but if it is to be extensive, it depends upon an increased confidence in the schools' ability to function well, something that has not yet happened.

Inequalities in Financing

A second major issue has been the inequality of school financing between different districts. Two recent court cases, *Serrano v. Priest* in California (1971) and *Rodriguez v. San Antonio Independent School District* in Texas (1971), have focused attention on within-state disparities in per pupil expenditures and in tax rates. The issue is whether the states have a responsibility to provide equal educational opportunity (insofar as it can be achieved through equal financing), without regard to the wealth or poverty of the local school district. The Supreme Court has decided in the Rodriguez case that the issue is not a Constitutional one, and so it has reverted to state legislatures, several of which have renewed their attempts to redress interdistrict financing inequalities.

The problem lies in part in increasing differences of wealth between districts, due to the increasing separation of place of residence from place of work. This separation has meant both an increasing income homogeneity within the area served by a school district, and increasing disparities of industrial taxable wealth in different districts. This led, rather early in the history of American public education, to state aid through supplementation formulas, but these formulas have not overcome the disparities. The problem is not simple, of course. A state commitment to full equalization of educational expenditures (assuming that this is desirable) would destroy the incentive of a local district to tax itself for education. But, even given this constraint, many state formulas are less effective in equalizing expenditures than they might be. Some states give a similar amount per pupil regardless of a district's tax base; other formulas use questionable measures of fiscal need (usually based on property wealth without reference to income). In general, state aid formulas sometimes exacerbate financing inequalities, sometimes reduce them slightly, but have not reduced them greatly.[22]

Another aspect of the equal funding problem is that the costs of education vary in different areas. Equal expenditures in a large city and in a rural area would effectively give greater support for education in the rural area, where teachers' salaries, building costs, vandalism costs, and most other costs are lower. Equal expenditures on physically handicapped and nonhandicapped children might be totally insufficient for the former while meeting the latter's needs adequately. Equal expenditures on children from educationally deprived families and educationally rich families may leave the former in a poor competitive position. But if so, then how much compensation is appropriate, and where should it come from?

It is not even clear which schools are in greater financial need. It is commonly believed that they are the schools of the central city districts, and this seems to have been true a decade ago.[23] But more recent data for one state indicate that the average suburban school district not only taxes itself more heavily for schools (as well as for other expenditures) but also has lower per pupil expenditure than its central city.[24] Some

---

[22] See Betsy Levin, *Alternatives to the Present System of School Finance: Their Problems and Prospects* (Washington, D.C.: The Urban Institute, 1973), pp. 886-89, and John E. Coons, William H. Clune, and Stephen D. Sugarman, *Private Wealth and Public Education* (Cambridge, Mass.: Belknap Press of Harvard University Press, 1970).

[23] See Seymour Sacks and David Ranney, "Suburban Education: A Fiscal Analysis," *Urban Affairs Quarterly*, 1966, pp. 103-19.

[24] John J. Treacy and Russell L. Harris, "Contemporary Suburban Schools— The Needy?" *Southern Economic Journal*, vol. 40, 1974, pp. 640-46.

suburban districts do have higher expenditures than the central city, but for many metropolitan areas, the average is lower.

Thus, the problem is not only how to overcome inequalities in school financing, but also how to determine what the appropriate goal is. If the state took full responsibility for providing equal educational opportunities for all the children in it, what level of financing would be appropriate for each locality? In the case of divided responsibility, what portion should the state, rather than the locality, assume? These problems, which were not perceived as social problems when responsibility resided locally, will worsen when and if responsibility comes to reside principally at the national level.

Statewide responsibility for educational opportunity can be approached through both the source of funding and the distribution of expenditures. For changes in the source of funding, two alternatives have been suggested, both involving a shift from local to state taxation: (1) an increase in state sales or income taxes, and (2) the creation of statewide property taxes. The first alternative has been explored for California, with the following conclusion:

> A recent study of a sample of districts in California concluded that in order to produce the same amount of education revenues raised through the local property tax for the school year 1968-1969, a five percent increase in the state sales tax would be required. This would increase California's present state sales tax from its four percent rate to a total of nine percent. This study also revealed that to replace all local school property taxes through an increase in the state income tax would necessitate an increase of 125 percent in the income tax.[25]

The use of a statewide property tax may also lead to unexpected results. Taxes in central cities and rural areas would ordinarily go up, while those in suburban districts would go down.

The distribution of expenditures under statewide responsibility can, itself, be separated into two questions. First is the question whether the level of per pupil educational expenditure is to be decided at state level or at local level. Traditionally, the decision has been made at the local level, modified by state supplementation. Full state funding of education, proposed as one policy option, would transfer this decision to the state level.

Second is the question whether local or statewide resources (that is, unequal or equalized resources) are to be used in school financing. The

---

[25] Levin, *Alternatives,* op. cit., pp. 911-12.

local property tax, with its existing inequalities, is the traditional resource base.

Some states, following the court cases on school financing, have assumed statewide responsibility by answering these two questions in different ways. The result is a form of financing called "power equalizing," following Coons, Clune, and Sugarman.[26] In power equalizing, the local school district determines the rate of taxation, but there is statewide equalization of per pupil property tax bases. Thus, in pure power equalizing at the district level, each district in the state that votes the same tax rate will obtain the same per pupil expenditure (achieved through a redistribution of property tax revenues among districts), though different districts may vote different rates to provide different levels of per pupil expenditure. This form of financing equalizes the resources available to each district, but the locality decides what the level of educational expenditures is to be. Because of this attractive combination of qualities, power equalization of some form appears likely to be used increasingly to finance education.

This is all apart from the question of compensatory financing because of differences in student need (e.g., for handicapped children, for children from educationally disadvantaged backgrounds, for gifted children, for children from different linguistic cultures). Compensatory financing is explicit and intentional unequalization of the resources available for different children. If the criteria for unequalization can be decided, then any of the preceding policies of financing can be modified to incorporate it. Thus power equalization, for example, can be modified to power *un*-equalization insofar as it is based on differences in the educational needs of different children.*

Implications for Education

The resolution of these issues of educational finance are important in relation both to the control over education and to school desegregation. If, in order to equalize educational opportunity or to overcome problems with the level of funding, more revenue comes from the state or federal level, the lines of local school districts will be blurred and more control will reside at the state or federal level. This, in turn, will increase the likelihood of metropolitan-wide approaches to racial segregation. At the

---

[26] *Private Wealth and Public Education,* op. cit.

*See chapter 2 for further discussion of the impact of power equalization, particularly on urban school districts. [Eds.]

same time, the threat of system-wide racial balance as ordered in recent court cases has very likely solidified resistance among whites to metropolitan-wide school districts except in those few places where they already exist, and has counterbalanced the tendency of local districts to push for new forms of state supplementation. Power equalization may be an attractive form of state supplementation for many local districts, because control would remain at the local level, thus providing state responsibility for equal financing, without the destruction or overriding of school district boundaries.

When we ask what differences in educational outcomes might result from changes in the distribution or level of educational finance, there are very few answers at hand. The evidence reveals that differences in financial resources have few observable effects on educational outcomes. This means that differences within the range of educational finance found within a state have little discernible effect on achievement or other educational outcomes for children. It does not mean, of course, that very great reductions or very great increases in a school district's expenditures may not have some impact on educational outcomes. But since very great changes in the level of financing in either direction do not seem likely, the educational consequences of recent and future court and state legislative decisions on equalization of educational expenditures will probably be modest.

IV. THE INTERNAL FUNCTIONING OF THE SCHOOL

Perhaps the most significant change that has taken place in recent years within the school and the classroom itself is a relaxation of the school's once well-defined authority over the child, a crumbling of the legitimacy with which schools have governed the daily lives of children.

One extreme form that this loss of legitimacy took beginning in the late 1960s was the creation of "free schools" or "experimental schools." In an earlier period, attendance at such schools, unaccredited and very unlike regular public schools, would have been regarded as a form of truancy, and punished as truancy. But these alternative schools have been tolerated by the public school system and the community, and sometimes have even been imitated within the public school itself on the ground that schools more relevant to current problems were needed to prevent the continuing alienation of youth. The alternative schools usually consisted of a mixture of poor blacks and middle-class whites, although the initial stimulus for establishing such schools came more from the alienated middle-class youth than from the disadvantaged poor youth.

Nearly all these schools were short lived although a few, initiated within the public school system in the late 1960s, still survive. At the same time, in response to the threat posed by alternative schools, the regular public schools have accommodated greatly to the demands for less traditional means of education. This is particularly pronounced in the junior and senior years of high school, for which a variety of nonacademic courses or "experiences" have been introduced.

Another sign of the loss of legitimacy in the school's authority over students is the relaxation of school discipline. This ranges from non-enforcement of truancy laws, and—in a few schools—nonrequired class attendance, to the abandonment (under the pressure of successful court challenges) of dress codes, of restrictions on hair styles, and of the traditional authority to suspend students without "due process."[27] The rather successful movement toward defining, codifying, and thereby legitimizing, a set of rights for students in public schools shows in another way the contraction of the schools' realm of authority.

The origins of this decline in the legitimate authority of the school are difficult to locate in the complex cause-and-effect nexus of recent years. It arises partly from the increased willingness of the courts to intervene for the protection of student rights. It arises partly from the youth movement of the 1960s. Clearly, however, it also arises partly from, and in turn reinforces, public loss of confidence in the schools. When that confidence was high, parents did not challenge a principal's or teacher's action, and would not support such a challenge by their children. But the reduced legitimacy of the school's authority in the eyes of parents makes such challenges more frequent, and reinforces the loss of legitimacy.

What began in the 1960s was the acceleration of a long-term decline in the legitimacy of school authority. What is not certain, however, is whether that decline will continue, or whether a period of consolidation and stability will restore the legitimacy of school authority over the behavior of students. If the decline continues, then the viability of secondary and, to a lesser extent, elementary education probably de-

---

[27] The requirement for due process involving prior hearings with evidence before a student is expelled or suspended implies that education is a "liberty" that cannot be denied without due process of law. The Supreme Court has not yet ruled on whether education is such a liberty, although in *Rodriguez* education was ruled not to be a "fundamental interest," as noted earlier. The incidence of such cases, which address issues that were once held, without question, to be within the principal's authority, further indicates how much authority over education is now exercised in the courts.

pends on devising an educational structure wholly different from the present structure, in which children and their families would have greater choice between schools and the schools, in turn, would have greater authority over their students, whose presence would be less compulsory and more voluntary.

Some studies of such different structures have been undertaken, particularly at the secondary level. In the early 1970s, four commissions or panels were convened, two under government auspices, to examine changes in the structure and content of secondary education. The reports of these groups all recommended similar changes: increased variability in the form of secondary education and greater choice for students; increased opportunities for responsibility for youth, inside the school and out; and a reduction of the isolation between young people in school and activities in the community outside the school.[28] Some of these recommendations are being implemented by a number of schools. As a consequence, a different relationship between high schools and their students is emerging, with a different set of rights and obligations compatible with the change in legitimacy.

In some respects, the present is a period in which productive changes can take place in secondary education, in part because the schools have a less compliantly captive audience than in the past. But without some such changes, the traditional high school may confront increasing problems as time goes on.

One measure of these problems is the incidence of violence, crime, and delinquency in the schools. Whether this should be regarded as an indicator of decline in the school's authority over children and youth, or simply as a measure on its own account, it is a highly informative measure. Outright violence and criminal behavior is, of course, not common in most schools, but what interests us here are the recent changes that have occurred in various forms of disorder.

For that purpose, we can use the results of a study by the Senate Subcommittee to Investigate Juvenile Delinquency, based on a questionnaire survey of the district superintendents of 477 of the largest U.S. school districts. The superintendents were asked to give the incidence of a

---

[28] *Youth: Transition to Adulthood*, report of the Panel on Youth of the President's Science Advisory Committee, 1973; *The Greening of the High School*, report on a conference sponsored by Educational Facilities Laboratories and I/D/E/A, 1973; *The Reform of Secondary Education*, by B. Frank Brown and others, a report of the National Commission on the Reform of Secondary Education, 1973; *Report of the National Panel on High School and Adolescent Education*, sponsored by the U.S. Office of Education, 1974 (unpublished).

number of categories of delinquent behavior over the three school years 1970-71 to 1972-73. The resulting figures are presented in table 9. The changes are striking: in almost every area of delinquent activity in every region there has been an increase over the three years and in most areas this increase is very great indeed. Thus although 1970 appeared to constitute a high point in the youth revolt of the 1960s in the colleges, after which collective violence in the colleges declined, it appears not to have constituted a high point in the incidence of individual acts of violence at younger ages.

Table 9

PERCENTAGE CHANGES FROM 1970-71 TO 1972-73 IN INCIDENCE OF DELINQUENT AND CRIMINAL BEHAVIOR IN SCHOOLS

Behavior	U.S.	Northeast	North Central	South	West
Homicide	+18.5	+20.1		+25.4	+26.6
Rape & Attempt	+40.1	+37.9	+60.0	+28.4	+52.3
Robbery	+36.7	+39.3	− 8.0	+51.7	+98.3
Assaults on Students	+85.3	− 2.2	+20.5	+276.9	+77.4
Burglary, Larceny	+11.8	− 2.9	+ 2.1	+28.1	+ 2.7
Weapons	+54.4	+20.6	+ 6.7		+90.3
Drugs, Alcohol	+37.5	+14.8	+97.4		+18.1
Dropouts	+11.7	+ 8.0		+18.8	
Vandalism		−12.0			+15.7
Expulsions		− 9.7		− 5.9	
Assaults on Teachers	+77.4		+52.4	+316.4	+ 6.4
Number of districts responding	477 a	(82)	(117)	(187)	(91)
Response rate	68.0%	59.4%	68.0%	71.6%	69.8%

a. The introduction to the report states that 516 school districts responded to the survey; the total regional responses, however, equal 477. This discrepancy may be a result of incomplete information on some of the returned questionnaires.

Source: "Our Nation's Schools—A Report Card: 'A' in School Violence and Vandalism," Report of Senate Subcommittee to Investigate Juvenile Delinquency, Committee on the Judiciary, April 1975. This preliminary report did not list rates of increase for all categories, with the result that the table contains some blank cells.

The general picture that results from the various kinds of changes described here is one of a major reduction in the ability of educational institutions to function in their traditional role. The present conditions appear to be unstable, either leading to a return to the broader exercise of legitimate authority by the schools, or else to an institutional form that can operate more effectively than current schools under conditions of shrunken legitimacy.

V. ACHIEVEMENT IN SCHOOLS

For some years, educators and the general public have expressed disappointment in the achievement levels exhibited by children in the public schools. With some, this disappointment has focused on the low scholastic achievement of children from disadvantaged backgrounds. For others, the focus has broadened to include American children generally, as in the results of the International Education Achievement studies in mathematics in 1967, which showed that the average score for American 13-year-olds was lower than that for any other nation studied.[29]

Here, we will not re-examine results that are well known, such as (1) the fact that some ethnic minorities, who on the average come from economically and educationally disadvantaged backgrounds, perform considerably less well on standardized achievement tests than do majority whites; (2) the fact that achievement levels in many cities have been declining over a period of years; and (3) the fact that average achievement levels increase from the inner city radiating out to the suburbs, declining again beyond the suburbs in rural areas.

Rather, we want to ask only two questions:

1. Has educational achievement increased or decreased over the past several years?
2. Does the persistent decline in scholastic achievement in the central city reflect merely a change in the composition of the city's population, with higher-performing students moving out and the lower-performing ones remaining behind, or does it represent an actual decline in the performance of children of comparable backgrounds, which would appear even if there were no population change in the city?

---

[29] See Torsten Husén, ed., *International Study of Achievement in Mathematics: A Comparison of Twelve Countries,* 2 vols. (Stockholm: Almqvist and Wiksell, 1967).

The data for answering these questions are not as good as one might desire. There are no tests administered nationally in all districts, and only a few states maintain standardized testing programs in which the same tests are administered in all state schools. However, most individual school districts administer standardized tests at various grade levels, and have done so for a number of years. Thus it is possible to examine changes in these test series for a period of years to help answer the questions we have raised.

There are further problems, however. Most school districts change their tests periodically, and, in addition, test publishers sometimes change the norms for their tests. Finally, it is difficult to obtain district-wide or statewide average test scores from many districts and states. Consequently, the evidence on these questions must be pieced together from various sources, none wholly satisfactory.

Fortunately, however, there are some general consistencies in the data from district to district and in the two states (New York and California) for which statewide scores were supplied by the state department of education. The following combination of trends appears in nearly every set of achievement data available from states and cities:[30]

1. In the lower grades (grade 1, 2, or 3), achievement scores remain about constant or increase slightly over the period of years 1966-74 (or for some part of this interval in those places with shorter series).

   Examples:
   Baltimore: grade 3 achievement increases slightly in reading comprehension 1969-73, and remains constant in mathematics 1969-73.

   New York City: grade 3 achievement remains constant in reading comprehension 1966-73, and increases in mathematics 1966-73. The same results occur in other districts in New York State, grouped by type and size of locality.

   Los Angeles, San Diego, and Oakland: in California state-mandated tests of reading comprehension, each of these cities increases slightly from 1970-73 (4 years) at grade 1, and from 1971-73 (3 years) at grade 2. For grade 3, one test was used

---

[30] See Appendix for achievement data used in the following discussion. Table A-1 in the appendix lists the tests used in each locality as well as the measure used for reporting results.

for 1970 and 1971, another for 1972 and 1973. This reduces possible comparisons, but there appears to be constancy in grade 3.

San Francisco: on the same reading tests, constancy 1970-73 in grade 1; constancy 1971-73 in grade 2; and constancy (1970, 1971) and (1972, 1973) in grade 3.

Dade County, Fla. (Miami): grades 1, 2, and 3 show slight increases in reading comprehension and mathematics 1969-73.

New York State: statewide figures show that grade 3 achievement remains constant in reading comprehension 1966-73, and increases slightly in mathematics, 1966-73.

California State: statewide figures show that grade 2 reading comprehension increases slightly from 1970-74, and grade 3 appears constant (1970, 1971) and (1972-74).

These results are extremely encouraging on several counts. First, they show that instead of a declining achievement in the early grades over this period of years, there is either constancy or a slight increase. Second, they show that this is true even in the large central cities shown here with large and increasing proportions of minority students. The evidence indicates, then, that not only are majority white students in the early grades doing better than their counterparts did a few years ago, but that minority children are doing better as well. In fact, their increased achievement is enough to overcome any negative effect on city averages that might stem from the declining numbers of middle-class whites in the schools. The state results (New York and California) reinforce the inference that these are real changes and not due to population shifts between the central city and the suburbs.

2. In the higher grades (from grade 4 or 5 through grade 12) achievement scores *decline* over the period 1966-74 (or some part of it in those places with shorter testing periods). The higher the grade level, the greater the decline. This is true both in cities of various sizes and in whole states.

Examples:
Baltimore: in grades 5, 6, and 9, there is a decline in reading comprehension, least at grade 5 and greatest at grade 9, from 1969-73. Mathematics shows the same result.

New York City: grade 6 achievement declines in mathematics

from 1966-73 and declines even more sharply in reading comprehension during the same span. These results also apply to other districts in New York State, grouped by type and size of locality.

Los Angeles, San Diego, and San Francisco: in California state-mandated tests of reading comprehension and mathematics at grade 5 and 12, each of these cities shows a decline from 1970-73.

Oakland: same as above, except no decline in grade 12.

Dade County Fla.: grades 4, 5, 6, 9 show declines, greater with each higher grade, in reading comprehension 1970-74. In mathematics, grades 4 and 5 are constant, 6 and 9 show a decline (9 is a greater decline) for 1970-74.

New York State: grade 6 declines in reading comprehension 1966-73, and even more sharply in mathematics, 1966-73.

California State: grades 6 and 12 decline in reading comprehension and mathematics 1970-74.

These results in the higher grades are just as striking as those for the earlier grades, but in the opposite direction, and stronger in magnitude. During the same period when achievement increased in the early grades, it declined in the later grades. Furthermore, this appears to be true not only for minority students but also for students in all types and sizes of localities in New York State, and for the whole states of New York and California as well. Thus the central city declines in achievement do not appear to be explainable by the increased movement of middle-class families out of the city.

This combination of constant or improving results in lower grades (1, 2, 3) and worsening results in higher grades appears inexplicable. Yet the effect, at least at the later grades, appears definite. This deteriorating performance at upper grades does not, of course, lead to the optimism suggested by the results from earlier grades, but rather to pessimism. As we have noted, it cannot be explained by the movement of middle-class higher-achieving students out of central cities, for it is a decline in all types of localities (at least in New York State), in California as a whole, and also in Dade County which encompasses both Miami and its suburbs. The result suggests that schools are becoming less effective for children from all social backgrounds, producing levels of performance that are progressively worse as the child's schooling continues.

This suggestion is reinforced when we examine successive cohorts, looking at their growth as shown by test results in earlier and later years. These comparisons are summarized in table 10, for New York State and its subdivisions, Dade County, Florida, and Baltimore, Maryland. California is not included because of variation in the forms of tests used there. (The scores themselves are given in the appendix.)

In New York State and in all its classes of school districts, each cohort shows a lower percentile on national norms at grade 6 than at grade 3, with only one exception in 80 pairs of cohort scores. In addition, the later cohorts, those which began school in the late 1960s, show a greater decline in percentile position than do the earlier cohorts, both in reading and in mathematics. The increase in percentile decline is somewhat greater in mathematics than in reading, but is evident in both.

In Dade County, Florida, where tests were given in each grade through grade 6, the growth in grade equivalents from one year to the next shows the same decline. First, the growth in reading for all cohorts is almost without exception less than one grade equivalent per year. And as in New York, each successive cohort shows, with few exceptions, smaller growth than the preceding one. In mathematics, the yearly growth for the early cohorts was greater than one grade equivalent per year. But there is a precipitous decline in growth, except for grade 1-2, so the later cohorts show less growth than one grade equivalent per year.

In Baltimore, where tests were given at grades 3, 5, 6, and 9, growth can be measured for grades 3-5, grades 5-6, and grades 6-9. These comparisons show in general less than one year of growth per school year; and again there is a decline in growth with successive cohorts— a decline that is most pronounced at the highest grades.

These results show that children who entered school in the late 1960s are learning less reading and mathematics than were their counterparts who entered school earlier—although, as the earlier comparisons of absolute test scores at grade 1 in Dade County and in California (see appendix) showed, they began grade 1 at least as well prepared as their earlier counterparts.

The explanation suggested by the other data in this chapter centers on the decline in discipline, the increase in disorder, and the general decline in the legitimacy of the school's demands. Since the effects of these changes are felt largely *after* grades 1, 2, and 3, and increasingly with higher grades, they could be responsible for the progressive decline in achievement in later grades. If the increasing disorder *is* responsible

Table 10

ACHIEVEMENT GROWTH IN SELECTED SCHOOL SYSTEMS

| | Cohorts beginning grade 1 in year | | | | | | | |
	1964	65	66	67	68	69	70	71	72
NEW YORK STATE (differences in percentile position)									
grade 3-6 Reading	− 3	− 5	− 8	− 7	− 5*				
Math	− 7*	−10*	−13	−13	−14				
New York City									
grade 3-6 Reading	− 2	− 3	− 6	− 3	− 6*				
Math	+ 1*	− 3*	− 7	− 8	−11				
Large N.Y. Cities									
grade 3-6 Reading	− 5	− 5	− 8	− 6	− 3*				
Math	− 7*	− 7*	−10	−15	−14				
Medium N.Y. Cities									
grade 3-6 Reading	− 5	− 4	− 7	− 8	− 6*				
Math	− 9*	−11*	−11	−14	−15				
Small N.Y. Cities									
grade 3-6 Reading	− 3	− 5	− 7	− 7	− 4*				
Math	− 9*	−10*	−14	−15	−15				
Villages									
grade 3-6 Reading	− 4	− 6	− 7	− 7	− 5*				
Math	− 9*	−12*	−13	−16	−15				
Large Rural									
grade **3-6** Reading	− 5	− 5	− 7	− 8	− 4*				
Math	− 8*	−10*	−13	−15	−15				
Small Rural									
grade 3-6 Reading	− 3	− 5	− 7	− 7	− 3*				
Math	− 5*	− 7*	−10	−13	−11				

					Cohorts beginning grade 1 in year				
	1964	65	66	67	68	69	70	71	72
DADE CO., FLORIDA (growth in grade equivalents)									
grade 1-2 Reading						.95	.95	.87	.86*
Math						1.09	1.16	1.12	1.03*
grade 2-3 Reading					.88	.85	.74	.79*	
Math					1.24	1.24	.98	.84*	
grade 3-4 Reading				.96	.98	.83	.77*		
Math				1.26	1.23	1.04	.94*		
grade 4-5 Reading			.95	1.05	.96	1.02*			
Math			.98	.88	.81	.74*			
grade 5-6 Reading		.99	.89	.80	.83*				
Math		1.30	1.43	1.26	.97*				
BALTIMORE, MARYLAND (growth in grade equivalents)									
grade 3-5 Reading				1.9	1.6	1.6	1.5*		
Math				1.9	1.7	1.6	1.5*		
grade 5-6 Reading		1.1	1.0	0.9	0.8				
Math		1.1	0.9	0.8	0.8				
grade 6-9 Reading	2.1	1.8	1.5*						
Math	1.9	1.7	1.8*						

* For the cases marked with an asterisk, the test in the earlier year was a different form of (though the same test as) the test given in the later year. Because the forms are intended to be equivalent, this should have no effect if the tests are correctly normed.

(a result which could be tested if measures of disorder and achievement could be obtained at the district level for 2 or more years), then the early grade results make the later declines even more disheartening: they suggest that if order and discipline had been continuously maintained, or if the schools had been capable of adapting to their reduced legitimacy, if violence had not grown in the schools, the educational promise of the early grades would have been nourished and reinforced throughout all of the years of public school.

Concluding Remarks

The general picture of public education, particularly in the cities, is not encouraging. It is a center of social conflict between different groups in society and between different parts of the educational structure itself. In addition, its internal functioning, particularly at upper grades, is in a state of flux, with uncertain realms of authority and declining levels of achievement. The institution appears to be at a point just prior to sweeping changes which might revivify its functioning. It is likely that those changes, if they occur, will reflect above all a change in the conception of what functions the school is to perform—particularly at the secondary level—and under what authority it is to perform those functions.

The fact that schools are in this uncertain state, which appears to call for very fundamental changes, could be encouraging for the major social issues that surround education—particularly the issue of racial integration. If the functioning of schools, particularly at the secondary level, came to be modified in the direction that the recent commissions on youth and secondary education have proposed—that is, toward a far greater physical and functional integration with the everyday activities of adults—then the goal of racial integration in education might be achieved in a far more natural and less disruptive way.

This is only one hint of the possibilities that are inherent in the present difficulties of education. It indicates that not only are creative solutions to education's problems necessary, but also that really fundamental changes may, while solving the problems to which they are addressed, also aid in the solution of others.

Given the current difficulties and problems, however, it would be misleading to end on such an optimistic note. The hard reality of the present is that schools in America are beset by more problems, and are functioning less well, than they have been in the recent past.

APPENDIX A: ACHIEVEMENT TEST RESULTS

Table A-1

TESTS AND MEASURES USED

	Locality	Test Used	For Grade(s)	Date	Measure
1.	Baltimore	Iowa Test of Basic Skills, 1964 Edition	3 through 9	1969-1973	Mean grade equivalent
		Iowa Test of Basic Skills, 1971 Edition	3, 5, 7, 9	1974	Mean grade equivalent
2.	New York City	Pupil Evaluation Program, Form A	3, 6 Reading	1966-1972	Percentile rank
		Pupil Evaluation Program, Form C	3, 6 Reading	1973	Percentile rank
		Pupil Evaluation Program, Form A	3, 6 Mathematics	1966-1968	Percentile rank
		Pupil Evaluation Program, Form C	3, 6 Mathematics	1969	Percentile rank
3.	Other districts in New York State	[Identical to New York City]			
4.	Los Angeles	Cooperative Primary Reading Test	1	1969-1973	Median scores
		Stanford Reading Test	2	1969	Median scores
5.	San Diego	Cooperative Primary Reading Test	2	1970-1973	Median scores
		Stanford Reading Test	3	1969-1971	Median scores
6.	Oakland	Cooperative Primary Reading Test	3	1972-1973	Median scores
		Comprehensive Tests of Basic Skills	6	1969-1973	Median scores
7.	San Francisco	Iowa Tests of Educational Development	12	1969-1973	Median scores
8.	Dade Co., Fla. (Miami)	Stanford Achievement Test, 1964 Edition	All	1969-1973	Mean grade equivalent
		Stanford Achievement Test, 1973 Edition	All	1973-1974	Mean grade equivalent
9.	New York State	[Identical to New York City]			
10.	California State	[Identical to Los Angeles, San Diego, Oakland and San Francisco]			Quartile percentile rank

Source: All tables in this appendix are based on data received from local and state boards of education.

Table A-2

BALTIMORE ACHIEVEMENT RESULTS (1969-74)
(mean grade equivalent)

Grade	1969	1970	1971	1972	1973	1974
			Reading Comprehension			
3	2.7	2.9	2.9	2.9	3.0	2.8
5	4.6	4.6	4.6	4.5	4.5	4.4
6	5.7	5.7	5.6	5.5	5.5	
9	8.0	8.0	7.9	7.8	7.5	7.1
			Arithmetic Skills			
3	3.1	3.2	3.2	3.2	3.1	3.1
5	4.9	5.0	5.0	4.9	4.8	4.7
6	5.9	6.0	5.9	5.8	5.7	
9	7.9	8.1	8.0	7.8	7.7	7.7

Table A-3

NEW YORK CITY ACHIEVEMENT RESULTS (1966-73)
(percentile rank)

Grade	1966	1967	1968	1969	1970	1971	1972	1973
				Reading				
3	36	35	38	35	35	35	38	35
6	37	36	37	34	32	32	32	29
				Mathematics				
3	29	31	37	37	38	38	40	37
6	34	30	32	30	28	30	29	27

Table A-4

OTHER DISTRICTS IN NEW YORK STATE, BY SITE AND TYPE,
ACHIEVEMENT RESULTS (1966-73)

(percentile rank)

Type of District and Grade	1966	1967	1968	1969	1970	1971	1972	1973
Reading								
Large Cities								
Gr. 3	45	43	43	41	38	38	40	41
6	47	44	42	40	38	35	35	35
Medium Cities								
Gr. 3	53	51	53	53	50	49	51	52
6	54	52	51	48	47	46	45	44
Small Cities								
Gr. 3	53	53	54	54	52	53	54	57
6	53	52	52	50	48	47	47	48
Village and Large Central Districts								
Gr. 3	60	60	60	60	59	59	60	63
6	59	58	57	56	54	53	53	54
Large Rural								
Gr. 3	56	56	56	56	55	55	54	58
6	55	53	54	51	51	49	48	51
Small Rural								
Gr. 3	53	53	54	53	53	51	53	54
6	52	50	50	50	48	47	46	50
Mathematics								
Large Cities								
Gr. 3	46	44	43	48	45	45	46	47
6	49	48	46	39	37	33	33	31
Medium Cities								
Gr. 3	55	54	54	56	54	54	55	55
6	51	50	48	46	43	43	42	39
Small Cities								
Gr. 3	57	56	58	58	57	57	58	59
6	54	52	51	48	46	44	43	42
Village and Large Central Districts								
Gr. 3	63	63	63	65	63	64	65	65
6	58	56	54	54	51	50	49	48
Large Rural								
Gr. 3	59	60	60	60	59	59	59	60
6	59	54	53	51	50	47	45	44
Small Rural								
Gr. 3	57	57	57	58	56	56	57	57
6	59	56	54	52	50	47	45	45

Table A-5

CALIFORNIA CITIES ACHIEVEMENT RESULTS (1970-73)
(median score)

City and Grade	1969-70	1970-71	1971-72	1972-73
		Reading		
Los Angeles				
Gr. 1	23.2	21.0	21.9	22.3
2	40.2	23.6	24.7	25.1
3	59.1	57.2	34.0	34.5
6	56.2	56.2	53.3	53.4
12	20.2	20.1	19.1	18.9
San Diego				
Gr. 1	22.3	23.2	24.2	24.8
2	46.1	27.7	28.3	28.6
3	66.6	66.5	38.0	37.5
6	64.7	65.1	62.7	63.6
12	24.4	24.6	22.6	22.9
Oakland				
Gr. 1	21.5	23.2	23.4	23.4
2	36.6	25.3	26.2	25.1
3	55.6	56.9	34.6	33.7
6	54.7	54.4	51.3	51.5
12	16.8	16.4	15.8	16.0
San Francisco				
Gr. 1	21.3	21.5	20.7	21.2
2	35.2	23.3	23.4	23.6
3	53.6	54.1	31.0	31.9
6	55.1	54.8	50.9	51.9
12	19.9	19.7	18.7	17.4
		Arithmetic		
Los Angeles				
Gr. 6	71.4	69.0	65.1	64.9
12	12.2	12.0	11.7	11.4
San Diego				
Gr. 6	77.9	77.1	73.8	75.2
12	14.9	15.0	14.5	14.0
Oakland				
Gr. 6	67.6	66.6	62.3	63.4
12	10.9	10.3	10.2	10.2
San Francisco				
Gr. 6	71.8	69.2	64.4	64.8
12	13.3	13.3	12.6	11.5

Table A-6

DADE COUNTY, FLA. (MIAMI) ACHIEVEMENT RESULTS
(1969-73)
(mean grade equivalent)

Grade	1969-70	1970-71	1971-72	1972-73	1973-74
			Reading		
1	1.78	1.84	1.89	1.94	1.95
2	2.72	2.73	2.79	2.76	2.80
3	3.64	3.60	3.58	3.53	3.55
4	4.80	4.60	4.58	4.41	4.30
5	5.75	5.76	5.65	5.54	5.43
6	6.92	6.74	6.65	6.45	6.37
9	9.69	9.71	9.39	9.27	9.09
			Mathematics		
1	1.90	1.94	2.01	2.05	2.05
2	2.84	2.99	3.10	3.13	3.08
3	3.92	4.08	4.23	4.08	3.97
4	5.02	5.18	5.31	5.27	4.92
5	5.96	6.00	6.06	6.12	6.01
6	7.41	7.26	7.43	7.32	7.09
9	9.66	9.59	9.56	9.35	9.19

Table A-7

NEW YORK STATE ACHIEVEMENT RESULTS (1966-73)
(percentile rank)

Grade	1966	1967	1968	1969	1970	1971	1972	1973
				Reading				
3	47	47	49	48	46	46	48	48
6	47	46	47	44	42	41	41	41
				Mathematics				
3	49	49	52	52	51	52	53	53
6	48	45	46	42	39	39	39	37

Table A-8

CALIFORNIA STATE ACHIEVEMENT RESULTS, 1970-1974
(second quartile percentile rank)

Grade	1909-70	1970-71	1971-72	1972-73	1973-74
Reading					
2	38	50	53	53	53
3	36	38	52	52	52
6	48	46	44	44	44
12	52	49	49	47	47
Mathematics					
6	47	43	38	38	38
12	48	48	48	48	48

Chapter 6

Transportation

Michael A. Kemp
Melvyn D. Cheslow

I. WHAT ARE THE PROBLEMS?

In June 1975, the Gallup Poll asked a national sample of city dwellers, "What do you regard as your community's worst problem?" In the responses, transportation-related concerns ranked above the problems of education, poor housing, and high taxes, and were outranked only by crime and unemployment.[1] It is obvious—from both survey findings like these and the amount of attention given to the subject by local politicians and the press—that city residents are indeed rankled by urban transportation problems. While this concern may not be felt as *deeply* as those about increasing crime or the fear of unemployment, it is a *broad* concern, felt and shared by many. Very large numbers of people must travel to, from, or within the city every day, and frequently at peak hours. Whether they travel by rail or road, by public or private transport, attitude surveys usually show that by far the major public grouse about the urban transportation system is with its *performance*. It is the cumulative

The authors are grateful to Alan Altshuler, Michael Beesley, Eric Beshers, Ellen Bozman, Herrington Bryce, Francine Rabinovitz, Martin Wohl, and to their colleagues Robert McGillivray and Gerald Miller for perceptive comments on earlier drafts.

[1] *Washington Post,* July 27, 1975.

effect of many relatively minor dissatisfactions and frustrations, repeated daily, that creates the public concern reflected in the surveys.[2]

Since such a large share of urban travel in the United States is by automobile, public attention focuses most strongly on traffic congestion on streets and highways—particularly during peak-hour journeys to and from work when congestion is heaviest and most frequently encountered. But the gap between the performance of the system and the desires or expectations of travelers also exists for other means of travel—transit vehicles are considered too slow, too infrequent, too dirty, too inconvenient, or too difficult to use; and taxis are "never around" when one is needed.

It may always have been that way. Travel, after all, is rarely an end in itself, so time spent in traveling is often considered "wasted." Perhaps *any* daily routine which consumes such large blocks of time for seemingly nonproductive purposes inevitably invites dissatisfactions. There is, however, some evidence to suggest that conditions in recent years have generally been improving rather than worsening, at least as far as highway travel into and out of central cities is concerned. The indices of highway performance most frequently cited are peak and off-peak average speeds, but typically these are measured only for "radial" journeys—that is, journeys which have either their origin or destination within the downtown area. Since circumferential and cross-town journeys form an increasingly important proportion of urban automobile travel, the average speeds of radial journeys give only a limited (and probably biased) indication of how well the highway system as a whole is performing. This limitation accepted, a 1970 survey of changes in travel time in 38 cities[3] suggests that many average speeds *have* improved for radial travelers, particularly during off-peak hours and for those making relatively long journeys. Certainly the data from Los Angeles, Detroit, Houston, Washington, Milwaukee, San Diego, and several other cities in the survey support such a conclusion. These improvements have occurred despite large increases in traffic volumes, and they are mostly the result of expanding the capacity of the highway system. But how far the improvements in travel times for radial journeys

---

[2] When a 1969 national survey of American adults (Harris & Associates, 1969) asked, "All in all, do you feel transportation in and around cities in this country is getting better, worse, or is about the same as it was five years ago?" roughly 30 percent responded "better," while 40 percent responded "worse." When this latter group, in turn, was asked to give reasons for their answers, about two-thirds cited road congestion and inadequacy as the major cause, and most of the remaining third mentioned problems with buses, trains, and taxis.

[3] Koltnow (1970). Meyer et al. (1965) provide an earlier review of evidence on improved highway speeds.

(mostly along expressways or arterial routes) are matched by improvements on *local* streets in urban areas is largely a matter for conjecture.

Trends in the level of service provided by bus transit over recent years are similarly hard to assess. Suburb-to-downtown services have shared in the enhanced radial highway speeds and, in an increasing number of locations, have benefited from the designation of exclusive rights of way and from other schemes to give them priority in mixed traffic. Rough estimates of average vehicle speeds for bus systems usually show small improvements between 1960 and 1970.[4] During the same decade, the route miles offered[5] increased in many cities. The average size of buses has also been increasing slightly. On the other hand, the annual vehicle miles of service[6] provided by buses and trolley coaches dropped by over 31 percent nationally between 1950 and 1970. The overall picture is one of less frequent (albeit slightly faster) service, spread more thinly over an enlarged route network.

The situation with rail transit systems is similar. Expanded route networks and slightly higher speeds have been accompanied by a national decline in the number of annual car miles of service. However, most of the reductions in service—for both bus and rail—have occurred in off-peak periods, following drops in ridership at those times. The average peak-hour traveler to and from downtown—the passenger whom transit systems are designed to serve best—has probably experienced little decline in service, if any at all.

During the very recent past there has been a more pronounced upturn in the quality of transit service in a number of younger, "growing" cities.[7] The improvements have been sparked chiefly by public takeover of the industry, and by an initial willingness of state and local governments to subsidize transit operations to an extent greater than that needed merely to make up deficits on existing services. The national statistics for transit are beginning to reflect the current fervor for innovation in the industry— between 1972 and 1975 the annual vehicle miles of service increased by roughly 13 percent. To what extent this will continue to lead to upgraded service for the average passenger, it is too early to tell.

So the trends in the overall performance of urban transportation sys-

---

[4] Miller (1974), at table I-43, page I-83.

[5] That is, the total miles of street along which bus service is offered.

[6] *Vehicle miles* (or in more accurate transit industry parlance, *revenue vehicle miles*) represents the total of all mileage operated in revenue service by all vehicles.

[7] See chapter 1 and chapter 2 where "growing" and "declining" cities are defined and discussed.

tems are mixed. On the highways—where most people are traveling—there has been a slow, steady improvement, as far as one may judge. On transit there *have* been declines in service, but mostly in the off-peak hours. Why, then, are the most frequent and vocal urban transportation complaints about performance?

The most likely answer is that, while conditions may have improved, they still fall short of the public's expectations and aspirations. The level of those expectations has probably been less influenced by travel conditions remembered from the past (since they are unlikely to have been better) than by the *best* levels of service to be experienced today. In other words, the psychological norms for urban travel are those set by the private automobile under uncongested conditions—the 50 to 60 mile per hour speeds, the flexibility, the comfort, the privacy, the reliability, and so on.

Such a theory is easy to rationalize, and a great deal of empirical evidence seems to support it. There are now at least two generations of citizens in the United States who have been accustomed to private automobile travel from birth: it is not surprising, therefore, that the automobile should shape our norms for traveling. There is much evidence, too, from research into the factors influencing consumer demand for travel to suggest that people place a high value on those service features which the automobile alone provides.

The Goals of Public Policy in Urban Transportation

It is the widespread discontent with existing travel options which has probably done most to shape governmental policies in urban passenger transportation. The overriding and (until recently) unquestioned objective of public policy, implicitly or explicitly, has been to make things better or easier for the traveling public—to enhance public mobility or at least see that mobility levels do not deteriorate as traffic volumes grow.[8] This predominant emphasis on improving mobility, and sometimes the objective itself, have come under increasing question in recent years. One reason for this is that the public has grown increasingly aware of the social costs associated with some of the measures taken to improve the transpor-

---

[8] The word "mobility" is used here to denote the ability of a person to reach a set of desired destinations at an acceptable outlay of time and money. Obviously, however, there is a relationship between a person's travel "desires" and his anticipations of the time and money necessary to fulfill them; he can substitute closer destinations for distant ones which are too costly to reach. In essence, then, increased mobility is indicated by a general decrease per mile in the real price of traveling (that is, both the money payments and the money value which the average citizen assigns to time spent traveling).

tation system, while legal means of redress have become more available to those who suffer most from the disbenefits.

In view of the superior level of service offered by the private car, it is not surprising that in the marketplace of travel alternatives consumers have overwhelmingly chosen the automobile [9] (as we document in section 2, below). Nor is it surprising that public agencies have pursued enhanced mobility mainly by catering to increased automobile use. But for most travel by private car, the average occupancy is usually no more than one or two persons per vehicle, which means that automobile travel generates more harmful emissions, uses more energy, and monopolizes more road and parking space per passenger mile than do other modes of transportation, most specifically the transit bus. The environmental movement and the nation's mounting energy problems have served to increase public awareness that car travel creates costs for society at large which are not being fully borne by the car users themselves.

Not only does automobile use create social costs; so too does urban highway construction. Providing roads and parking space consumes more land and can strongly affect urban form. The aesthetic and social implications of highway building, difficult as they are to quantify, are very inadequately considered in deciding whether, what, and where to build. Of course, locating any major public facility may be expected to create rancor among residents affected adversely in nearby areas. But more generally, critics argue that policy about highway construction cannot and should not be divorced from some normative notions about desirable urban form.

Meanwhile, the growth rate of public demand for travel shows few signs of moderating. At some stage, however, the financial and social costs of further highway expansion presumably outweigh the benefits. Unless all of those costs are properly appraised, the argument runs, road building may change the nature of the city in ways which many people find undesirable. In recent years, legislation has provided mechanisms for dissident groups to stall or thwart highway construction programs.

Moreover, if one accepts the theory that public dissatisfactions with the performance of the transportation system derive mostly from the discrepancy between congested peak-hour commuter travel and travel by private car under uncongested conditions, an important insight follows. Unless public expectations and aspirations are adjusted downwards, the dis-

---

[9] It can be argued, and we partly concur, that marketplace choices have been distorted by pricing automobile use below the level indicated by economic efficiency considerations. We discuss this issue later.

satisfaction is likely to continue regardless of the efforts being made to improve the transportation system. On the highways, the social and financial costs of expanding capacity to the point where peak-hour speeds can approximate those in the off-peak would be prohibitive; particularly so when one considers the high latent demand for highway travel which often appears when new facilities are introduced. As for public transportation, there are technological as well as cost limitations: we do not have any existing mode of travel (except, possibly, very high-grade taxi service) which can match the service features of the private car, even under peak-hour conditions.

In sum, the effect of such considerations has been to raise public doubts about past governmental policies. Of course, in most of the important areas of policy there is no clear consensus among the general public on what the goals should be, or on what priorities should be given to different (and sometimes conflicting) objectives. This is as true for urban transportation as for policy issues concerning education, crime, or the social services. Lacking a consensus, there are many viewpoints on which problems should receive the most attention. For some people, for example, the key objective of governments should be to encourage further mobility —or, at the least, to preserve existing mobility levels. Others, believing that the costs (particularly those associated with high automobile ownership and use) already outweigh the benefits, hold that our current average mobility is adequate, or even too high. For others, the main objective should be to help the "transportation disadvantaged," and particularly to focus on the problems of the carless. For still others, the overriding concern is the survival of public transportation alternatives under seemingly hostile market conditions.

One of the problems underlying this disagreement on priorities is that the commodity involved—"mobility"—is so amorphous. Mobility for what? Travel is seldom an end in itself, but rather a means to other ends, and those "other ends" are practically innumerable. Is it clear that it is in the interest of governments to foster greater freedom of movement, as a "good thing" in itself? The answer is apt to be largely judgmental, and depends intrinsically on an individual's views of what constitutes the good life and the optimal ways of ordering society.

The economist has a theoretically satisfying approach to deciding what level of public sector financial and regulatory involvement in urban transportation seems wise. Leaving aside questions of equity, governments should pursue those policies for which the benefits most outweigh the costs. But the net benefits of enhanced mobility are largely dependent on

how much the general public values improvements in mobility as compared with changes in other aspects of urban life—and those relative
values are difficult to measure.

Certainly there is much circumstantial evidence to suggest that the
public places a relatively high value on greater mobility. Instance the
continuing increase of spending on travel as a proportion of the total
household budget.[10] Instance, too, the relatively steep increase in spending on automobiles and their use as incomes rise; the low sensitivity of
travel behavior to increases in the price of traveling; the high level of
latent demand manifest as new highway segments are opened; the continued high rate of growth in such national indicators as vehicle miles of
travel per capita—all suggest a fairly strong appetite for travel.[11]

How far will the demand continue to grow as new facilities are provided? At what stage do the financial and social costs of catering to
greater mobility exceed the value which the public places on it? These
are questions essential to deciding how much weight should be given to
investments in mobility enhancement as an objective of public policy. By
and large, they are questions to which the analysts have no clear answers.

But for the public at large, many or all of these concerns are often dis-
tilled into just one key issue: whether society should continue to invest
in highway expansion or instead devote the resources to mass transit.
Much of the public debate on this question is oversimplified. A recent
survey of editorial articles showed that the discussion of investment
options tends to be highly polarized.[12] Construction of more transit facilities and further expansion of highways are implicitly viewed as mutually
exclusive, perfect substitutes for each other. Moreover, the transit alternative in larger cities is frequently envisaged (explicitly or implicitly) as
"rapid transit," and that term in turn is usually taken to mean only the
construction of fixed-rail facilities. Presenting the issues in such polarized

---

[10] Around 1910, only 6 percent of personal consumption expenditures was spent
on transportation, mainly on public transit. From 1920 through the 1940s this proportion stayed around 10 percent, and since then has increased to a present level
of 14 percent.

[11] Two comments are relevant here. First, in part the growth in public demand for travel has been exaggerated by the fact that it has been underpriced—a
topic which is discussed later. But second, it is noteworthy that the strong fervor
for "automobility" is a cross-cultural one, manifest in countries at widely different
stages of economic development. It is certainly not confined only to the relatively
affluent nations.

[12] Olsson and Kemp (1975). The survey covered all editorial articles on urban
transportation issues appearing in a broadly representative sample of 155 news-
papers over a nineteen-month period in 1973-74.

terms, most of the editorial positions surveyed can be categorized as pro-transit and anti-highway.

The broad question of past, present, and future priorities for public investment in urban transportation does provide an appropriate central focus for this chapter, even though the issues may have been clouded by the oversimplifications of the press. How have past governmental policies shaped current urban travel patterns? What policy options might enhance or maintain mobility levels with relatively low disbenefits? Most specifically, what forms of governmental investment in urban transportation make the most sense? In the following pages, these questions are explored, if not fully answered. In addition, we discuss (in varying depth) four other closely-related issues which face governments in the 1970s:

- how do we insure that *all* members of the population can share a minimum acceptable level of mobility;

- how do we pay for transportation service, and how do we distribute the costs;

- how can we better mesh transportation policies with other closely-related urban goals (for urban form and the shape of urban growth, for example) ; and

- at what level of government—local, state, or federal—are various decisions about policy best made?

II. URBAN TRANSPORTATION IN THE MID-1970s

A discussion of urban passenger transportation requires some understanding of how and where city-dwellers are currently traveling, and of the recent trends which have produced these patterns of behavior. To-day's passenger transportation in U.S. cities has been shaped by two major influences—by the decisions of individual consumers in the marketplace, and by governmental regulatory and fiscal actions which have affected market forces. For the most part, public policy has served in some ways to accommodate and to reinforce the trends of the marketplace.

The most significant processes shaping urban travel patterns since the end of the Second World War have been the interwoven phenomena of increasing private automobile ownership and migration from the city to the suburbs. It is not necessary to understand the detailed causality of these processes—how far, for example, the easy acquisition of cars by low- and middle-income households made suburbanization possible, or how far decentralization of residences and workplaces made the automobile a household necessity—to accept the importance of their combined effects. Indeed, there is much evidence to suggest that urban Americans have aspired strongly to *both* low-density living and increased personal mobility throughout the whole of the twentieth century. Over the last thirty years, increasing numbers of families have gained the financial resources necessary to indulge these aspirations, and their individual consumption decisions about where to live and work and how to travel have been predominantly responsible for major transportation changes. These market trends have been reinforced both by the decentralization of employment and possibly also by governmental policies regarding personal taxation, housing credit, land use planning, and transportation investment.

Personal Travel Characteristics

What *are* the salient features of urban passenger transportation in the mid-1970s, and what have been the major changes in recent decades? It is, of course, no surprise that most urban travel is now made by private automobile. Consider that, in 1940, public transit was responsible for roughly 30 percent of the urban vehicular passenger miles.[13] This percentage almost doubled during the Second World War, but dropped immediately after the war as gasoline rationing ceased and the production of automobiles was re-established. In 1960, 88 percent of the urban passenger miles were by automobile with 12 percent by public transport.[14] By 1970, almost 94 percent of the passenger miles were made by car, and only 6 percent were made by varying forms of public transport.

It has been widely suggested that transit's share of the market has been falling primarily because of increasing urban decentralization and the inability of transit to provide efficient and acceptably-priced service to the lower density areas.[15] However, transit was able to remain financially healthy until long after suburbanization and the patronage decline were both well established.[16]

---

[13] A passenger mile is one person traveling one mile. Three people traveling each one mile and one person going three miles both yield three passenger miles. The estimate for 1940, based in part on suspect data, may not be entirely comparable with subsequent estimates for 1960 and 1970.

[14] U.S. Department of Transportation (1972). These numbers are slightly high since motorcycle and bicycle journeys are not considered.

[15] See, for example, Meyer et al. (1965).

[16] See U.S. Department of Transportation (1967) and American Public Transit Association (1976, and earlier years).

The Pattern of Car Ownership

Of major influence in lowering transit's share of the market has been the rapid increase in private automobile ownership. For instance, by 1920 there were 8 million cars in the United States, one for every 13.1 persons; by 1930 there were 23 million, one for every 5.3 persons, and possibly about half of these cars were in urban areas. Ownership and the use of motor vehicles declined during the early years of the depression of the 1930s, but the decline appears to have been much less sharp than the decline in real personal incomes. When automobile production resumed after the Second World War, ownership increased rapidly, and has continued to grow, up to the present time. We now have one automobile for every 2.1 persons in the country, and the ratio of cars to people continues to rise.

The proportion of families not owning a car also decreased rapidly after World War II. In 1950, 41 percent owned no car; in 1955, the figure was 30 percent; and by 1960, only 23 percent. Since 1960, the proportion of carless families has continued to decline, and was reported to be 17 percent in 1970. The figures indicate, however, a tapering-off in the growth of auto-owning families. Offsetting this, there has been a strong growth in the proportion of families owning *more than* one car. Multi-car families grew from 7 percent in 1950 to 29 percent by the early 1970s.[17]

While these statistics relate to the entire nation, the picture for metropolitan areas is very similar. Between 1960 and the early 1970s the proportion of carless households declined from 31 to 22 percent.[18] A similar pattern emerges when central cities and suburbs are examined separately. Thirty-eight percent of central city households were without cars in 1960, decreasing to 34 percent by the early 1970s. In the suburbs, carless households declined from 18 percent to 13 percent over the same period. It appears that about half of the drop in carless families was associated with movement from the center cities to the suburbs, although one cannot say that this movement, rather than other factors, *caused* the decline.

It is important, also, to realize that while the *proportion* of urban households without an automobile is falling, in *absolute numbers* the carless households have grown. In 1970 there were roughly 325,000 more

---

[17] University of Michigan "Survey of consumer finances" data.

[18] U.S. Department of Commerce (1970, 1973). These data are from a source different from the national data cited previously, and they relate to *households* rather than *families*.

metropolitan households without a car than in 1960, an increase of over 4 percent.

The growth of multiple car households in metropolitan areas has been slightly greater than for the nation as a whole—from 14 percent in 1960 to over 30 percent by the early 1970s. There are differences again between central cities and suburbs, but both types of areas showed large gains. The growth in multi-car households in central city areas (from 10 percent in 1960 to 21 percent in the early 1970s) is particularly noteworthy; there population densities are high, destinations are close, parking space is at a premium, car ownership costs are high, and transit service is comparatively good.

As the ownership of automobiles has increased, the number of licensed drivers has kept pace. In 1940, about 45 percent of the population of driving age had licenses. By 1972, the level had increased to 78 percent.[19] Most of this increase has come from women and elderly men, but people in these groups are still much less likely to be licensed drivers than are men in the 21 to 59 age bracket.

Driving Has Grown Cheaper

One of the major factors fueling the growth in private automobile ownership and use has been increasing personal incomes. Evidence suggests that as a family gains more disposable income, automobile ownership and use is typically given high priority in its pattern of increased spending. High-income families, consequently, are much more car-oriented than the lower-income families, as table 1 illustrates.

Table 1
EXAMPLES OF CAR OWNERSHIP AND USE WITH
INCREASING INCOME

	Year	All house-holds	Households with gross annual income		
			less than $3,000	$7,500 to $9,999	$15,000 or more
Proportion of households with at least one car	1972	80%	41%	91%	96%
Average annual mileage per car	1969-70	11,600	6,600	12,200	15,000

Sources: U.S. Department of Commerce (1973); Strate (1972).

[19] Maring (1974).

The acquisition and use of automobiles have doubtless been influenced by the fact that both have been growing progressively less expensive in real terms over the last 25 years. While the general consumer price index increased by 102 percent over that period, the index of new car prices increased by only 48 percent, implying a relative price reduction of 26 percent for new cars. Even very recently, automobile prices have been increasing more slowly than retail prices generally. Between September 1973 and September 1975 new car prices rose by 16 percent, while the consumer price index grew by 21 percent.

Gasoline prices have fallen in constant dollar terms, too. In the period from 1950 to 1973, the real price of gasoline declined by 26 percent. In the most recent past, however, this trend has been reversed; between Fall 1973 and Fall 1975, the real price rose by over 26 percent.

Geographical Variations in Travel Patterns

The increased acquisition and use of automobiles, together with urban decentralization, have brought about changes in the geographical aspects of urban travel which are not widely understood. Many of the popular notions about urban travel come from information presented in the press.

Table 2
TRANSPORTATION CHARACTERISTICS OF
DIFFERENT-SIZED METROPOLITAN AREAS (1970)

| | | Type of metropolitan area | | |
	U.S. Total	major cities	medium-sized cities	small cities	other areas
Resident population	100%	27%	31%	13%	29%
Residence of people working in CBDs	100%	45%	49%	1%	5%
Transit passengers	100%	72%	23%	2%	3%
Households without automobiles	100%	42%	28%	13%	17%
Proportion of households having no car	17%	26%	15%	18%	11%

Definitions of area types:
   major cities: urbanized parts of the largest 12 metropolitan areas
   medium-sized cities: urbanized parts of 227 smaller metropolitan areas
   small cities: cities and towns with population under 50,000
   other areas: rural areas, and non-urban parts of metropolitan areas

Source: Derived from Costello (1973).

Often the creators of these presentations focus on travel as seen in the very largest cities, especially New York and Los Angeles, because the problems are more striking, and because they themselves live there and are familiar with them. But not everyone lives in these very large urban areas. As shown in table 2, only 27 percent of the nation's population lives in the urbanized parts of the largest twelve standard metropolitan statistical areas (SMSAs). These twelve "major cities" account for 72 percent of the transit passengers and 42 percent of the households with no cars, and their residents hold 45 percent of the country's jobs located in the dense downtown central business districts (CBDs).[20] These urban areas usually have relatively high densities, CBD-oriented employment, and sufficiently pervasive transit services for transit to be considered a reasonable alternative to private automobile travel for a sizable segment of the population.

However, the urbanized areas in the 227 smaller SMSAs are rather different. These "medium-sized cities" comprise 31 percent of the nation's population, but only 23 percent of the transit riders and 28 percent of the households without cars. These areas are much more captive to the automobile than are the twelve largest cities.

Then there are the still smaller towns and cities with populations under 50,000. They have 13 percent of the population and 12 percent of the automobiles in the country—but only 2 percent of the transit riders. These "small cities" are obviously oriented toward the private car to an even greater extent than are either the major or the medium-sized cities.

In all of the urban parts of the country taken together, only 8 percent of the employed people work in central business districts. On the other hand, 34 percent of urban workers work in the suburbs. Even in the four large cities which have extensive rapid transit systems oriented toward downtown—New York, Chicago, Philadelphia, and Boston—only 13 percent of the employed residents work in the CBD. In those four cities 43 percent work in the central city but outside the CBD, and another 38 percent work in suburban jurisdictions. So an extensive number of commuting trips are oriented toward the suburbs, and these trips are made predominantly by automobile. Only 4 percent of commuters to the suburbs use transit.

Transit mainly serves the downtown-oriented commuter. Nationally

---

[20] These statistics are from an unpublished paper by Costello (1973) which reviews data from the 1970 Census of Population and from the American Transit Association. It is known that the 1970 Census may have seriously underestimated CBD workplaces.

speaking, around 40 percent of CBD workers use public transport, and even in the medium-sized cities, 20 percent of CBD employees use public transport to and from work. To summarize, transit principally serves the very largest urban areas and the central business districts of the smaller ones. But since only a small proportion of all employees work in the CBD, transit serves a small fraction of all workers. And the trends in urban decentralization are such that the proportion continues to grow smaller.

The Role of Governments in Urban Transportation

While the changes in urban travel patterns which have been discussed are primarily the aggregate result of marketplace decisions by individual consumers, they have been influenced also by government policies regarding urban transportation. Governments, at federal, state, and local levels, have played two basic roles; one regulatory, and the other fiscal. Regulation has shaped the forms of urban public transport which are available today, and public financing policies have strongly influenced priorities for investment in transportation facilities.

Regulation of Public Transport

There are many ways in which government regulation impinges on urban transportation. Federally-imposed standards, for example, are increasingly influencing aspects of private automobile design. States and municipalities regulate road usage through traffic laws and by requiring, for instance, driver licensing, vehicle registration, and safety inspections. Most importantly, state and local governments regulate the provision of public transportation.

Past and present regulation has done much to shape the forms of public transport available in cities today, as an historical perspective can illustrate.[21] When the new electric street railways replaced horse-drawn vehicles late in the nineteenth century, they brought with them an important (but temporary) economy of scale to urban passenger transport. The use of a single powerhouse to generate electricity for the city-wide grid allowed the power to be distributed to wherever the peak passenger load might be. In consequence, a competitive form of public transportation (the horse-drawn car and cab) was quickly replaced in most cities by a city-wide electric streetcar monopoly, providing a product superior in comfort and speed but operating along less flexible linear routes. With

---

[21] Eckert and Hilton (1972).

monopolization came public regulation of fares and entry into the industry.

A threat to the dominance of the street railway companies arose in 1914 in the form of the jitney. Private car ownership was growing. The flat nickel fare of the streetcars meant that the short-distance passenger was cross-subsidizing the long. The short-distance patrons were thus vulnerable to poaching by private automobile owners who drove their vehicles along streetcar routes, stopping when hailed, and providing a speedier and more comfortable service at no higher fare. Fueled by rising unemployment in the fall of 1914, the jitney movement spread rapidly, particularly in the mild climate cities of the west and south. By the second quarter of 1915, it was estimated that there were about 62,000 jitneys operating throughout the country. An element of competition was restored to urban passenger transport.

However, the street railway companies, losing revenue sharply because of the diverted traffic, took quick action to have jitney service outlawed. Because of their superior political influence, the street railways managed to have anti-jitney legislation enacted in virtually every city of the country. By the early 1920s, very few jitneys survived. The most significant residue of the episode was, however, the enhanced monopoly status of the streetcar companies. When the street railways went into decline, to be replaced by motor buses often operated by the same companies, the monopoly rights survived. In the 1970s, transit is still organized on a monopoly basis operating along linear routes, even though the technological rationale for the monopoly largely disappeared with the streetcar.

The "jitney craze" also had a spillover effect on another important mode of urban transport—the taxicab. The desire to prohibit jitney service strengthened the public regulation of taxis, particularly with regard to entry into the industry and the legality of carrying more than one group of passengers simultaneously. In most cities today, the ordinances allow cab service to be provided only by franchised firms or by a limited number of vehicles, and "shared riding" is expressly prohibited.[22]

The Fiscal Role of the Federal Government

Just as local regulation has had a lasting impact on urban transportation, so have government financing policies, particularly those of the federal government. As we shall show, the end result of financing legislation is that the federal government has set urban transportation policy. The

---

[22] Kirby et al. (1975).

policy is not precisely spelled out, and parts may be inconsistent, but the policy is there implicitly.

The federal government has been providing funds for highway construction since 1916, and for *urban* highways specifically since the depression years. The Highway Trust Fund, established in 1956 as a financing mechanism for the new "National System of Interstate and Defense Highways," introduced at the federal level of government the concept of dedicating receipts from user taxes (on gasoline, tires, and cars) for road construction. Transit, on the other hand, received no significant federal support until 1965, when a program of grants for approved capital expenditures was introduced. The federal role which has evolved has several features worthy of note. The federal government is concerned with fund-raising by taxation and with financing by grant-in-aid programs. These functions are explicitly laid out in legislation and are administered by the executive branch. The legislation includes matching ratios for funds required from local sources, and allocation formulae which specify the geographic distribution of the funds expended in the grant programs. The formulae are usually compromises between rural and urban interests for highways, and between those cities which have extensive rail transit systems and other cities for transit programs.

The legislation also includes some standards which states or localities must meet in order to receive the grants tied to them. These standards are both organizational—requiring, for instance, the establishment of state highway departments or metropolitan "clearinghouse" agencies through which all of a city's requests for capital grants must be channeled—and functional, requiring certain planning activities by the local agencies. In setting guidelines for the legislated standards, the agencies of the executive branch can further constrain the actions of the states or localities. The standards approach has been used by the Congress in an almost commonplace way to require activities of states and localities which it has no *direct* authority to require. Recently this approach was used in the 1974 Highway Act, for example, to require any state which received federal highway aid to reduce its maximum speed limit to 55 miles per hour.

The provision of federal funds to states and localities also affects their consideration of the costs of alternative transportation programs. For instance, a local government must currently pay 100 percent of the cost of routine highway and transit maintenance, at least 50 percent of the operating subsidy for approved transit services, 30 percent of the cost of construction of non-Interstate highways, 20 percent of transit capital expenditures, and only 10 percent of the costs for construction of Interstate highways. To the local government, the Interstate system is therefore a relatively inexpensive alternative compared with constructing other roads or with maintenance.

Not only has the federal provision of grants influenced the choices for highway spending, but it has also affected the expenditures on public transit. Between 1950 and 1965 while transit patronage was falling, states and localities were being given federal aid to construct highways which would attract riders to automobiles. Since federal aid to transit began in 1965, the amount of support (about $3.0 billion in total by fiscal year 1974) has been small compared with that for urban highways (roughly $15.4 billion over the same period). Moreover, the federal refusal until recently to give aid for transit operating costs has pushed localities toward buying buses and building rail systems in preference to improving the routing, scheduling, maintenance, and management of systems.[23] The federal legislation has further influenced the way that grants can be used by requiring, in effect, that the transit unions approve of any program before aid can be given.

The discrepancy in the levels of federal financial support for highways and transit is not necessarily economically unsound of itself, for the relative volumes of funding provided do *not* represent the relative magnitudes of net federal subsidy to the one or the other. The federal highway funds are derived entirely from user charges, whereas transit support comes entirely from general revenues.[24] The question of the level of subsidization is a complex one, and to some extent an emotionally charged one, too. Studies suggest that highway *provision* as a whole is not being publicly subsidized (since the costs of provision approximately equal user payments), although highway *use* may be subsidized in several ways.

The point is not that the public spending on highways and transit is uneven, but that the relative magnitudes of spending on the two implicitly shape urban transportation policy. The result of the various financing formulae, geographical allocation formulae, legislated standards, and bureaucratic guidelines is that the federal government is setting policy for urban transportation.

Shifts in the Balance of Decision Making

Local planning for urban transportation is performed by many diverse organizations: state and local departments of transportation and highway

---

[23] This is *not* to suggest that federal operating subsidies would encourage operating efficiency in the industry. We strongly suspect that they reduce the overall incentive to be efficient.

[24] Indeed, the legislation requires the local contribution to transit matching funds to come from sources *other* than the farebox.

departments, regional "clearinghouse" agencies, and local transit agencies. In the interaction between so many levels of government there is high potential for misunderstanding, disagreement, and turf disputes. Indeed, many observers claim that, because of this diffused decision-making structure, decisions are not being made for improving urban transportation.

Some have suggested that the federal government must take a stronger, more normative role in planning for urban transportation. By setting appropriate standards for federal aid, it should become more involved in local decisions about what modes of travel should be provided, the mix of public and private transportation, the amount of new construction necessary, and which—if any—new systems should be developed and introduced. The advocates feel that the social benefits arising from the decisive improvement of transportation would justify the increased federal involvement. They point to decision making for national defense and space programs, which in both cases is centralized in the federal establishment, and which permits national commitments to be made and put into action. If urban transportation improvement were a national goal, they argue, it would be possible to take the actions necessary to accomplish the goal.

Other groups hold that the way to improve urban transportation decision making is to *reduce* the federal role. They argue that the indirect policy making of the federal government has created biases and distortions and has led to many of the problems which now exist. They propose that federal grants should be continued, but that there should be one formula for all grants, that conditions on the use of the money should be relaxed, and that the highway trust fund should be phased out.

Some of these people advocate a general revenue-sharing approach, whereby the state and local governments would be permitted to use a block grant for any purpose they desire, transportation or otherwise, without a requirement for matching funds. Others favor revenue sharing specifically earmarked for transportation, but still without a matching funds requirement. Still others would broaden the highway trust fund into a unified transportation trust fund under which transportation-related receipts would be dedicated to transportation expenditures.

Although there are many vocal proponents of the argument to increase the federal role, the most recent legislative activity evidences a movement toward less involvement. The change is occurring very slowly, and could easily be reversed. But for now, the legislative trend is toward removing some of the existing limitations on the use of federal grants.

For instance, the 1970 Highway Act allowed states to spend federal highway money on specific improvements which would aid buses, such as fringe parking lots. Later, the 1973 act allowed states to spend a portion of the Trust Fund monies on any type of transit capital improvement in urban areas. This freedom only applied to $800 million per year, but it was a clear change of direction. Many hailed the section of the highway act which allowed this transfer as the "breaking of the trust fund." The 1974 National Mass Transportation Assistance Act not only extended authority for capital grants but also allowed some federal grants to cover transit operating costs for the first time.

More recently, in mid-1975, legislation developed by the executive branch was submitted to Congress which would limit the highway trust fund to supporting the Interstate system. This legislation would have allowed the Interstate system to be completed, but would transfer all but one cent per gallon of the federal gasoline taxes to the general fund. It also proposes the reduction of a portion of the federal fuel tax in return for an equal increase in state fuel taxes. Although this particular bill did not find many congressional supporters when first introduced, the trend is such that legislation similar to it seems likely to be passed eventually.

III. DISCONTENT WITH THE AUTOMOBILE

The private automobile provides the dominant share of all urban travel, and highway conditions for the automobile appear to show a slow but steady improvement, but nevertheless there remain strong dissatisfactions with the performance of the highway system. Why then does the public apparently doubt the advisability of continuing with past policies to improve mobility levels? Briefly, the doubts derive from citizen and governmental concerns about the social, health, safety, aesthetic, and economic impacts of expanded use of private automobiles. Most specifically, the car is a relatively heavy consumer of space and energy, and a relatively heavy contributor to urban noise and air pollution.

It is sometimes difficult to maintain perspective while discussing this issue, as several popularly-targeted diatribes published over recent years bear witness.[25] Of course, one can speculate whether life in the United States would be any worse had the automobile never been invented, or question whether the quality of life in Los Angeles is preferable to that of less car-oriented cities like Venice or Prague. Ultimately, these are matters of personal values and taste. Our personal view is that both the auto-

---

[25] A listing of titles alone provides a good indication of the level of polemicism: instance "Autokind vs. Mankind," "Road to Ruin," "Dead End," and "Superhighway, Superhoax."

mobile itself, and its ready availability to such a large segment of the population, have provided considerable social and economic net benefits to society as a whole.

The Growth of a Citizen Lobby

At the same time, the "love affair with the automobile" certainly has created social costs. By the 1960s many citizens were discovering that the benefits of attaining greater mobility were also accompanied by disbenefits, of which some groups received a disproportionate share. For example, the large-scale construction of new transportation facilities affects the lives of the residents of nearby areas in two major ways. For surface facilities, swathes of land must be acquired for right-of-way; and the new facility, when constructed, may markedly alter social, economic, land use, and travel patterns in its vicinity in ways which local residents find detrimental. Both processes can disrupt the community to varying degrees.[26]

Up to now, most public protest about disruption has focused on urban freeways—largely because highway construction has been the most common way of expanding the capacity of the transportation system on a large scale. It was the residents of areas which were to be adversely affected by new highway facilities who first began to contest road building policies. The cause was joined by others who did not expect to experience the disbenefits personally but who were against the facilities for other social or political reasons. Urban development had reached a point in large metropolitan areas where highway routes took land already used for residential and commercial purposes; some neighborhoods were destroyed. Critics pointed to the displacement of established homeowners, to the increased local noise and noxious emissions, to greater congestion and decreased pedestrian safety on some local streets, to the sometimes adverse social and aesthetic consequences of new urban highways. In the late 1960s this problem took on racial overtones, too. Since the highway alignment of least political resistance and lowest cost often passed through inner-city ghetto areas, the issue was often characterized as "building white men's roads through black men's bedrooms."

Furthermore, for some travelers the benefits were lower than had been

---

[26] There is a third form of adverse effect on the area which, surprisingly, attracts less public concern. This is the temporary disruption caused by the construction itself, which in some cases lasts for several years and can cause some groups—for example, local retail merchants—to suffer substantial, permanent, and uncompensated losses.

anticipated: new facilities were often congested soon after they were built. In addition to disaffected citizens, there were transit operators experiencing growing deficits, and local government leaders who wanted to use highway monies for transit. These various groups of people did not agree on exactly what changes they wanted, but they all wished at least some modification of a trend which saw more highways being built and more automobiles being used.

The 1969 National Environmental Protection Act (NEPA) provided a mechanism by which these groups could try to change the highway program. In the words of the act:

> all agencies of the federal government shall . . . include in every recommendation or report on proposals for . . . major federal actions significantly affecting the quality of the human environment, a detailed statement . . . on the environmental impact of the proposed action.[27]

Citizens went to court to require environmental impact statements to be filed for highway projects. Before 1969 only three or four cases involving highways were brought to court each year. In 1970, however, the number jumped to 18, and presently about 45 cases are being brought annually. Some of these suits are by individuals with particular grievances about the acquisition of their land, but many are by groups of citizens with broader concerns. Prior to 1971, the plaintiff in a court case had himself to be hurt financially (generally by more than $10,000) to bring suit, but in that year the Supreme Court ruled that this criterion was not necessary in NEPA cases against the government, thus allowing class action suits to be filed by various citizen groups. In the early 1970s many of the court cases were for failure to provide an environmental impact statement at all. After highway agencies lost their arguments that the statements were unnecessary, they proceeded to perform the studies required. New studies also stopped or delayed many other projects which had not been taken to court. Moreover, in many cases either the highway agency or a local government felt that not only an environmental impact study but a completely new plan or design for a project would be desirable.

At present, the citizen groups are still filing suits concerning impact statements, but the orientation has changed. They now argue that agencies have been "arbitrary and capricious" in their studies. Suits are also brought on other grounds such as civil rights. So far as this issue

---

[27] Anderson (1973) provides a review of the 1969 act and its interpretation by the courts.

is concerned, the mid-1970s is a time of transition and uncertainty, and transportation observers differ in their prognoses. Some firmly believe that the era of large-scale highway expansion in urban areas is over, and that most of the plans currently in contention will eventually be abandoned, either through judicial restraint or political pressures.[28] Others, among them many state and federal highway engineers, are less convinced that all urban expressway construction has been effectively stalemated. They believe that plans can be adapted to conform fully with the legal constraints and then will be allowed to proceed. However, in August 1975 the federal Secretary of Transportation disapproved the construction of one highly contentious urban link of the Interstate highway system,[29] after a protracted legal battle between the State Highway Commission and local citizens, and this may presage the abandonment of more plans for urban freeway segments—for radial routes if not for circumferential routes as well.

Compensation May Be The Key

It is a little difficult to gauge and place in perspective the current extent of public concern on the construction issue. Limited survey research and referendum evidence (albeit now rather dated) suggests that self-interest is the primary motivating factor: most people are not averse to the expansion of transportation facilities *per se,* so much as they are concerned that their own neighborhood should not be the one to suffer the disadvantages.[30]

And while most of the attention has in the past focused on the adverse impacts of new *highway* facilities, the problems of neighborhood disruption apply with equal force to the construction of fixed-guideway public transportation systems. Experience in those cities currently building rapid rail facilities shows that the locations of rail lines and of stations are among the most controversial issues involved; homeowners do not want either the lines or the stations in the vicinity of their own property.[31]

According to one viewpoint, the problems of neighborhood disruption

---

[28] This has already happened to some proposed urban segments of the Interstate system in California, Maryland, Massachusetts, and the District of Columbia.

[29] Secretary Coleman's decision against the extension of Route I-66 inside the Washington Beltway marked the first time that a segment of the Interstate system has been turned down by a Secretary of Transportation.

[30] Charles River Associates (1970).

[31] Although no express busways requiring the acquisition of exclusive rights-of-way are yet being built, doubtless the same problems would apply to them.

can be alleviated by more adequately compensating those who suffer losses because of decisions about locating public facilities. Everyone has a price, this argument says in effect, and society should be willing to pay the price necessary for all who are affected to believe that they have not been left worse off by the change. This price is a valid part of the total costs of the project, which should be weighed against the benefits in deciding whether the project is worthwhile. This viewpoint has much merit, although in practice it is difficult to fix monetary values on many adverse impacts, to identify the losers and the extent of their individual loss, and to devise appropriate legal and administrative procedures.

At least so far as residents actually displaced by right-of-way acquisition (a relatively easy loss to identify and measure) are concerned, the recent years have seen some progress in compensation practices. For example, under 1970 federal legislation, relocation assistance to private households displaced by the Federal-aid Highway Program now comprises the fair market value of the property, moving expenses, and, under prescribed conditions, a supplemental payment of up to $15,000 to meet the higher costs of replacement housing. Displaced firms receive comparable assistance.

To what extent these upgraded compensation practices for displacement have moderated public concern over the effects of facility construction as a whole is undetermined. We suspect probably little, since, despite the compensation, antipathy to forced relocation still runs high at the time the move has to be made. Surveys of relocated households in Ohio and Texas have shown almost two-thirds to be unfavorable to the move at first. The dissatisfaction drops to a third or less of the households over time, however; and delays in the receipt of relocation payments appears to be more a cause for concern than do the amounts of those payments.[32]

The other adverse impacts of facility location are less easy to compensate for. One possible indication of the magnitude of the loss is the change in property value, determined as objectively as possible. Recent legislation in the United Kingdom uses declines in property values as the basis of compensation for the discomfort and inconvenience of transportation noise. Changes in property values, however, do not indicate the total losses due to the facility location; they are unable or unlikely to take full account of the social impacts, for example. Moreover, it must be remembered that the highway or transit facility provides benefits to

---

[32] U.S. Department of Transportation (1974b).

the neighborhood as well as costs. In many cases, improved accessibility to the area has led to a general enhancement, rather than decline, in property values (except for property immediately abutting the facility).[33] Indeed, some states are contemplating legislation to tax land value gains which can be clearly associated with the siting of highway interchanges.

Automotive Emissions, Energy Consumption, and Safety

Although it is the disruption created by new highways that has kindled the revolt against the automobile, the dissatisfaction is fueled by other concerns as well. As for the more direct detrimental side-products of automobile usage—such as increased exposure to accident hazards and to the health hazards of air pollution exacerbated by automotive emissions— government policy should be aimed at abating these hazards to the extent that the benefits of abatement outweigh the costs. The magnitude of benefits are indicated by the public's willingness to pay to ameliorate the disagreeable side-products. But citizens have no means, as individuals, either to bribe motorists to refrain from creating nuisances or to charge them for doing so. Only government agencies can act effectively on the public's behalf. Public policy should be framed so as to simulate market forces as closely as possible, by reflecting the public's valuation of reduced levels of noise or air pollution, or of reduced probabilities of accidental death or severe injury. One possible remedial policy would be to charge automobile users (the people who by their own decisions create the problems for society as a whole) a price which reflects the costs of abating the harmful side-products of automobile usage to an extent determined by the public's valuation of such abatement.

Unfortunately, the theoretical elegance of this construct is not matched by pragmatic ease of applicability. One problem is that we know very little about the public's valuation of variations in air quality, safety, quietness, or other types of amenity. The fact that there is no real market

---

[33] "A number of studies of land values along major highways have been made, most of them varying as to type of highway improvement, size of community, study methods, etc. Analysis of 183 individual study segments shows that median annual increases in land prices along highways ranged from 6 percent to nearly 18 percent in the 5 to 10 year study period. Gains in value were much more common than losses; for the highway study segments analyzed, 94 percent gained and 6 percent lost. Also, the amount of the gains in areas influenced by the highway generally exceeded gains in areas remote from the highway influence" (U.S. Department of Transportation, 1970). It should be pointed out, however, that highway impact studies have often been poorly designed; for a cogent critique of this type of study, see Charles River Associates (1972).

where these commodities are traded (except insofar as such considerations are internalized into locational decisions, and are reflected very imperfectly in land or property values) means that the most usual and important method of ascertaining "values"—observing market behavior—is not easily applicable. Another problem is that the full extent of the harm (particularly in matters of health) has not, in many instances, been fully appreciated by society until long after the injury has been irrevocably inflicted. It is yet more difficult to appraise the public's valuation of avoiding hazards to which they are not even aware that they are exposed! Furthermore, the vociferousness of citizens' groups—a measure of concern most evident to the legislator—may in fact be a very poor indication of the general public's willingness to pay for amelioration.

Problems with Current Policies

Because of the paucity of information necessary for sound policy making, legislative reactions to automotive emissions and safety have tended to be broad-brush and somewhat arbitrary. This is, of course, not surprising; it is very common to find agreement that legislation is necessary but to lack clear guidelines for framing the legislation. From a few studies which have examined the effects of recent federal regulation of the automobile, there are indications that some of the legal controls which have been imposed are of questionable value.

For example, the contribution of car exhaust gases to air pollution varies highly from area to area depending both on the concentration of traffic and on local meteorological conditions. Nationally-imposed uniform emissions standards may thus not be appropriate for cars other than those to be driven in problem areas. A 1972 study for the U.S. Office of Science and Technology predicted that in 1976 about three out of every ten purchasers of new automobiles would be paying a large extra initial cost and a higher operating expense for stringent emission control features which might be unnecessary in their areas.[34]

The same study found reasons to doubt the overall wisdom of the emission control measures laid down by the 1970 Clean Air Act amendments; it estimated that the costs of control would exceed the benefits to be gained over the decade of 1976 through 1985. A more recent study carried out under the auspices of the National Academy of Sciences drew a similar conclusion:

In brief, the benefits derivable from meeting *currently established* automobile emission standards may not immediately exceed the expected

---

[34] Goldmuntz et al. (1972), the so-called RECAT Report.

costs of these standards; a desirable benefit/cost ratio can be achieved with reasonable certainty in the short run only if a two-car strategy[35] or some relaxation of projected oxides of nitrogen standards is adopted. In essence, the key to being reasonably certain of a favorable benefit/cost ratio is to reduce the costs of the program.[36]

Findings like these do *not* imply that the benefits to be gained by reducing automotive emissions are small. On the contrary, automobiles account for very significant proportions of the hydrocarbon, oxides of nitrogen, and carbon monoxide emissions in many urban areas, and if a substantial reduction can be achieved in automotive emission rates it should produce a major improvement in urban air quality. The problems lie with the relative costs and the efficacy of the particular measures incorporated in the 1970 Clean Air Act. The cost-benefit studies carried out to date, imperfect as they are, indicate that some relaxation or postponement of the emissions standards of the act (particularly the standard for nitrogen oxides emissions) would be advisable.

Moreover, it seems that the effectiveness of many strategies designed to modify vehicle *usage* patterns in an attempt to reduce emissions—for example, by decreasing the amount, speed, or stop-and-go characteristics of urban traffic—is relatively small. This has implications for the so-called "transportation control policies" required for major metropolitan areas by the Clean Air Act. While these control policies may be locally effective when applied to the central portions of a city, as a broad generalization they are likely to be dominated in near-term impact by the cumulative effect of an increasingly cleaner population of automobiles brought about by the current (or even relaxed) emissions standards for new cars.[37]

Highway safety is also a pressing problem. Motor-vehicle-related deaths have been on the order of 50,000 to 55,000 a year for the past ten years, roughly 48 percent of all accidental deaths. One estimate sets the economic costs of motor vehicle accidents in 1974 at over $19 billion.[38]

---

[35] A "two-car strategy" is one which mandates two sets of emissions standards, the more stringent of which would apply in problem areas. Vehicles not conforming to the more stringent standards would be prohibited from operating in the problem areas. Such a strategy is likely to encourage the development of a car designed primarily for in-city driving.

[36] U.S. Congress (1974).

[37] Grad et al. (1975).

[38] National Safety Council (1975). Motor-vehicle-related accidents and deaths declined sharply following the OPEC oil embargo of 1973-74 and the consequent national introduction of a 55 m.p.h. speed limit. While some part of the decline may be due to adjustments in driving patterns occasioned by higher fuel prices, it is likely that the speed limit reduction is the primary cause.

However, the death and accident rates per registered vehicle and per vehicle mile have been falling steadily throughout this century.

A major governmental response to the safety problem—beyond legislating basic rules of the road—has again been to influence automobile design through the setting of standards. Economic evaluation of these standards has produced mixed findings. The 1972 study for the Office of Science and Technology[39] concluded that regulation through the Federal Motor Vehicle Safety Standards, as practiced to date, had yielded economic benefits which out-weighed the costs. But the study questioned certain specific standards (for flammability and passive restraint systems, for example), and pointed to other safety improvements of high, but as yet unrealized, potential benefit to society: for example, improved emergency treatment of accident trauma and the elimination of drunk drivers. It may be that legislators see less political risk in seeking safety improvements through improved technology than in getting drunk drivers off the roads or in requiring higher driving skills before issuing licenses.

In fact, we have tended to look toward technological advance as the panacea for many of the problems associated with the private car, perhaps because goading the automobile manufacturers carries less political risk than antagonizing the ordinary voter by restricting or increasing the price of his driving. But even if the technological improvement being sought appears possible, the best public policy for attaining it may be far from clear:

> Regulation should not be based upon a blind faith in technology. Establishing standards beyond the known state of the art on the theory that industry can do anything if enough pressure is put on it is not likely to result in wise governmental decision making or to provide the greatest net benefits to society. Furthermore, crash efforts to meet fixed time limits can delay the development of alternative and perhaps better technology. While regulatory agencies should not hesitate to push reluctant industries to make use of available technology, they should not presume that major breakthroughs in technology are there simply for the taking if enough money is expended. The regulation of automobiles is not a game in which higher costs are imposed on the industry; it is the public which must bear the costs.[40]

To question the efficacy of past legislative attempts to cope with the problems created by the automobile is not, however to deny the need to find solutions. And legislators are currently searching for an appropri-

---

[39] Goldmuntz et al. (1972).
[40] Ibid.

ate policy response to yet another side-product of car use—its consumption of energy. The privately-owned motor vehicle has been viewed as a prime target for energy conservation for a number of reasons. First, it accounts for about one-third of the nation's petroleum use, a fuel for which the United States is becoming increasingly dependent on foreign sources. Second, it is felt that the private automobile represents a high potential for fuel conservation at relatively low cost. The problem for public and private policy is to find strategies for exploiting that potential with a minimum of adverse political and economic impacts—on the mobility of the public, and on particularly vulnerable industries such as automobile manufacture, recreation, and tourism.

For example, a general shift toward smaller, lighter weight cars could help, but if that shift implies lower automobile running costs, the fuel savings gained by greater efficiency in the average car might be offset by greater usage. Highway safety levels might be impaired. If automobile use is reduced for long distance intercity travel, people may shift to air transport—which, at existing load factors, consumes more energy per passenger mile. It is obvious that this is, again, an area where good policy making requires an understanding of complex market behavior, which (by and large) has yet to be achieved.

IV. BUILDING NEW TRANSPORTATION SYSTEMS

If because of dissatisfaction with the automobile and with highway construction society seeks to place less emphasis on the private car, what are the alternatives? Can transit services be substituted for greater highway capacity in cities? Can the different types of public transportation provide "adequate" mobility?

Some insight into these questions can be gained by examining past and current (as well as potential) governmental policies aimed at improving urban mobility. The policies can be summarized under three major alternatives:

- invest in new transportation facilities, or expand the capacity of existing systems;

- search for new technologies; and

- manage the existing systems more efficiently so that their effective capacity is expanded or that their costs (both financial and social) are decreased.

Investing in New or Expanded Facilities

Since the early 1950s, by far the greatest emphasis in urban transportation policy has been on investing in new facilities and expanding the capacity of existing systems by further construction. Consequently, the focus in transportation planning has been principally on the investment decision. The large-scale metropolitan-area transportation planning studies, carried out since the 1950s in all medium-sized and large cities, started primarily as highway investment studies, and their focus and procedures have since been adjusted only slightly by changes in government thinking. The first change in emphasis was a desire to take better account of the interactions between land use policy and transportation policy—but the aspirations and rhetoric in this direction have been in advance of the technical ability. The second modification in procedure has been to ensure that public transit investment options are weighed alongside potential highway investments. The major objective of these studies has, however, remained the same: to evaluate potential new transportation system investment alternatives at the metropolitan area or regional level.

The emphasis on capital-intensive approaches is reflected in the urban transportation spending patterns at federal, state, and local levels. Given the signals from the market (the magnitude of automobile user tax revenues, for example) and the urban public's dissatisfactions with present travel conditions, it is not difficult to see why this has been the case. There have also been financial incentives for local governments to opt for highway construction—incentives which have not been paralleled for capital investments in any other mode of urban travel. When local politicians can be sure of getting between 50 and 90 percent of road building costs from the federal government, it is clear why they prefer to build highways rather than take a wait-in-line chance to share in the much smaller federal funds available for mass transportation support.

As federal legislation throughout the 1960s and 1970s has sought to redress this imbalance with more funds for urban public transportation, again the emphasis has been strongly placed on capital investment. The Urban Mass Transportation Act of 1964 limited federal financial assistance largely to a program of capital grants, on the grounds that capital investment to modernize, improve, extend, and construct transit systems was the industry's greatest need and that operating assistance could be dissipated by labor demands and wasteful managerial practices.[41] Federal

---

[41] The provisions of the 1964 act closely reflected the conclusions of a contemporary report on federal urban transportation policy by Fitch et al. (1964).

grants matched local funds on a two-to-one basis, a ratio which was increased to four-to-one in 1973.

Federal Programs Influence Local Choices

This emphasis on capital investment support by the federal government has had at least two effects on the transit industry, both due to the fact that local governments and transit agencies can make decisions to spend dollars which cost them only twenty cents each—or less, if state financial help is also available. First, there is evidence from a study of the Chicago and Cleveland bus transit systems that the capital grants program has encouraged overcapitalization and the premature replacement of old equipment (rather than its continued repair and maintenance), and has not been able to prevent the grants from being dissipated by labor union demands for greater benefits.[42]

Second, when the direct cost to a community of building a new transit system, or of extending or modernizing an existing system, is only one-third or one-fifth of the total monetary costs, the choice between competing alternative plans is apt to be distorted in the direction of the most ambitious and most expensive plan. There are also powerful local political forces supporting such a bias:

> The newly-formed transit authority very quickly perceives that its success will be judged by how quickly they [sic] get a system planned, financed, designed, and under way. They also intuitively comprehend that getting anything built at all will require a successful bond referendum which, in turn, is much more easily achieved with a system which is big, bold, glamorous, fast, extensive, and, above all, which appears to serve as much of the affected area as possible from the day the system first opens. Since even a small start on one short line will likely be the biggest public works project in the history of the area, it's much easier to sell the full system if it appears to serve more people. In short, it's easier to sell a billion dollar project than a hundred million dollar project.[43]

Since most major new systems are planned at the metropolitan area level, they require the cooperation and financial support of a number of local jurisdictions. The paramount consideration in the design of the project, therefore, is typically to secure the highest possible degree of acceptance by the governments involved; the functional utility of the system, in terms of its ability to carry people efficiently when and where they want

---

[42] Tye (1973).

[43] Deen et al. (1975).

to travel, is only a secondary factor. Since the suburban governments will usually be the richest, their involvement is crucial to the project. Lines are consequently planned deep into the suburbs in preference to providing more intensive coverage in the central city. For the new rail transit system currently under construction in the Washington metropolitan area, for example, the primary determinant of route alignments was a desire to provide a politically acceptable number of route miles within each of the participating jurisdictions.

It is significant in this context that the Urban Mass Transportation Administration has not required a cost-benefit analysis as a precondition for the approval of capital grants under the program.[44] Indeed, transportation planning consultants highly experienced in providing technical assistance to local governments report that any serious economic work on the question of how much transit makes sense for an area is usually brushed off. This is because, first, political considerations dominate economic considerations in planning the project; and second, "economic analysis is in disrepute partly because it must necessarily depend on some heroic and less than totally agreed-on assumptions, and partly because it has been bent by authorities who used it as a tool for justifying actions they fervently desired to take for other reasons."[45]

New Rapid Rail Systems?

These financial and political influences on transit planning go some way toward explaining why some 65 percent of the capital grant funds since the inception of the program have been devoted to rail rapid transit systems (predominantly those in Boston, Chicago, New York City, San Francisco, and Washington), and why a number of cities without such systems (Atlanta, Baltimore, Honolulu, Los Angeles, and Miami, for example) have been developing plans to build them. The economic wisdom of investing in new fixed-rail systems or in extensions of existing systems has been seriously questioned by many observers and remains a topic of considerable controversy among transportation analysts.

The critics of further investment in new rapid rail right-of-way raise several objections.[46] First, in a number of ways fixed-guideway systems in

---

[44] Revised guidelines for the program, published in 1975, require the analysis of a range of alternative investment options, and introduce cost-effectiveness considerations. While UMTA will now provide funds no greater than the matching share of the most cost-effective alternative, there is no requirement that the benefits of that alternative should exceed the costs.

[45] Deen et al. (1975).

[46] See, for example, Meyer et al. (1965), Wohl (1970), and Hilton (1974).

general do not match well with what is known about the demand for urban travel. Studies have consistently shown that a key concern of people making travel decisions is the *door-to-door* journey time. Furthermore, people view the time spent in getting to and from a vehicle, in waiting for a vehicle to arrive, or in transferring between vehicles, as more onerous than the time actually spent traveling inside the vehicle. Fixed-guideway systems can provide in-vehicle time savings—but unless they operate over a very pervasive network, they ignore the important access and distribution legs of the journey. It is only over fairly long journeys (say suburb-to-downtown commuting) that the speed advantage of rail transit has much meaning for potential travelers. Fixed-guideway systems, too, are by nature very inflexible; they cannot respond inexpensively to geographical changes in travel patterns.

More specifically, the critics question certain aspects of the design of the generation of rapid rail systems currently being planned or under construction. By comparison with the existing systems in older cities (New York, Boston, and Chicago, in particular), these new systems have lines extending further into the suburbs, have fewer stations in the downtown and central city areas, and have stations spaced significantly further apart on average. In other words, the target market for these new systems appears to be the suburban resident who works in the central city. This focus, however, bucks the trends in urban travel patterns. The suburb-to-downtown commute forms an increasingly smaller proportion of the total travel to work in major cities. According to the 1970 Census of Population, for the thirty or so cities with populations of over one million, only 14 percent of the metropolitan area employment consists of central city workers living in the suburbs, and only 4 percent consists of suburban residents working in the central business district. The great majority of central city workers—about 75 percent on average for the cities of over a million people—in fact live in the central city. Moreover, the households without automobiles—the people who might be expected to make most use of a rapid transit system—appear also to be concentrated heavily within the central city rather than in the suburbs.

So these new systems, argue the critics, are designed to cater to a segment of the travel market which is relatively small today, and which can be expected to decline in relative importance so long as the current trends in the decentralization of residences and workplaces continue. Further, the target market for these heavily-subsidized systems—the suburb-to-downtown commuter—forms a comparatively affluent stratum of the urban community.[47] In San Francisco, over 48 percent of the 1975 riders of the new Bay Area Rapid Transit (BART) system, for example, have an annual family income of $15,000 or more;[48] by contrast, probably no more than 35 percent of the residents of BART's three-county service area have family incomes that high.

Another objection is raised about the demand for rapid rail transit. Experience with new lines or extensions in (for example) Chicago, Cleveland, and Boston has shown that these investments rarely produce the ridership response anticipated by their promoters. The total patronage, the level of diversion of peak-hour private automobile travelers onto the new line, and the reductions in automobile traffic on parallel highways have all characteristically failed to live up to prior expectations.

The final cause for concern relates to the *costs* of rapid rail services. Since the 1960s an increasing number of studies of the costs of various modal technologies appropriate for carrying people to and from work have concluded that rapid rail transit is relatively a very expensive method except in a few corridors with a very high density of demand.[49] In particular, some of the cost studies strongly suggest that, under most levels of demand, rapid rail investment options are likely to be much more costly than high quality express bus service running on exclusive right-of-way.

It is this question of relative costs which has perhaps aroused the sharpest contention between promoters and critics of investment in rail transit.[50] The promoters doubt whether it is technologically possible to match rail's level of service with buses, and raise questions about the costs of coping with the buses in central business districts. Currently there are no extensive grade-separated rights-of-way for buses in any downtown area, and there is some question whether the costs assumed by the studies for such facilities are realistic.

The rapid rail advocates also point to other major assumptions inherent in the cost studies, and they question how far analysis based on the average costs and performance for a cross-section of existing systems is relevant to the relative costs of new system alternatives tailored to a particular local situation. Finally, they point out that the financial costs

---

[47] Kain and Meyer (1970).

[48] Unpublished data from a one-day on-board survey conducted by BART in May 1975.

[49] See, for example, Meyer et al. (1965), Deen and James (1969), Miller et al. (1973), Smith (1973), Boyd et al. (1973), and Bhatt (1975).

[50] See Vuchic (1974).

should not be the sole consideration in the investment decision—factors such as the relative levels of energy consumption and contribution to air pollution, as well as local goals for urban form, should be taken into account.

Nor is rapid rail transit the only fixed-rail alternative available. Some observers are increasingly talking about the potential for "light rail" transit: essentially, modernized streetcar or similar systems operating substantially over exclusive rights-of-way. While streetcars and trolleycars have been allowed, for the most part, to decline and disappear in the United States and the United Kingdom, in many European cities they have been preserved and modernized. How far a completely new light rail system may be an appropriate option in an urban context in the United States remains to be seen, but it seems likely that the idea will somewhere be put into practice within the next decade.

Public Support for Transit Investments

If the wisdom of building new rapid rail transit systems (except along a few very dense corridors) is in such doubt, why do these systems appear so attractive politically? We have already discussed how both federal programs and local political pressures provide an incentive for the transit planning agency to opt for the largest, most pervasive, and most grandiose schemes; but why have these schemes been accepted by the voters who have been asked to approve the financing proposals?

There have been a number of recent analyses of transit financing referenda.[51] but they throw only limited light on this question. Most showed that voting patterns or attitudes about transit financing could be most readily explained by perceived self-interest; support for the proposed systems was strongest in those areas most accessible to the facilities or else among those groups likely to benefit most by "getting other people off the highways." The studies have also analyzed the variations in support between different demographic and socioeconomic groups of the population. Evidence from Atlanta[52] suggests that what has been termed "public regardingness"[53]—the tendency of some groups of the population to vote in a fashion inconsistent with narrow self-interest out of altruism or concern

---

[51] Most notably Stipak (1973) on the 1968 Los Angeles referendum; Bowman et al. (1972), Schroeder and Sjoquist (1974), and Neidell (1974) on the 1968 and 1971 Atlanta referenda; and Corsi et al. (1975) on a Milwaukee referendum.

[52] Bowman et al. (1972).

[53] Wilson and Banfield (1964).

for "the public interest"—is of much lower importance than considerations of benefits to be experienced personally.

As we have seen, in choosing between alternative plans the transit agency gives great weight to maximizing voter acceptance by planning lines into all cooperating local jurisdictions. In this key choice, there typically has been little public participation. Once a firm decision is made about the type of system to be built, the full efforts of the transit agency go into promoting the project among the voters. The potential ridership for the system is often overestimated, and the operating and construction costs underestimated.[54] The project chosen is implicitly presented as the *only* transit alternative for the metropolitan area, and the public is given the impression that to be "pro-transit" requires support for the specific proposals being promoted. This false identification is probably reinforced by the oversimplification and polarization often evidenced in the press discussion of these issues.

So the public debate is effectively shifted away from the key questions of what sort of transit investments and services make sense for a city, to the simple approval or rejection of a particular, highly-promoted scheme. It is our impression, however—based on little factual information—that this situation may be changing. The 1974 referendum in Los Angeles, for instance, appeared to stimulate locally a great deal of informed public analysis of the transit agency's proposals. Recently revised regulations for the disbursement of federal capital grants call for increased public involvement at early stages of the planning process. It may be that some referenda have been approved in the past partly because of general feelings of disaffection with the highway and automobile system, but it is possible that in the future particular transit proposals will receive as intensive public scrutiny as planned urban freeway segments.

The Search for New Urban Transport Technologies

A second major emphasis of public policy in seeking ways to enhance mobility has been to seek technical advances in carrying passengers. The last ten years, however, have witnessed an almost complete *volte-face* by the federal government to this approach.

In the late 1960s and early 1970s potential technological advances were being promoted as a panacea for transportation problems in the cities.

---

[54] See Hamer (1976). The BART system was promoted to the public with a clear statement that, once built, it would generate revenues adequate to cover all operating costs. Operating deficits are, in fact, now projected to exceed $44 million in fiscal year 1976.

An expensive and wide-ranging study commissioned by the Department of Housing and Urban Development in 1966—the "Study in new systems of urban transportation"—pointed to the potential. The federal government responded positively. Between 1966 and 1973 roughly 40 percent of the research and development funds authorized under the Urban Mass Transportation Act were devoted to the development of new systems. This infatuation with the potential of new technology also coincided with a major decrease in the nation's spending on aerospace technology, and a number of manufacturers in the aerospace industry saw ground passenger transportation as an appropriate area for diversification.[55] The catch phrase of the times appeared to be "If we can get men onto the moon, why can't we move people across town more efficiently?"

Cost Overruns and Technical Problems

By 1974, however, widespread disillusionment with the notion of new technology as a panacea was very evident—and perhaps for the wrong reasons. The disaffections derived in large part from technological problems on the one hand and from escalating costs on the other. It gradually came to be publicly recognized that the problem of sending a handful of highly-trained technocrats into space is inherently different from the efficient daily movement of hundreds of thousands of members of the general public. The former is largely an exercise in applied physics; the latter requires durable, mass-produced vehicles and systems which can withstand a daily interaction with large numbers of non-orchestrated human beings.

Technological problems developed with a number of key, highly visible new systems—the computer control system for the Bay Area Rapid Transit system, the intercity TurboTrain turbine-powered train, a prototype automated "personal rapid transit" system at Morgantown (West Virginia). Cost overruns, too, have created a great deal of publicity. For the Morgantown project, for example, the estimated costs for a simple baseline system comprising six stations and 75 vehicles grew from $13.5 million in 1971 to roughly $115 million by 1974. The plans have been cut back to provide a three-station, 45-vehicle system with 2.2 miles of guideway at a total cost of about $64 million. Estimates of operating costs have also increased markedly.[56]

---

[55] Companies such as Boeing, LTV Aerospace Systems, Rohr Industries, and United Technologies Corporation have been involved in the development of new ground transportation technology.

[56] *Business Week,* March 16, 1974.

Developments such as these have done much to dampen the ardor for continued heavy public and private investment in developing new technology. There is evidence of some disenchantment by the federal government. By fiscal year 1975, the proportion of Urban Mass Transportation Administration research and development money allocated to new systems had fallen to roughly 17 percent, and cities contemplating using UMTA capital grant funds to invest in systems at the frontier of technology (Denver and Pittsburgh, in particular) were beginning to sense discouraging sounds from the Department of Transportation. Among the general public, however, it is clear that there is still strong faith in technological solutions to urban transportation problems. When a major oil company ran an advertising campaign in 1974-75 soliciting ideas on public transportation, well over a half of the 30,000 suggestions submitted related to technology.[57]

Perhaps a more important reason to be skeptical of new technology as a panacea—since technological difficulties and cost overruns ought largely to be anticipated—is that the travel modes into which most development money has so far been sunk are predominantly fixed-guideway systems. As has been already stressed, the quality of service offered by fixed-guideway systems (unless using a very pervasive network) is inherently lower than that offered by the private car. If the aim is to entice passengers to public transportation without imposing strong disincentives to automobile use, a mode of public transportation must be able to compete in the dimensions of service to which people respond—*door-to-door* travel time, flexibility, reliability. How far can fixed-guideway systems provide this sort of competition?

It would be wrong, however, to be totally negative about technological progress, for we believe that there are some advances to be foreseen. The technologies for which we have most hope are those which—in line with what is known about the determinants of urban travel demand—would cater to the complete door-to-door journey. One possibility of this type (still requiring substantial development) is the so-called *dual mode* system of public or private transportation in which vehicles would operate under driver control on local streets, and would also operate under automatic control on an exclusive right-of-way for the high speed segment of the journey. Another promising concept is that of *dial-a-ride*, already in existence in several North American cities.[58] Dial-a-ride systems aim to

---

[57] Atlantic Richfield Company (1975).

[58] Kirby et al. (1975).

provide door-to-door service on demand between points within a specified area in response to telephone requests, using shared vehicles.

V. BETTER MANAGEMENT OF EXISTING FACILITIES

From capital-intensive approaches to improving urban mobility, we turn to consider an alternative—making more efficient use of the facilities already available. Public policies of this nature are currently being pursued in three directions:

- improving the vehicle or passenger capacity of the transportation system, by making improvements in the way the system itself performs;
- discouraging peaking in the use of the system; and
- encouraging the diversion of travelers out of low-occupancy vehicles and into high-occupancy vehicles.

On the highways, traffic management techniques (for example, improved signalling at intersections, the elimination of cross-traffic turns, better routing and signposting for through traffic, one-way street systems, parking restrictions, and so on) have the potential for increasing traffic speeds and road capacity, and for reducing accidents. Some of that potential is being realized, while a number of the ideas of greatest promise (such as computerized area-wide interactive systems of traffic signals, and the ramp metering of vehicles entering freeways) have yet to be implemented in any large-scale fashion. The reduction in congestion which can come about as a result of these measures, however, is not necessarily a total gain for users of the roads. Abolishing cross-traffic turns and creating one-way streets may improve traffic speeds but at the same time lead to an increase in the average lengths of journeys; in net, the resultant travel time savings may be small (or even negative), more fuel may be consumed, and harmful exhaust emissions may increase.[59]

In the transit industry, there is some evidence of a slowly growing movement to rationalize routes and schedules so as better to match today's patterns of demand. Computerized techniques to aid both in transit planning and in the practicalities of coordinating vehicles and personnel efficiently are beginning to be used.

As for the active discouragement of peaking, government action has been mostly limited to acknowledging that it could help reduce congestion. The staggering of working hours can most easily be coordinated

---

[59] Thomson (1968) provides an evaluation of the costs and benefits of a major traffic management program.

when a small number of major employers operate several different facilities concentrated in one area; the federal government enclave in Washington, D.C. is a prime example. Wider adoption of the "flexitime" or "gliding time" concept, under which individual employees at a particular location are given some flexibility in fixing their own working hours, could also reduce the peaking of travel demands.

Much of the government effort to make more efficient use of existing transportation facilities has been aimed at encouraging the diversion of travelers out of low-occupancy vehicles (such as the private automobile with only one or two passengers) into high-occupancy vehicles—in particular, into transit vehicles and car pools. At typical peak-hour loads, each passenger-mile by transit contributes less to traffic congestion, air pollution, and fuel consumption than does a passenger-mile in a private car. It is therefore argued that the higher the proportion of journeys made by transit in preference to the private automobile (particularly under congested conditions), the lower will be the total costs to the community and the higher will be the net benefits. In other words, according to this theory every person who can be lured out of a car and into a transit vehicle in the peak hours is a step toward making the existing transportation system as a whole function more efficiently. The problem for public policy is, of course, how to bring about these diversions.

The Concept of Traffic Limitation

One large family of policy options directed at using scarce road space efficiently under circumstances of heavy demand has been generically dubbed "traffic limitation."[60] Michael Thomson, who has comprehensively surveyed the methods of traffic limitation (both those currently in use and potential), draws a useful distinction between three approaches:

- *traffic restriction*, whereby people are prevented by physical or legal means from fulfilling certain travel desires;

---

[60] "In every city of the world the volume of traffic is limited, intentionally or unintentionally, by measures adopted by governments, both central and local. If these measures were relaxed, there would be more traffic; if they were strengthened, there would be less. In other words, the volume of traffic in a city is not something like the rainfall that has to be accepted; it is amenable to some control or influence by government. Furthermore, depending upon the methods used, control may be exercised selectively over particular classes of vehicle, in particular areas or streets, at particular times, and for particular purposes. . . . Few people, of course, are wholly for, or wholly against, traffic limitation; most people want there to be some traffic but not too much. What constitutes 'too much' is something which every city must decide for itself in the light of its own economic and geographical circumstances, its heritage, aspirations and values." Thomson (1972).

- *traffic restraint,* whereby people are discouraged, but not prevented, from fulfilling certain travel desires; and
- *traffic avoidance,* whereby action is taken to keep the desire from arising in the first place.[61]

About the last of these approaches—traffic avoidance—we will say little. This can only be regarded as a long-term goal, for it is posited on the hypothesis that better land use planning and improved methods of electronic communication may be able to reduce the desire to travel.

Establishing Traffic-Free Zones

Traffic restriction includes the creation of physical barriers to movement by the complete or the partial closure of certain roads, and the creation of legal barriers prohibiting traffic of particular sorts at particular times. In the United States neither approach has been pursued very strongly; in Europe, where the preservation of historic city centers (often with narrow streets) is more frequently weighed against providing for greater volumes of traffic, restriction is more common. A growing number of European cities are opting for restriction schemes, some of a very ingenious nature, to create automobile-free zones or to divert through traffic out of city centers.[62]

How can the imposition of new physical impediments to automobile movement be construed as enhancing mobility? In one sense, of course, it cannot: total journey times to points in the restricted area can be expected to increase, and people will be forced to substitute walking for driving, whereas in the previous "free choice" situation they opted for the latter. The existence of large traffic-free zones forces vehicles to take circuitous routes around them, adding to journey times, fuel consumption, operating costs, and traffic volumes outside the areas.

Many argue, however, that the overall benefits—particularly those relating to the improved environment in the restricted area—outweigh the costs. Indeed, *pedestrian* movement within the city center may be greatly improved, and cities which have created traffic-free zones generally report citizen enthusiasm rather than dissatisfactions. People are more willing to walk when they can do so freely without having to compete for space with motor vehicles. The primary opposition to restriction schemes in Europe—before their introduction—comes from retailers in the affected

---

[61] Ibid.

[62] Surveys of current techniques may be found in Kühnemann and Witherspoon (1972), Orski (1972), and Thomson (1972).

area. After their introduction, however, business is often increased.[63]

Whether similar outcomes would result if traffic-free zones were introduced in the centers of major or medium-sized North American cities is unclear. In Europe, urban decentralization has not advanced to the same degree as here; the European city center is still the dominant focus of the city's business, commercial, and retail activity. In particular, downtown retail trade in Europe does not face the same level of heavy competition from large suburban shopping malls.[64] How far pedestrianization of U.S. central business districts might help to "revitalize" those areas, or alternatively how far it would encourage their decay, is uncertain.

Congestion Pricing as a Form of Traffic Restraint

The concept of *traffic restraint* comprises policies designed to influence travel patterns without imposing restrictions—it is, therefore, concerned with creating incentives and disincentives to encourage those individual travel choices which will contribute to the efficient operation of the system. One may usefully distinguish between *direct* and *indirect* methods of restraint, and between *fiscal* and *physical* measures.

Direct restraints focus directly on the choice which they are intended to encourage or discourage. The most potent example of a direct fiscal restraint would be the imposition of "congestion pricing." The theory behind this concept can be briefly summarized. Travel patterns are the direct result of choices made by the individual—choice of the mode of travel, choice of route, choice of destination, choice of departure time— on the basis of such considerations as the prices, the relative travel times, the relative convenience, and so on. However, in making these choices the potential traveler does *not* take into account the effect which his own traveling has on other people. A journey which is of only marginal value to the one car driver making it can (under congested conditions) cause delays to other people whose time is more important to them.[65] In other words, the total costs of the journey to the rest of society are greater than the costs perceived by the traveler. Society would consequently benefit if it could induce those whose journey value is small to forego their journeys. One way of doing this would be to impose an additional

---

[63] Orski (1972).

[64] It can, of course, be argued that traffic-free shopping is one of the features which has encouraged the success of the large suburban malls.

[65] Similarly, it can contribute to the deterioration of other people's environment through noise and exhaust emissions.

price on each traveler so as to make his own perceived cost equal to the extra costs he imposes on society.

Therefore, many economists have long argued that on the highways under congested conditions the present system of pricing by user taxes (which price each vehicle mile at approximately average cost) leads to economic inefficiencies.[66] Under a more efficient pricing scheme, peak-hour automobile commuters in particular would typically face much higher prices than they currently do, matching the contribution their vehicles make to the social costs of congestion, and travelers by other travel modes using the congested facility would also face an increased price. The two major problems in the way of imposing these congestion prices[67] are, first, the technological problem of finding means to assess and charge the price; and second, the political problem of public acceptance.

The technological problem is the lesser of the two. Equipment already exists which, without much further development, could be used to impose a fairly flexible and accurately determined price which varied at different times of day and in different areas to reflect variations in congestion. Oversimplifying, one promising type of equipment would detect the presence of individual vehicles in congested conditions and compute an appropriate price for each one, to be billed by a computer at a later time.[68] But implementing such a system is likely to be very costly and fraught with practical problems, not least among them being the invasion of privacy inherent in a scheme which allows a government agency to track the movement of individual vehicles past specific locations.

Since this very precise form of congestion pricing appears to be beyond reach as a near-term policy, other less congestion-sensitive methods of imposing financial disincentives to the marginal-value use of the automobile have been considered. The most promising of these "approximate" methods is the use of an "area license." In order for a vehicle to operate legally on the streets within a designated area at a designated period of the day (the area and the time periods would, of course, be defined with regard to congestion levels), it would be required to display a special

---

[66] See, for example, Vickrey (1963, 1965) or McGillivray (1974). The support for the concept, however, rests on theoretical, somewhat "perfect world" analysis. We just do not know enough about the practicalities of imposing congestion pricing —or the extent of its impacts—to be dogmatic about the matter. See Wohl (1972).

[67] In this context the terms "congestion price," "congestion toll," "peak load pricing," and "road pricing" are often used interchangeably.

[68] Bhatt (1974) has surveyed the technology which is currently available to do this.

license, purchasable by the year, the month, the day, or even perhaps by the hour.[69] A simple scheme of this kind was introduced in Singapore in May 1975, and there has also been much discussion of the adoption of area licensing for central London.

Another method of fiscal restraint which is relatively easy to implement in the near term would be the imposition of parking taxes or surcharges. This is an indirect method in that the target of the restraint is not the use of the vehicle or the highway directly so much as the consumption of a complementary good—parking space. But parking surcharges will fail completely to discourage the people who contribute to central area congestion by driving through without parking. Studies show that typically between 50 and 70 percent of vehicles on central business district streets at peak times are passing right through the area rather than parking.[70]

The problem of public acceptability is the major stumbling block to the adoption of any of these fiscal restraint measures. The concept of congestion pricing is inherently difficult to explain to the layman, and when the idea *is* explained adequately, there is usually little public enthusiasm for it. Since the sensitivity of travel behavior to urban transportation prices is low, the prices it would be necessary to charge on the grounds of economic efficiency are high—say on the order of an additional $2.00 to $3.00 per day for a typical round trip journey between home and work in urban areas—and many people appear to think that this is a heavy price to pay for reduced congestion and improved air quality. A 1973 series of television programs in the New York metropolitan region did a reasonably competent job of explaining the rationale for peak load pricing; yet in an associated mail survey of viewers, 55 percent of those responding opposed the idea, while only 34 percent expressed support.[71]

Given the lack of public enthusiasm and the many uncertainties, it is not surprising that local governments have been somewhat reticent about promoting the idea—despite the potentially large revenues which would accrue. Legislators seldom want to be blamed for price increases; our

---

[69] Some ingenious variations on this basic concept have been suggested. For example, licenses distinguished by color and varying in price could allow differential access to areas of a large city suffering varying degrees of congestion: the most expensive license would permit access to all areas, the next most expensive to all areas but the central business district, and so on. Roth (1967) has proposed a "transferable annual license," produced in limited numbers by the public authority, and brokered on a rental basis by private entrepreneurs at whatever price the market will bear.

[70] Kulash (1974).

[71] Regional Plan Association (1974).

society has an ingrained notion that politicians should always be against higher prices. During 1973, for example, the U.S. Environmental Protection Agency suggested parking surcharges in several major cities as part of the transportation control plans required by the 1970 Clean Air Act Amendments.[72] The reaction in the local areas affected, and in the U.S. Congress, was intense. The agency eventually bowed to "firm Congressional guidance" and rescinded the surcharges early in 1974. While local areas still have the option to include parking surcharges in their transportation control plans, few are expected to do so.

We do, however, sense some slight shift in public attitudes toward these ideas in the United States. Five years ago they were largely dismissed out of hand by all but their most ardent advocates. But the requirements of the 1970 Clean Air Act amendments have stimulated some consideration of fiscal methods of traffic restraint. There are small signs that more local and government officials and politicians are growing less negative about this class of option—but the average citizen is probably still far from being convinced.

Using Transit Fares to Restrain Traffic

Some transportation economists have argued that, given a failure to levy congestion charges on private cars, a second-best way to minimize congestion in mixed traffic may be to adjust the price of the principal competing mode of travel—bus transit—to offset the inability to vary the automobile price.[73] This second approach is one which *has* been put into practice in recent years, although typically with little reference to the pricing formulae of the theoretical economists.

Since 1973, a vogue has developed within the transit industry for major system-wide fare cuts. Atlanta, Cincinnati, San Diego, and Los Angeles are among the many cities where significant fare cuts have been made, financed by operating subsidies from state and local governments. In other cities (Seattle, Dayton, and Dallas, for example), fares have been abolished completely for travel within the downtown area. There is some political pressure (particularly from the transit unions) to move to fare-free transit on a wider scale, and the 1974 National Mass Transportation Assistance Act authorized funds for a program of fare-free transit demonstrations.

However, if one rules out the possibility of negative prices—that is,

---

[72] Horowitz and Kuhrtz (1974).
[73] See, for example, Sherman (1971, 1972) and Glaister (1974).

actually paying people to ride the buses—then the potential for influencing highway congestion through the transit farebox is slim. Since the public sensitivity to urban transportation prices is low, it requires a very large adjustment in the relative prices of private automobile travel and bus transit before a significant level of diversion is achieved. There is only a limited scope for creating such a large price differential by adjusting the transit fare alone—the limit is the level of the existing fare. By contrast, the extent to which private automobile prices might be increased is not bounded in the same way.

Furthermore, there is some limited evidence to suggest that fare reductions are a relatively costly way of achieving those diversions which do occur, and that in many cases intelligently planned transit service improvements would be capable of achieving the same level of diversion at lower cost. Certainly, patronage appears to be more sensitive to improvements in the average door-to-door travel times than it is to reductions in fare.

Congestion as a Method of Physical Restraint

Traffic restraint may be accomplished by physical means as well as fiscal, and the most common form of physical restraint is congestion itself. Congestion causes delays, and hence economic losses in that travelers must devote more time to their journeys than they would under uncongested conditions. On the other hand, the people contributing to congestion are mostly there by choice; despite the time delays, they value the objectives of their journeys more highly than they value the time costs. Certainly there are economic benefits for society when congestion is reduced—but those benefits may be less than the total costs (financial and social) of taking action to reduce the congestion, say by new construction or by traffic limitation.

So congestion itself may be used as a constraint on road use, and careful planning can help to reduce the harmful side-effects. For example, highways may be deliberately designed for low speeds, or the highway network may be built or managed so that the congestion occurs at the least harmful locations where the impacts on pedestrian and bus movement, on the environment, or on road safety are minimized. Traffic management techniques can be used to meter access to freeways—so as to transfer the congestion delays from the freeways themselves to the access ramps—or to reallocate existing road space in order to give priority to high-occupancy vehicles (buses and car pools) in mixed traffic.

The most common form of preferential treatment is the reservation of a highway, bridge, or tunnel lane (sometimes by physical separation of the lane where that is practicable) for the exclusive use of high-occupancy vehicles; whether on the freeway or downtown, this can create marked travel-time advantages for the favored vehicles. Other traffic management priorities are also being introduced in a gradual fashion: for example, buses may be allowed to make turns or use routes denied to other traffic, to preempt traffic signals, or to gain preferential access to freeways. Measures like these appear to be among the most successful in giving a competitive advantage to high-occupancy vehicles.

There are also some limited incentives to major employers to encourage car pooling for the work journey; this is particularly true where parking space provided for employees on company property could be put to more profitable use. A number of private companies consequently provide preferential parking facilities for car or van pools, take steps to encourage the formation of pools by providing means for matching potential ride-sharers, or by overseeing the acquisition and operation of company-owned vehicles for pooling. Some local governments have also taken to promoting car pools and providing matching services.

Other Forms of Traffic Limitation

There are, of course, several other means of restraining traffic which deserve a brief mention in this context. They include:
- *direct fiscal restraints*—
  increased fuel taxes, or wider use of highway tolls;
- *indirect fiscal restraints*—
  financial disincentives to automobile ownership through taxation,[74] or heavy public subsidization of public transportation modes; and
- *indirect physical restraints*—
  limitation of parking space provision in congested areas, or controls on parking to allow discrimination between drivers, vehicles, different durations of parking, or times of day.

Promoting Competition in Urban Transportation

For some observers, one of the root problems with the current pattern of urban transportation is that public policy has encouraged the develop-

---

[74] For example, these could include high excise taxes on automobile purchase (which might be graduated in such a way as to favor, say, low-polluting energy-efficient cars), or high annual licensing fees. Credit for automobile purchase could also be restricted by regulation, as is done on occasion in some European countries.

ment of monopolized, linear transit systems, inflexible and incapable of responding adequately to the complexity of today's urban travel patterns:

> The decision to put down the jitneys amounted to a decision to stand with monopolized linear transit systems indefinitely in the future. Cost conditions turned steadily in favor of buses relative to streetcars, but the decision to forego the alternative of a competitive bus industry meant that the conversion to bus was done by the transit monopolies, which customarily continued to run the buses over the old linear routes. This produced an organization so inferior to the automobile in speed and comfort and so unresponsive to changes in the urban pattern that the transit monopolies could only decline. Further, the monopolistic organization stimulated a strong union in the field. . . . Accordingly, the transit monopolies proved expensive to operate, relative to what the foregone competitive alternative would have been. In particular, their labor costs were so high that in most cities only radial routes from central business districts were practical. Demand for such trips declined. . . . By the 1950s, most transit systems were so unprofitable that the private sector would no longer operate them, and now in the 1970s virtually all large systems are municipally owned. Currently, the transit monopolies have declined to the point that many of the municipalities are questioning their ability to continue operation.
>
> The economics of the transit industry are not, as often stated, "unique" or "peculiar." Rather, they are very ordinary: the industry has simply been failing a market test over a long period, beginning before World War I. Except in a few large cities, the linear transit systems would have been eliminated by the jitneys had the jitneys been allowed to survive, probably by the mid-1920s. The elimination of the jitneys meant that private automobiles, rather than competitive buses, became the best alternative to the transit monopolies. The consequence was an excessive number of trips by private automobile and, in particular, a low rate of occupancy of automobiles, because the anti-jitney legislation prohibited filling the empty seats at a price.[75]

The implied remedy for this malady would be a return to free market conditions in urban passenger transportation—more specifically, abolish the monopoly rights of transit companies and remove entry restrictions and certain service prohibitions on taxicabs and jitneys. Such a policy would be a radical one, certain to meet powerful political opposition from the interests which stand to lose from it, and it is certainly not without its own costs. One can foresee the creation or intensification of a number of problems if current bus services were to be replaced wholesale by a large number of individual entrepreneurs. Insofar as the change might lead to a greater number of lower occupancy vehicles on the roads, congestion could increase. There are also problems, as there have been with

---

[75] Hilton (1974).

taxi operations, of overseeing the adequate maintenance of vehicles so that public safety and air quality are not unduly impaired, and of requiring an adequate level of financial responsibility from individual and small-scale operators.

Because of the anti-jitney legislation of the 1920s, we have no current North American experience with the large-scale operation of jitneys. The few small systems surviving today are largely confined to two types of environment: tourist resorts, and poverty or ghetto areas where they often operate illegally or on a semilegal basis.[76] In those Latin American, Middle Eastern, and Far Eastern countries where they continue to operate pervasively, they are viewed as something of a mixed blessing.[77]

But despite the potential problems, we do see many potential benefits from the deregulation of several facets of urban passenger transportation, and the encouragement of greater competition in public transport services. The taxicab is already a very important mode in terms of the numbers of passengers it carries; its importance could be enhanced by the relaxation of the local regulations which in most large cities limit entry into the market and strongly constrain the range of services which cabs are allowed to offer.

Perhaps some change of attitude is required here, too. We have become so used to regarding the transit operator as the predominant supplier of passenger transport that local governments typically look to transit as the only instrument with which to pursue public transport policy. This is short-sighted. In some circumstances it may be true that the transit operator is best placed to, say, provide special services for the elderly and handicapped or initiate dial-a-ride services. Generally, however, it is not true. Conventional transit's high labor costs, high overhead structure, and predilection for large vehicles puts the transit operator at a disadvantage in supplying such special services. It is no coincidence that the most successful dial-a-ride operations in existence today in North America are privately owned and are operated by taxicab companies.[78]

VI. PAYING FOR PUBLIC TRANSPORTATION

An urban transportation problem of increasing importance is that of finding ways to finance publicly owned facilities. Significantly, this is not a problem which inhibits highway construction and maintenance, since

---

[76] Kirby et al. (1975).

[77] See, for example, Ozdirim (1973). The Istanbul authorities would like to prohibit jitneys (*dolmus*) because the drivers refuse to obey traffic laws, and drive so negligently that they are a significant hindrance to traffic flow and safety.

[78] Kirby et al. (1975).

highway users have been prepared to pay these costs through user charges. The management of the federal Highway Trust Fund has been largely on a pay-as-you-go basis; in most years the disbursements for road building have not exceeded the receipts from user taxes. The states, too, finance most of their highway expenditures from imposts on users and from bond issues. Several studies of the national costs of road construction, maintenance, and servicing have concluded that highway user receipts fully cover those costs, although there may be some cross-subsidization from urban to rural highways.[79]

Moreover, there are strong market indications that highway users would be prepared to pay more if further funds were needed. A one cent increase in the federal motor fuel tax, for example, could raise over $1 billion a year, almost 5 percent of the nation's annual highway expenditures, without producing any significant adjustments in travel patterns.

The Problems of the Transit Industry

It is with public transit, however, that the financial problems lie. "Transit services inevitably lose money." That precept, although like most generalizations not entirely accurate, appears to have gained almost universal acceptance over recent years—by the transit industry itself, by politicians, by the press, and seemingly also by the public at large. While there are still a handful of North American cities where the transit system manages to break even (at least as far as operating costs go), for the industry as a whole the generalization certainly holds true.

The total operating expenses (including taxes and depreciation)[80] for the U.S. transit industry have exceeded farebox and other revenues in every year from 1963 onward. Since 1967 the operating costs have been growing at an average compound rate of about 4.5 percent per year, and the deficits by over 41 percent per year—both expressed in constant dollars. By 1975, the industry nationally was incurring an annual operating loss of $1.7 billion—over 30 cents per paying passenger.[81]

But even these stark figures do not indicate all of the deficits, for the national balance sheet adds in the surpluses of profit-making systems along with the deficits of those suffering losses. If one were just to add together all of the losses, and take an economist's view of the annual costs

---

[79] However, highway *use* creates social costs such as air pollution, congestion delays, and accidents which are not fully borne by the users.

[80] Most economists (as distinct from accountants) would not include depreciation or interest expense as an *operating* cost. We do so here only because the published data do not allow one to do otherwise.

[81] American Public Transit Association (1976).

of equipment, then the total deficits for U.S. transit systems appear to be substantially higher than the industry figures suggest.[82]

For the most part, the operating deficits have been borne by state and local governments: the federal government began to provide operating support only in 1975. The cost increases are due in part to the fact that as transit companies have been brought into public ownership, the local governments themselves have often encouraged expansion in service.[83] But the rate at which the deficits are growing has begun to startle some local governments, particularly as they face the fiscal downturns of 1974-75. In metropolitan areas where privately owned systems have been bought up and services have subsequently been upgraded, it is not unusual for local politicians to find that over a period of only two or three years the funds necessary for transit support rise from zero to become one of the largest and fastest-growing items in the budget. Special sales taxes, property taxes, sometimes state gasoline tax revenues, federal revenue sharing funds—all are popular sources of local funding for transit subsidies. But as the burden has mounted, city governments have become some of the most vocal advocates of increased federal and state government operating assistance.

Why Shouldn't the Users Pay?

One obvious response to this problem is to ask why the public sector should be expected to provide support at all. Why shouldn't fares be increased so that the users pay the full cost of providing the transit service which they consume?

The level of transit fares appears to have become a political sacred cow. There is little doubt that fares figure prominently in the minds of politicians and in the press, and that the emphasis reflects concerns perceived among the constituencies of those groups. To the transportation analyst, however, the weight given to public discussion of fare levels is puzzling, for it appears out of line with what he observes about the relative importance of prices in influencing local travel patterns. As we have noted before, there is much evidence to suggest that local travel behavior is not very sensitive to the price of traveling, and that other features of transportation service (in particular, door-to-door travel times) are more important determinants of the general public's traveling decisions. Con-

---

[82] Boyd and Wells (1973) have made such a calculation for 1970.

[83] In 1969, 12 percent of the nation's transit systems were publicly owned, but they carried 77 percent of transit riders. By 1975, these proportions had grown to 35 percent and 90 percent respectively.

sider, for example, that in 1970 between 50 and 60 percent of all U.S. workers living in urbanized areas drove *alone* to work each day by private automobile. Many have a transit alternative which would be considerably cheaper for them if money cost were their major consideration.

Consider, too, that the taxicab charges fares which, on average, are between five and ten times higher per passenger mile than are transit fares. Yet in 1970, fleet taxis alone carried more passengers nationally than all of the nation's rapid rail and commuter rail services combined, and earned gross revenues some 35 percent higher than the total passenger revenues of the whole bus and rail transit industry. Or consider New York City, where traffic congestion problems are severe, commuting and parking costs are very high, and transit fares are heavily subsidized. Yet for the weekday traffic entering downtown Manhattan, between 1963 and 1971, the daily person trips by public transit declined by about 8 percent while those by private automobile and taxi grew by roughly 12 percent. Indeed, during the morning peak hours (7 A.M. to 10 A.M.) person trips by car and taxi increased by about 28 percent while overall the number of people entering the area in that time period showed a slight decline.

People are clearly telling us by their behavior that, at least under present economic conditions, they are prepared to pay for *quality* transportation service. In particular and despite peak hour highway congestion, they appear to value highly those service features which the private automobile (or taxi) gives them but which transit generally does not: privacy, flexibility, comfort, convenience, reliability, and so on. Indeed, the public tells us so verbally as well as behaviorally. In surveys which have asked people what improvements they would most like to see in public transportation, lower fares usually appear at about the middle of the list, below more reliable, more frequent, and more convenient service.

If this is the case, why *is* so much discussion given to the level of transit fares? Perhaps part of the answer is another disappointment of expectations. Transit fares are no longer the nickels and dimes which were common throughout the first half of the century.[84] While they have not escalated as rapidly as the operating costs, they have increased substantially in real terms. Between 1950 and 1970 consumer prices as a whole rose about 61 percent, and transportation prices generally rose by 65 percent; transit fares, on the other hand, increased by over 175 percent. By 1970 the

---

[84] New York City transit system fares, for example, were maintained at a nickel from the turn of the century until July 1948.

average fare had reached roughly 28 cents, while the actual average economic cost per ride (excluding the capital costs of way and structures) was probably between 35 and 40 cents. So fares are now much more expensive than the level to which people grew accustomed over a very long period of time.

A fare increase is very visible, too. Under private ownership, fare hikes were requested by the transit company and approved by the public regulatory commission—usually appointed officials. As transit comes under public ownership, however, it customarily falls to the *elected* officials to make decisions about fare levels. The "responsibility" for the price increase is clearly known, whereas for many other aspects of the public's travel the connection between the conditions experienced and the actions of the elected legislators is less clear. And riders experience fare changes much more sharply and uniformly than any other transit change that is likely to occur at a single point in time or as the result of a single public decision.

A further reason why fares receive such emphasis in public debate is that the general public image of transit patronage is one of riders drawn predominantly from the less well-to-do sections of the community. To some extent this is correct, although there are important qualifications which are discussed later. Suffice it to say here that below-cost transit fares are promoted partially as a form of welfare payment, and in particular, as a possible means of broadening the range of job opportunities for low-income people.

Can Fare Subsidies Be Economically Justified?

But the most usual argument advanced for keeping fares low is that to increase them would lead to loss of patronage. A term frequently used in this context is the "vicious spiral": higher fares lead to fewer passengers, decreases in service, further patronage losses, revenue decreases, and ultimately to a further need to raise fares again. The fallacy in the "spiral" hypothesis is that it is not necessary to reduce the service when the ridership falls following the original fare hike. The transit operator typically reasons that, since the fare increase will reduce patronage, he needs less service to carry the passengers who remain on the system. But, because of the sensitivity of travel behavior to changes in journey times, the reductions in service may reasonably be expected to lead to further loss of riders. Hence, the patronage decline caused by the fare hike becomes magnified by the effects of the service cutbacks.

A frequently-heard contention is that "transit can no longer pay for itself out of the farebox." If this is intended to mean that it would be impossible to fix on a price at which farebox revenues were fully able to cover the operating costs, we can see little evidence that the statement is true. But the important question is not whether transit services *can* be self-financing, so much as whether they *should* be expected to be.

To that question there is no single, clear answer. There are, indeed, benefits to be gained by low fares. They can serve some welfare purposes, and they can help to reduce urban transportation problems by attracting onto transit some people who would otherwise travel by private automobile. But two questions need to be answered before fare subsidies can be economically justified. How large are these benefits, and do they exceed the costs of subsidization? And even if the benefits do exceed the costs, are low fares the most cost-effective way of achieving them? Empirical evidence gives some clues but does not answer these questions definitively.

The Burden on City Governments

However, the economic justification of subsidizing transit is not the question of most current importance. Transit services *are* now publicly supported, and there appears to be little near-term prospect that legislators will want to withdraw from that position. The most relevant question is not "whether?" but "how much?"

Transit operating deficits will, in all likelihood, continue to increase. The industry is labor-intensive, with only limited potential for improvements in productivity. Labor costs account for roughly two-thirds of all operating costs. The transit unions are strong, and public policy has served to bolster their strength.[85] Since 1945, despite the marked decline of the industry, transit labor has experienced significant gains in real earnings. Between 1970 and 1975, for instance, the average annual earnings per transit employee rose by 52 percent, while the cost of living generally showed a 39 percent rise. This is equivalent to a gain in real

---

[85] Tye (1973) argues that, since any net farebox revenues cannot be used to provide the local matching share for a federal capital grant, this reduces the incentives for transit management to keep down operating costs. Moreover, since the grant program makes transit more capital-intensive, it serves to make the demand for vehicle drivers less sensitive to their wage rate, and thereby strengthens union power. Section 13(c) of the Urban Mass Transportation Act requires federally-supported projects to be approved by the transit union, consequently limiting the use of capital as a direct substitute for labor. Lurie (1960) draws evidence from the Boston transit industry to conclude that the presence of government regulations has there served to strengthen union power.

earnings averaging 1.8 percent annually. Yet over the same period, the productivity—as measured by vehicle miles per employee—has fallen by almost 9 percent.

Since there are few indications that the unions' bargaining power will be reduced, and fuel prices (albeit a small fraction of total operating costs) will continue to increase, it seems inevitable that transit deficits will continue to grow in the absence of *major* fare increases. So far, the deficit increases are generally being tolerated, but a few city governments are beginning to rethink their commitments to prop up the transit industry.

Up to now, this phenomenon has been most noticeable in the suburban jurisdictions of metropolitan areas, where the transit service is likely to be most sporadic and least relevant to the residents' travel desires. The financing arrangements for metropolitan area transit operating agencies vary widely. Some agencies (that in Minneapolis-St. Paul, for instance) effectively have their own authority for assessing property taxes. In other cities, participating local jurisdictions are bound together in an agreement from which the withdrawal of any one member would be politically difficult. But in many cities, the relationship between the operating agency and the supporting governments is a less constraining one; the transit agency contracts with each jurisdiction to provide specified services. It is in these situations, where the political costs of withdrawing from the compact are relatively slight, that individual jurisdictions are beginning in isolated cases to tell the transit operator not to bother to send the bus by any longer.

The situation in El Cajon and La Mesa (two jurisdictions in the San Diego metropolitan area) provides an example.[86] The two city councils decided that the costs of some existing bus services were too expensive, and they contracted individually with a local taxicab company to provide subsidized shared-ride service. After an experimental period it was concluded that service levels had been improved significantly, the costs per ride to the local governments were lower than with transit, and the ridership response had been strong.

In the major cities, too, there are indications that the transit agencies' demands for more public funds are meeting with increasing resistance. In late 1975, for example, transit authorities in Chicago and Washington, D.C., were considering making cutbacks in services. It seems likely that the financial strain which transit subsidization is increasingly placing

---

[86] Cruz (1974).

on local governments—particularly those in the older, declining cities—will be a very significant factor influencing the future role of the U.S. transit industry. While many cities are still continuing to increase their financial support, the general public is becoming more aware that the money not collected in the farebox is being collected through taxes. How far citizens will continue to be willing to pay for a service which the majority of them do not regularly use is an open question.

One possible source of revenue to support transit might be highway use. At the national level, as section 2 of this chapter documents, there has been a slight shift in recent years towards allowing more local decision-making in the use of federal funds for transportation purposes. There has been much debate about "opening up" the highway trust fund in such a way that the tax monies can be diverted to transit support. That proposal has been fought vigorously by many politically powerful groups which point out that the trust fund revenues are no greater than are required to complete the Interstate system (roughly 30 percent of the estimated total cost remains to be funded) and to provide for major maintenance of the Interstate and federal-aid highway systems.

At the state and local level, some areas have already legislated mechanisms for diverting highway use-related revenues directly to transit support. In Michigan, for example, the state's gasoline tax was raised by two cents in 1973 and a portion of the increase was dedicated to transit. California, unlike other states, applies a general *sales* tax to gasoline and uses a portion of the revenues for transit. In the Chicago metropolitan area, the Regional Transportation Authority (RTA) which operates the transit system has the authority to levy a 5 percent gasoline tax over its six-county service area. The RTA has not yet voted to impose the tax, however; although the revenues are supposed to be spent in the counties from which they were raised, suburban government representatives on the RTA Board fear that most of the money would go to the central city.

VII. MOBILITY FOR THE TRANSPORTATION DISADVANTAGED

For some observers, further advances in general public mobility should no longer be the primary focus of public policy. Rather, they argue, concern should be directed towards the uneven distribution of mobility throughout the urban population.[87] Because automobile ownership and

---

[87] This viewpoint has been most forcefully expressed by Webber (1974).

use is now so widespread, those without access to a car are at a distinct disadvantage. Much of our pattern of urban living presumes a level of geographic mobility which is obtainable only by having an automobile available. A lack of this geographic mobility severely restricts social mobility, and is possibly a contributing cause to poverty. Well over a half of the families with incomes below the officially designated poverty line do not own a car.

Over the last decade, governments have become increasingly aware of the problems of the "transportation disadvantaged" and the need for some policy response. People with impaired mobility fall into two basic group—those whose impairment derives from physical causes (the physically handicapped and, to a lesser extent, the elderly), and those who are disadvantaged due to social and economic causes. Most government attention has been directed to the former group.

Physical Barriers to Mobility

Physical disabilities frequently preclude driving automobiles. Thus, in the urban areas, a large proportion of the ambulatory elderly and handicapped (about 6 out of 10 by one estimate) [88] are dependent on public transportation as the main means of getting about on their own. In 1970 there was an estimated national total of about 7.6 million handicapped and elderly people living in urban areas, without drivers' permits but physically capable of using public transit were transit services available to them.

Amendments made in 1970 to the Urban Mass Transportation Act stated that

> It is hereby declared to be the national policy that elderly and handicapped persons have the same right as other persons to utilize mass transportation facilities and services; that special efforts shall be made in the planning and design of mass transportation facilities and services so that the availability to elderly and handicapped persons of mass transportation which they can effectively utilize will be assured; and that all Federal programs offering assistance in the field of mass transportation should contain provisions implementing this policy.

The courts have interpreted this provision as requiring the rapid rail systems currently planned or under construction with federal aid to provide complete access to the facility by the elderly and handicapped. This implies many design considerations (such as elevators at all stations,

---

[88] Derived from data in U.S. Department of Transportation (1973b).

standards for vehicle acceleration and retardation, special entry gates to the system, and so on) which are very expensive. For example, it is estimated that the additional capital and maintenance costs for the Washington Metro system attributable to these features are about $4.9 million per year at 1973 prices.[89] Estimates of the daily usage of the system by the elderly and handicapped in 1990 vary from 5,400 to 23,500 trips. Thus, the additional costs of these provisions will be between 70 cents and roughly $3 (in 1973 dollars) per ride in 1990, assuming that none of those trips would be taken were the accessibility provisions not made.[90] This expense is, of course, over and above the average cost per ride for the Metro system as a whole—probably on the order of $1.50 to $2.00 (at 1973 prices) per ride by 1990.[91]

It is readily apparent that the total costs of providing complete access to a rapid rail system for the handicapped and elderly are very high, particularly when one considers that another mode of transportation to and from the subway system will be necessary in most cases. In the Washington example, the total rapid rail costs per elderly or handicapped ride—somewhere between $2.20 and $5.00 perhaps (at 1973 prices)—are some two to four times the average cost of a taxicab ride in the city. It can be argued, therefore, that the public provision of fare-free taxicab service for these people would provide a higher level of service at substantially lower costs.[92]

But the provisions of the Urban Mass Transportation Act do not apply to new rail rapid transit facilities alone. There is apprehension within the transit industry as to how the law will be interpreted for bus fleets purchased with federal money. By late 1975, the matter had not been adequately tested in the courts and the Urban Mass Transportation Administration had yet to issue definitive regulations.

Leaving aside the dictates of national legislation, it is not at all obvious that to look to conventional scheduled bus or rail transit is the most pertinent policy response to the mobility problems of the physically handicapped. In general, it seems more appropriate to provide possibly subsidized para-transit alternatives. Not only would low-fare taxicab or dial-

---

[89] Estimates based on data in U.S. Department of Transportation (1973a).

[90] So far as the elderly are concerned, such an assumption probably implies an understatement of the incremental costs per ride.

[91] These estimates include both operating costs and annualized capital costs.

[92] It is likely, however, that the door-to-door, more personalized nature of cab service would attract a greater demand than the rapid rail service, so that the difference in the *total* annual costs of the alternative programs would be less pronounced than that suggested by the "per ride" cost comparisons.

a-ride services be substantially less costly to society than a large-scale adaptation of transit facilities, but the service level is also likely to be higher and more in tune with the individual needs of the physically handicapped. Service would be provided from door to door, without a need to change vehicles. There would be less walking, less waiting, less jostling, no stairs, and a higher level of personal security. Other potential solutions include greater public investment in mobility training for the handicapped and elderly themselves, improved personal equipment for mobility (electric wheelchairs, modified private automobiles, and so on) and adequate training to use it, and better street design to overcome the problem of getting over curbs.

Social and Economic Barriers to Mobility

Government agencies have so far shown less interest in the problems of those whose transportation disadvantages are due to social and economic causes rather than to physical disabilities—mostly the carless, the poor, the unemployed, and the young. Although the *proportion* of urban households without access to a car has been falling, the *number* of households without an automobile has been increasing. Between the 1960 and 1970 censuses the number of metropolitan area households with no car available increased by over 4 percent, and in the urban jurisdictions outside the central cities the number grew by almost 17 percent. Insofar as attention has been paid to the problems of families without automobiles, society has once again tended to look to conventional public transit (in those cities where it is available) to provide solutions.

In fact, urban transit systems have developed in such a way that, as a broad generalization, they tend to serve the travel demands of the urban poor very imperfectly. Most transit systems have radial routes oriented toward the central business district. But the numbers (and the proportion) of jobs within the central business districts of many cities— particularly the older, declining cities of the northeast and midwest— have been decreasing. Most residents of the central city work within the central city but outside the central business district.[93] The radial nature of transit routes often means that, although the direct distances to work for poverty area residents may be short, their transit journeys are time-consuming and involve transferring between vehicles.[94]

[93] According to the 1970 Census of Population, the proportion of central city residents working in the CBD averaged only 15 percent for metropolitan areas with populations of 1 million or more. While there is a great deal of variation between cities in this statistic, only in New York City does the proportion exceed 25 percent.

[94] Piovia et al. (1973).

Moreover, as industries requiring relatively high proportions of semi-skilled and unskilled labor have decentralized, the "reverse commute"—inner city residents commuting to both factory jobs and domestic service in the suburbs—has grown more pronounced. Many of these new areas of employment are poorly served by peak hour public transit.

In general, it is likely that bus services could be markedly improved for poverty area residents in the larger metropolitan areas—by altering routes and schedules so that they better reflect travel patterns, and by allowing the economically disadvantaged greater participation in planning the public transport services provided for them. Because transit has often been so slow to adapt to changing travel patterns, some improvements for all passengers might be possible for a relatively small change in operating costs by reallocating vehicles and personnel. A 1969 study of the bus system in Washington, D.C., and suburban Maryland presents a case in point.[95] Analysis of the expenses and the current passenger journeys on the system indicated that, for a net *reduction* of 1.7 percent in the daily operating costs, it would be possible to rearrange routes and schedules in a way which should

- reduce door-to-door travel times for roughly three times as many passengers as those whose journeys would take longer;
- reduce the number of journeys requiring transfers between vehicles by 12 percent in the peak and 17 percent at midday;
- reduce the number of journeys requiring more than one transfer by 37 percent overall; and
- reduce the number of vehicles needed for peak hour operation by 4.7 percent.

If these findings are correct, they are very suggestive; the potential for making similar low cost improvements in other systems is probably high. But for the most part, improved transit service is likely to imply increases in operating costs. In some cities (such as New York, Chicago, Pittsburgh, and Chattanooga), the inadequacies of existing conventional transit services in catering to cross-town travel have led to flourishing illegal or semi-legal taxi and jitney services based in poverty areas.[96] On routes where traffic volumes are unlikely to be high, it will probably be less costly to legalize and encourage (perhaps even to subsidize) these com-

---

[95] Voorhees and Associates, Inc. (1969). The Washington system rationalization was never implemented, partly because of the administrative costs involved in making the changes at a detailed operational level.

[96] Kirby et al. (1975).

petitive small vehicle services rather than to look to conventional transit.[97]

A series of federally-funded transit demonstration programs was initiated in the late 1960s to provide bus services from low-income areas to concentrations of low-skill employment. Very similar results were evidenced in a number of the cities in which demonstrations were mounted:

> Of fifteen cities which undertook such projects, twelve have reported on their financial performances. All reported losses, ranging from thirty-nine cents per passenger trip in Chicago to $7.40 in St. Louis. The sponsor of the St. Louis project reported that many who used the bus to find jobs bought automobiles quickly and forsook the bus.[98]

Many of the routes established under this program were discontinued, although some were combined with reduced service or increased fares after federal financial support was withdrawn. The experience of the program does cast doubt on the suitability of conventional bus transit to service cross-town and reverse commute trips to decentralized employment locations.

But that may be too sweeping a conclusion. One study of transportation access and unemployment in the Central Brooklyn Model Cities area concluded that accessibility to jobs did significantly affect the unemployment levels of the unskilled labor force living in the area.[99] While it would require major and costly transit service improvements to make a detectable difference in the level of unemployment, it was found to be economically justifiable for the public sector to finance those improvements—since unemployment rolls would fall, the total amount of public subsidies to the unskilled worker would decrease. But even a very ambitious upgrading of transit service would not be able to bring the local unemployment down to the average level for the metropolitan area.

The Welfare Role of Transit Service

It is not uncommon for the advocates of public subsidies for transit operations to suggest that transit services as a whole cater disproportionately to low-income groups, and that subsidies will therefore help the transportation disadvantaged. Such a suggestion has some truth in it, although it requires careful qualification. Not much is known about the

---

[97] We are aware that such a proposal is fraught with political and administrative difficulties. They are not insurmountable, however, and there have been some recent indications that government thinking may be moving slowly in this direction.

[98] Hilton (1974).

[99] Falcocchio and Cantilli (1974).

income circumstances of transit riders, and as might be expected there appears to be a large amount of variation from one type of service to another, and from city to city. If one looks at national statistics on transit ridership to work, and particularly if New York City is included, transit riders as a group do not appear to be much different from the population as a whole.[100] However, when attention is shifted away from work journeys some other consistencies emerge. Bus passengers, particularly in medium-sized or small cities, tend to be disproportionately female, disproportionately drawn from minority groups, and more likely to be from lower-income families than is the population at large. These trends grow more pronounced as city size decreases.[101]

Thus, the nature of the transit service is a major determinant of the types of people who will ride it. Long haul bus or rail commuter service, particularly from the suburbs to downtown, attracts a relatively affluent clientele, while local bus services are disproportionately patronized by the relatively poor. There are likely to be many local exceptions, however.

If the welfare role of transit service provision *as a whole* is open to doubt, how about the welfare implications of transit *pricing?* In general, it seems true that transit fares are regressive, in that on average they absorb a larger share of the incomes of the poor than they do of the wealthy. How far fare subsidies redress this situation, however, is critically dependent on the means used to raise the subsidy funds. Studies of the incidence of benefits and costs for specific subsidy schemes sometimes raise doubts that the poor gain to a greater extent than the more affluent. Thus, one recent analysis of the net incidence of various existing and theoretical transit subsidy schemes in Canada concluded that:

> . . . several but not all existing subsidies and methods of financing them are regressive. Of course, since urban transit subsidies are a minor item in government expenditures, the redistribution of income resulting from these subsidies is small. Nevertheless, one immediate implication is that the evidence does not support the popular impression that in general subsidization of urban public transit contributes to the well-being of low-income groups.[102]

---

[100] Wohl (1970) has collated information from the 1960 Census of Population, the 1963 Census of Transportation, and surveys of users of specific facilities in a discussion of some of these issues.

[101] These observations are made on the basis of data from the 1969-70 *Nationwide Personal Transportation Survey,* and from rider surveys conducted under the Urban Mass Transportation Administration's Technical Studies Program. Some of this evidence is presented in U.S. Department of Transportation (1974a).

[102] Frankena (1973).

One particular type of transit subsidy does, however, merit special mention. A subsidy mechanism in which the subsidy funds are essentially vested in the passengers may be directed more precisely at the transportation disadvantaged.[103] Under such a scheme, passengers may buy tickets for public transport rides through a public agency at prices which reflect the welfare goals espoused by the community—for example, the price might fall with decreasing family income or for trips to a decaying downtown area. One of the advantages of such a scheme is that it affords a high degree of specificity in price discrimination. Another advantage is that it allows one to separate completely the economic efficiency arguments for subsidization from the welfare arguments. If specific price discrimination is used to take care of the welfare goals of subsidization, then the level of subsidy and the setting of fares to the rest of the population can be decided solely on the basis of making the urban transportation system work most efficiently.

A further advantage is that different types of tickets, representing differing types of passengers or journeys, could be redeemed by the public agency at varying monetary values when presented by the transit operator. In this way it can be made financially attractive to the transit agency to provide good service to particular population subgroups and indeed—if the tickets can be honored by more than one transportation provider (buses and various taxicab companies, for example)—to compete actively for the patronage of these people. In these smaller communities where transit is not available, the price of using taxis can be reduced to come within the budget of low-income families—at a total cost to society lower than would be required to support scheduled transit. A "transportation stamp" program introduced throughout West Virginia in 1974 has some of the characteristics of such a subsidy scheme, but the full potential of the idea has yet to be tested.

Such a program would have the disadvantages of any program which transfers welfare in kind; it would restrict freedom of use of the subsidy, and it would require some form of means test or other test for qualification. Economists usually disparage income transfers in kind as inferior to a cash transfer. Political reality, however, seems to indicate that in this transportation context indirect subsidies have a much greater near-term feasibility than less restrictive programs. The transit industry and transit labor, both powerful lobby groups, currently see that (with hard work) they have established some "squatters' rights" to a pool of public

---

[103] Kirby and McGillivray (1975).

money, and they are unlikely to let it be dissipated through a nondedicated general income transfer program. The transfer of a portion of these funds to a subsidy mechanism vested in the user seems to be a far more practical political goal.

Finally, brief mention should be made of a more novel approach to the problems of carless families which has been proposed. Some have advocated the public sector encouragement of automobile ownership and operation for this group, perhaps by assistance with credit and insurance, or even by direct subsidy—a proposal which has been characterized as "buying Volks for poor folks." While such a program would obviously have several disadvantages, it deserves greater discussion and analysis.

VIII. PERSPECTIVES ON URBAN TRANSPORTATION

The earlier sections of this chapter have attempted to cover a large amount of ground. We have explored urban travel patterns in the 1970s, and the public sector's involvement with urban transportation. We have described dissatisfactions with the outcomes of past and current policies and have discussed other policy options—for enhancing mobility, for helping the transportation disadvantaged, for coordinating governmental roles. We have referred to the advantages and disadvantages of both the private automobile and conventional transit in many of these contexts.

We turn now to review the central themes and conclusions which can be drawn from the discussion, and to suggest possible directions for urban transportation in the future—that is, a time horizon of from five to fifteen years from now. We do not consider the more extreme changes which might evolve from technological breakthroughs, major adjustments in social values, or large-scale changes in urban form.

The Importance of Market Forces

One theme which has pervaded much of our discussion is the importance of marketplace decisions. The most salient features of current urban travel patterns, and the current state of our transportation systems, have been shaped primarily by consumer demand—and influenced peripherally by other factors such as public policy (which has often served to reinforce market trends) and the quality of system management. The marketplace has to be the starting point to understanding today's situation, and to assessing what seems likely to happen in the future.

For most urban travel, the private automobile has a monopoly because it has no competitor. In many small urban areas and in the suburbs of many large metropolitan areas, the only passenger transportation available is the private car. Taxi service, when available, may be too expensive for day-to-day use by most households. Many urban residents who do have transit services available do not even consider them as a viable alternative. We have seen that, in making travel decisions, most of the public values highly such considerations as reliability, flexibility, safety, comfort, privacy, and convenience—all are features of the private car which no existing mode of public transportation is capable of matching. Of course, the consumer's values may have been strongly influenced by policies of the automobile manufacturing industry and by a willingness of public agencies to encourage car travel—but the origins of the consumer behavior are of less relevance than the fact that these values are now well established.

At the same time, the public's "love affair" with the automobile is probably more accurately described as a "love-hate relationship." The last ten years have witnessed a remarkable shift in transportation investment policies, largely sparked by the general public's concern about the social costs of automobile use. The political process has responded in a marked way to considerations of air quality, community disruption, safety, and energy consumption.

And yet the same public continues to use the automobile profligately, and shows few signs of adjusting the values by which personal decisions are made. The elected representatives, moreover, perceive the public to be highly resistant to any governmental effort to reduce automobile use. How can one rationalize this paradox? Altshuler has provided a convincing explanation:

> The consumer does not want government to interfere with his life. He is receptive to having government provide improved service—e.g., transit—but he will oppose having government disrupt his neighborhood, harm his environment, or make it more difficult for him to drive. *The status quo is the thing.* Citizens oppose new highways because they disrupt existing neighborhoods, social patterns, and natural ecologies. They oppose programs to reduce auto travel because such programs would disrupt established life styles and travel habits. They can adjust to inconvenience if they have to, but they are angry if they feel that their elected representatives could have averted the need—or, even worse, deliberately created it.[104]

---

[104] Altshuler (1975). Emphasis added by the present authors.

Is there, or will there be, a genuine need to impose inconveniences and sacrifices on the traveling public? Do the concerns for environmental quality and stable neighborhoods necessarily imply some adjustment in the public's values as seen in the marketplace? Is there, in sum, a need for greater government interference in the market?

Of course, there is disagreement on the answers to these questions. If a market failure is necessary in order to justify government intervention, many observers feel that this failure is evident in urban transportation. They argue that individual consumers can see in abstract that society might gain from curtailing the use of private automobiles and relying more on other modes, but unless large numbers of people do so, an individual adjusting his own behavior will not benefit. Further, the benefits to be gained from following some sharply radical policies—creating auto-free pedestrian areas, for instance—are not indicated by current marketplace forces. Consequently, this viewpoint holds that major changes in direction have to be made by governments prepared to take a leap of faith and to intervene authoritatively in the market.

Media commentators often point to this problem, explicitly or implicitly, in suggesting that American cities would be better places in which to live if they were more like European cities. The principle of reduced dependence on the automobile is an easy one to embrace in the abstract; the difficulty (which the commentators only rarely address except in a superficial way) lies in framing public policies which would provide an alternative. Transit provides an inferior level of service and is applicable, even were services to be greatly expanded, to only a fraction of urban travel. New technology will not provide a solution in the near term. There are policy options which would allow us to make more efficient use of existing transportation facilities, but they do require strong government intervention in ways which are likely to be politically unpopular, and they may also bring some adverse impacts on urban life. Given the paucity of real alternatives, then, what is the likely future for the private automobile?

The Role of the Private Automobile

One possibility is that travel behavior in the marketplace may make some adjustments, without the need for any radically new policy initiatives by governments. Current forces seem likely to lead to changes in the relative price and convenience of travel by car. Recent increases in gasoline prices have meant that the real price of automobile use has begun to increase after years of steady decline. Existing government regulations relating to emissions control, noise control, and safety are beginning to increase the costs of automobile acquisition. The effects of these price changes could be augmented by increased congestion on urban highways, due to a diminished construction program brought about by changes in public priorities. These forces could induce consumers to use available public transportation more than in the recent past, and to reduce their use of private cars.

While such a scenario sounds credible, it does not take into account the possible technological adaptation of the automobile. Fuel efficiency standards for private cars produced from the 1978 model year onward have been mandated by the 1975 Energy Act. Automobile manufacturers are already responding to the higher prices of fuel and of the cars themselves by designing new models which are more efficient in fuel consumption and in interior space utilization. The first attribute will decrease the impact of higher fuel prices and might actually lower annual fuel costs for some drivers. The second attribute will allow smaller, lighter weight vehicles to be built with the same interior dimensions as the larger current cars. These smaller cars will partially mitigate the increasing costs of vehicle production and keep new car prices from rising at the current rates.

The end-product of federal pollution control regulations may be automobiles which are not considered health hazards, but this result probably would not occur until the late 1980s, after almost the entire vehicle fleet becomes very low-polluting. There also may be increased federal regulation of automobile safety, fuel consumption and noise. The resultant "fully regulated" car would be more costly than at present and probably would run more poorly, but it would still be a privately-owned personal transportation mode (with its concomitant attractions) which would create social costs much lower than those of today's automobile.

An alternative scenario could develop if the public becomes more distressed by the automobile's social costs and less satisfied with its benefits. Even with the fully regulated car, a steady increase in car ownership and vehicle mileage may still make the social costs unacceptable. Public values may change. World politics (or perhaps even the depletion of natural resources) could produce sharp reductions in fuel supply before synthetic fuels, or shale oil extraction, or alternative motor vehicle power plants reach an adequate stage of development. Any of these forces could set into motion actions to limit automobile use. The federal government is already requiring local governments to "consider" traffic limitation measures as a condition for receiving transit funds, and this requirement might be extended eventually to highway funding. Possible restrictions include, for instance, regulations creating auto-free zones in dense commercial areas or requiring multiple-occupancy of cars using certain highways. Alternately, they might work through the market by charging high prices for automobile use in dense areas. Such limitations would be most palatable when alternative transportation modes were available—hence they would be most likely to be introduced in the largest cities which have broad conventional transit service, or the medium-sized metropolitan areas which have good transit service at least in some corridors. But, even under this scenario, most urban travel would probably still take place in the private automobile.

The Future for Urban Highways

Although there seems likely to remain an attachment to the private automobile by consumers, the commitment for further freeway construction in urban areas is unlikely to be as strong. At present, the institutions and financing exist to continue building both Interstate and other freeways. The supporters of more construction will certainly work to continue the program, and in the immediate future their position will probably be strong enough for some new construction to proceed. But pressures to halt construction are increasing, and our expectation is that the building of new urban freeways will be reduced, first in the largest metropolitan areas and eventually in the smaller ones as well. The result of this change will probably be that the lane miles of freeways per vehicle will eventually decrease in urban areas, leading at peak hours to reduced average speeds on commuter facilities.

But other highway construction not requiring major purchases of rights-of-way in developed areas will still continue. Many new arterials will be constructed from existing narrower roads; interchanges will be built. Widening and straightening of roads will be a major emphasis. There will also be road construction in new developments to be built at the fringes of existing metropolitan areas.

With a reduction in the rate of new freeway construction should come an increased effort to improve the operation of existing highways. The extent to which improvements in traffic management proceed will depend on changing much of the state legislation which channels state gasoline taxes exclusively into new construction. Federal laws have already changed in this direction—the 1973 Highway Act allows non-Interstate funds to be used for improvements in traffic operations.

Highway maintenance will also get more emphasis in the future. Thus far, federal funds have not been available for routine maintenance and this may have influenced state priorities toward new construction. Both the safety and efficiency of roads can be improved by keeping shoulders in good condition, filling potholes, resurfacing, repainting lane markings. If there is a movement toward smaller cars in the future, there will be more consumer concern for good road surfaces; reducing vehicle weight probably implies reducing the ride quality.

The Role of Public Transportation

If the automobile's predominance in urban transportation is unlikely to be threatened by market trends under current public policies, and if radically restrictive governmental action does not develop, are there any other options which might induce changes in travel patterns? One alternative would be to increase the relative attractiveness of public transport, in the hope that car users might be enticed out of their vehicles.

This hope has motivated much of the public sector's involvement with transit services, and it underlies the current interest in building new systems, cutting fares, and expanding and improving service. The response in the marketplace has been mixed, although strong ridership gains in a small number of cities with innovative transit managements suggest that there is indeed a potential for transit to increase its share of the market. But at what cost? A substantial increase in subsidization for both the purchase and operation of buses would be necessary before the number of buses on the road doubled or tripled. An increase in vehicles by a factor of four or five (at the least) would be necessary before one could expect inroads to be made in car ownership levels, since transit now provides only 6 percent of the passenger miles in urban areas. But, as we have seen, the rapidly escalating expense of providing existing transit services is already leading some communities to question their value-for-money.

Indeed, two potential problems exist for improved transit service. One is that consumers won't use it, and the other is that they will. On the one hand, the service may not be sufficiently attractive to entice drivers out of their cars. Private vehicles will continue to have important amenities such as privacy, flexibility, and the ease of carrying baggage, which will keep them the primary choice for many trips. Even if car travel becomes more costly and congested, it is not clear to what extent public transit will be able to divert riders to it.

On the other hand, improved transit *might* lead to increases in ridership. If this occurs, then there may be a problem of increased operating deficits. The economics of transit operation in the 1970s are such that peak-hour service can be expanded only at very high cost, and usually at an increased deficit for the transit operator. The only way to counter this problem is to gain riders during the off-peak as well, and it is difficult to accomplish this. Most travel during off-peak hours in urban areas is so dispersed that a fixed-route transit service cannot readily attract much of it.

It is in the older and larger cities, where travel densities are the highest, that continuation of transit service is most beneficial. The large declining cities, however, are the least equipped to bear the escalating deficits. There are political and economic limits to the extent to which fares may be productively increased. In some of the major cities, therefore, we foresee a cutback on services, most likely in the evenings and at weekends; continued heavy subsidization; increased diversion of highway-related revenues for transit support; and continued heavy pressure on state and federal governments to increase their shares of the financial burden.

However, in some small cities (and in some of the medium-sized cities, too) where transit's share of the market is small, transit may increasingly be allowed to die. In its place, there may remain only the automobile and increased deprivation for carless families. Maybe the demise of monopoly transit operators in small cities could lead to an opening up of the public transport markets, and to competitive, privately-owned companies operating smaller vehicles filling the void. Some communities are already becoming more reliant on expanded (and possibly even subsidized) taxicab services.

New Rapid Rail Systems

The problem of the high costs of providing transit service can be seen most acutely, of course, when considering the construction of completely new transit systems. For a number of cities, the lure of an extensive new rapid rail system with metallically-gleaming cars has been too much to resist—despite the heavy costs. Indeed, for those who are able to use the new rail systems, the service should be a significant improvement over what they have had before. Rail service can be very attractive if it is planned and run as part of a door-to-door transportation system. Many may find, however, that the feeder bus service which is supposed to transport them from their local neighborhoods to the rail transit station is no better than the conventional bus service which they have rejected in the past.

But it is folly to talk about the attractiveness of rapid rail service without at the same time considering the price which has to be paid for that attractiveness. We personally doubt whether there can be many corridors in those urban areas currently without rail transit where the building of a new rapid rail line would be economically justified—even after the social costs of automobile and bus travel have been taken into account. Moreover, under existing programs there are certainly insufficient federal funds to provide 80 percent of the costs of constructing rapid rail systems in all of the cities which have shown an interest in having one.

Other Public Transportation Alternatives

New bus-based (or possibly even light rail) rapid transit lines are a different matter. They are less costly and more flexible, and can be built and opened incrementally. It seems likely that in the near future we shall see increasing numbers of urban freeway and local street lanes designated for the exclusive use of express buses, and special busways will be constructed. Most of the problems with bus-based systems occur at the downtown end of the route; in the central area, some cities may opt to build busways underground or create bus-only streets.

The so-called para-transit modes—taxicabs, jitneys, dial-a-ride services, prearranged ride-sharing, rental cars, and so on—have the advantage that they generally provide a higher quality of transportation service than that provided by conventional transit. Since consumers have shown that they are prepared to pay for quality service, we suspect that market forces will produce an increase in demand for these services. This is particularly likely if automobile travel is reduced because of fuel scarcities or strong traffic limitation policies by governments. And publicly-subsidized para-transit modes of transportation will grow increasingly important as a means of travel for the transportation disadvantaged, particularly the handicapped and the carless. The political and institutional barriers which currently limit the supply of cab and jitney services in many large cities are likely to be progressively broken down—just as there has already been a *de facto* breakdown of cab regulations in New York City.[105]

We do not envisage that public transportation will be much influenced during the next ten years by esoteric forms of new technology. Without a large-scale federal initiative, similar perhaps to the Apollo moon program, it is unlikely much will be accomplished with advanced systems such as dual-mode or "personal rapid transit."

It seems more likely that in the next ten years or so new technology will be applied to the private automobile. Electronic systems may be introduced which control the fuel system, the braking system, and even aid vehicle spacing with respect to other cars. And there might be a breakthrough in battery research which could make an electric car economically feasible.

Can We Continue to Improve Mobility?

We have suggested, then, that the automobile is likely to become more costly to the consumer, but may become less obtrusive to neighborhoods and the environment. Limitations on its use could be introduced in some areas. New highway construction in urban areas quite probably will be reduced, while existing facilities will be improved. Transit and paratransit services will provide somewhat improved service for some travelers, but for most people even the less attractive automobile will still be more attractive than public transportation.

The likely net effect of these changes will be to improve mobility— that is, reduce the money and time costs of traveling—for some trips and worsen it for others. The growing numbers of urban citizens who do not have access to an automobile may find their mobility improved in the future if transit or para-transit services are significantly upgraded; otherwise, the degree of their deprivation may increase, particularly in those small or medium-sized cities in which transit is allowed to die. The travelers who use automobiles in the less dense areas will probably experience improved mobility due to the improvement of local highways. For drivers who are induced to switch to transit because of either higher automobile costs, automobile use restrictions, or improved transit, mobility may or may not be better than its present level. However, travel will certainly cost more in the largest metropolitan areas and in the dense corridors of medium-sized areas for those who continue to travel by private automobile. Peak-hour congestion in radial commuter corridors may increase.

---

[105] Kirby et al. (1975).

Some citizens whose mobility worsens may be angered by this trend; others, perhaps many others, may be satisfied with the situation, since it will be accompanied by a better environment and less community disruption.

The scenario which we have outlined basically one of continued heavy dependence on the redesigned private car, with only limited new intervention by the public sector—appears to us to be a strong possibility for a number of reasons. As we have seen, there appears to be less political risk for legislators in goading the automobile manufacturers than in pursuing policies which call for the general public to adapt its lifestyle. Moreover, market forces are already pushing the manufacturers to produce design responses to public concern about the price and availability of fuel.

A second reason why we expect no great shift in travel patterns in the near future is that there are as yet few signals from the marketplace that consumers are willing to adjust their values and aspirations. In Western Europe, where the prices of car ownership and use relative to alternative methods of travel are significantly higher than in the United States, the forces for "automobility" are also strong. Travel behavior is not very sensitive to price changes. Most consumers appear to be more willing to make adjustments elsewhere in their budgets than to cut down on their traveling. A fiscal or regulatory stimulus aimed at changing travel patterns consequently needs to be large to be effective—and the larger the stimulus, the less feasible it is politically.

But the assumption that governments will not be willing to create effective physical or financial restraints on the ownership or use of private vehicles may prove untrue, despite the high political risks now perceived in antagonizing the car driver. In a small number of foreign cities there is some movement toward embracing strong physical restraints or congestion-pricing ideas. Were effective traffic restraint policies to be pursued in U.S. cities, many of our prognoses would be invalid. If automobile ownership and use is made much more unattractive, it is not clear exactly how travel patterns would respond. Current behavior in the marketplace provides few clues as to how consumers would respond to a very marked change in the price or convenience of car travel.

REFERENCES

Altshuler, Alan A. (1975). "The Consumer and Urban Transportation Decision Making in the United States," Paper presented to the Conference on Public Transportation and People, Paris, France, unpublished.

American Public Transit Association (1976). *Transit Fact Book, '75-'76 Edition*, Washington, D.C., American Public Transit Association.

Anderson, Frederick R. (1973). *NEPA in the Courts*, Baltimore, Md., Johns Hopkins University Press.

Atlantic Richfield Company (1975). *Paying the Fare*, Ideas on Public Transportation, vol. 2, Los Angeles, Calif., Atlantic Richfield Company.

Bhatt, Kiran U. (1974). *Road Pricing Technologies: A Survey*, Paper 1212-11, Washington, D.C., The Urban Institute.

―――― (1975). "A Comparative Analysis of Urban Transportation Costs," *Transportation Research Record* 559, Washington, D.C., Transportation Research Board.

Bowman, Lewis; Ippolito, Dennis S.; and Levin, Martin L. (1972). "Self-interest and Referendum Support: the Case of a Rapid Transit Vote in Atlanta," in Harlan Hahn, *People and Politics in Urban Society*, Urban Affairs Annual Review, vol. 6, Beverly Hills, Calif., Sage.

Boyd, J. Hayden; Asher, Norman J.; and Wetzler, Elliot S. (1973). *Evaluation of Rail Rapid Transit and Express Bus Service in the Urban Commuter Market*, Washington, D.C., U.S. Government Printing Office.

Boyd, J. Hayden; and Wells, John D. (1973). *An Estimate of the 1970 U.S. Urban Transit Deficit*, Paper P960, Arlington, Va., Institute for Defense Analyses.

Charles River Associates (1970). "Public Attitudes toward Urban Expressway Construction," Cambridge, Mass., Charles River Associates.

―――― (1972). "Measurement of the Effects of Transportation Changes," Cambridge, Mass., Charles River Associates.

Corsi, Thomas M.; Schmitt, Robert P.; and Beimborn, Edward A. (1975). "Voter Response to Highway and Transit Referenda: a Case Study in Milwaukee County, 1974," *Proceedings of the Transportation Research Forum* 16, Oxford, Ind., Richard B. Cross Co., pp. 80-90.

Costello, Martin (1973). "Geographic Distribution of Factors Affecting Automobile Use," Research paper SP25, Cambridge, Mass., U.S. Department of Transportation, Transportation Systems Center.

Cruz, Manny (1974). "The Taxi: One City's Transit System," *Nation's Cities* 12, no. 12, pp. 41-45.

Deen, Thomas B., and James, Donald H. (1969). "Relative Costs of Bus and Rail Rapid Transit Systems," *Highway Research Record* 293, Washington, D.C., Highway Research Board, pp. 33-53.

Deen, Thomas B.; Kulash, Walter M.; and Baker, Stephen (1975). "Critical Decisions in the Rapid Transit Planning Process," *Transportation Research Record* 559, Washington, D.C., Transportation Research Board.

Eckert, Ross D., and Hilton, George W. (1972). "The Jitneys," *The Journal of Law and Economics* 15, pp. 293-325.

Falcocchio, John C., and Cantilli, Edmund J. (1974). *Transportation and the Disadvantaged*, Lexington, Mass., D. C. Heath.

Fitch, Lyle C., and Associates (1964). *Urban Transportation and Public Policy*, San Francisco, Calif., Chandler.

Frankena, Mark (1973). "Income Distributional Effects of Urban Transit Subsidies," *Journal of Transport Economics and Policy* 7, pp. 215-30.

Glaister, Stephen (1974). "Generalized Consumer Surplus and Public Transport

Pricing," *The Economic Journal* 84, pp. 849-67.

Goldmuntz, Lawrence A., and Associates (1972). *Cumulative Regulatory Effects on the Cost of Automotive Transportation* (RECAT), Washington, D.C., U.S. Office of Science and Technology.

Grad, Frank P., and Associates (1974). *The Automobile and the Regulation of Its Impact on the Environment,* Norman, Okla., University of Oklahoma Press.

Hamer, Andrew Marshall (1976). *The Selling of Rail Rapid Transit,* Lexington, Mass., D. C. Heath.

Harris, Louis, and Associates (1969). "How Urban Americans View Their Transportation System," New York, N.Y., Louis Harris and Associates.

Hilton, George W. (1974). *Federal Transit Subsidies,* Washington, D.C., American Enterprise Institute for Public Policy Research.

Horowitz, Joel, and Kuhrtz, Steven (1974). *Transportation Controls to Reduce Automobile Use and Improve Air Quality in Cities,* Washington, D.C., U.S. Environmental Protection Agency.

Kain, John F., and Meyer, John R. (1970). "Transportation and Poverty," *The Public Interest* 18, pp. 75-87.

Kirby, Ronald F.; Bhatt, Kiran U.; Kemp, Michael A.; McGillivray, Robert G.; and Wohl, Martin (1975). *Para-Transit: Neglected Options for Urban Mobility,* Washington, D.C., The Urban Institute.

Kirby, Ronald F., and McGillivray, Robert G. (1975). "Alternative Subsidy Techniques for Urban Public Transportation," Working Paper 5050-4-1, Washington, D.C., The Urban Institute.

Koltnow, Peter G. (1970). "Changes in Mobility in American Cities," Washington, D.C., Highway Users Federation for Safety and Mobility.

Kühnemann, Jörg, and Witherspoon, Robert (1972). *Traffic-free Zones in German Cities,* Paris, France, Organization for Economic Cooperation and Development.

Kulash, Damian (1974). *Parking Taxes for Congestion Relief: A Survey of Related Experience,* Paper 1212-1, Washington, D.C., The Urban Institute.

Lurie, Melvin (1960). "Government Regulation and Union Power: a Case Study of the Boston Transit Industry," *Journal of Law and Economics* 3, pp. 118-35.

Maring, Gary (1974). "Highway Travel Forecasts," Washington, D.C., U.S. Department of Transportation, Federal Highway Administration.

McGillivray, Robert G. (1974). *On Road Congestion Theory,* Paper 1212-8-1, Washington, D.C., The Urban Institute.

Meyer, John R.; Kain, John F.; and Wohl, Martin (1965). *The Urban Transportation Problem,* Cambridge, Mass., Harvard University Press.

Miller, D. R.; Goodwin, B. C.; Hoffman, G. A.; and Holden, W. H. T. (1973). "Cost Comparison of Busway and Railway Rapid Transit," *Highway Research Record* 459, Washington, D.C., Highway Research Board, pp. 1-10.

Miller, David R., ed. (1974). *Urban Transportation Factbook,* two vols., Detroit, Mich., Urban Transportation Information Service.

National Safety Council (1975). *Accident Facts, 1975 Edition,* Chicago, Ill., National Safety Council.

Neidell, Lester A. (1974). "Analysis and Demand Implications of the Rapid Transit Vote in Atlanta," *Transportation Journal* 13, no. 4, pp. 14-18.

Olsson, Mary Lou, and Kemp, Michael A. (1975). "Urban Transportation and the Press: a Survey of Editorial Opinion," Working Paper 0722-01-1, Washington, D.C., The Urban Institute.

Orski, C. Kenneth (1972). "Car-Free Zones and Traffic Restraints: Tools of Environmental Management," *Highway Research Record* 406, Washington, D.C., Highway Research Board, pp. 37-46.

Ozdirim, M. (1973). "The Problems in Big Towns Created by Traffic Increase," in *Techniques of Improving Urban Conditions by Restraint of Road Traffic*, Paris, France, Organization for Economic Cooperation and Development.

Piovia, Esther S.; Hill, Robert B.; and Leigh, Wilhelmina (1973). "Journey to Work Patterns of Transportation Consumers among the Urban Disadvantaged," Washington, D.C., National Urban League.

Regional Plan Association (1974). "The Metropolis Speaks," *Regional Plan News* 95, pp. 13-18.

Roth, Gabriel (1967). *Paying for Roads: The Economics of Traffic Congestion*, Harmondsworth, U.K., Penguin.

Schroeder, Larry D., and Sjoquist, David L. (1974). "An Analysis of the Theory of Voting Using Two Rapid Transit Referenda," Working paper 7475-23, Atlanta, Ga., Georgia State University, Department of Economics.

Sherman, Roger (1967). "Club Subscriptions for Public Transport Passengers," *Journal of Transport Economics and Policy* 1, pp. 237-42.

——— (1971). "Congestion Interdependence and Urban Transit Fares," *Econometrica* 39, pp. 565-76.

——— (1972). "Subsidies to Relieve Urban Congestion," *Journal of Transport Economics and Policy* 6, pp. 22-31.

Smith, Edward (1973). "An Economic Comparison of Urban Railways and Express Bus Services," *Journal of Transport Economics and Policy* 7, pp. 20-31.

Stipak, Brian (1973). "An Analysis of the 1968 Rapid Transit Vote in Los Angeles," *Transportation* 2, pp. 71-86.

Strate, Harry E. (1972). "Annual Miles of Automobile Travel," *Nationwide Personal Transportation Study* Report 2, Washington, D.C., U.S. Department of Transportation, Federal Highway Administration.

Thomson, J. M. (1968). "The Value of Traffic Management," *Journal of Transport Economics and Policy* 2, pp. 3-32.

Thomson, J. Michael (1972). *Methods of Traffic Limitation in Urban Areas*, Paris, France, Organization for Economic Cooperation and Development.

Tye, William B. (1973). "Economics of Urban Transit Capital Grants," *Highway Research Record* 476, Washington, D.C., Highway Research Board, pp. 30-35.

U.S. Congress, Senate Committee on Public Works (1974). *The Costs and Benefits of Automobile Emission Control*, Air Quality and Automobile Emission Control, vol. 4, Washington, D.C., U.S. Government Printing Office.

U.S. Department of Commerce (1970). "Special Report on Household Ownership of Cars, Homes, and Selected Household Durables: 1970, 1969, and 1960," *Consumer Buying Indicators* Report P65-33, Washington, D.C., U.S. Government Printing Office.

——— (1973). "Household Ownership of Cars and Light Trucks: July 1972," *Consumer Buying Indicators*, Report P65-44, Washington, D.C., U.S. Government Printing Office.

U.S. Department of Transportation (1967). *Highway Statistics: Summary to 1965*, Washington, D.C., U.S. Government Printing Office.

——— (1970). "Benefits of Interstate Highways," Washington, D.C., U.S. Department of Transportation, Federal Highway Administration.

——— (1972). *1972 National Transportation Report*, Washington, D.C., U.S. Government Printing Office.

——— (1973a). "The Additional Cost of Providing Mobility for the Elderly and Handicapped on the Washington Metropolitan Rail Rapid Transit System," Washington, D.C., U.S. Department of Transportation, Urban Mass Transportation Administration.

——— (1973b). "The Handicapped and Elderly Market for Urban Mass Transit," Washington, D.C., U.S. Department of Transportation, Urban Mass Transportation Administration.

—— (1974a). *A Study of Urban Mass Transportation Needs and Financing,* Washington, D.C., U.S. Government Printing Office.

—— (1974b). *Social and Economic Effects of Highways,* Washington, D.C., U.S. Department of Transportation, Federal Highway Administration.

Vickrey, William (1963). "Pricing in Urban and Suburban Transport," *American Economic Review* 52, pp. 452-65.

—— (1965). "Pricing as a Tool in Coordination of Local Transportation," in National Bureau for Economic Research, *Transportation Economics,* New York, N.Y., Columbia University Press.

Voorhees, Alan M., and Associates, Inc. (1969). *A Systems Analysis of Transit Routes and Schedules,* Washington, D.C., Washington Metropolitan Area Transit Commission.

Vuchic, Vukan R. (1974). "A Critique of the Study, 'Evaluation of Rail Rapid Transit and Express Bus Service in the Urban Commuter Market,'" unpublished mimeograph.

Webber, Melvin M. (1974). "Post-automobile Transport," in Transportation Research Forum, *Proceedings of the International Conference on Transportation Research, 1973, Chicago, Ill.,* Oxford, Ind., Richard B. Cross Co., pp. 289-94.

Wilson, James Q., and Banfield, Edward C. (1964). "Public-regardingness as a Value Premise in Voting Behavior," *The American Political Science Review* 58, pp. 876-87.

Wohl, Martin (1970a). "Users of Urban Transportation Services and Their Income Circumstances," *Traffic Quarterly* 24, pp. 21-43.

—— (1970b). "Urban Transport We Could Really Use," *Technology Review* 72, no. 8, pp. 30-37.

—— (1972). "Congestion Toll Pricing for Public Transport Facilities," in Selma Mushkin, ed., *Public Prices for Public Products,* Washington, D.C., The Urban Institute.

INDEX

INDEX